February 27–28, 2019
Santa Cruz, CA, USA

I0018765

**Association for
Computing Machinery**

Advancing Computing as a Science & Profession

HotMobile'19

Proceedings of the 20th International Workshop on
Mobile Computing Systems and Applications

Sponsored by:
ACM SIGMOBILE

Supported by:
NSF, Microsoft, Samsung, and Google

Association for Computing Machinery

Advancing Computing as a Science & Profession

The Association for Computing Machinery
2 Penn Plaza, Suite 701
New York, New York 10121-0701

ISBN: 978-1-4503-6273-3 (Digital)

ISBN: 978-1-4503-6740-0 (Print)

Additional copies may be ordered prepaid from:

ACM Order Department
PO Box 30777
New York, NY 10087-0777, USA

Phone: 1-800-342-6626 (USA and Canada)
+1-212-626-0500 (Global)
Fax: +1-212-944-1318
E-mail: acmhelp@acm.org
Hours of Operation: 8:30 am – 4:30 pm ET

Welcome to ACM HotMobile 2019

Welcome to the twentieth edition of the International Workshop on Mobile Computing Systems and Applications -- HotMobile 2019. This is a special year for HotMobile as it is the 25th anniversary: in 1994, the first workshop in this series was held in Santa Cruz, CA. In the past 25 years, Mobile Computing has profoundly changed the world and our life. By 1994, Personal Computing had recently emerged as the giant of the computing industry; Microsoft was still working toward Bill Gates' dream of "a computer on every desk and in every home"; GSM, the second generation (2G) of cellular data networks, was being deployed. People had to wait for two more years for the first Nokia Communicator, arguably the first smartphone. A lot of people were working on wireless local-area network but the first 802.11 protocol would be released only three years later. Today, Mobile Computing is Personal Computing. We carry around mobile devices in various form factors that are more powerful by orders of magnitude than the PCs of that era; and our mobile devices are connected with wireless broadband faster than best home and office Internet back then by orders of magnitude.

HotMobile 2019 provides a unique opportunity to reflect on the fascinating progression of mobile computing over the past quarter century, and to look forward to the next 25 years. In addition to the usual HotMobile program, HotMobile 2019 features a number of activities that exploit this opportunity. We are delighted that the Program Chair of the first HotMobile, Professor Mahadev Satyanarayanan, has invited many of the 1994 workshop participants to join us this year. HotMobile 2019 returns to the Dream Inn in Santa Cruz, CA, where it started in 1994.

Our technical program features a keynote talk by Dr. Edmund Nightingale from Microsoft, 26 technical papers, a Pioneer's Panel organized by Professor Satyanarayanan as well as a Demo & Poster session. The Program Committee of 17 scholars selected the 26 papers out of 57 submissions. All submissions received at least three and usually four reviews. After online discussion, the PC met at Rice University for a whole day to make the final decisions. Due to the time constraints of the workshop, 6 of the 26 accepted papers are given shorter time for oral presentation. Nevertheless, all 26 papers are excellent and are included in the proceedings in the same way. Along with the posters and demos, these technical papers cover a broad scope of Mobile Computing with varied boldness and maturity.

A workshop like HotMobile always relies on teamwork by the larger community. We are grateful to the many authors who chose to submit their work to HotMobile. We thank the scholars on the program committee and the organizing committee who volunteered a lot of their personal time to serve the community. We thank ACM SIGMOBILE for sponsoring the workshop, as well as our corporate sponsors including Microsoft, Samsung, and Google. We also thank the National Science Foundation and ACM SIGMOBILE for funding student travel grants to ensure strong student participation in the workshop.

Alec Wolman
HotMobile'19 General Chair
Microsoft Research

Lin Zhong
HotMobile'19 Program Chair
Rice University

Table of Contents

Keynote

Session 1: Video Analytics

Session 2: Security, Privacy and Isolation

Session 3: Ideas for the Future

Session 4: Machine Learns

Session 5: Human Matters

Session 6: Internet of Things

Session 7: Sensing & Streaming

Poster and Demo Session

ACM HotMobile 2019 Workshop Organization

General Chairs: Alec Wolman *(Microsoft Research, USA)*

Program Chair: Lin Zhong *(Rice University, USA)*

Publication Chair: Shadi Noghabi *(Microsoft Research, USA)*

Posters and Demos Chairs: Wenjun Hu *(Yale University, USA)*
Kyungmin Lee *(Facebook, USA)*

Student Travel Grant Chair: Felix Lin *(Purdue University, USA)*

Sponsorship Chair: Iqbal Mohomed *(Samsung Research, USA)*

Publicity Chair: Ali Razeen *(University of British Columbia, Canada)*

Web Chair: Mateusz Mikusz *(Lancaster University, UK)*

Steering Committee Chair: Nigel Davies *(Lancaster University, UK)*

Steering Committee: Ramón Cáceres *(Google, USA)*
Mahadev Satyanarayanan *(Carnegie Mellon University, USA)*
Roy Want *(Google, USA)*
Elizabeth Belding *(University of California, Santa Barbara, USA)*
Nic Lane *(University of Oxford and Nokia Bell Lab, UK)*
Minkyong Kim *(Samsung Electronics, South Korea)*
Aruna Balasubramanian *(Stony Brook, USA)*

Program Committee: Aakanksha Chowdhery *(Google, USA)*
Alastair Beresford *(University of Cambridge, UK)*
Aruna Balasubramanian *(Stony Brook, USA)*
Ben Greenstein *(Google, USA)*
Eric Rozner *(University of Colorado Boulder, USA)*
Eyal de Lara *(University of Toronto, Canada)*
Felix Xiaozhu Lin *(Purdue University, USA)*
Haitham Hassanieh *(University of Illinois at Urbana-Champaign, USA)*
Mahadev Satyanarayanan *(Carnegie Mellon University, USA)*
Mahanth Gowda *(Penn State University, USA)*
Robert LiKamWa *(Arizona State University, USA)*
Robin Kravets *(University of Illinois, USA)*
Silvia Santini *(Università della Svizzera italiana , CH)*
Wenjun Hu *(Yale University, USA)*
Xia Zhou *(Dartmouth College, USA)*
Xinwei Hu *(Huawei, China)*

ACM HotMobile 2019 Sponsors & Supporters

Sponsors:

Supporters:

A View from Industry: Securing IoT with Azure Sphere

Ed Nightingale
edn@microsoft.com
Microsoft

ABSTRACT

Every year, 9 billion new devices powered by single-chip computers–MCUs–are deployed; all with little to no cybersecurity and most with no network connectivity. These devices are in your home, in your office, and in every industrial or commercial setting on the planet. Azure Sphere offers to improve MCU computing by bringing cloud connectivity, intelligence, and high security to these devices. The Azure Sphere solution consists of three components: a new class of cross-over MCUs incorporating Microsoft silicon security technology, a new OS built around a custom Linux kernel, and a cloud-based security service that guards every Azure Sphere-based device on the planet for its deployed lifetime.

In this talk, I will explain the market scenarios Azure Sphere addresses, dig into the silicon and software architecture that compose the Azure Sphere solution, review some of the project's history, and demo the Azure Sphere experience. Finally, I will look towards the future and discuss research problems out on the horizon. Specifically, I'll explore some scenarios around the convergence mobility, IoT and facial recognition via machine learning where strong security and privacy guarantees are especially important.

ACM Reference Format:
Ed Nightingale. 2019. A View from Industry: Securing IoT with Azure Sphere. In *The 20th International Workshop on Mobile Computing Systems and Applications (HotMobile '19), February 27–28, 2019, Santa Cruz, CA, USA.* ACM, New York, NY, USA, 1 page. https://doi.org/10.1145/3301293.3302378

1 BIO

Ed Nightingale has been part of Azure Sphere from its inception and has filled many different roles as the product has grown from research to product.

Currently, Ed is the Partner Director of Engineering for Azure Sphere where he is responsible for the overall software and hardware engineering effort on the team. Prior to Azure Sphere, Ed was a systems researcher and software engineer. Ed has authored papers in top systems conferences such as OSDI and SOSP. He has co-authored 20 conference and journal publications, has won 6 best paper awards, and even helped to set the world record in disk-to-disk sorting (http://sortbenchmark.org). He has also worked as an engineer and as an engineering manager running a large-scale distributed storage service. Ed really enjoys building operating systems and large-scale distributed systems.

Towards Drone-sourced Live Video Analytics for the Construction Industry

Shilpa George
Carnegie Mellon University
shilpag@cs.cmu.edu

Junjue Wang
Carnegie Mellon University
junjuew@cs.cmu.edu

Mihir Bala
University of Michigan
mihirkb@umich.edu

Thomas Eiszler
Carnegie Mellon University
teiszler@cs.cmu.edu

Padmanabhan Pillai
Intel Labs
padmanabhan.s.pillai@intel.com

Mahadev Satyanarayanan
Carnegie Mellon University
satya@cs.cmu.edu

ABSTRACT

This paper investigates the use of drones for live inspection in the construction industry. The key technical challenge is the real-time registration of the drone video feed to the architectural plan. We present and evaluate three different approaches for registration and propose an edge-based prototype using visual features. Our evaluations show that GPS alone is not sufficient for accurate registration, but with visual features, accuracies within ten centimeters can be achieved.

ACM Reference Format:
Shilpa George, Junjue Wang, Mihir Bala, Thomas Eiszler, Padmanabhan Pillai, and Mahadev Satyanarayanan. 2019. Towards Drone-sourced Live Video Analytics for the Construction Industry. In *The 20th International Workshop on Mobile Computing Systems and Applications (HotMobile '19), February 27–28, 2019, Santa Cruz, CA, USA.* ACM, New York, NY, USA, 6 pages. https://doi.org/10.1145/3301293.3302365

1 Introduction

The U.S. construction industry is estimated to be over $1.8 trillion by 2022 [4]. A recent McKinsey report [1] estimates that productivity in this industry has only improved at about 1% per year over the past 20 years. The use of drones for inspection of progress at construction sites, with prompt detection and reporting of construction errors, has emerged as a promising approach to improving productivity [6].

The use of drones in construction faces two challenges. First, performing real-time analytics on drone-sourced videos requires more processing power than what is available on a small, lightweight and inexpensive drone. Second, drones typically run Linux or an embedded RTOS, while engineering and architectural software such as Autodesk Revit and Navisworks are only implemented for Windows. Direct, real-time registration of drone observations on engineering drawings offers the highest potential for productivity improvement, yet this is not feasible today. Even when mobile devices such as tablets are used at construction sites today, they are only used to view a PDF file of engineering drawings. This is only slightly better than viewing a hard-copy printout.

In this paper, we describe our experience in using edge computing to enable drone-sourced video analytics for live building inspection. The substantial computing resources of a cloudlet are used to meet the high computational demands. At the same time, the virtualization capability of a cloudlet is used to run a Windows virtual machine (VM) that contains the original engineering and architectural drawings for the construction site as well as the Autodesk software that was used to create those drawings. *Accurate real-time registration of drone observations on drawings* emerges as a key challenge in this setting. We focus on addressing the following problem: When the analytics pipeline detects a construction defect in the drone-sourced video, where exactly on the corresponding drawing should the error be noted? While localization has been studied extensively [11] [14], our focus is not on absolute coordinates but on coordinates relative to an engineering drawing. One can view this problem as an inverted form of augmented reality (AR): rather than annotating the real world with virtual observations (classic AR), our goal is to annotate a virtual world (engineering drawing) from real-world observations. A person living in the virtual world (e.g., an engineer or architect at a remote Internet location), should be able to see annotations created in real-time by a drone flight.

The main goal of this paper is to illustrate the potential of using drones for live video analytics in construction industry by showcasing building inspection as a use case. We briefly introduce the current uses of drones in construction industry in Section 2 and describe the case study conducted and its setup in Section 3. We explore the performance of live registration and the accuracy obtained using various techniques from Section 4 to Section 6. In Section 6 we present our proposed solution of using feature-based registration. We describe related work in Section 8. In Section 9 we have a discussion and describe areas of future research and finally conclude in Section 10.

2 Background: Drones in Construction

The use of drones in the construction industry is still in its infancy. Drones have been used to inspect hard-to-reach parts of a constructions site, and to take ad-hoc aerial photographs of the site. Systematic use of drones to improve productivity of the construction process is just beginning.

One of the most sophisticated uses of drones in construction to date involves the production of a 360° time-lapse video of the construction progress. This is accomplished by periodic precisely-controlled flights around a site to capture high-resolution imagery from all directions. After each flight, the captured data is sent to

Figure 1: Completed Tepper Building (October 2018)

Figure 2: Revit 3D model of Tepper Building

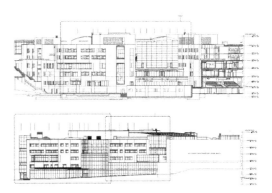

Figure 3: Two Revit Elevation Views of Tepper Building

the cloud for offline processing. As the position of the drone in flight can never be perfectly controlled, the offline processing will visually match the captured images to each other and to images from past flights. These are then stitched together and presented as an HTML5 visualization that lets one view the progress of the construction from any direction and over time. Although this is a valuable capability, it has two key limitations. First, the process is inherently offline. Second, manual effort is needed to register drone observations on engineering drawings.

Our goal is to overcome both these limitations through a a live, interactive drone-based inspection system. During a drone flight, captured video is streamed to a ground-based cloudlet. The system generates a synthetic view, registering and superimposing the live drone view on top of the corresponding portions of the engineering drawings. An important benefit of live video analytics over offline analytics is that it is possible to actuate the drone in real time. This allows zooming in/out the camera or changing the flight path of the drone based on current observations, thus enabling immediate follow-up of trouble spots, and re-imaging (typically closeups) of specific features. Accurate online positioning is critical for other construction applications such as live thermal mapping, where thermal imagery could be used to identify leaks, and inspect them up close within the same drone flight.

3 Case Study: CMU Tepper Building

The Tepper Building is a new 315,000 square feet building that was completed in September 2018 to house the Business School at Carnegie Mellon University. Fig. 1 shows this building shortly after completion of construction. Our use of drones in this construction project occurred close to its completion, in the late spring and summer of 2018.

We obtained detailed engineering plans of this building from the architectural firm that designed the building. These plans were provided as a set of files for the Revit software package. The plans include both 3D models of the building, as well as 2D elevations from different directions (e.g., Fig. 2 and Fig. 3). Industry standards specify the accuracy of these inputs to be within one-quarter inch

(roughly 0.6 cm) of actual construction. This quantity serves to bound the drone positioning accuracy that we seek to achieve — there is no point in being more accurate than the plans themselves!

For drone flights, we used a DJI Phantom 4 Pro UAV that is equipped with a variety of sensors (GPS, altimeter, etc.) and a 4K steerable video camera. During each flight, we capture both the video and sensor data, and stream these to a ground-based cloudlet. The cloudlet has a copy of the building model, and attempts to register and overlay the drone video on top of the model view. The cloudlet we used to develop our prototype has an eight-core Intel® Core™ i7-5960X processor (3.00GHz) with 32 GB of memory and an NVIDIA GeForce GTX 960 GPU.

Figure 4 illustrates our overall system architecture. The drone communicates over DJI's proprietary Lightbridge 2 wireless technology [5] with a controller held by a human operator. The wireless channel carries flight control signals from the controller to the drone. In the other direction, it carries video, GPS and other sensor data. The controller relays the video and other sensor streams over WiFi or 4G LTE to the ground-based cloudlet. Two VM instances are configured on the cloudlet. One VM instance runs the Gabriel platform that was originally developed for wearable cognitive assistance [10], but is repurposed here for drone video analytics. This VM also runs a SIFT-based localization pipeline (discussed in Section 6) on the arriving video frames. The extracted value is passed on to the Autodesk VM instance. In an ideal implementation, the latter VM instance would just run the Revit software. However, our initial experiments showed that the current Revit implementation is too slow in redrawing its model to reflect drone updates. We are tracking down the source of this performance slowdown. In the interim, to achieve real-time tracking, we feed the Revit model to a Unity engine that is able perform real-time redisplay in response to drone-sourced location updates to Revit files.

Using this experimental setup, we aim to answer the following questions:

(1) When relying solely on GPS and position sensors, what is the accuracy of positioning? Is this sufficient to accurately register the drone camera view to the building model?

(2) Assuming near-perfect computer vision, how accurately can we estimate the positions of certain building features relative to reference features?

(3) Using real-world computer vision how close can we come to the above ideal?

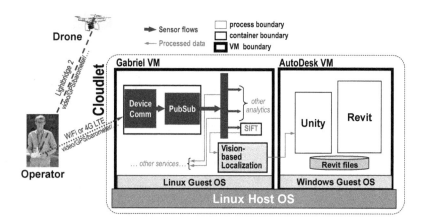

Figure 4: System Architecture

Ground Truth (m)	GPS-based Measurement (m)	Absolute Error (m)
7.62	9.34	1.72
7.62	9.11	1.49
7.62	6.27	1.35
14.94	16.72	1.78
14.94	13.68	1.26
14.94	13.52	1.42

Average error is 1.50 m
Standard deviation is 0.21 m

Figure 5: Measured GPS Horizontal Error

4 Built-in Drone Position Sensors

If we can accurately determine the position and orientation of the drone, then we can calculate the view frustum of its camera. Assuming the building model has been calibrated to real-world coordinates, we can then determine precisely where the drone camera view intersects the model, and thus localize any visible issues onto the model. In this section we explore if the measurements from GPS and position sensors of the drone are accurate enough to satisfy our requirement.

The specifications of DJI Phantom 4 Pro drone gives Hover Accuracy Range, a loosely related metric to GPS positioning accuracy, to be 0.5 m in the vertical direction and 1.5 m in the horizontal direction. While this specification helps set the expectation for its GPS-based positioning accuracy, exact numbers need to be measured.

Horizontal Accuracy: To measure the horizontal accuracy of the drone's GPS receiver, we compared the distance of two known locations to the calculated distance from the drone's GPS readings using the Haversine formula. Fig. 5 shows the horizontal GPS accuracy results. The average distance measurement error is 1.50 m with a standard deviation of 0.21 m.

Altitude Accuracy: The DJI mobile SDK makes available only the relative altitude with respect to the take-off location rather than absolute altitude from the sea level. To evaluate the accuracy of such relative altitude, we tied ropes of 4 different lengths with a small weight to the drone. We recorded the altitude reading while taking-off by flying the drone straight up to a position in which the rope is tightened and vertical to the ground with the weight barely touching the ground. We then flew the drone briefly for a minute and took another measurement when landing. We took three experiments for each rope length. Fig. 6 shows the measured altitude results. The average take-off altitude errors ranges from 6 cm to 18 cm. The landing altitude errors, ranging from 17 cm to 48 cm, are significantly larger than take-off errors due to sensor drift.

Thus, GPS and barometers alone cannot provide the needed accuracy for our view registration task. Note that in this paper we have not measured orientation errors; these can only further degrade the registration accuracy.

5 Near-Ideal Computer Vision

Instead of trying to accurately determine the drone's absolute position, we investigate whether visual features can be used to directly register the drone's views on the engineering drawings. To control variables and get an idea of the theoretical limits of this approach, we use artificial easily-detected features in this section. In particular, fiducial markers [7] [9] [17] have been widely used for positioning and pose estimation for many computer vision and augmented reality applications. These markers leverage judiciously designed patterns to achieve reliable detection of key points and represent the simplest, most accurate visual approach.

We place a few markers at known positions on the wall as reference markers. We use the detected coordinates of reference markers in a test image together with their wall position to calculate the transform matrix (a homography [19]) that relates the pixels in the test image to wall coordinates. Using the calculated homography, we are able to transform any image points to wall coordinates.

To evaluate the accuracy of our method, we placed 100 ArUco markers [9] on a building's sidewall, as shown in Fig. 7. These markers are printed on four pieces of tabloid size paper as 5x5 grids. Each marker is 4.6 cm by 4.6 cm in size and 0.8 cm away from adjacent markers in the same grid. The horizontal and vertical distance among grids are 61.0 cm. We took 54 test images from different viewpoints with our drone. We chose 8 corner markers as reference points and evaluated the view registration errors for the rest of detected markers in each test image. For each test marker, the calculated coordinates of its four corners are compared against their wall positions. Fig. 9 shows the cumulative distribution function (CDF) of the registration errors along the horizontal and vertical directions of the wall. Over 90% of the errors are less than 1 cm while the worst cases are less than 6 cm. These results come close to the allowed errors (0.6 cm) of the engineering drawings and demonstrate the potential of using visual features for precise view registration.

6 SIFT: Real-World Computer Vision

In the real world, it is not possible to have fiducial markers placed around the building to aid inspection. However, there are many

Ground Truth (m)	Take-Off Altitude Error (m)	Landing Altitude Error (m)
0.63	0.13 ± 0.10	0.17 ± 0.17
1.27	0.06 ± 0.02	0.41 ± 0.39
1.85	0.18 ± 0.15	0.28 ± 0.15
2.49	0.17 ± 0.15	0.48 ± 0.12

Figure 6: Drone Altitude Error

Figure 7: Fiducial Markers Drone Image

Figure 8: Tepper Reference Image

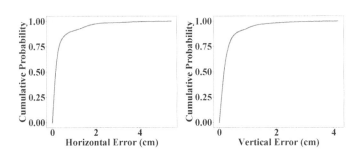

Figure 9: Registration Error using Fiducial Markers

naturally-occurring distinctive features such as corners of windows, brick patterns and other architectural components which allow humans to easily find correspondences between the building image and the engineering drawing. A variety of computer vision techniques have been developed to find distinctive regions in an image. In particular, Scale Invariant Feature Transform (SIFT) features [15] describe distinctive regions that characterize an image. These features are robust to transformations such as scale, rotation, and illumination, which often occur in drone images. SIFT has been widely used in various computer vision tasks such as image stitching, image registration, object detection, tracking, and robot localization.

Matching SIFT features across two inputs requires them to have similar visual appearances; however, the engineering drawing does not have similar visual features as a camera image. This makes it impossible to directly match the drone's camera view to the virtual engineering drawing. To overcome this challenge we add a layer of indirection. We first capture a handful of references images — these are wide-angle images of the exterior of the building taken from a few different locations. Fig. 8 shows an example reference image of the Tepper Quad building. These reference images are manually registered to the drawings using key features such as corners of walls and windows. During the drone flight, we can now use SIFT matching to find correspondences between the live camera view and the reference images, and then transitively, find the matching coordinates in the engineering drawing.

In our implementation, the cloudlet stores a database of reference images that span the exterior of Tepper building along with an offline, pre-computed set of SIFT features from these images. For an incoming frame or query image from the drone, we first use its GPS coordinates to perform coarse localization and narrow down the number of reference images against which the frame has to be matched. The cloudlet then extracts SIFT features of the query frame and performs approximate nearest neighbor search using the FLANN library [16] to match its features to the SIFT features of the reference images. Thus, for each of the typically three thousand or so features extracted from the query frame, we obtain a candidate match and reference image id. A simple voting scheme is used to retrieve the top 4 reference images having the largest number of candidate matches to the query image.

To register the drone view to the reference image we find the projective transform that maps feature correspondences between the two images. Projective transform or homography requires that the points chosen in a scene be coplanar; this assumption generally holds in our case as facades of a building are largely planar. To estimate the parameters of the homography transform we use the RANSAC algorithm [8]. RANSAC also helps us refine our feature matches as it removes spurious matches that do not fit our hypothesis. Fig. 11 shows an example SIFT feature match between a query image and a reference image. The red bounding box shows the region on the reference image to which the query image maps using the computed homography transform. A query image is considered to be correctly registered if the best homography returned by RANSAC has at least 20 inlier points.

Once we register the drone view to a reference image, we need to find its position on the engineering drawing. As we had already computed and saved the mapping from the reference image to the engineering drawing, we simply need to multiply the homography obtained above by this mapping to produce a single transform from query image pixels to coordinates of the engineering drawing. Fig. 10 gives the overall flow of our registration algorithm.

7 EVALUATION

We evaluate the accuracy of our localization approach by calculating the error between the estimated position of particular points and the ground truth positions in the engineering drawings. For this, we selected distinct points such as corners of windows on the engineering drawing whose positions in the coordinate system are known. We manually find the pixel coordinates of these points in query images, compute their positions in the engineering drawing based on the output of our registration algorithm, and compare these values to the actual locations in drawings. Fig. 12 shows the CDF of positioning error for 548 points over 167 query frames. Most of the time, our system is able to localize the camera view to the engineering drawing to within 10 cm of accuracy, and within 20 cm over 95% of the time. Note that our system is not able to

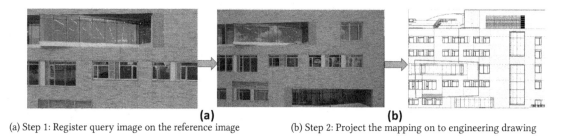

(a) Step 1: Register query image on the reference image   (b) Step 2: Project the mapping on to engineering drawing

Figure 10: Registration pipeline

Figure 11: Example of SIFT feature matching between query image (left) to reference image (right).

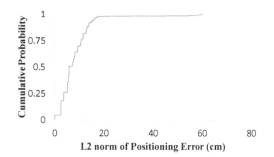

Figure 12: Registration Error using SIFT matching

find a valid mapping for every frame. As mentioned above, if a sufficient number of inliers is not found, no output is produced. Approximately 20% of the frames tested resulted in no solution. Just as the accuracy of the approach is important, the decision on the placement of the compute needs consideration. Can the compute be done solely on the drone with the results of its position shipped back? Or is there a need to offload to a cloudlet?

One concern is whether the localization pipeline can be executed fast enough for use on the live drone feed. In particular, SIFT feature extraction is notoriously compute intensive, which impedes real-time use. In our prototype, we use a GPU implementation of the SIFT algorithm [2] that can process a 1280x720 image in 14-15 ms on our GPU. Approximate nearest neighbor matching takes about 75 ms. The complete pipeline, therefore, takes on average 97 ms for a 720p image when run on a cloudlet which has an eight-core, 3 GHz Intel® Core™ i7-5960X processor with 32 GB of memory and an NVIDIA GeForce GTX 960 GPU. Thus, with the assistance of the ground-based cloudlet, we are able to accuately localize the drone over ten times per second, enabling real-time use at reasonable flight speeds.

In contrast, if we attempt to run the SIFT-based localization algorithm on drone hardware, performance drops by an order of magnitude. On an Intel® Joule™ 570x module, a 1.7 GHz quad-core embedded SoC comparable to processors used in high-end smartphones and more capable than typical drone platforms, our algorithms completes in 857 ms for a 720p image. The significant difference in drone-based and edge-based processing capability is corroborated in Wang et al. [20] in an object detection context.

Therefore, for this application, the ground-based edge computing infrastructure serves two improtant purposes. Not only do the cloudlets significantly speed up the localization by an order of magnitude, they also allow execution of Windows-based proprietary architectural software in VMs.

A video demo of our prototype can be found in https://youtu.be/odOXFBpMdG8.

8 Related Work

Image-based localization is a widely researched area in computer vision and robotics. Some of its applications include urban navigation, location recognition, and augmented reality on mobile devices. For localization, we have used a feature-based image retrieval approach taken by Irschara et al. [11] and Sattler et al. [18]. Other popular approaches include SLAM [12] and PTAM [13] where they simultaneously construct the 3D model of the environment and localize the camera pose within this map in real-time. Our work differs from them in that, while these works map to points in the physical world, we register the live view to the architectural model which is the golden standard in construction. Recent approaches to image-based localization that use deep-learning [3] are still in early stages and do not perform as well as feature based methods.

9 Discussion and Future Work

The construction industry has seen a more rapid adoption of drones than any other commercial sector. From site surveying to maintenance, drones are being utilized in all stages of a construction lifecycle. Most use-cases of the drone today are restricted to offline processing, where the data captured from the drone are uploaded to the cloud to create topographic maps, 3D mesh files or other formats for visualization. While offline analytics has its advantages, live-analytics using drones in construction is an area of topical interest. Live-analytics of drone feed enables the potential to actuate the drone in real time. Our work is a first step towards realizing that vision.

A major impediment to drone-sourced live video analytics is the lack of processing power available on a lightweight and compact drone. In this work, we leverage edge computing and existing techniques in computer vision to realize live-registration of drone view onto virtual architectural drawings. Live-registration is a key step in realizing many applications such as live-mapping, monitoring, and real-time error detection. Decisions that used to take hours or days can be done in minutes using live video analytics.

Of course, our work represents just the initial forays into this application space. Many interesting near term and long term research questions are raised by our work. Our current prototype uses manually-registered reference images. It may be possible to automate this aspect, for example by using long-term mean GPS readings to accurately locate the reference images, or by using precisely-placed fixed cameras. In addition our system uses homographic transforms, which make sense when dealing with planar surfaces; more sophisticated mappings may be needed to robustly handle partially constructed walls, or curved facades. Likewise, although SIFT features are robust to rotations in the camera plane, they are not effective with out of plane rotations. More robust features will be needed for proper matching when the drone is obliquely facing a wall. In addition, it may be possible to train a DNN to directly detect architecturally significant features that can be directly mapped to the engineering drawing without requiring intermediate reference images. Finally, the ultimate goal of inspection is to find any variance between the partially-constructed building and the plans; automating such anomaly detection will require further investigation.

10 Conclusion

This paper investigated the potential use of drones in the construction industry, and demonstrated a working prototype of a live inspection use case. Key to this is the use of live visual registration to the architectural plans made possible with support of ground-based cloudlet infrastructure. We believe the combination of semi-autonomous drones and live video analytics will be a source of significant productivity gains for the construction industry in the near future.

ACKNOWLEDGEMENTS

We thank our shepherd, Lin Zhong, and the anonymous reviewers for their guidance in improving the presentation of our work. We greatly appreciate the technical assistance of the following organizations: Hangar, Renaissance 3 Architects, PJ Dick, and Carnegie Mellon University Campus Design and Facility Development. This research was supported in part by the Defense Advanced Research Projects Agency (DARPA) under Contract No. HR001117C0051 and by the National Science Foundation (NSF) under grant number CNS-1518865. Additional support was provided by Intel, Vodafone, Deutsche Telekom, Verizon, Crown Castle, NTT, and the Conklin Kistler family fund. Any opinions, findings, conclusions or recommendations expressed in this material are those of the authors and do not necessarily reflect the view(s) of their employers or the above-mentioned funding sources.

REFERENCES

[1] Filipe Barbosa, Jonathan Woetzel, Jan Mischke, Maria João Ribeirinho, Mukund Sridhar, Matthew Parsons, Nick Bertram, and Stephanie Brown. 2017. *Reinventing Construction: A Route to Higher Productivity*. Technical Report. McKinsey Global Practices Institute.

[2] Mårten Björkman, Niklas Bergström, and Danica Kragic. 2014. Detecting, segmenting and tracking unknown objects using multi-label MRF inference. *Computer Vision and Image Understanding* (2014).

[3] Eric Brachmann, Alexander Krull, Sebastian Nowozin, Jamie Shotton, Frank Michel, Stefan Gumhold, and Carsten Rother. 2017. DSAC-differentiable RANSAC for camera localization. In *IEEE Conference on Computer Vision and Pattern Recognition (CVPR)*, Vol. 3.

[4] BusinessWire. 2018. United States $ 1.77 Billion Construction Industry Analysis 2013-2018 with Forecasts to 2022. https://www.businesswire.com/news/home/20180410006055/en/United-States-1.77-Billion-Construction-Industry-Analysis. *(Typo in title: should be $1.77 Trillion)*.

[5] DJI, Inc. 2017. Lightbridge 2 — Professional Quality Live Streaming From the Sky. https://www.dji.com/lightbridge-2.

[6] DroneDeploy. 2018. 2018 Commercial Drone Industry Trends. https://www.dronedeploy.com/resources/.

[7] Mark Fiala. 2005. ARTag, a fiducial marker system using digital techniques. In *Computer Vision and Pattern Recognition, 2005. CVPR 2005. IEEE Computer Society Conference on*, Vol. 2. IEEE, 590–596.

[8] Martin A Fischler and Robert C Bolles. 1981. Random sample consensus: a paradigm for model fitting with applications to image analysis and automated cartography. *Commun. ACM* 24, 6 (1981), 381–395.

[9] Sergio Garrido-Jurado, Rafael Muñoz-Salinas, Francisco José Madrid-Cuevas, and Manuel Jesús Marín-Jiménez. 2014. Automatic generation and detection of highly reliable fiducial markers under occlusion. *Pattern Recognition* 47, 6 (2014), 2280–2292.

[10] Kiryong Ha, Zhuo Chen, Wenlu Hu, Wolfgang Richter, Padmanabhan Pillai, and Mahadev Satyanarayanan. 2014. Towards Wearable Cognitive Assistance. In *Proceedings of the Twelfth International Conference on Mobile Systems, Applications, and Services*. Bretton Woods, NH.

[11] Arnold Irschara, Christopher Zach, Jan-Michael Frahm, and Horst Bischof. 2009. From structure-from-motion point clouds to fast location recognition. In *Computer Vision and Pattern Recognition, 2009. CVPR 2009. IEEE Conference on*. IEEE, 2599–2606.

[12] Michael Kaess, Hordur Johannsson, Richard Roberts, Viorela Ila, John J Leonard, and Frank Dellaert. 2012. iSAM2: Incremental smoothing and mapping using the Bayes tree. *The International Journal of Robotics Research* 31, 2 (2012), 216–235.

[13] Georg Klein and David Murray. 2007. Parallel tracking and mapping for small AR workspaces. In *Mixed and Augmented Reality, 2007. ISMAR 2007. 6th IEEE and ACM International Symposium on*. IEEE, 225–234.

[14] Jesse Levinson, Michael Montemerlo, and Sebastian Thrun. 2007. Map-Based Precision Vehicle Localization in Urban Environments.. In *Robotics: Science and Systems*, Vol. 4. Citeseer, 1.

[15] David G Lowe. 2004. Distinctive image features from scale-invariant keypoints. *International journal of computer vision* (2004).

[16] Marius Muja and David G Lowe. 2009. Fast approximate nearest neighbors with automatic algorithm configuration. *VISAPP (1)* 2, 331-340 (2009), 2.

[17] Alessandro Mulloni, Daniel Wagner, Istvan Barakonyi, and Dieter Schmalstieg. 2009. Indoor positioning and navigation with camera phones. *IEEE Pervasive Computing* 2 (2009), 22–31.

[18] Torsten Sattler, Bastian Leibe, and Leif Kobbelt. 2011. Fast image-based localization using direct 2d-to-3d matching. In *Computer Vision (ICCV), 2011 IEEE International Conference on*. IEEE, 667–674.

[19] Richard Szeliski. 2010. *Computer vision: algorithms and applications*. Springer Science & Business Media.

[20] Junjue Wang, Ziqiang Feng, Zhuo Chen, Shilpa George, Mihir Bala, Padmanabhan Pillai, Shao-Wen Yang, and Mahadev Satyanarayanan. 2018. Bandwidth-efficient Live Video Analytics for Drones via Edge Computing. In *Proceedings of the Third IEEE/ACM Symposium on Edge Computing (SEC 2018)*. Bellevue, WA.

Scaling Video Analytics Systems to Large Camera Deployments

Samvit Jain[†*], Ganesh Ananthanarayanan[†], Junchen Jiang[¶†], Yuanchao Shu[†], Joseph Gonzalez[*]

[†]Microsoft Research, [*]University of California at Berkeley, [¶]University of Chicago

ABSTRACT

Driven by advances in computer vision and the falling costs of camera hardware, organizations are deploying video cameras *en masse* for the spatial monitoring of their physical premises. Scaling video analytics to massive camera deployments, however, presents a new and mounting challenge, as compute cost grows proportionally to the number of camera feeds. This paper is driven by a simple question: can we scale video analytics in such a way that *cost grows sublinearly*, or even remains constant, as we deploy more cameras, while *inference accuracy remains stable*, or even improves. We believe the answer is yes. Our key observation is that video feeds from wide-area camera deployments demonstrate significant content correlations (e.g. to other geographically proximate feeds), both in space and over time. These *spatio-temporal correlations* can be harnessed to dramatically reduce the size of the inference search space, decreasing both workload and false positive rates in multi-camera video analytics. By discussing use-cases and technical challenges, we propose a roadmap for scaling video analytics to large camera networks, and outline a plan for its realization.

CCS CONCEPTS

• **Computer systems organization** → *Distributed architectures*; • **Networks** → *Network algorithms*; • **Information systems** → *Data analytics*; • **Computing methodologies** → *Computer vision tasks*.

KEYWORDS

video analytics; spatio-temporal correlations; neural networks; edge computing; streaming video

ACM Reference Format:
Samvit Jain, Ganesh Ananthanarayanan, Junchen Jiang, Yuanchao Shu, Joseph Gonzalez. 2019. Scaling Video Analytics Systems to Large Camera Deployments. In *The 20th International Workshop on Mobile Computing Systems and Applications (HotMobile '19), February 27–28, 2019, Santa Cruz, CA, USA*. ACM, New York, NY, USA, 6 pages. https://doi.org/10.1145/3301293.3302366

1 INTRODUCTION

Driven by plummeting camera prices and the recent successes of computer vision-based video inference, organizations are deploying cameras at scale for applications ranging from surveillance and flow control to retail planning and sports broadcasting. Processing video feeds from large deployments, however, requires a proportional investment in either compute hardware (i.e. expensive GPUs) or cloud resources (i.e. GPU machine time), costs from which easily exceed that of the camera hardware itself [1, 25]. A key reason for these large resource requirements is the fact that, today, video streams are analyzed *in isolation*. As a result, the compute required to process the video grows linearly with the number of cameras. We believe there is an opportunity to both stem this trend of linearly increasing costs, *and* improve accuracy, by viewing the cameras *collectively*.

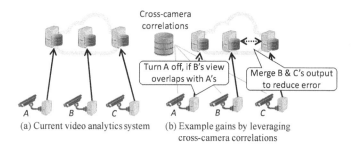

(a) Current video analytics system   (b) Example gains by leveraging cross-camera correlations

Figure 1: *Contrasting (a) the traditional per-camera video analytics with (b) the proposed approach that leverages cross-camera correlations.*

This position paper is based on a simple observation—cameras deployed over any geographic area, whether a large campus, an outdoor park, or a subway station network, demonstrate significant content correlations—both spatial and temporal. For example, nearby cameras may perceive the same objects, though from different angles or at different points in time. We argue that these cross-camera correlations can be harnessed, so as to use *substantially fewer resources* and/or achieve *higher inference accuracy* than a system that runs complex inference on all video feeds independently. For example, if a query person is identified in one camera feed, we can then exclude the possibility of the individual appearing in a distant camera within a short time period. This eliminates extraneous processing and reduces the rate of false positive detections (Figure 1(a)). Similarly, one can improve accuracy by combining the inference results of multiple cameras that monitor the same objects from different angles (Figure 1(b)). Our initial evaluation on a real-world dataset with eight cameras shows that using cameras collectively can yield resource savings of *at least 74%*. More such opportunities are outlined in §3.

Given the recent increase in interest in systems infrastructure for video analytics, we believe the important next step for the community is designing a software stack for *collective* camera analytics. Video processing systems today generally analyze video streams independently even while useful cross-camera correlations exist [19, 38]. On the computer vision side, recent work has tackled specific multi-camera applications (*e.g.* tracking [30, 35, 40]), but has generally neglected the growing cost of inference itself.

We argue that the key to scaling video analytics to large camera deployments lies in fully leveraging these latent cross-camera correlations. We identify several architectural aspects that are critical to improving resource efficiency and accuracy but are missing in current video analytics systems. First, we illustrate the need for a new system module that learns and maintains up-to-date *spatio-temporal correlations* across cameras. Second, we discuss online pipeline reconfiguration and composition, where video pipelines incorporate information from other correlated cameras (*e.g.* to eliminate redundant inference, or ensemble predictions) to save on cost or improve accuracy. Finally, to deal with any missed detections arising from our proposed optimizations, we note the need to process small segments of historical video at faster-than-real-time rates, alongside analytics on live video.

Our goal is not to provide a specific system implementation, but to motivate the design of an accurate, cost-efficient *multi-camera* video analytics system. Our hope is to inspire the practical realization of these ideas in the near future.

2 CAMERA TRENDS & APPLICATIONS

This section sets the context for using many cameras collaboratively by discussing (1) trends in camera deployments, and (2) the recent increased interest in cross-camera applications.

Explosive growth of smart camera installations: Organizations are deploying cameras *en masse* to cover physical areas. Enterprises are fitting cameras in office hallways, store aisles, and building entry/exit points; government agencies are deploying cameras outdoors for surveillance and planning. Two factors are contributing to this trend:

1. *Falling camera costs* enable more enterprises and business owners to install cameras, and at higher density. For instance, today, one can install an HDTV-quality camera with on-board SD card storage for $20, whereas three years ago the industry's first HDTV camera cost $1,500 [32]. Driven by the sharp drop in camera costs, camera installations have grown exponentially, with 566 PT of data generated by *new* video surveillance cameras worldwide *every day* in 2015, compared to 413 PT generated by newly installed cameras in 2013 [32].

   There has been a recent wave of interest in "AI cameras" – cameras with compute and storage on-board – that are designed for processing and storing the videos [4, 28]. These cameras are programmable and allow for running arbitrary deep learning models as well as classic computer vision algorithms. AI cameras are slated to be deployed at mass scales by enterprises.

2. *Advances in computer vision*, specifically in object detection and re-identification techniques [29, 40], have sparked renewed interest among organizations in camera-based data analytics.

For example, transportation departments in the US are moving to use video analytics for traffic efficiency and planning [23]. A key advantage of using cameras is that they are relatively easy to deploy and can be purposed for multiple objectives.

Increased interest in cross-camera applications: We focus on applications that involve video analytics *across* cameras. While many cross-camera video applications were envisaged in prior research, the lack of one or both of the above trends made them either prohibitively expensive or insufficiently accurate for real-world use-cases.

We focus on a category of applications we refer to as *spotlight search*. Spotlight search refers to detecting a specific type of activity and object (*e.g.* shoplifting, a person), and then tracking the entity as it moves through the camera network. Both detecting activities/objects and tracking require compute-intensive techniques, *e.g.* face recognition and person re-identification [40]. Note that objects can be tracked both in the forward direction ("real-time tracking"), and in the backward direction ("investigative search") on recorded video. Spotlight search represents a broad template, or a core building block, for many cross-camera applications. Cameras in a retail store use spotlight search to monitor customers flagged for suspicious activity. Likewise, traffic cameras use spotlight search to track vehicles exhibiting erratic driving patterns. In this paper, we focus on spotlight search on live camera feeds as the canonical cross-camera application.

Metrics of interest: The two metrics of interest in video analytics applications are inference *accuracy* and *cost* of processing. Inference accuracy is a function of the model used for the analytics, the labeled data used for training, and video characteristics such as frame resolution and frame rate [18, 19, 38]. All of the above metrics also influence the *cost* of processing – larger models and higher quality videos enable higher accuracy, at the price of increased resource consumption or higher processing latency. When the video feeds are analyzed at an edge or cloud cluster, cost also includes the bandwidth cost of sending the videos over a wireless network, which increases with the number of video feeds.

3 NEW OPPORTUNITIES IN CAMERA DEPLOYMENTS

Next, we explain the key benefits – in efficiency and accuracy – of cross-camera video analytics. The key insight is that scaling video analytics to many cameras does not necessarily stipulate a linear increase in cost; instead, one can significantly improve cost-efficiency as well as accuracy by leveraging the spatio-temporal correlations across cameras.

3.1 Key enabler: Cross-camera correlations

A fundamental building block in enabling cross-camera collaboration are *spatio-temporal correlation* profiles across cameras. At a high level, these spatio-temporal correlations capture the relationship between the content of camera A and the content of camera B over a time delta Δt.[1] This correlation manifests itself in at least three different forms. Firstly, the same object can appear in multiple cameras, *i.e.* content correlation, at the same time (*e.g.* cameras in

---

[1]The correlation reduces to "spatial-only", when $\Delta t \rightarrow 0$.

the same room) or at different points in time (*e.g.* cameras placed at two ends of a hallway); Secondly, multiple cameras may share similar characteristics, *i.e. property* correlation, *e.g.* the types, velocities, and sizes of contained objects. Thirdly, one camera may have a different viewpoint on objects than another, resulting in a *position* correlation, *e.g.* some cameras see larger/clearer faces since they are deployed closer to eye level.

As we will show next, the prevalence of these cross-camera correlations in dense camera networks enables key opportunities to use the compute (CPU, GPU) and storage (RAM, SSD) resources on these cameras *collaboratively*, by leveraging their network connectivity.

3.2 Better cost efficiency

Leveraging cross-camera correlations improves the *cost efficiency* of multi-camera video analytics, without adversely impacting accuracy. Here are two examples.

C1: Eliminating redundant inference

In cross-camera applications like spotlight search, there are often far fewer objects of interest than cameras. Hence, ideally, query resource consumption over multiple cameras should not grow proportionally to the number of cameras. We envision two potential ways of doing this by leveraging content-level correlations across cameras (§3.1).

- When two spatially correlated cameras have overlapping views (*e.g.* cameras covering the same room or hallway), the overlapped region need only be analyzed once.
- When an object leaves a camera, only a small set of relevant cameras (*e.g.* cameras likely to see the object in the next few seconds), identified via their spatio-temporal correlation profiles, need search for the object.

In spotlight search, for example, once a suspicious activity or individual is detected, we can selectively trigger object detection or person re-identification models only on the cameras that the individual is likely to traverse. In other words, we can use spatio-temporal correlations to narrow the search space by *forecasting* the trajectory of objects.

We analyze the popular "DukeMTMC" video dataset [31], which contains footage from eight cameras on the Duke University campus. Figure 2 shows a map of the different cameras, along with the percentage of traffic leaving a particular camera *i* that next appears in another camera *j*. Figures are calculated based on manually annotated human identity labels. As an example observation, within a time window of 90 minutes, 89% of all traffic leaving Camera 1 first appears at Camera 2. At Camera 3, an equal percentage of traffic, about 45%, leaves for Cameras 2 and 4. Gains achieved by leveraging these spatial traffic patterns are discussed in §3.4.

C2: Resource pooling across cameras

Since objects/activities of interest are usually sparse, most cameras do not need to run analytics models all the time. This creates a substantial heterogeneity in workloads across different cameras. For instance, one camera may monitor a central hallway and detect many candidate persons, while another camera detects no people in the same time window.

Such workload heterogeneity provides an opportunity for dynamic offloading, in which more heavily utilized cameras transfer

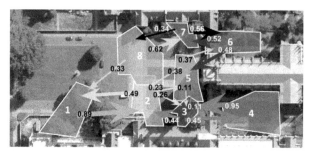

Figure 2: *Camera topology and traffic flow in the DukeMTMC dataset [31].*

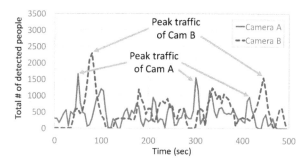

Figure 3: *Number of person detections on two cameras in [31] in each 5-second window over a span of 500 seconds. Note the heterogeneity in traffic patterns.*

part of their analytics load to less-utilized cameras. For instance, a camera that runs complex per-frame inference can offload queries on some frames to other "idle" cameras whose video feeds are static. Figure 3 shows the evident imbalance in the number of people detected on two cameras across a 500 second interval. By *pooling* available resources and balancing the workload across multiple cameras, one can greatly reduce resource provisioning on each camera (*e.g.* deploy smaller, cheaper GPUs), from an allocation that would support peak workloads. Such a scheme could also reduce the need to stream compute tasks to the cloud, a capability constrained by available bandwidth and privacy concerns. *Content* correlations (§3.1) directly facilitate this offloading as they foretell query trajectories, and by extension, workload.

3.3 Higher inference accuracy

We also observe opportunities to improve inference accuracy, without increasing resource usage.

A1: Collaborative inference

Using an ensemble of identical models to render a prediction is an established method for boosting inference accuracy [14]. The technique also applies to model ensembles consisting of multiple, correlated video pipelines (*e.g.* with different perspectives on an object). Inference can also benefit from hosting dissimilar models on different cameras. For instance, camera A with limited resources uses a specialized, low cost model for flagging cars, while camera B uses a general model for detection. Then camera A can offload its video to camera B to cross-validate its results when B is idle.

Table 1: *Spotlight search results for various levels of spatio-temporal correlation filtering. A filtering level of $k\%$ signifies that a camera must receive $k\%$ of the traffic from a particular source camera to be searched. Larger k (e.g. $k = 10$) corresponds to more aggressive filtering, while $k = 0$ corresponds to the baseline, which searches all of the cameras. Results aggregated over 100 tracking queries on the 8 camera DukeMTMC dataset.*

Filtering level (%)	Detections processed	Savings (vs. baseline)	Recall (%)	Precis. (%)
0%	76,510	0.0	**57.4**	60.6
1%	29,940	60.9	55.0	81.4
3%	22,490	70.6	55.1	**81.9**
10%	19,639	**74.3**	55.1	**81.9**

Cameras can also be correlated in a *mutually exclusive* manner. In spotlight search, for example, if a person p is identified in camera A, we can preclude a detection of the same p in another camera whose view does not overlap with A. Knowing where an object is likely *not* to show up can significantly improve tracking precision over a naïve baseline that searches all of the cameras. In particular, removing unlikely candidates from the space of potential matches reduces false positive matches, which tend to dislodge subsequent tracking and bring down precision (see §3.4).

A2: Cross-camera model refinement

One source of video analytics error stems from the fact that objects look differently in real-world settings than in training data. For example, some surveillance cameras are installed on ceilings, which reduces facial recognition accuracy, due to the oblique viewing angle [26]. These errors can be alleviated by retraining the analytics model, using the output of another camera that has an eye-level view as the "ground truth". As another example, traffic cameras under direct sunlight or strong shadows tend to render poorly exposed images, resulting in lower detection and classification accuracy [12], whereas cameras without lighting interference yield better inference performance. Since lighting conditions change over time, two such cameras can complement each other, via collaborative model training. Opportunities for such cross-camera model refinement are a direct implication of position correlations (§3.1) across cameras.

3.4 Preliminary results

Table 1 contains a preliminary evaluation of our spotlight search scheme on the Duke dataset [31], which consists of 8 cameras. We quantify resource savings by computing the ratio of 1) the number of person detections processed by the baseline (*i.e.* 76,510) to 2) the number of person detections processed by a particular filtering scheme (*e.g.* 22,490). Observe that applying spatio-temporal filtering results in significant resource savings and much higher precision, compared to the baseline, at the price of slightly lower recall.

4 ARCHITECTING FOR CROSS-CAMERA ANALYTICS

We have seen that exploiting spatio-temporal correlations across cameras can improve cost efficiency and inference accuracy in multi-camera settings. Realizing these benefits in practice, however, requires re-architecting the underlying video analytics stack. This section articulates the key missing pieces in current video analytics systems, and outlines the core technical challenges that must be addressed in order to realize the benefits of collaborative analytics.

4.1 What's missing in today's architecture?

The proposals in §3.2 and §3.3 require four basic capabilities.

#1: Cross-camera correlation database: First, a new system module must be introduced to learn and maintain an up-to-date view of the spatio-temporal correlations between any pair of cameras (§3.1). Physically, this module can be a centralized service, or a decentralized system (with each camera maintaining a local copy). Different correlations can be represented in various ways. For example, content correlations can be modeled as the *conditional probability* of detecting a specific object in camera B at time t, given its appearance at time $t - \Delta t$ in camera A, and stored as a discrete, 3-D matrix in a database. This database of cross-camera correlations must be dynamically updated, because the correlations between cameras can vary over time: video patterns can evolve, cameras can enter or leave the system, and camera positions and viewpoints can change. We discuss the intricacy of discovering these correlations, and the implementation of this new module, in §4.2.

#2: Peer-triggered inference: Today, the execution of a video analytics pipeline (what resources to use and which video to analyze) is largely pre-configured. To take advantage of cross-camera correlations, an analytics pipeline must be aware of the inference results of other relevant video streams, and support *peer-triggered inference* at runtime. Depending on the content of other related video streams, an analytics task can be assigned to the compute resources of *any* relevant camera to process *any* video stream at *any* time. This effectively *separates* the logical analytics pipeline from its execution. To eliminate redundant inference (C1 of §3.2), for instance, one video stream pipeline may need to dynamically trigger (or switch off) another video pipeline (Figure 4.c). Similarly, to pool resources across cameras (C2 of §3.2), a video stream may need to dynamically offload computation to another camera, depending on correlation-based workload projections (Figure 4.d). To trigger such inference, the current inference results need to be shared in real-time *between* pipelines. While prior work explores task offloading across cameras and between the edge and the cloud [9, 20], the trigger is usually workload changes on a single camera. We argue that such dynamic triggering must also consider events on the video streams of other, related cameras.

#3: Video pipeline composition: Analyzing each video stream in isolation also precludes learning from the content of other camera feeds. As we noted in §3.3, by combining the inference results of multiple correlated cameras, *i.e.* composing multiple video pipelines, one can significantly improve inference accuracy. Figure 4 shows two examples. Firstly, by sharing inference results across pipelines in real-time (Figure 4.e), one can correct the inference error of another less well-positioned camera (A1 in §3.3). Secondly, the inference model for one pipeline can be refined/retrained (Figure 4.f) based on the inference results of another better positioned camera (A2 in §3.3). Unlike the aforementioned reconfiguration of video

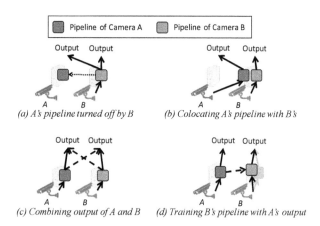

(a) A's pipeline turned off by B   *(b) Colocating A's pipeline with B's*

(c) Combining output of A and B   *(d) Training B's pipeline with A's output*

Figure 4: *Illustrative examples of peer-triggered inference (a, b) and pipeline composition (c, d).*

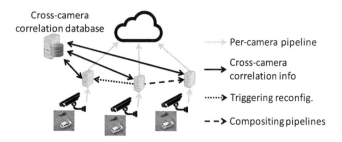

Figure 5: *Envisioned cross-camera architecture.*

pipelines, *merging* pipelines in this way actually impacts inference output.

#4: Fast analytics on stored video: Recall from §2 that spotlight search can involve tracking an object *backward* for short periods of time to its first appearance in the camera network. This requires a new feature, lacking in most video stream analytics systems: fast analysis of stored video data, *in parallel* with analytics on live video. Stored video must be processed with very low latency (*e.g.* several seconds), as subsequent tracking decisions depend on the results of the search. In particular, this introduces a new requirement: processing many seconds or minutes of stored video at *faster-than-real-time* rates.

Putting it all together: Figure 5 depicts a new video analytics system that incorporates these proposed changes, along with two new required interfaces. Firstly, the correlation database must expose an interface to the analytics pipelines that reveals the spatio-temporal correlation between any two cameras. Secondly, pipelines must support an interface for real-time communication, to (1) trigger inference (C1 in §3.2) and (2) share inference results (A1 and A2 in §3.3). This channel can be extended to support the sharing of resource availability (C2) and optimal configurations (C3).

4.2 Technical challenges

In this section, we highlight the technical challenges that must be resolved to fully leverage cross-camera correlations.

1) Learning cross-camera correlations: To enable multi-camera optimizations, cross-camera correlations need to be extracted in the first place. We envision two basic approaches. One is to rely on domain experts, *e.g.* system administrators or developers who deploy cameras and models. They can, for example, calibrate cameras to determine the overlapped field of view, based on camera locations and the floor plan. A data-driven approach is to *learn* the correlations from the inference results; *e.g.* if two cameras identify the same person in a short time interval, they exhibit a *content correlation*.

The two approaches represent a tradeoff— the data-driven approach can better adapt to dynamism in the network, but is more computationally expensive (*e.g.* it requires running an offline, multi-person tracker [30] on all video feeds to learn the correlations). A hybrid approach is also possible: let domain experts establish the initial correlation database, and dynamically update it by periodically running the tracker. This by itself is an interesting problem to pursue.

2) Resource management in camera clusters: Akin to clusters in the cloud, a set of cameras deployed by an enterprise also represents a "cluster" with compute capacity and network connectivity. Video analytics work must be assigned to the different cameras in proportion to their available resources, while also ensuring high utilization and overall performance. While cluster management frameworks [13] perform resource management, two differences stand out in our setting. Firstly, video analytics focuses on analyzing video *streams*, as opposed to the batch jobs [37] dominant in big data clusters. Secondly, our spatio-temporal correlations enable us to *predict* person trajectories, and by extension, forecast future resource availability, which adds a new, temporal dimension to resource management.

Networking is another important dimension. Cameras often need to share data in real-time (*e.g.* A1, A2 in §3.3, #3 in §4.1). Given that the links connecting these cameras could be constrained wireless links, the network must also be appropriately scheduled jointly with the compute capacities.

Finally, given the long-term duration of video analytics jobs, it will often be necessary to *migrate* computation across cameras (*e.g.* C2 in §3.2, #2 in §4.1). Doing so will require considering both the overheads involved in transferring state, and in loading models onto the new camera's GPUs.

3) Rewind processing of videos: Rewind processing (#4 in §4.1)— analyzing recently recorded videos—in parallel with live video requires careful system design. A naïve solution is to ship the video to a cloud cluster, but this is too bandwidth-intensive to finish in near-realtime. Another approach is to process the video where it is stored, but a camera is unlikely to have the capacity to do this at faster-than-real-time rates, while also processing live video.

Instead, we envision a MapReduce-like solution, which utilizes the resources of many cameras by (1) partitioning the video data and (2) calling on multiple cameras (and cloud servers) to perform rewind processing in parallel. Care is required to orchestrate computation across different cameras, in light of their available resources (compute and network). Statistically, we expect rewind processing to involve only a small fraction of the cameras at any point in time, thus ensuring the requisite compute capacity.

5 RELATED WORK

Finally, we put this paper into perspective by briefly surveying topics that are related to multi-camera video analytics.

Video analytics pipelines: Many systems today exploit a combination of camera, smartphone, edge cluster, and cloud resources to analyze video streams [18, 19, 22, 33, 38]. Low cost model design [11, 19, 34], partitioned processing [6, 16, 39], efficient offline profiling [18, 33], and compute/memory sharing [17, 21, 24] have been extensively explored. Focus [15] implements low-latency search, but targets historical video, and importantly does not leverage any cross-camera associations. Chameleon [18] exploits content similarity across cameras to amortize query profiling costs, but still *executes* video pipelines in isolation. Our specific goal is to meet the joint objectives of high accuracy and cost efficiency in a *multi-camera* setting. In general, techniques for optimizing individual video pipelines are orthogonal to techniques for cross-camera analytics, and could be co-deployed.

Camera networks: Multi-camera networks (*e.g.* [2, 3]) and applications (*e.g.* [10]) have been explored as a means to enable cross-camera communication (*e.g.* over WiFi), and allow power-constrained cameras to work collaboratively.

Our work is built on these communication capabilities, but focuses on building a custom data analytics stack that spans a cluster of cameras. While some camera networks do perform analytics on video feeds (*e.g.* [5, 7, 8, 39]), they have specific objectives (*e.g.* feature augmentation [7], camera network topology inference [8], minimizing bandwidth utilization [39]), and fail to address the growing resource cost of video analytics, or provide a common interface to support various vision tasks. Our objective is to provide system-level support for these capabilities.

Geo-distributed data analytics: Analyzing data stored in geo-distributed services (*e.g.* data centers) is a related and well-studied topic (*e.g.* [27, 36]). The key difference in our setting is that camera data exhibits spatio-temporal correlations, which as we have seen, can be used to achieve major resource savings and improve analytics accuracy.

6 CONCLUSIONS

The increasing prevalence of enterprise camera deployments presents a critical opportunity to improve the efficiency and accuracy of video analytics via spatio-temporal correlations. The challenges posed by cross-camera applications call for a major redesign of the video analytics stack. We hope that the ideas in this paper both motivate this architectural shift, and highlight potential technical directions for its realization.

ACKNOWLEDGMENTS

We would like to acknowledge the helpful discussions and feedback from Victor Bahl and Alec Wolman. In addition to NSF CISE Expeditions Award CCF-1730628, this research is supported by gifts from Alibaba, Amazon Web Services, Ant Financial, Arm, CapitalOne, Ericsson, Facebook, Google, Huawei, Intel, Microsoft, Scotiabank, Splunk and VMware.

REFERENCES

[1] 2018. WyzeCam. https://www.wyzecam.com/.
[2] Kevin Abas et al. 2014. Wireless smart camera networks for the surveillance of public spaces. *IEEE Computer* (2014).
[3] Hamid Aghajan and Andrea Cavallaro. 2009. *Multi-camera networks: principles and applications.* Academic press.
[4] Amazon. 2017. AWS DeepLens. https://aws.amazon.com/deeplens/.
[5] Shayan M. Assari et al. 2016. Human Re-identification in Crowd Videos Using Personal, Social and Environmental Constraints. In *ECCV*.
[6] Tiffany Chen et al. 2015. Glimpse: Continuous, Real-Time Object Recognition on Mobile Devices. In *ACM SenSys*.
[7] Y. Chen et al. 2018. Person Re-Identification by Camera Correlation Aware Feature Augmentation. *IEEE TPAMI* 40, 2 (Feb 2018), 392–408.
[8] Yeong-Jun Cho et al. 2017. Unified Framework for Automated Person Re-identification and Camera Network Topology Inference in Camera Networks. In *ICCV*.
[9] Eduardo Cuervo et al. 2010. MAUI: Making Smartphones Last Longer with Code Offload. In *ACM MobiSys*.
[10] Bernhard Dieber et al. 2011. Resource-aware coverage and task assignment in visual sensor networks. *Transactions on Circuits for Video Technology* (2011).
[11] Biyi Fang et al. 2018. NestDNN: Resource-Aware Multi-Tenant On-Device Deep Learning for Continuous Mobile Vision. In *ACM MobiCom*.
[12] Ting Fu et al. 2017. Automatic Traffic Data Collection under Varying Lighting and Temperature Conditions in Multimodal Environments: Thermal versus Visible Spectrum Video-Based Systems. *Journal of Advanced Transportation* (2017).
[13] Benjamin Hindman et al. 2011. Mesos: A platform for fine-grained resource sharing in the data center. In *NSDI*.
[14] Geoffrey Hinton et al. 2015. Distilling the Knowledge in a Neural Network. In *NIPS Deep Learning and Representation Learning Workshop*.
[15] Kevin Hsieh et al. 2018. Focus: Querying Large Video Datasets with Low Latency and Low Cost. *USENIX OSDI*.
[16] Chien-chun Hung et al. 2018. VideoEdge: Processing Camera Streams using Hierarchical Clusters. In *ACM SEC*.
[17] Angela H Jiang et al. 2018. Mainstream: Dynamic Stem-Sharing for Multi-Tenant Video Processing. In *USENIX ATC*.
[18] Junchen Jiang et al. 2018. Chameleon: Video Analytics at Scale via Adaptive Configurations and Cross-Camera Correlations. In *ACM SIGCOMM*.
[19] Daniel Kang et al. 2017. NoScope: Optimizing Neural Network Queries over Video at Scale. In *VLDB*.
[20] Robert LiKamWa et al. 2013. Energy Characterization and Optimization of Image Sensing Toward Continuous Mobile Vision. In *ACM MobiSys*.
[21] Robert LiKamWa et al. 2015. Starfish: Efficient Concurrency Support for Computer Vision Applications. In *ACM MobiSys*.
[22] Sicong Liu et al. 2018. On-Demand Deep Model Compression for Mobile Devices: A Usage-Driven Model Selection Framework. In *ACM MobiSys*.
[23] Franz Loewenherz et al. 2017. Video Analytics Towards Vision Zero. In *ITE Journal*.
[24] Akhil Mathur et al. 2017. DeepEye: Resource Efficient Local Execution of Multiple Deep Vision Models Using Wearable Commodity Hardware. In *ACM MobiSys*.
[25] Microway. 2018. NVIDIA Tesla P100 Price Analysis. https://www.microway.com/.
[26] NPR. [n. d.]. It Ain't Me, Babe: Researchers Find Flaws In Police Facial Recognition Technology. https://www.npr.org/sections/alltechconsidered/2016/10/25/499176469.
[27] Qifan Pu et al. 2015. Low latency geo-distributed data analytics. In *ACM SIGCOMM*.
[28] Qualcomm. 2018. Vision Intelligence Platform. https://www.qualcomm.com/news/.
[29] J. Redmon et al. 2016. You Only Look Once: Unified, Real-Time Object Detection. In *IEEE CVPR*.
[30] Ergys Ristani and Carlo Tomasi. 2018. Features for Multi-Target Multi-Camera Tracking and Re-Identification. In *IEEE CVPR*.
[31] Ergys Ristani et al. 2016. Performance Measures and a Data Set for Multi-Target, Multi-Camera Tracking. In *ECCV Workshop*.
[32] SecurityInfoWatch. 2016. Data generated by new surveillance cameras to increase exponentially in the coming years. http://www.securityinfowatch.com/.
[33] Haichen Shen et al. 2016. MCDNN: An Approximation-Based Execution Framework for Deep Stream Processing Under Resource Constraints. In *ACM MobiSys*.
[34] Haichen Shen et al. 2018. Fast Video Classification via Adaptive Cascading of Deep Models. In *IEEE CVPR*.
[35] Bi Song et al. 2010. Tracking and activity recognition through consensus in distributed camera networks. *Transactions on Image Processing* (2010).
[36] Ashish Vulimiri et al. 2015. Wanalytics: Geo-distributed analytics for a data intensive world. In *ACM SIGMOD*.
[37] M. Zaharia et al. 2010. Spark: cluster computing with working sets. In *USENIX HotCloud*.
[38] Haoyu Zhang et al. 2017. Live Video Analytics at Scale with Approximation and Delay-Tolerance. In *USENIX NSDI*.
[39] Tan Zhang et al. 2015. The Design and Implementation of a Wireless Video Surveillance System. In *ACM MobiCom*.
[40] Liang Zheng et al. 2017. Person Re-Identification in the Wild. In *IEEE CVPR*.

Towards a Distraction-free Waze

Kevin Christensen
Carnegie Mellon University
kchrist1@andrew.cmu.edu

Christoph Mertz
Carnegie Mellon University
cmertz@andrew.cmu.edu

Padmanabhan Pillai
Intel Labs
padmanabhan.s.pillai@intel.com

Martial Hebert
Carnegie Mellon University
mhebert@andrew.cmu.edu

Mahadev Satyanarayanan
Carnegie Mellon University
satya@cs.cmu.edu

ABSTRACT

Real-time traffic monitoring has had widespread success via crowd-sourced GPS data. While drivers benefit from this low-level, low-latency road information, any high-level traffic data such as road closures and accidents currently have very high latency as such systems rely solely on human reporting. Increasing the detail and decreasing the latency of this information can have significant value. In this paper we explore this idea by using a camera along with an in-vehicle computer to run computer vision algorithms that continuously observe the road conditions in high-detail. Abnormalities are automatically reported via 4G LTE to a local server on the edge, which collects and stores the data, and relays updates to other vehicles inside its zone. In this paper we develop and test such a system, which we call *LiveMap*. We demonstrate its accuracy on detecting hazards and characterize the system latency achieved.

CCS CONCEPTS

• **Information systems** → **Mobile information processing systems**; *Sensor networks*; • **Networks** → **Application layer protocols**; *Mobile networks*; • **Computing methodologies** → **Object detection**; *Neural networks*.

KEYWORDS

Vehicular Systems; Automotive Systems; Edge Computing; Cloudlet; Cloud Computing; Cellular Wireless Networks; 4G LTE; 5G ; Distracted Driving; Crowd-sourcing; Neural Networks; Object Detection

ACM Reference Format:
Kevin Christensen, Christoph Mertz, Padmanabhan Pillai, Martial Hebert, and Mahadev Satyanarayanan. 2019. Towards a Distraction-free Waze. In *The 20th International Workshop on Mobile Computing Systems and Applications (HotMobile '19), February 27–28, 2019, Santa Cruz, CA, USA*. ACM, New York, NY, USA, 6 pages. https://doi.org/10.1145/3301293.3302369

1 INTRODUCTION

Over 100-million active users benefit from Waze every month [17]. This crowd-sourced application allows drivers and passengers to report road events to a collecting entity that merges information and

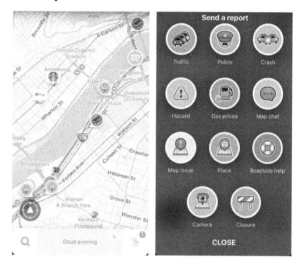

Figure 1: a) Left: A screenshot of Waze app with road events overlayed on GPS navigation map. b) Right: A screenshot of the Waze hazard reporting interface.

overlays it on GPS navigation maps via the mobile Waze app [4]. Figure 1 shows the Waze app interface.

In 2013 Google purchased Waze for 1.15 billion dollars [17], which is an indication of the perceived value for its service. Unfortunately the benefits of Waze come at the cost of user distraction, which is known to be a major source of traffic accidents [5][8]. Since the majority of vehicles have just the driver in the car with no passengers, Waze reports are typically made by a driver who incurs distraction in creating and submitting the Waze report. In short, the service is valuable but dangerous to not only the driver but also to nearby drivers, pedestrians, and bicyclists. With advances in computer vision and edge computing, we ask the question: "Can we have the benefits of Waze without user distraction?" Our approach to solve this problem utilizes an in-vehicle camera with an in-vehicle computer termed the Vehicle Cloudlet, to run computer vision algorithms to observe the road conditions. Abnormalities are then reported via 4G LTE to a local server on the edge, termed the Zone Cloudlet. The Zone Cloudlet synthesizes the data, stores it in a database, and notifies other Vehicle Cloudlets inside its zone of responsibility. The Zone Cloudlet is situated on the edge in order to improve bandwidth scalability and provide more localized control of user data and privacy, as well as for potential national security reasons to decentralize such information [15]. This is in contrast to Vehicle-to-Vehicle (V2V) Communication systems [16][21], which focus on addressing issues such as immediate collision detection and avoidance, as well as highway platooning. V2V communication exhibits additional security concerns, such as message accuracy and reliability, etc. The Zone Cloudlet in contrast can address such issues by vetting information before sharing it with other vehicles. Note that this pipeline would also enable autonomous vehicles to make reports as well since it does not require a human in the loop. In this paper we focus on the development of an architecture for such a system, and demonstrate it detecting hazards such as potholes, which are frequently found locally for testing.

In prior work [10], we have shown that a 4G LTE network is sufficient to support such a large-scale system with tens of thousands of participating vehicles, as demonstrated through simulations in SUMO [12] (Simulation of Urban Mobility). While that work focused on the scalability challenges of using LTE, in this work we focus on the architecture, implementation, and characterization of the automated hazard reporting system.

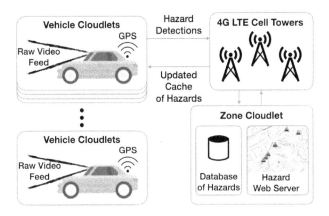

Figure 2: System Overview. Vehicle Cloudlets run hazard detection on live video feed, reporting any hazards to the Zone Cloudlet for dissemination to other vehicles and for display through a web interface.

2 BACKGROUND AND RELATED WORK

To the best of our knowledge, no previous work has attempted to create a Waze-like real-time data collection system for road monitoring without a human in the loop. From a broader perspective, there is a substantial amount of work relating to road condition monitoring [7][18][6][13]. However, none of these can handle the wide variations in hazard types and durations of events such as accidents, debris on the road, potholes, etc. Many of these systems focus on road infrastructure monitoring such as detecting potholes or general road health inspection.

A common approach for detecting potholes is to use an accelerometer with signal processing. The most notable of these, the Pothole Patrol [7], utilizes an accelerometer and on-board filtering to determine likely locations of a pothole. Such a system has several drawbacks, the most significant being that it requires the vehicle to physically run over the pothole for detection. This is harmful to both the vehicle and uncomfortable for the driver. For this reason, it is not uncommon for drivers to swerve in order to deliberately miss running over a pothole. Furthermore, it is limited to a very specific type of road monitoring — that is, whatever the car physically hits. A non-destructive alternative is to instead use image processing.

There has also been prior research in the field of vehicular distributed network system architectures. CarTel [11] has explored the development of such a system. They detail and prototype a system that utilizes vehicles to collect sensor data, store it locally, and prioritize the dissemination of sensor data to a local server. The main disadvantage of their system is that, as described, they have no significant on-board compute and cannot locally process data-rich media, such as images. Thus, their system is limited to selective transmission as the only approach to dealing with low-bandwidth situations. Furthermore, as it relies on opportunistically connecting to local Wi-Fi hotspots, it suffers from frequent loss of network connectivity. The main advantage of LiveMap is that it can process media rich sensor data such as video feed on-board the vehicle, and can greatly save bandwidth by transmitting only distilled, interesting data, thus enabling effective use of relatively low bandwidth, but ubiquitous 4G LTE networks.

A few companies offer commercial products that are relevant to our research. Waze [4] utilizes user input in order to add detailed input to their maps. As previously discussed, the main shortcoming of such a system is that it creates dangerous situations by distracting the driver, and tends to incur high latencies and unreliable updates due to reliance on human reporting. In contrast, LiveMap is safe, autotmated, and real-time. Another relevant company is Roadbotics [3]. Roadbotics uses cameras to capture video data of roads from the windshield, and uploads it to a server where machine learning algorithms score road conditions over 10-foot intervals. In comparison to Roadbotics, LiveMap operates in real-time, is not specific to detecting road quality, and can generalize to any hazards detectable through computer vision.

3 SYSTEM ARCHITECTURE

LiveMap is designed to scale to a large number of vehicles [10], and as such it is critical that our system scales with increased bandwidth such that we do not saturate the 4G LTE network. Sending video streams from every vehicle would quickly prove to be intractable, and moving the Zone Cloudlet to the cloud would also degrade the scalability of our system. Instead, we harness compute ability both in the vehicle and in the infrastructure on the edge to reduce network use.

The key idea behind LiveMap is that it performs the heavy video analytics computations on-board the vehicle. Each participating vehicle is required to have an on-board camera and GPS module, as well as a computer, called the Vehicle Cloudlet. As the vehicle drives around, it runs a Convolutional Neural Network (CNN) to detect various hazards. When a hazard is detected with a confidence level greater than a threshold, the Vehicle Cloudlet reports it to the Zone Cloudlet via a message containing the GPS coordinates, the image with bounding box(es) around the hazard(s), as well as the timestamp and other metadata pertaining to the drive. The Zone Cloudlet is responsible for handling the incoming data, storing it in a database, and notifying the vehicles in the vicinity of the hazard. See Figure 2 for a high-level overview of LiveMap.

Figure 3: Map of Hazards. Icons for each hazard appear real-time. Clicking on each icon displays more hazard information.

There are several challenges associated with choosing when and how often to report hazards. One such challenge is in avoiding identical reports. Imagine a vehicle stuck in traffic behind an accident; until the accident clears the system will repeatedly detect the same accident. Now imagine there are many cars that view this accident. This single event may be reported thousands of times. Such careless report sending policies would quickly saturate the network with useless duplicate data.

To address this issue of duplicating data, we employ a policy that if a vehicle detects a hazard of the same type in close proximity to one that has previously been reported, it will not send the report. This achieves the desired result of saving bandwidth by avoiding duplicate reports, with the small cost of perhaps missing a few instances of the same class. We argue that this is indeed an acceptable tradeoff with the following example: Suppose several objects fall from a truck in one area on the highway, creating hazardous debris. A car driving by will detect multiple frames of debris, but will only send one report. In general, this single report for multiple related hazards should suffice. Another such issue that complicates this design decision is the issue of hazard removal. Different types of hazards may have various temporal lifespans. For instance, some hazards like car accidents are usually cleaned up and removed within a matter of hours, while potholes can exist for several months. At the Zone Cloudlet, detecting when a hazard is no longer present can be tricky. A naive solution would be to wait until reports of the hazard stop arriving. This idea is flawed due to our previous design decision to not report duplicate hazards. It is difficult to know if a hazard has "expired" or if the duplicate elimination policy is preventing further reports. It is possible the Zone Cloudlet may never hear again about a long-lasting hazard.

To address this second issue, we use a polling scheme. In this polling scheme, the Zone Cloudlet occasionally sends a message to vehicles near a previously-reported hazard asking them if they still see the hazard, and optionally whether or not to send an image. The Vehicle Cloudlets then send a "yes" or "no" reply back after validating the continued presence of the hazard, minimizing the bandwidth consumed for verifying the hazard presence. The rate at which such verification polls are sent would be inversely proportional to the expected duration of the hazard, based on the mean or median duration of the hazard class type. This can be further optimized

as the system collects more data and can generate more accurate predictions of when best to poll while minimizing network usage.

4 IMPLEMENTATION

4.1 Zone Cloudlet

The Zone Cloudlet is situated on the edge, and in our experiments is implemented on a server on the Carnegie Mellon University (CMU) campus. It has a number of responsibilities, which can be classified into two main functionalities: 1) hazard message operations and 2) web server operations. Within the class of hazard message operations, the Zone Cloudlet must accept and handle incoming hazard reports from vehicles, and transmit update data to vehicles. See Figure 4.

When the Zone Cloudlet receives a hazard report, it queries its database for any matching hazards previously reported within the tolerance of the GPS module (typically around 3-5 meters). If no active matches are found (i.e., this is not a duplicate report), it adds the hazard to its database. It then sends a message to all vehicles in its area of responsibility with the GPS coordinates of the hazard, and an image of the hazard with a bounding box around it.

For our implementation, we opted to use the Message Queuing Telemetry Transport (MQTT) protocol, an ISO standard built on top of TCP/IP [1]. MQTT is a publisher-subscriber-based messaging protocol intended for the "Internet of Things," and is designed around the idea that machine-to-machine communication will have limited network bandwidth and will suffer from intermittent connectivity. This fits our application requirements, since moving vehicles will invariably be in a dead zone at one time or another, and the 4G LTE network has limited bandwidth. For a Vehicle Cloudlet to receive updates from the Zone Cloudlet, it simply has to look up its GPS coordinates, find the nearest Zone Cloudlet, and subscribe to the updates being published by the Zone Cloudlet. In order to avoid major safety concerns, we limit communication in LiveMap as follows: the Zone Cloudlet is the message broker, and the Vehicle Cloudlets are the clients; no vehicle-to-vehicle communication is performed, and all messages to the Vehicle Cloudlets must come from the Zone Cloudlet.

The second class of operations has to do with the presentation of hazard information, which is done via a web-based interface. The Zone Cloudlet doubles as a web server, and actively delivers hazard information on a map overlay to connected web clients. When a client, say a city official, connects to the web server, the Zone Cloudlet sends all present hazards to the client, which are displayed on the map as icons. The user can then click on the icon and have additional information displayed, such as GPS coordinates and the image with bounding box of the detected hazard. When a new hazard is added to the database, a notification is sent via web sockets to all connected clients in real-time. An example screenshot of the web-based hazard display is shown in Figure 3. We use Leaflet [2] as our map serving framework, and Node.js to dynamically deliver content. This web server display can effectively serve as a quality control measure. Since the details of all hazards can be displayed on the map as images with bounding boxes encapsulating the hazards, a city official can easily verify the accuracy of hazard detections with a click on each hazard icon. This provides an interface for human oversight of the system, letting an official reject any false positives before notifying the appropriate response teams, for example.

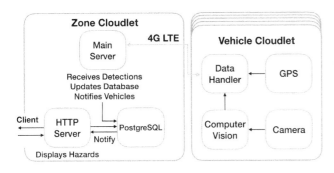

Figure 4: System Architecture. The Zone Cloudlet handles incoming hazard reports and notifies other vehicles. It also runs an HTTP server that displays a map of detected hazards.

4.2 Vehicle Cloudlet

The Vehicle Cloudlet performs image processing to find hazards. It utilizes a Convolutional Neural Network (CNN) to perform object detection to identify road abnormalities, and then sends a message to the Zone Cloudlet with accompanying data. When it detects a hazard, it checks its local database of current hazards for a nearby hazard of the same type. If it doesn't find any, it adds it to its database and sends a message to the Zone Cloudlet. In doing this it avoids repeatedly sending notifications of known hazards. When the Vehicle Cloudlet receives a hazard notification from the Zone Cloudlet, it adds it to its database. In previous work [10] we have shown detection of deer on the roadside (https://youtu.be/_GrP42359z8). We have also recently demonstrated the system detecting traffic cones (https://youtu.be/TToOb2rTNZU), which often signal lane closures. The list of objects that can be detected is extensible: new object classes can be added to the system by providing a classifier trained on the object data. Some other items that may be useful to detect include road closure signs, road debris, construction equipment, and accidents. New detectors can be incrementally added as they become available.

Not all types of hazards are of equal importance. Vehicle Cloudlets would contain a list of hazard types with a possibly dynamic importance ranking for each hazard type. Hazards that are ranked with high importance would be sent immediately, while those that are less serious can be deferred until the Vehicle Cloudlet is connected to WI-FI in a garage, for example. This feature would save bandwidth without sacrificing completeness.

The accuracy and recall capability of the sensing is a function of compute capability, which is a function of cost. We explore the trade-off between accuracy/recall and cost by experimenting with two different designs and implementations for the Vehicle Cloudlet. One configuration is a powerful server with state-of-the-art compute capability but can run reliably off of a car alternator. We call this the Big Vehicle Cloudlet (BVC). It can afford to use a more computationally expensive and memory intensive CNN architecture for detection, employing dual GPUs with high bandwidth and large memory. The second option uses a mobile phone as the Vehicle Cloudlet, which has significantly less compute capability and memory, but is an order of magnitude lower in cost. We term this the Small Vehicle Cloudlet (SVC). We outline both implementations below and highlight the key differences between them.

Table 1: Latency Measurements in ms

Config	Detection	Transmission	End-to-end
BVC	38.6 (3.1)	205.6 (50.2)	244.2 (50.3)
SVC+ZC	391.6 (67.1)		597.2 (83.7)

BVC: Big Vehicle Cloudlet, SVC: Small Vehicle Cloudlet
ZC: Zone Cloudlet, std. deviation in parentheses
Note that the latency for BVC is per GPU

4.3 Big Vehicle Cloudlet

The first system we test is a ruggedized server, configured with 2 Intel® Xeon® Processors, 2 Nvidia Tesla V100 GPUs, and a liquid cooling system. This system configuration can afford to run a large CNN model with a large number of weights, which is both memory and compute intensive. On this system, we run Faster R-CNN [14] as our object detector, which provides state-of-the-art accuracy, but is computationally demanding. The image processing is run on both GPUs independently in order to double the processing frame rate. Each GPU has a copy of the CNN weights and can run inference on an individual image independently. The output image is the original image overlaid with bounding boxes indicating where a hazard was detected. If a hazard is detected and is not a duplicate, the Vehicle Cloudlet prepares a message and sends it to the Zone Cloudlet. If the image is not interesting and no hazards were detected, the system simply discards the image.

This setup provides the best scalability, as we have moved all of the compute to the vehicle, and the aggregate compute capability will scale with number of vehicles. Furthermore, the BVC is well-positioned to address privacy concerns that arise from recording people in such video feeds. The BVC has enough compute to denature images as done in [19].

4.4 Small Vehicle Cloudlet

The second system we test uses a smartphone-class device as the Vehicle Cloudlet. As this platform is not capable of running the large CNN used for hazard detection, we employ the early discard method proposed by [20] that uses lightweight computations to selectively send only the interesting images to the Zone Cloudlet, which would then run the hazard detection algorithm. The small vehicle cloudlet is limited to making send-don't send decisions using a small and simple neural network model. The expensive hazard detection algorithm is then run on the Zone Cloudlet. This significantly reduces costs of the vehicles, but comes at the expense of scalability, since we move the hazard detection to the centralized Zone Cloudlet.

We implement the Small Vehicle Cloudlet using a Nexus 6 smartphone, and run MobileNet [9] as the image classifier. This has significantly lower computational requirements than Faster-RCNN, and can process roughly three frames per second on this platform.

5 EXPERIMENTAL RESULTS

There are three aspects of performance that we consider when evaluating LiveMap. The first is the end-to-end system latency for LiveMap given a new hazard. This is the time it takes from the point at which a vehicle detects a hazard, sends it to the Zone Cloudlet, and the Zone Cloudlet sends out the newly captured data to nearby

Figure 5: Examples of pothole detections with bounding boxes.

Table 2: Detection Results

Config	FPS	mAP	Event Recall	Avg. Mbps
BVC	30	52.7	92.3%	0.46
SVC+ZC	2.8	52.7*	84.6%	0.91

BVC: Big Vehicle Cloudlet, SVC: Small Vehicle Cloudlet,
ZC: Zone Cloudlet, *Zone Cloudlet only

vehicles. The second evaluation criterion is the hazard detection accuracy and recall. Ideally we want high accuracy (quality detections with a high ratio of true positives among all detections), as well as high recall (most hazards are actually reported). Lastly, we need to quantify the bandwidth savings by moving compute into the vehicle.

System latency can be further broken down into two categories: 1) detection latency, or the time it takes to process a single image, and 2) message round-trip latency, or the time it takes to send a message to the Zone Cloudlet and receive an acknowledgement. The detection latency is dependent on the Vehicle Cloudlet server, while the transmission latency is the same for both configurations since they will both be using 4G LTE for transmission. Note that for the Small Vehicle Cloudlet, the detection latency includes both the local image classification, which gives a send-don't send result, as well as the actual hazard detection code, which places bounding boxes around hazards, running on the Zone Cloudlet. To test the detection latency, we simply record the time the system takes to process each frame over a one minute interval. See Table 1 for Transmission Latency and Detection Latency results. Note that the Big Vehicle Cloudlet has two GPUs, but Table 1 shows latency *per* GPU. On an end-to-end basis, using the Big Vehicle Cloudlet incurs less than half of the latency as using the Small Vehicle Cloudlet.

The camera frame rate is 30 fps, therefore the ideal processing latency is below 33 ms to achieve real-time performance. Per-frame processing times greater than 33 ms would imply that frames are dropped, or not processed. By utilizing 2 GPUs and alternating frames assigned to each, the Big Vehicle Cloudlet can avoid dropping any frames. While it is great to process every frame, it is often not necessary in order to detect hazards.

Our second metric attempts to quantify how well the system actually detects road hazards. We consider this in two different ways. For the Big Vehicle Cloudlet we measure the mean Average Precision (mAP), which is a common metric for evaluating bounding-box-based object detection algorithms. We use the standard mAP_{50} which defines a correct detection if the intersection over union of the detected and the ground truth bounding boxes is greater than 50%. Note that we use this metric to evaluate BVC's detection algorithm,

which is also run on the Zone Cloudlet for the SVC configuration. We obtain this metric over all test images.

Frequently a hazard will be encountered more than in just one frame. In fact, we expect to encounter any given hazard in multiple frames. Even if detection failed in one frame, the system may still be able to identify the hazard in another one. To address this, we employ an event-level recall metric, which we define as the number of distinct hazards correctly identified over the total number of hazards. For the Big Vehicle Cloudlet we filter out duplicate detections based on GPS location. If we detect a hazard of the same class in the same location, we can filter out the message as it was likely the same instance of the hazard previously detected. Note that we cannot utilize this for the Small Vehicle Cloudlet, as it simply categorizes the image as interesting or not interesting, and furthermore runs at a much slower frame rate.

Deep Neural Networks require large amounts of annotated data for training. For our prototype, it was not feasible to collect a large training set of accidents or debris on the road. Rather, we focused our proof-of-concept on detecting hazards for which we could collect data, namely potholes. We annotated approximately 3,000 pothole images to train our detector from a set of set of driving videos we collected. Data collected consists of footage in the greater Pittsburgh region across various lighting and weather conditions, as well as from various viewpoints. We kept aside a portion of the data for testing. We show the metrics in Table 2 and example positive detections in Figure 5. Due to the limited processing rate of the SVC configuration, many frames are dropped. This reduces its consumed bandwidth, but also reduces its event recall.

Finally, the third metric is the average bandwidth saved by utilizing compute in-vehicle. We run both the Big and Small Vehicle Cloudlets on the same recorded driving video, and record the amount of data transferred over TCP. We compare these to a third baseline option, in which the compressed H.264 video is streamed to a central server for processing. Figure 6 summarizes our results. Here, the video stream rate of the baseline is plotted as a red line. The GPS-based duplicate suppression is heavily dependent on the speed of the vehicle, and the rate at which we encounter hazards. Therefore, we test the Big Vehicle Cloudlet with several different radii parameters for redundant hazard checking, ranging from 1 meter to 25 meters. We show the theoretical best detector as the green star in the bottom right for reference, which exhibits perfect accuracy and recall, as well as the lowest possible bandwidth (i.e., each unique hazard is reported exactly once). Note that the consumed bandwidth is inversely proportional to the detection accuracy.

We can see that the Big Vehicle Cloudlet performs the best in terms of recall with GPS filtering of radii 1m, 3m, and 5m. Using a larger GPS filtering radius decreases bandwidth consumed at the cost

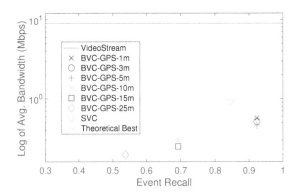

Figure 6: Bandwidth uplink in Mbps. Y-axis shown in log scale.

of hazard recall. The Small Vehicle Cloudlet provides a reasonable compromise between the two. The SVC requires more bandwidth since it uses a "filtering out" approach, and sends the image without knowing what the predicted class type is due to its limited memory and compute capabilities. We cannot use such spatial filter strategies because the SVC does not know what class of hazard was just detected. This is the main drawback of such a filtering out approach, and it therefore tends to send images more frequently on average. Additionally, since it operates at a low frame rate, it may be susceptible to missing hazards that are only visible briefly, a situation not reflected by these experiments. Overall, moving compute inside the vehicle reduces the average bandwidth consumed by around 95% compared to the baseline. Streaming the data costs nearly 9 Mbps uplink while our system used less than 0.5 Mbps with 5 meter GPS filtering. Extrapolating from this, if the average vehicle is driven for 1 hour a day, over the course of a month streaming video would require approximately 121 GB per vehicle, whereas our method would consume only 6.3 GB.

In Figure 6 we can see that even the theoretical "perfect detector," which exhibits perfect precision and recall, still sends a significant amount of data detecting potholes. Further restricting the report rate for non-urgent hazards would further reduce this number as well, as potholes in some cities may be categorized as non-urgent and can be transmitted when connected to WI-FI.

6 CONCLUSION

We have proposed a system architecture, LiveMap, that automates the detection and reporting of road hazard information utilizing in-vehicle compute and recent advances in computer vision. We have built and demonstrated a prototype system using both powerful and modest in-vehicle computers coupled with edge computing services. Both variants are able to detect and report potholes with no human involvement. Furthermore, we reduce the bandwidth consumed by such a system by over twenty-fold compared to video streaming to the cloud for processing. Future work includes expanding the types of hazards we can detect as well as developing reporting protocols to allow prioritization of hazard classes, and efficient dissemination of collected hazard information. In order to address privacy concerns, we plan on utilizing the compute in the BVC to selectively blur license plates and faces in images. We plan on

adding such functionality to the first production release of LiveMap. Another future goal is to develop algorithms that are able to reliably fuse together reports of the same hazard from different vehicles that are off due to GPS inaccuracies and localization inaccuracies, and yet can determine that perhaps a line of traffic cones is signaling a road closure. Lastly, there is value in being able to detect street-view changes, not just hazards. Such examples include detecting new or removed buildings, road signs, and more. We plan on investigating these aspects in future versions of LiveMap.

ACKNOWLEDGMENTS

We thank Tom Eiszler and John Kozar for their technical assistance. We also thank our shepherd, Aruna Balasubramanian, and the anonymous reviewers for their guidance in strengthening this paper. This research was supported in part by the Defense Advanced Research Projects Agency (DARPA) under Contract No. HR001117C0051 and by the National Science Foundation (NSF) under grant number CNS-1518865. Additional support was provided by Intel, Vodafone, Deutsche Telekom, Verizon, Crown Castle, NTT, and the Conklin Kistler family fund. Any opinions, findings, conclusions or recommendations expressed in this material are those of the authors and do not necessarily reflect the view(s) of their employers or the above-mentioned funding sources.

REFERENCES

[1] Eclipse paho. https://www.eclipse.org/paho/.
[2] Leaflet. https://leafletjs.com/.
[3] Roadbotics. https://www.roadbotics.com/, Accessed: 2018-09-17.
[4] Waze. https://www.waze.com/, Accessed: 2018-09-17.
[5] N. E. Boudette. Biggest spike in traffic deaths in 50 years? blame apps.
[6] D. B. A. Chacra and J. S. Zelek. Fully automated road defect detection using street view images. In *2017 14th Conference on Computer and Robot Vision (CRV)*, pages 353–360, May 2017.
[7] J. Eriksson, L. Girod, B. Hull, R. Newton, S. Madden, and H. Balakrishnan. The pothole patrol: Using a mobile sensor network for road surface monitoring. In *Proceedings of the 6th International Conference on Mobile Systems, Applications, and Services*, MobiSys '08, pages 29–39, New York, NY, USA, 2008. ACM.
[8] L. L. Firm. Is the waze driving app too distracting?
[9] A. G. Howard, M. Zhu, B. Chen, D. Kalenichenko, W. Wang, T. Weyand, M. Andreetto, and H. Adam. Mobilenets: Efficient convolutional neural networks for mobile vision applications. *CoRR*, abs/1704.04861, 2017.
[10] W. Hu, Z. Feng, Z. Chen, J. Harkes, P. Pillai, and M. Satyanarayanan. Live synthesis of vehicle-sourced data over 4G LTE. In *Proceedings of the 20th ACM International Conference on Modelling, Analysis and Simulation of Wireless and Mobile Systems*, MSWiM '17, pages 161–170, New York, NY, USA, 2017. ACM.
[11] B. Hull, V. Bychkovsky, Y. Zhang, K. Chen, M. Goraczko, A. K. Miu, E. Shih, H. Balakrishnan, and S. Madden. CarTel: A Distributed Mobile Sensor Computing System. In *4th ACM SenSys*, Boulder, CO, November 2006.
[12] D. Krajzewicz, J. Erdmann, M. Behrisch, and L. Bieker. Recent development and applications of SUMO - Simulation of Urban MObility. *International Journal On Advances in Systems and Measurements*, 5(3&4):128–138, December 2012.
[13] M. G. N. Angelini, J. Brache and G. Shevlin. Gps coordinate pothole mapping. Technical report, Worchester Polytechni, 2006.
[14] S. Ren, K. He, R. B. Girshick, and J. Sun. Faster R-CNN: towards real-time object detection with region proposal networks. *CoRR*, abs/1506.01497, 2015.
[15] M. Satyanarayanan. Edge computing for situational awareness. In *2017 IEEE International Symposium on Local and Metropolitan Area Networks (LANMAN)*, pages 1–6, June 2017.
[16] M. L. Sichitiu and M. Kihl. Inter-vehicle communication systems: a survey. *IEEE Communications Surveys & Tutorials*, 10(2), 2008.
[17] C. Smith. 14 interesting waze statistics and facts (june 2018).
[18] S. Varadharajan, S. Jose, K. Sharma, L. Wander, and C. Mertz. Vision for road inspection. In *IEEE Winter Conference on Applications of Computer Vision*, pages 115–122, March 2014.
[19] J. Wang, B. Amos, A. Das, P. Pillai, N. Sadeh, and M. Satyanarayanan. A scalable and privacy-aware iot service for live video analytics. In *Proceedings of the 8th ACM on Multimedia Systems Conference*, MMSys'17, pages 38–49, New York, NY, USA, 2017. ACM.
[20] J. Wang, Z. Feng, Z. Chen, S. George, M. Bala, P. Pillai, S.-W. Yang, and M. Satyanarayanan. Bandwidth-efficient live video analytics for drones via edge computing. In *SEC '18: Proceedings of the Third ACM/IEEE Symposium on Edge Computing*, New York, NY, USA, 2018. ACM.
[21] F. Ye, M. Adams, and S. Roy. V2v wireless communication protocol for rear-end collision avoidance on highways. In *ICC Workshops - 2008 IEEE International Conference on Communications Workshops*, pages 375–379, May 2008.

A Hypervisor-Based Privacy Agent for Mobile and IoT Systems

Neil Klingensmith
University of Wisconsin
Electrical and Computer Engineering
naklingensmi@wisc.edu

Younghyun Kim
University of Wisconsin
Electrical and Computer Engineering
younghyun.kim@wisc.edu

Suman Banerjee
University of Wisconsin
Computer Science
suman@cs.wisc.edu

ABSTRACT

We present a design for a mobile and IoT data privacy agent that lives in software on end devices. Our privacy agent learns and enforces a user's privacy policy across all devices that he manages. Implemented as a hypervisor onboard the end device, our privacy agent sits between the device's hardware and its application software. It can inspect, modify, block, and inject I/O traffic between the device's main CPU and its peripherals. The key advantage of our architecture is that, unlike network middleboxes, the hypervisor can track all I/O transactions in *unencrypted* form. This makes our privacy agent potentially much more effective than those that only monitor network traffic because it can track and modify plaintext data. Our privacy agent also gives users the ability to impose a uniform privacy policy across all devices that they manage, which minimizes the burden and possibility of error that arise when setting privacy policy on individual devices. Since the notion of per-user (as opposed to per-app) privacy policy is relatively new, there has not been much opportunity for researchers to think about how to define and implement policy on that scale. We propose a method for learning a user's privacy policy one time and automatically implementing it in a context-aware fashion on multiple devices.

CCS CONCEPTS

• **Security and privacy** → **Embedded systems security**; *Mobile platform security*; • **Computer systems organization** → **Embedded software**.

KEYWORDS

Privacy; Mobile Systems; IoT; Hypervisors; Real-time

ACM Reference Format:
Neil Klingensmith, Younghyun Kim, and Suman Banerjee. 2019. A Hypervisor-Based Privacy Agent for Mobile and IoT Systems. In *The 20th International Workshop on Mobile Computing Systems and Applications (HotMobile '19), February 27–28, 2019, Santa Cruz, CA, USA*. ACM, New York, NY, USA, 6 pages. https://doi.org/10.1145/3301293.3302356

1 INTRODUCTION

Data from IoT devices is particularly vulnerable to intrusion because it cannot be curated by users in the same way as a social media feed.

Furthermore, because IoT devices often operate autonomously, we may forget that they are transacting in troves of our personal data, much of which is of a far more intimate nature than the cat pictures and status updates we share on social networks. This problem is compounded by the fact that users are increasingly interacting with multiple mobile and IoT devices. When, as many predict, we are routinely interacting with hundreds of autonomous devices, the problem of managing the privacy settings for each will be intractable.

In this work, we examine the possibility of deploying a verifiably independent privacy agent onboard IoT and mobile devices. It would implement a user's personal privacy policy across all IoT devices that the user manages. This privacy agent, under exclusive control of the user, can act as an intermediary between the device software and its cloud services platform. Our agent can inspect the flows and prune or modify potentially sensitive information before it can be released to the putatively untrusted cloud.

For users, the benefit of having a privacy agent is that they can assert control over the way their data is used. Instead of having to blanketly agree to the service providers' privacy policy for every IoT and mobile app, users would have the option of setting their own privacy policy for their devices.

We propose building a privacy agent that is implemented as a hypervisor onboard mobile and IoT devices. It lives between the system's hardware and its stock app, inspecting, modifying, and dropping data that is transmitted between the app and its peripheral hardware devices. Because these peripheral buses typically transmit data in unencrypted form, our privacy agent has access to data collected in plain text. Since it can see raw data, our privacy agent has the opportunity to implement targeted privacy policies that would not be possible with a network middlebox, which generally would only have access to encrypted data.

If a user has several devices outfitted with our hypervisor-based privacy agent, he can set his privacy policy once and allow all devices to implement it in a context-aware fashion. This would significantly alleviate the difficulty of deploying and managing many IoT devices, particularly if they are all different. However, without the user setting specific policy for each device individually, the system must infer those settings from a high-level description of how devices should behave in general. To our knowledge, this problem of inferring specific policy from a short description has not been investigated before. We discuss some ways of implementing this later in the paper.

For any intermediate privacy agent, there is a tradeoff between ease of deployment and effectiveness that is affected by how closely coupled it is to the IoT device itself. Existing work on the topic of intermediate IoT privacy policy has tended toward the more loosely coupled end of the spectrum because it has been the only approach with a reasonable hope of widespread adoption.

Cinch [1] is another system that used a hypervisor to intercept I/O traffic for security, not privacy. Cinch intercepts traffic on the USB bus and redirects it through a virtual network port so standard networking security measures can be used to validate I/O traffic. Cinch is mostly about validating I/O traffic to prevent attacks to the relatively vulnerable USB driver stack. It does not consider the possibility of selectively anonymizing I/O data which requires (1) that we make different assumptions about the data and (2) that we dedicate significant computational resources to anonymization.

Security vs. Privacy. In security, we generally assume that there are good guys—the users—and bad guys who are trying to disrupt service or steal (computational resources, data, bandwidth, etc.) from the users. In privacy, the delineation is not so clear. The assumption of privacy is that users supply data to service providers, usually of their own volition and in exchange for access to some service. But the service provider may be overly zealous in collecting information about users. In privacy, there are not bad guys—there are only information gluttons. Unlike security, the goal of privacy protections should not be to cut off the flow of information from users to service providers but to limit the flow in a way that acceptable to both user and service provider.

The reason that this seemingly subtle difference matters is that in privacy measures, if we do not like the way a service behaves, we cannot necessarily just shut it down as we would in a security countermeasure. Usually we need to find a solution to allow the service to continue to operate in some capacity. In this work we present a practical mechanism for selective data anonymization which allows the service to continue operating, but it gives users control over what and how much data they share about themselves.

One important technical challenge is to intercept and modify a datastream nonintrusively and with low latency.

2 ARCHITECTURE

Our approach is to run IoT end device software inside a specialized hypervisor. The hypervisor will run on the end IoT device itself. It will emulate the bare-metal hardware interface provided by the specific end device so that the software will not know that it is running inside a hypervisor. A diagram is shown in Figure 1. Hermes is an IoT-optimized hypervisor that could be used for this purpose.

The IoT privacy agent is either a guest that runs inside the hypervisor or an external cloud-based service. When it receives I/O traffic from the hardware, the hypervisor passes the raw data directly to the privacy agent for anonymization according to the user's privacy policy. If the agent is implemented in the cloud, the hypervisor would stream the I/O traffic over a UDP connection, allowing for more sophisticated anonymization software at the expense of latency[1]. The privacy agent can anonymize the data in four general ways before returning it to the hypervisor to be passed to the IoT app:

(1) **Passthrough:** communication between app and peripheral proceeds normally without intervention from the hypervisor. The hypervisor may record salient data to decide if it is necessary to take a different action.

(2) **Drop:** hypervisor drops the communication between app and peripheral. For example, the hypervisor blacks out the image from a video camera.

(3) **Modify:** Hypervisor allows data exchange between peripheral and app, but modifies it in transit. For example, the user's location as reported by a GPS receiver may be modified to make the app think that the user is in a different location.

(4) **Inject:** hypervisor creates fake traffic that appears to be coming from the peripherals to the app. For example, the hypervisor on a smart watch may create fake I/O events that appear to be coming from the accelerometer to spoof the activity tracker.

The privacy agent can observe all I/O traffic exchanged between the IoT device software and its peripherals. As traffic flows back and forth to the peripherals, data can be inspected or modified by the privacy agent's peripheral data processing module. The privacy agent's mode decision engine selects modes for the data parsing module to operate in: passthrough, modify, drop, or inject. The privacy agent's user interface module provides a mechanism to allow the users to define policies that will be implemented by the mode decision engine and peripheral data processing module.

Others have proposed implementing privacy mediators inside network middleboxes that would inspect (and potentially modify) network traffic as it traveled between IoT devices and their respective cloud services [2, 3]. Our approach has two key advantages. First, it will not break if network traffic is encrypted (which it almost surely will be). Second, the hypervisor can control not just the IoT device's interface to the cloud but also its interface to its own hardware. This means that if the user wishes, he could black out a video stream before it can even be processed by the IoT device software or anonymize an audio stream to remove personally identifying information [7].

Because Hermes, unlike IoT device software, is open-source, users can evaluate for themselves whether they think it is secure enough to entrust with their data. But if the IoT device manufacturer cannot be trusted to safeguard the user's data, how can we be certain that it does not modify the hypervisor or bypass its data processing functionality?

One option is to use trusted platform modules (TPMs), which can perform software integrity attestation. A remote machine that lives either on an edge device or in the cloud could interrogate the Hermes-enabled IoT device, using a TPM to validate that the hypervisor is intact. Another option is to have users program their own devices with the hypervisor, similar to rooting an Android phone. This would remove the possibility of IoT device manufacturers disabling the hypervisor.

2.1 Hermes

Hermes [6] is a hypervisor for MMU-less microcontrollers that enables high-performance bare metal applications to coexist with RTOSes and other less time-critical software on a single CPU. Hermes is a single monolithic interrupt service routine that intercepts all CPU exceptions before they can be processed by the operating system. Since it is a relatively small piece of code, it should be possible to verify that it is secure. On boot, the Hermes initialization code sets up the CPU's exception table to point to the Hermes ISR.

---

[1]We have demonstrated this technique in the lab for video traffic with a few tens of milliseconds of additonal latency and a low frame loss rate. We will not present the results of these experiments here.

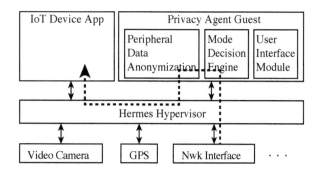

Figure 1: A diagram of the Hermes hypervisor, including our privacy agent, implemented as a guest running in parallel with the IoT device app. The dotted line shows that path traversed by I/O traffic from the hardware to the device's app.

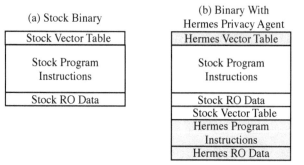

Figure 2: A diagram of the IoT device's software binary, before and after adding the Hermes hypervisor.

It then launches the guest operating systems in the ARM CPU's unprivileged execution mode. In benchmark tests, we have found that I/O responsiveness is far more deterministic under Hermes than under FreeRTOS, the most popular open-source real-time OS. Depending on the type of I/O event, guests running inside Hermes may experience higher I/O latency than apps running on the bare metal (without an operating system or hypervisor), but the increase is comparable to server and workstation virtualization platforms like VMWare and Xen.

2.2 Dynamic Taint Analysis

We propose using dynamic taint analysis similar to Panorama and TaintDroid [4, 9] to track how data flows from I/O peripherals to network connections or storage on IoT devices. Using the hypervisor's ability to inject data into the stock IoT or mobile app, we can insert a taint source at the hardware level and track the tainted data to a destination of interest.

Taint propagation, the process by which we track tainted data as it moves through memory buffers, relies on the hypervisor's ability to trap when a tainted memory region is accessed. Memory protection units (MPUs), available on higher-end ARM Cortex-M CPUs, would allow us to generate an exception when the IoT or mobile app accesses a tainted buffer.

MPUs are like extremely simple versions of memory management units. Their only function is to generate a memory protection exception when a process accesses a memory region that it does not own. Region permissions can be configured by the hypervisor to cause an exception any time the stock IoT or mobile app accesses a tainted buffer. The exception could then be handled by the hypervisor to record the access.

Using dynamic instruction analysis, the hypervisor would be able to generate a taint graph that shows how tainted data propagates from source to sink. This would be an additional tool that could be used to determine whether an app's behavior is consistent with the user's privacy policy.

2.3 Deploying a Virtualized Privacy Agent

Since the Hermes privacy agent lives in the IoT device's main memory, it must be built by someone who is technically proficient

enough to reflash an IoT device. For average users, installation be as easy as rooting a phone if the device has appropriate firmware loading capabilities. The process of building the rooted firmware image is the more technically challenging piece, and that is what we discuss here.

Because of the way that the ARM Cortex-M CPU handles some privilege violations, the IoT software's kernel may need to be patched to be compatible with Hermes. In the ARM Cortex-M core, some privileged instructions, when executed in user mode, will not cause an exception and will instead complete as a NOP instruction. For example, the mrs and msr instructions[2] are classified as privileged instructions, but when they are executed in unprivileged mode, they fail silently: the register write is not committed, and the processor continues normal execution.

The problem is that if a guest OS tries to modify the processor state with one of these privileged instructions, that state modification cannot be registered by Hermes since it does not cause an exception. The privileged instruction will complete like a nop instruction without modifying the CPU state. Critical CPU state changes like disabling interrupts will not work as intended.

This can cause some important changes to the CPU state to go unregistered (see reference [6] for details). As a workaround, we must patch the OS kernel, adding undefined instructions directly following the privileged instructions in order to be sure the hypervisor has an opportunity to trap the privileged instructions and emulate them. When the hypervisor encounters an undefined instruction exception, it will search backward in the instruction stream for an mrs or msr instruction and emulate it. If we run an unpatched kernel inside the hypervisor, it will crash because the intended CPU state modifications will not happen as intended.

To do this, we would need to disassemble the stock binary and insert undefined instructions following the problematic ones. This would also require some branch targets and read-only data references to be relocated.

On the ease-of-deployment spectrum, our solution tends toward the more tightly-coupled end, making it more difficult to deploy than a middlebox approach. To ensure wide-scale adoption, it would be best for our privacy agent to be flashed into firmware by the

---

[2] mrs and msr are most frequently used to enable/disable interrupts and modify stack pointers in an RTOS.

device manufacturer, either during factory programming or a field update.

However, like rooting an Android phone, it would be possible for users to reflash their own IoT and mobile devices. We envision the process of user programming the Hermes-based privacy agent to work as follows:

(1) Read the contents of the IoT device's main program memory into a binary file. This contains the device software's interrupt vector table, program instructions, and read-only data (Figure 2 (a)).

(2) Copy the stock vector table to a different location in the binary image. Replace it with the Hermes vector table[3]. Append the Hermes program instructions and read-only data to the binary file (Figure 2 (b)).

(3) Modify the program's instruction stream, inserting undefined instructions after privileged instructions to be emulated.

(4) Reflash new binary image to the IoT device.

Steps 1 and 4 may require specialized hardware to access the device's program memory. Other authors [5] have shown that it is possible to directly read and write an IoT device's main memory with no special hardware on some devices. Naturally, the process of reading and writing memory would be highly device-specific. Steps 2 and 3 could be carried out automatically by a script.

2.4 Driver Implementation

We have built three preliminary implementations of our privacy agent, one in the Linux kernel, one in FreeRTOS (an embedded OS for microcontrollers), and one in Hermes. Our goal was to understand how driver and hardware interfacing will affect the scalability of our proposed system. In all implementations we built a simple data path in which the mode decision engine and data anonymization blocks are stubs that just pass data through to the device app. Our demo app is an IoT video camera in all cases.

In the Linux kernel we found the process of modifying the USB video driver to be very time consuming and tedious, largely because the driver code lacks comments and documentation. Also, Linux's USB video driver is tightly coupled to video4linux, a logically separate kernel module that presents a video interface to userspace apps. We think that adding privacy agent functionality for other device types would be similarly complex and probably not scalable. Also, implementing the privacy agent in the OS requires the end device to run Linux, which may not be the case for all devices.

The issues in the FreeRTOS implementation were similar to those in Linux with the additional requirement that we needed the complete source code (application plus OS) in order to add our privacy agent. This is because microcontroller software is compiled into a single binary, so we cannot modify the OS while keeping the userland code in place.

The implementation in Hermes was much more seamless, mainly because we did not need to modify any existing drivers. Hermes sends video data to the privacy agent VM in raw form. The privacy agent can modify the data as needed and send it to the IoT device app without worrying about the particulars of how the device app

	Frame Loss Rate	Frame Jitter (σ)
FreeRTOS, Low I/O Load	0 fps	7.03 ms
FreeRTOS, High I/O Load	4.2 fps	47.91 ms
Hermes Low I/O Load	0 fps	4.85 ms
Hermes High I/O Load	0 fps	4.86 ms

Table 1: Performance comparison of Hermes and FreeRTOS in the video app. Low frame loss rate and jitter is better.

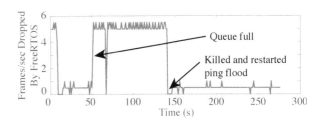

Figure 3: Number of frames dropped by FreeRTOS per second as a function of time while camera was running in the presence of a ping flood.

manages internal data structures. The processor's data sheet, typically freely available, specifies the peripheral's data format, which is what the IoT device app expects to receive from the peripheral. As long as the privacy agent VM generates data in the appropriate format, things will work correctly. Also, since Hermes is a virtualization environment, it presents the same interface to the IoT device runtime software as the hardware. This allows us to add the privacy agent as a separate module while leaving the IoT device software untouched.

2.4.1 Evaluation. In the FreeRTOS and Hermes implementations, we measured frame jitter and loss rate under varying I/O load conditions. Both were benchmarked on an Atmel SAME70 Xplained development board with an ARM Cortex-M7 CPU. The board has a VGA image sensor interface that can accept images in 16-bit RGB color format at a rate of about 10 frames per second. We present an evaluation both as a proof of concept for our privacy agent and as a demonstration that it can be used without diminishing performance (in most cases).

In both cases, we saw no frame losses under low I/O load. Figure 3 shows the number of frames dropped every second during a 276-second test of the FreeRTOS-based privacy agent. Note in the figure that a queue overflow in the RTOS caused a high rate of frame drops under high I/O load. This will not happen in the Hermes implementation because it can be configured to prioritize certain kinds of I/O traffic over others. **Under high I/O load, Hermes lost no frames, and the jitter did not increase** because the hypervisor prioritizes userland video frame processing over lower-priority networking interrupts. Table 1 shows a performance comparison between Hermes and FreeRTOS for the video app under low and high I/O load conditions. Figure 4 shows histograms of the inter-frame timing for the same test cases.

---

[3]The application's original (stock) vector table is needed to initialize it as a guest inside the Hermes hypervisor.

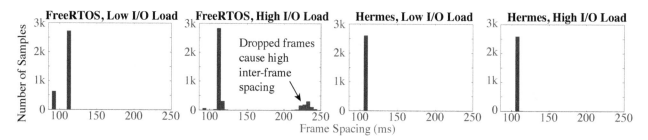

Figure 4: Histograms of inter-frame spacing for our privacy agent, implemented in different runtime environments. We call the standard deviation of these histograms the *jitter* in Table 1.

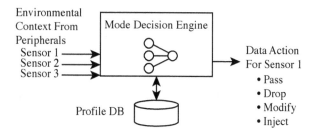

Figure 5: A diagram of the mode decision engine, which uses the privacy policy to decide what action to take with data collected from peripheral devices.

2.5 Privacy Policies

To make our system seamless, we need a way for users to quickly express their privacy policy, similar to [8]. The user's policy should be implemented across all the IoT devices under their control. A privacy policy should begin with a short (one paragraph or less) human-readable explanation of how a user wants his data managed. It should apply generally to all devices under a user's control. In the course of daily device use, the system may occasionally ask the user questions to clarify the policy. Answers will be stored locally and shared with the user's other devices. A neural network in the mode decision engine will make decisions about how data should be anonymized based on the user's responses to privacy policy questions. Its inputs will be (1) data collected from local peripheral devices and (2) the user's responses to targeted questions about data consumption.

2.5.1 Expressing a Privacy Policy. During setup, users are asked to choose a privacy profile that describes, in broad terms, their preferences regarding how the privacy agent will handle their data. Example profiles are:

- **Laissez Faire:** generally permit apps to do as they please with the user's data. Only flag data usage that may be in violation of an app's privacy policy, and alert the user in those cases.
- **Camera-shy:** track video and scrutinize its content. Optionally black out or blur the faces in video frames containing certain people.
- **Secret agent:** don't disclose user's identity (name, email, etc.) or GPS location to cloud services.

The user-selected profile serves as a starting point for the privacy agent. Running on the mobile device, it will take data collected from peripherals and pass it through the profile mode decision engine, which will decide how to handle it (see Figure 5). The mode decision engine will generate one of the four actions outlined above: passthrough, drop, modify, or inject. When the mode decision engine's neural network produces a low-confidence classification, it will query the user to clarify what the privacy policy should be in that situation. User queries will help the mode decision engine refine a personalized privacy policy from the coarse profile.

2.5.2 Implementing Privacy Policies. Some data will have a clear action associated with it: for example, in the camera-shy policy, frames with no faces or people should be passed through without modification. But some will fall in a gray area, like video frames with faces that the policy engine has not seen before. During the course of their device use, users will be asked targeted questions about whether to permit certain kinds of data collection by their mobile and IoT devices in order to clarify the user's policy. Answers to these questions will be stored in the profile database to inform future data handling decisions. The profile database's input-output pairs can be used to train the mode decision engine's classification algorithm. When the database is updated, the updates are pushed to the privacy agents on all devices under the user's control. The mode decision engines on each end device can then be retrained using the new database.

3 APPLICATIONS

Security Camera. suppose a user buys a security camera with cloud-based analytics that can identify suspicious activity within the home. The platform vendor (Nest, Belkin, etc.) advertises that the device comes equipped with the Hermes privacy agent, allowing the user to set his own data privacy policy for the device. This is the first Hermes-enabled IoT device that this user has installed, so he will need to configure his privacy policy for the Hermes privacy agent.

After installation, the user connects the device to the home WiFi network. He then visits a third-party website that validates the presence and integrity of the Hermes privacy agent using the a trusted platform module onboard the camera. This website also asks him to set his privacy policy profile, as outlined in Section 2.5.1. The user chooses both Secret Agent and Camera Shy profiles, and the privacy agent setup is complete.

The Hermes peripheral data parsing modules (Figure 1) monitor video frames as they pass from the camera hardware to the IoT device firmware. The data parsing module passes each frame through the mode decision engine, which interprets the user's privacy policy and decides what action to take (passthrough, drop, modify, or inject). Suppose that most frames contain nothing of interest, so the mode decision engine passes them unmodified to the IoT app, which sends them on to the device manufacturer's cloud-based analytics engine.

Then, the user wanders in front of the camera. The mode decision engine detects his face and notices that it is not in its profile database. It passes the frame up to the IoT app, but it also sends the user an email asking whether or not he wishes frames with his face to be passed, blurred, or blocked in the future. The user requests to have all frames with his face blocked in the future. From then on, the mode decision engine sends black frames to the IoT app software when it detects the user's face in the frame.

Smart Watch. suppose the user subsequently buys a Hermes privacy agent-enabled smart watch. He will again go through the device-specific setup process and the third-party Hermes integrity validation. This time, though, he will not need to configure his privacy profile—the existing profile database will be pushed from the camera to the watch after the integrity validation completes, and he can continue using his new smart watch without any further setup.

As the privacy agent captures I/O transactions and processes them through the mode decision engine, it notices that the user's coordinates are being continuously uploaded to the smart watch vendor's cloud-based server. It identifies this activity as a violation of the secret agent privacy profile, which does not permit transmission of the user's personally-identifying information. The privacy agent begins blocking all I/O transactions to and from the smart watch's GPS receiver and sends an email to the user to inform him that the GPS is being blocked, giving him the option to unblock it if he chooses.

When he receives this second email about GPS data collection by his smart watch, the user decides that the features enabled by GPS tracking are valuable enough to allow it. He enables GPS coordinate collection by the smart watch via the privacy agent's user interface. This decision is sent to the smart watch, which updates its profile database and pushes the updates to the other Hermes privacy agent-enabled devices in the user's home, including the security camera. Once the devices have received their updated profile databases, they retrain their mode decision engines with the new information.

4 CONCLUSION

In this work, we proposed building a mobile and IoT data privacy agent within an embedded hypervisor. The agent would sit between the device's data collection peripherals and the stock IoT software, modifying or pruning data in order to implement the user's individual privacy policy. Instead of asking users to set privacy policies individually for each IoT device, the privacy agent could learn the user's privacy preferences contextually by observing how the user interacts with devices and asking targeted questions about those interactions. A learned privacy policy would be used to configure new devices. This would make IoT device deployment much easier

by reducing the burden of configuring detailed privacy policies for every device. It would also give the user considerably more control in dictating his own privacy policy because the privacy agent would have the power to disable or modify data streams that the user is not comfortable sharing with the service provider.

The techniques we discussed in this work provide a platform to deploy data anonymization software on mobile and IoT devices without cooperation from device manufacturers or service providers. Data anonymization algorithms themselves are relatively new, and their capabilities and limitations are not well understood. In order for our techniques to be useful (and trustworthy), it will be important to think more about information theoretic limits of anonymization algorithms and how those limitations would affect the data transacted by our privacy agent.

5 ACKNOWLEDGMENTS

We would like to acknowledge the anonymous reviewers and our shepherd Dr. Eric Rozner for his detailed comments and guidance. The authors were supported in part by the US National Science Foundation through grants CNS-1719336, CNS-1647152, CNS-1629833, and CNS-1343363.

REFERENCES

[1] Sebastian Angel, Riad S. Wahby, Max Howald, Joshua B. Leners, Michael Spilo, Zhen Sun, Andrew J. Blumberg, and Michael Walfish. 2016. Defending against Malicious Peripherals with Cinch. In *25th USENIX Security Symposium (USENIX Security 16)*. USENIX Association, Austin, TX, 397–414. https://www.usenix.org/conference/usenixsecurity16/technical-sessions/presentation/angel
[2] Andy Crabtree, Tom Lodge, James Colley, Chris Greenhalgh, Kevin Glover, Hamed Haddadi, Yousef Amar, Richard Mortier, Qi Li, John Moore, Liang Wang, Poonam Yadav, Jianxin Zhao, Anthony Brown, Lachlan Urquhart, and Derek McAuley. 2018. Building accountability into the Internet of Things: the IoT Databox model. *Journal of Reliable Intelligent Environments* 4, 1 (01 Apr 2018), 39–55. https://doi.org/10.1007/s40860-018-0054-5
[3] Nigel Davies, Nina Taft, Mahadev Satyanarayanan, Sarah Clinch, and Brandon Amos. 2016. Privacy Mediators: Helping IoT Cross the Chasm. In *Proceedings of the 17th International Workshop on Mobile Computing Systems and Applications (HotMobile '16)*. ACM, New York, NY, USA, 39–44. https://doi.org/10.1145/2873587.2873600
[4] William Enck, Peter Gilbert, Byung-Gon Chun, Landon P. Cox, Jaeyeon Jung, Patrick McDaniel, and Anmol N. Sheth. 2010. TaintDroid: An Information-flow Tracking System for Realtime Privacy Monitoring on Smartphones. In *Proceedings of the 9th USENIX Conference on Operating Systems Design and Implementation (OSDI'10)*. USENIX Association, Berkeley, CA, USA, 393–407. http://dl.acm.org/citation.cfm?id=1924943.1924971
[5] Grant Hernandez, Orlando Arias, Daniel Buentello, and Yier Jin. 2014. Smart nest thermostat: A smart spy in your home. *Black Hat USA* (2014).
[6] Neil Klingensmith and Suman Banerjee. 2018. Hermes: A Real Time Hypervisor for Mobile and IoT Systems. In *Proceedings of the 19th International Workshop on Mobile Computing Systems & Applications (HotMobile '18)*. ACM, New York, NY, USA, 101–106. https://doi.org/10.1145/3177102.3177103
[7] Anantharaghavan Sridhar, Neil Klingensmith, and Suman Banerjee. 2016. dB-Hound: Privacy Sensitive Acoustic Perception in Home Settings: Poster Abstract. In *Proceedings of the 14th ACM Conference on Embedded Network Sensor Systems CD-ROM (SenSys '16)*. ACM, New York, NY, USA, 370–371. https://doi.org/10.1145/2994551.2996711
[8] Primal Wijesekera, Joel Reardon, Irwin Reyes, Lynn Tsai, Jung-Wei Chen, Nathan Good, David Wagner, Konstantin Beznosov, and Serge Egelman. 2018. Contextualizing Privacy Decisions for Better Prediction (and Protection). In *Proceedings of the 2018 CHI Conference on Human Factors in Computing Systems (CHI '18)*. ACM, New York, NY, USA, Article 268, 13 pages. https://doi.org/10.1145/3173574.3173842
[9] Heng Yin, Dawn Song, Manuel Egele, Christopher Kruegel, and Engin Kirda. 2007. Panorama: Capturing System-wide Information Flow for Malware Detection and Analysis. In *Proceedings of the 14th ACM Conference on Computer and Communications Security (CCS '07)*. ACM, New York, NY, USA, 116–127. https://doi.org/10.1145/1315245.1315261

Regulating Drones in Restricted Spaces

Abhishek Vijeev, Vinod Ganapathy, Chiranjib Bhattacharyya

Department of Computer Science and Automation and Robert Bosch Centre for Cyber-Physical Systems

Indian Institute of Science, Bangalore-560012, India

abhishekvijeev@iisc.ac.in,vg@iisc.ac.in,chiru@iisc.ac.in

ABSTRACT

Commercial and end-user drones come equipped with a wide array of sensors. Unregulated use of such drones in public airspaces poses a serious threat to the privacy of citizens. We make the case for *restricted spaces* for drones, which are geographic areas for which a *host* can specify its privacy policies. *Guest* drones must prove to the host that they are in compliance with the host's policies before entering the restricted space. We then make the case for an information-flow control-based policy enforcement framework on drones, and sketch the design of a prototype framework atop the Robot Operating System (ROS).

CCS CONCEPTS

• **Security and privacy** → **Mobile platform security**; **Information flow control**;

KEYWORDS

Drones; privacy; restricted spaces; trusted hardware

ACM Reference Format:

Abhishek Vijeev, Vinod Ganapathy, Chiranjib Bhattacharyya. 2019. Regulating Drones in Restricted Spaces. In *The 20th International Workshop on Mobile Computing Systems and Applications (HotMobile '19), February 27–28, 2019, Santa Cruz, CA, USA.* ACM, New York, NY, USA, 6 pages. https://doi.org/10.1145/3301293.3302370

1 INTRODUCTION

Commercial and end-user drones are becoming widely available. Such drones can be employed for a number of interesting and socially-beneficial use-cases, such as sensing, search and rescue, and product delivery. However, the wide availability of drones has also put a previously tightly-regulated resource, i.e., airspace, into the hands of commercial entities and end-users. We are already beginning to see an increasing number of cases where commercial drones can pose dire risks. Incidents involving "near-misses" between drones and aeroplanes are becoming increasingly common, with drones sightings being reported as high as 15,500 feet [34]. In August 2018, two DJI Matrice 600 drones were used to carry out an attack in Caracas during an address by the Venezuelan president at a military event [17]. London Gatwick airport was shut down

for approximately three days in December 2018, causing major disruption, after suspicious drones entered the restricted airspace of the airport.

Regulatory bodies, such as the Federal Aviation Authority (FAA), and other law-enforcement agencies are actively seeking to evolve tighter rules for the shared use of airspace by commercial and end-user drones [3, 7, 8, 11, 13]. The impact of regulations on the frequency of such drone-related incidents will only become clear over time. However, we posit that even in a regime where rules regarding the shared use of airspace are clearly formulated and enforced, the future deployment of drones (*e.g.,* those expected to be used by Amazon's Prime Air) will pose a serious risk to the privacy of citizens. Most commercial drones come equipped with cameras and other advanced sensors that can record the environment around them. These sensors are *essential* features of drones, *e.g.,* video feeds and images captured from the drone are used for either autonomous navigation or remote human control of the drone. However, these very sensors can be misused to compromise privacy.

In this paper, we propose to address these issues by developing the vision of *restricted spaces* for drones. A restricted space is an area geographically demarcated by its *host*, within which the host expects *guest drones* to conform to its usage policies. We present the design of a framework via which the host can communicate its privacy policies to a guest drone, and ensure that the policies are enforced on the guest drone.

2 RESTRICTED SPACES FOR DRONES

We now develop our vision of restricted spaces for drones. The host of the restricted space may configure its security policies to suit its privacy needs. We consider three examples below:

• *Process-Images-Locally*: The host may require that any images or video feeds captured by the drone be processed locally within the drone and should not be transmitted over the network. The host may additionally require that the images not be stored in the drone's persistent storage (from where an attacker may recover them later). Such a policy can be applied to autonomous drones that have sufficient processing power to locally process images/video for navigation.

• *Blur-Exported-Images*: If the drone is manually controlled or requires its image/video feed to be processed by a back-end cloud server, then the host may require the image/video feed to be processed by a filtering service that blurs sensitive portions of the image/video (*e.g.,* faces and car registration plates) before the being transmitted to the cloud server. The filtering service could either be a trusted application running within the drone, or a cloud-based service controlled by the host. In the former case the host can leverage trusted hardware on the drone to establish the existence of a filtering service on the drone.

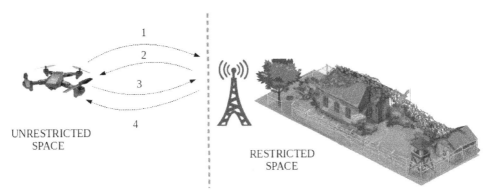

Figure 1: *Restricted spaces for drones.* **(1) When a *guest drone* wishes to enter a *host's* restricted space, it presents its credentials to the host and requests its security policy; (2) The host responds with its security policy, which the guest drone then analyzes to determine if the policy is acceptable to it; (3) If the policy is acceptable, the drone enforces the policy on its software stack, and sends a cryptographic proof to the host that it is in policy compliance; (4) The host verifies the proof and authorizes the drone to enter.**

- *Log-GPS*: The host may require the guest drone to only fly along pre-defined "drone lanes" when within its restricted space. The host can check this by requiring the drone to log its GPS feed during its stay in the restricted space, and to submit this GPS log for analysis as it leaves [20].

When a guest drone enters the restricted space from the outside, it must first "check-in" with the host to determine the host's security policy (see Figure 1). For instance, it could communicate with a Wi-Fi access point or tower controlled by the host. In a 5G or WiMax setting, for instance, the host could have communicated its policy to the 5G-provider, which tags the policy with the host's GPS markers. The drone can directly obtain the policy from the 5G-provider as it approaches the restricted space. During check-in, the drone presents its credentials (*e.g.*, its public key) to the host. The host sends its policy to the drone, which the drone can then choose to analyze to determine if it is acceptable.

If the guest finds the policy too restrictive, it can choose to reject the policy and not enter the host's restricted space. At this point, the host can take suitable action if the drone still chooses to enter its restricted space. The action taken depends on the nature of the host. For example, a defense establishment could choose to shoot down the drone; in contrast, a commercial establishment could choose to report the drone's credentials (or perhaps a close-up picture of the drone) to a regulatory body.

If the guest drone finds the policy acceptable, it applies the policy to the applications running on the drone. It then proves to the host that it is in compliance with the host's policies, and is then granted approval to enter the restricted space. To enable cryptographically-sound proofs, we assume that the drone is equipped with trusted hardware (see threat model below). Once it leaves the host's restricted space, it can "check-out" by choosing to resume execution without the host's policy restrictions. Depending on the host's policy, the drone may be required to submit some information (*e.g.*, its GPS log) during check-out, which the host can then post-process to check for compliance.

A drone will typically fly over multiple such restricted spaces during a single flight to its destination. It must conform to the policy restrictions of all the hosts enroute, or choose to take an alternative path to the destination.

Threat Model. We consider a threat model where hosts assume that guest drones are under adversarial control. Drones must submit their credentials and prove that they are compliant with the host's policies before they enter the restricted space.

To enable robust compliance proofs, we require that the drones be equipped with trusted hardware, such as the ARM TrustZone [4]. Such hardware is becoming increasingly available on commodity devices, and offers a hardware root of trust on the guest device. The hardware is endowed with a public/private key pair, and can produce digitally-signed attestations of the state of the software stack running on the guest drone. The guest's public key (together with its digital certificate) could also serve as the credential used by the host to identify the drone. The host verifies these attestations to determine the guest's security posture. We discuss the details of the attestation process in Section 3. We assume the existence of a regulatory authority that hosts can approach to report drones that enter the restricted space without complying with the host's policies.

Our threat model does *not* currently consider the following two important cases:

- Drones that are not equipped with trusted hardware.
- Covert use of drones.

Without trusted hardware on the drone, hosts do not have a mechanism to reliably identify the drone or verify that it is in compliance. We hypothesize that foolproof verification of the guest drone's security posture is impossible without trusted hardware. Fortunately, consumer devices are increasingly being equipped with ARM TrustZone, and indeed, future regulations may require that commercial drones have a reliable way to establish their identity, *e.g.*, akin to registration plates on vehicles.

A drone may covertly enter the restricted space and compromise the host's privacy. In cases where drones have a miniature form-factor, it may even be difficult for a host to determine that an unauthorized drone is present in its restricted space. Such covert use of drones poses a major risk to privacy, and new methods are needed to detect the presence of such drones.

① **Drone → Host:**	Pub_{drone} + certificate	
	Host verifies certificate	
② **Host → Drone:**	Policy_{host}, nonce	
	Drone checks policy	
③ **Drone → Host:**	Signed attestation quote	
	Host checks attestation/freshness	
④ **Host → Drone:**	Okay to enter	

Figure 2: The check-in protocol.

3 REGULATING DRONE BEHAVIOUR

In this section, we describe how the vision discussed above can be realized on drones equipped with the ARM TrustZone. The methods used by the host to determine whether a drone is in policy compliance also depend on the software stack running on the drone. We describe a concrete implementation for drones running the Robot Operating System (ROS) [24]. We make the case for *dynamic information-flow control* (IFC) as the core policy enforcement mechanism within the drone's software stack, and describe how ROS lends itself well to IFC.

3.1 Background on the ARM TrustZone

The TrustZone is a set of security extensions to the ARM architecture. A TrustZone processor executes in one of two "worlds," a *secure world* or a *normal world*, with the transition between the two mediated by a security monitor. The normal world executes complex applications within a rich computing environment, and is the world with which the end-user interfaces during regular operation of the platform. The secure world consists of security-related applications, and implements functionality such as secure boot, which prevents bootup of devices in which there are unauthorized modifications to the software stack. Device memory can be partitioned between the two worlds such that a partition is reserved for exclusive access by the secure world. This allows the secure world to store sensitive information, such as cryptographic keys, that are not accessible to the normal world, which is untrusted.

3.2 The Check-in Protocol

As shown in Figures 1 and 2, check-in is a four-step protocol:

① The drone identifies itself with its public key Pub_{drone} and the corresponding public key certificate. We assume that the Pub_{drone} uniquely identifies the drone and that it is registered with a suitable regulatory authority. The host verifies the certificate with the regulatory authority.

② The host sends its privacy policy together with a random nonce to the guest drone. The drone determines whether the policy is acceptable to it. In the subsequent discussion, for instance, we show that these policies can be expressed as information-flow control restrictions. If not, it can abort the protocol and navigate away from the restricted space.

③ If the policy is acceptable, the drone sends a signed *attestation quote* [27] back to the host. The attestation quote contains a digitally-signed hash-chain of the software stack installed in the drone's normal world, and is produced by the secure world. The nonce from step ② is also included as part of the signed attestation. The quote allows the host to check that suitable policy-enforcement software is installed on the drone. Note that the host uses Pub_{drone} from step ① to verify the digital signature, thus tying the message

received in step ③ to the drone from step ①. The presence of the nonce in the quote convinces the host that the response is fresh.

④ If all checks succeed, the host authorizes the drone to enter its restricted space.

The above protocol establishes to the host that the guest has policy-enforcement software installed on it. This software could itself execute in the untrusted normal world, with the secure world ensuring that the enforcement code cannot be disabled or modified at runtime. Several widely-deployed systems adopt this approach. For example, the Samsung Knox platform [5] uses this approach to protect against unauthorized modifications to key data structures of the normal world's operating system kernel. As discussed in the following sections, we adopt a similar approach, where the normal world tracks information-flow across applications and peripherals. The normal world contains the enforcement *mechanisms*, the code of which remains unchanged as the drone moves from one restricted space to another. Thus, the secure world simply needs to attest to the host that these mechanisms exist on the drone, and protect the normal world from unauthorized modifications. The *policy* to be enforced would vary based on the host, and the secure world places the policy to be enforced within normal world memory (from where the enforcement mechanism reads and enforces it) and write-protects it (see Figure 3).

3.3 Dynamic Information-flow Control

Dynamic information-flow control (IFC; also called taint-tracking) mechanisms regulate the flow of data objects within a system. IFC mechanisms work by attaching *taint labels* to data objects. The taint of an object changes as it is processed by various entities on the system. IFC employs flow rules that determine how labels can change and whether certain label transitions are allowed. When a data object reaches a *sink* (*e.g.,* an output channel), the label attached to the object can be used to determine whether it can be transmitted via the sink. IFC has successfully been applied in a number of domains, including most notably, to tracking data leaks from Android applications [12].

IFC is well-suited to our setting because it can be used to express a number of useful privacy policies. For example, the policies discussed in Section 1 can be expressed with IFC:

① The *Process-Images-Locally* policy can be enforced by tagging images obtained from the camera with a special label (*e.g.,* camera), and ensuring that data objects with the camera label cannot be stored on disk or accessed by the network interface.

② The *Blur-Exported-Images* policy can be enforced by ensuring that only a trusted blur-filter application, which executes in the normal world and is recorded as part of the attestation quote sent to the host, can change the label of a data object from camera to blurred-img. The network interface is allowed to transmit objects with a blurred-img label but not those with a camera label (see Figure 3).

③ The *Log-GPS* policy can be enforced by ensuring that all readings from the GPS sensor, *e.g.,* tagged GPS, pass through a trusted logging application. The logging application executes in the normal world and interfaces with the secure world to create a tamper-proof audit log. The logging application is authorized to change the label

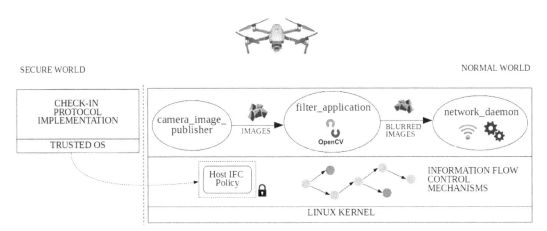

Figure 3: Policy enforcement within the guest drone. The normal world runs a version of ROS enhanced with IFC mechanisms. During check-in, the secure world attests to the host that the normal world runs an IFC-enforcing ROS version. The secure world places and write-protects the host's IFC policy in normal-world memory, and also protects ROS' security mechanisms from unauthorized modifications. In turn, ROS ensures that information-flow restrictions imposed by the host are followed. In this example, it ensures that only images that have been processed by a blur-filter can be read by the network interface.

of GPS sensor readings to audited-GPS, and other client applications on the drone (*e.g.*, control software) can only consume GPS readings with the tag audited-GPS.

Note that the normal world is only entrusted with the task of attaching labels to data objects and propagating these labels as the object is processed by various entities in the system. Label transitions could be implemented by trusted applications running atop the normal world, *e.g.*, the blur-filter and the logging application in the policies described above. These applications are *trusted by the host* in that the host requires the guest drone to execute them for policy compliance; it verifies the integrity of these applications using the attestation quote during check-in.

3.4 IFC on ROS

We built our IFC prototype on ROS. ROS is a set of middleware libraries that run atop Linux, and provides a convenient platform to author robotics applications. ROS is used by a number of drone manufacturers, *e.g.*, 3DR, Parrot, Gaitech, Erle, BitCraze, Skybotix, for developing robotics applications and supports a variety of hardware platforms. The ROS market, including drones and other kinds of robots, is forecasted to reach $400 million by 2026 [25]. A number of popular software packages for drones also build atop ROS. For example, FlytOS [1], which is an operating system for drones, and MAVROS [2], which is a communication driver for autopilots such as PX4 and ArduPilot that use the MAVLink communication protocol (a widely-used protocol for communicating with small drones), are built atop ROS.

ROS is a publish/subscribe system in which applications can either be publishers or subscribers (or both). Every publisher produces data objects on a certain *topic*. Subscribers can choose to listen to messages that fall under a set of topics. When applications start up on ROS, they register themselves as publishers or subscribers for a certain set of topics. ROS libraries then bootstrap communication by matchmaking publishers and subscribers based on the topics they advertised when they started up. It does so by setting up an IPC channel between the corresponding publishers and subscribers.

All underlying communication then directly happens between the Linux processes that implement the publishers and subscribers. For example, the camera application could publish images under the topic camera, and all image-processing applications could choose to subscribe to this topic. ROS ensures that all messages associated with this topic (and only messages associated with this topic) are sent to all subscriber image-processing applications.

The architecture of ROS lends itself well to IFC. Because messages are already tagged with topics, we can directly leverage these topics as IFC labels. The IFC policy simply determines the topics of the data objects that subscribers can consume. Label transitions on data objects by trusted applications are implemented by registering the application as a subscriber for the topic of the input data object and a publisher for the output data object. For example, the trusted blur-filter application used to enforce the *Blur-Exported-Images* can register as a subscriber for the camera topic and publish objects with the topic blurred-img.

We were able to implement a rudimentary IFC mechanism atop ROS by adding just under 200 lines of Python code to the ROS codebase, and used it to enforce the example policies discussed above. Most of this code relates to parsing the host's policy and setting restrictions on the topics that applications can publish/subscribe. ROS's topic-matching algorithms in its publish-subscribe system then automatically take care of enforcement.

3.5 Challenges and Future Directions

We are continuing work to build an end-to-end IFC in drones. Our ROS-based implementation is only one part of the end-to-end system. While ROS bootstraps communication between publishers and subscribers, the underlying communication happens directly via sockets and IPC between Linux processes. An adversary could still bypass ROS-level IFC enforcement by directly setting up communication channels between Linux processes.

We are currently investigating IFC enforcement from within the normal-world OS to ensure that such attacks are not possible. In such a system, the kernel attaches labels to data objects managed by the OS and propagates these labels as data is copied. We are currently building atop the IFC model proposed by Flume [18], which attaches labels to files, sockets, and other OS-level abstractions, and exposes a label interface to applications. We are adding support for IFC within the Linux kernel, and integrating ROS to run atop IFC-enabled Linux. With this support, applications running on the drone can specify their label requirements using a familiar interface, such as ROS-level topics. ROS communicates these to the OS, which manages and propagates the labels as the application executes. While this effort is a work in progress, our modifications to Linux and ROS largely mirror Weir [22], which implemented IFC atop Android using a Flume-like label model.

3.6 Deployment Considerations

The discussion thus far has assumed that a guest drone checks in with the host and obtains an IFC policy. A practical deployment must also consider the challenges involved in performing check-in. We discuss two possible deployment models:

① *Designated entry corridors.* A host may require that drones that wish to enter its restricted space do so via designated entry corridors. The host could then deploy physical infrastructure (*e.g.,* NFC or Wi-Fi access points) that records the identity of the guest drone and communicates the host's policy to the drone. Having a designated entry corridor also helps ensure that the drone has an area in which to wait and establish compliance with the host in case network connectivity is intermittent. This model is applicable in settings such as office and apartment complexes, defense establishments and in university campuses.

② *Cooperation with wireless provider.* A host could communicate the geographic coordinates of its restricted space to 5G or WiMax providers that service the area and also specify its IFC policy. A guest drone can then directly obtain this information from the 5G/WiMax provider. One of the risks with this approach is that if network connectivity is unreliable, then the drone may not reliably receive the host's policy prior to entry. A possible way to mitigate this risk is to pre-load a database of restricted spaces and the corresponding policies before the drone takes flight. This model is applicable for delivery drones where the set of locations to be visited is known *a priori.*

These models are ineffective for adversarial drones (or covertly deployed ones) that fly unauthorized over the host's restricted space. These cases currently fall outside of our threat model. Additional methods are needed to detect/prevent adversarial drones. Of course, even for the case where drones are used overtly, the techniques proposed in this paper are designed to benefit hosts rather than the owners/operators of drones. Lacking additional incentives or regulations, there is little motivation for drone manufacturers to incorporate the hardware and software stack modifications that we propose. However, given the increasing social and governmental concern over privacy, we hypothesize that such incentives and regulations are likely to emerge over time. For example, if a large commercial drone operator deploys these mechanisms, it may incentivize its competitors to also deploy them on their drones.

4 RELATED WORK

Restricted Spaces. The work most closely related to ours is that of Brasser *et al.* [6], which develops the notion of restricted spaces for ARM TrustZone-enabled mobile devices. While Brasser *et al.*'s work directly inspired this paper, there are a few key ways in which this paper deviates from that work. Brasser *et al.*'s work focused on host control over peripherals in guest devices, *e.g.,* to ensure that interfaces such as the camera, Wi-Fi, and Bluetooth on the guest device are used in accordance with the host's policies. Their work used host-initiated remote memory operations as the core mechanism for policy enforcement on guest devices. The ability of hosts to remotely modify memory operations results in a potential security backdoor via which malicious hosts may modify unsuspecting guest devices. Brasser *et al.* therefore introduced the notion of a vetting service that guest devices could use to verify that the host's memory updates do not maliciously modify the guest device.

In contrast to their work, this paper focuses on information-flow control between applications executing atop drones, and uses an enhanced ROS stack on the guest drone for policy enforcement. This change overcomes two key drawbacks in Brasser *et al.*'s approach. First, Brasser *et al.* employed peripheral control for policy enforcement, *i.e.,* a peripheral would simply be turned off as specified by the host's policies. We extend Brasser *et al.*'s approach beyond peripheral control to fine-grained control over data produced and consumed by peripherals. For example, autonomous drones rely critically on the use of their camera for navigation, and it would be infeasible to turn the camera off. In contrast, our finer-grained approach allows the camera to operate, but instead places restrictions on how the pictures/video captured by the camera are used.

Second, Brasser *et al.*'s work used remote memory operations on guest devices to inject policy-enforcement code. This approach is intrusive on the guest device and requires additional supporting infrastructure if the guest does not trust the host, *e.g.,* the vetting service mentioned above. In contrast, our approach builds the policy-enforcement mechanism directly into the drone (*e.g.,* atop ROS), and the host's restrictions are simply encoded as policies to be enforced by the drone. The host does not inject any new code into the drone and no vetting service is required.

Drone and UAV Security. Prior work on drone and unmanned aerial vehicle (UAV) security has largely focused on exploitable vulnerabilities in either the communication channels or the hardware/software stack on the drone. Such attacks have focused on exploiting unencrypted communication over wireless media to implement eavedropping, cross-layer attacks, signal jamming, denial of service, and dropping Wi-Fi communication with ground control, to name a few [14, 15, 23, 30, 31]. Other attacks on drones involve GPS spoofing attacks to fool the drone into moving to a different destination (possibly with the intention of hijacking the drone) [16, 29]. Such attacks are a concern for delivery drones, which may be captured and analyzed to obtain sensitive details related to delivery data [28].

More recent work has investigated how ARM TrustZone may be used to enhance drone security. PROTC [19] is a system that leverages the TrustZone to address the lack of system-level protection for a drone's peripherals. PROTC ensures that applications runnning on the drone are able to securely access its periperhals even when the operating system of the drone has been compromised. Liu *et al.* [20] investigate the problem of ensuring a drone has not strayed into no-fly zones. To do this, they leverage the TrustZone to keep a tamper-proof log of the drone's GPS locations, which then provide an alibi to a third-party auditor that the drone was in compliance. However, they do not consider the problem of ensuring that the drone respects a host's privacy policies when it is within permitted airspace.

ROS Security. There has been a modest amount of research into identifying the key security vulnerabilities of ROS, and proposals by which these can be overcome [9]. McClean *et al.* [21] analyzed ROS and identified a number of vulnerabilities such as plain text communication between nodes, unprotected TCP ports, unencrypted data storage and a lack of an authentication mechanism for nodes.

Some of the key security vulnerabilities within ROS are inherent in the publish-subscribe paradigm that it employs. Publishers are unable to control the consumption of their data, and subscribers are unable to verify the integrity of received messages. Rodriguez *et al.* [26] have proposed to use message level encryption between nodes and find that it is a feasible solution even for low-power robots. Prior work has also proposed integration of the ROSC++ package with TLS to provide end-to-end encrypted communication channels [9]. Dieber *et al.* [10] develop an authentication mechanism that allows publishers and subscribers verify each others' identities and establish the integrity of messages exchanged between them. These and similar enhancements are under consideration as part of the Secure ROS [32, 33] framework, which is under active development.

5 SUMMARY

Drones are now widely available and are soon proposed for use in commercial settings. These drones will pose a massive threat to security and privacy unless active steps are taken now to develop suitable policy regulations and enforcement technologies. This paper takes a step in that direction by proposing the notion of restricted spaces for drones and demonstrating an IFC-based mechanism to enforce privacy policies on drones.

Acknowledgments. We thank the reviewers for their comments and Silvia Santini for shepherding the paper. This work was supported in part by a Ramanujan Fellowship from the Government of India and by the Robert Bosch Centre for Cyber-Physical Systems.

REFERENCES

[1] FlytOS: Operating system for drones. https://flytbase.com/flytos/.
[2] MAVROS – MAVLink extendable communication node for ROS with proxy for ground control station. http://wiki.ros.org/mavros.
[3] 112th Congress. FAA Modernization and Reform Act of 2012, February 2012. https://www.congress.gov/112/plaws/publ95/PLAW-112publ95.pdf.
[4] ARM. Security technology building a secure system using TrustZone technology (white paper). *ARM Limited*, 2009.
[5] A. Azab, P. Ning, J. Shah, Q. Chen, R. Bhutkar, G. Ganesh, J. Ma, and W. Shen. Hypervision across worlds: Real-time kernel protection from the ARM TrustZone secure world. In *ACM Conference on Computer and Communications Security*, 2014.
[6] F. Brasser, D. Kim, C. Liebchen, V. Ganapathy, L. Iftode, and A-R. Sadeghi. Regulating ARM TrustZone devices in restricted spaces. In *ACM International Conference on Mobile Systems, Applications, and Services*, 2016.
[7] A. Cavoukian. *Privacy and drones: Unmanned aerial vehicles*. Information and Privacy Commissioner of Ontario, Canada Ontario, 2012.
[8] Civil Aviations Authority (CAA). CAP 722, Unmanned Aircraft System Operations in UK Airspace - Guidance, March 2015. https://publicapps.caa.co.uk/docs/

33/CAP%20722%20Sixth%20Edition%20March%202015.pdf.
[9] B. Dieber, B. Breiling, S. Taurer, S. Kacianka, S. Rass, and P. Schartner. Security for the Robot Operating System. *Robotics and Autonomous Systems*, 98, 2017.
[10] B. Dieber, S. Kacianka, S. Rass, and P. Schartner. Application-level security for ROS-based applications. In *2016 IEEE International Conference on Intelligent Robots and Systems*, 2016.
[11] Directorate General of Civil Aviation. Requirements for Operation of Civil Remotely Piloted Aircraft System (RPAs), August 2018. http://dgca.nic.in/cars/D3X-X1.pdf.
[12] W. Enck, P. Gilbert, B-C. Chun, L. P. Cox, J. Jung, P. McDaniel, and A. Sheth. Taintdroid: An information-flow tracking system for Realtime privacy monitoring on smartphones. In *ACM/USENIX Symposium on Operating System Design and Implementation*, 2010.
[13] Federal Aviation Administration (FAA). Small Unmanned Aircraft Systems (sUAS), June 2016. https://www.faa.gov/documentLibrary/media/Advisory_Circular/AC_107-2.pdf.
[14] K. Hartmann and C. Steup. The vulnerability of UAVs to cyber attacks-an approach to the risk assessment. In *IEEE International Conference on Cyber Conflict*, 2013.
[15] A. Y. Javaid, W. Sun, V. K. Devabhaktuni, and M. Alam. Cyber security threat analysis and modeling of an unmanned aerial vehicle system. In *IEEE Conference on Technology for Homeland Security*, 2012.
[16] A. J. Kerns, D. P. Shepard, J. A. Bhatti, and T. E. Humphreys. Unmanned aircraft capture and control via GPS spoofing. *Journal of Field Robotics*, 31(4), 2014.
[17] C. Koettl and B. Marcolini. A closer look at the drone attack on Maduro in Venezuela, August 2018. https://www.nytimes.com/2018/08/10/world/americas/venezuela-video-analysis.html.
[18] M. Krohn, A. Yip, M. Brodsky, N. Cliffer, F. Kaashoek, E. Kohler, and R. Morris. Information flow control for standard os abstractions. In *ACM Symposium on Operating Systems Principles*, 2007.
[19] R. Liu and M. Srivastava. PROTC: Protecting drone's peripherals through ARM TrustZone. In *3rd Workshop on Micro Aerial Vehicle Networks, Systems, and Applications*, 2017.
[20] T. Liu, A. Hojjati, A. Bates, and K. Nahrstedt. Alidrone: Enabling trustworthy proof-of-alibi for commercial drone compliance. In *IEEE International Conference on Distributed Computing Systems*, 2018.
[21] J. McClean, C. Stull, C. Farrar, and D. Mascareñas. A Preliminary Cyber-Physical Security Assessment of the Robot Operating System (ROS). In *Unmanned Systems Technology XV*, volume 8741, 2013.
[22] A. Nadkarni, B. Andow, W. Enck, and S. Jha. Practical DIFC enforcement on Android. In *USENIX Security Symposium*, 2017.
[23] J-S. Pleban, R. Band, and R. Creutzburg. Hacking and securing the AR. Drone 2.0 quadcopter: investigations for improving the security of a toy. In *Mobile Devices and Multimedia: Enabling Technologies, Algorithms, and Applications 2014*, volume 9030, 2014.
[24] M. Quigley, K. Conley, B. Gerkey, J. Faust, T. Foote, J. Leibs, R. Wheeler, and A. Y. Ng. ROS: An open-source Robot Operating System. In *ICRA workshop on open source software*, 2009.
[25] Transparency Market Research. Robot Operating System Market - Snaphshot, 2018. https://www.transparencymarketresearch.com/robot-operating-system-market.html.
[26] F. J. Rodríguez-Lera, V. Matellán-Olivera, J. Balsa-Comerón, Á-M. Guerrero-Higueras, and C. Fernández-Llamas. Message Encryption in Robot Operating System: Collateral Effects of Hardening Mobile Robots. *Frontiers in ICT*, 5, 2018.
[27] R. Sailer, X. Zhang, T. Jaeger, and L. van Doorn. Design and implementation of a TCG-based integrity measurement architecture. In *USENIX Security Symposium*, 2004.
[28] S-H. Seo, J. Won, E. Bertino, Y. Kang, and D. Choi. A security framework for a drone delivery service. In *2nd Workshop on Micro Aerial Vehicle Networks, Systems, and Applications for Civilian Use*, 2016.
[29] D. P. Shepard, J. A. Bhatti, T. E. Humphreys, and A. A. Fansler. Evaluation of smart grid and civilian UAV vulnerability to GPS spoofing attacks. In *Radionavigation Laboratory Conference Proceedings*, 2012.
[30] E. Vattapparamban, İ. Güvenç, A. İ Yurekli, K. Akkaya, and S. Uluağaç. Drones for smart cities: Issues in cybersecurity, privacy, and public safety. In *2016 International Wireless Communications and Mobile computing Conference*, 2016.
[31] W. Wang, Y. Sun, H. Li, and Z. Han. Cross-layer attack and defense in cognitive radio networks. In *IEEE Global Communications Conference*, 2010.
[32] R. White, G. Caiazza, H. Christensen, and A. Cortesi. Using and developing secure ROS1 systems. In *Robot Operating System*, 2019.
[33] R. White, D. Christensen, I. Henrik, and D. Quigley. SROS: Securing ROS over the Wire, in the Graph, and through the Kernel. *arXiv preprint arXiv:1611.07060*, 2016.
[34] A. Young. Passenger jet carrying 240 people nearly hits a drone at 15,000ft, 2018. https://www.dailymail.co.uk/news/article-6172229/Passenger-jet-carrying-240-people-nearly-hits-drone-15-000ft.html.

Receiving Data Hidden in Music[*]

Manuel Eichelberger
ETH Zurich
manuelei@ethz.ch

Simon Tanner
ETH Zurich
simtanner@ethz.ch

Gabriel Voirol
ETH Zurich
voirolg@ethz.ch

Roger Wattenhofer
ETH Zurich
wattenhofer@ethz.ch

ABSTRACT

This paper presents a method for transmitting data within music played from loudspeakers. The data is hidden in the music by leveraging the psychoacoustic masking effect, so that humans are not disturbed by the data transmission. The system achieves data rates of over 900 bits per second. The client side of the system could be implemented as a smartphone app, which receives data wherever users are without requiring any setup, making the system user-friendly.

CCS CONCEPTS

• **Human-centered computing** → **Ubiquitous and mobile devices**; • **Hardware** → **Sound-based input / output**;

KEYWORDS

audio, data transmission, masking effect, psycho-acoustics

ACM Reference Format:
Manuel Eichelberger, Simon Tanner, Gabriel Voirol, and Roger Wattenhofer. 2019. Receiving Data Hidden in Music. In *The 20th International Workshop on Mobile Computing Systems and Applications (HotMobile '19), February 27–28, 2019, Santa Cruz, CA, USA*. ACM, New York, NY, USA, 6 pages. https://doi.org/10.1145/3301293.3302360

---

[*]The authors of this paper are alphabetically ordered.

---

1 INTRODUCTION

Wireless communication standards such as Wi-Fi or Bluetooth demand a setup process. A smartphone user must explicitly allow the protocol, and potentially pair the device, which may entail entering passwords or pressing buttons in the right order. While this is acceptable when setting up a permanent communication channel, it is a hassle in countless ad hoc communication situations.[1]

In situations with (background) music, a user simply starts an app, and immediately receives data hidden within the music. Such a zero-setup scheme may have many interesting applications in situations where music is present anyway, or where music can be played without being disturbing. The transmitter hides the data inside the music and the smartphone can receive the data, as the microphone can be accessed without any setup. For example, a speaker in a store or a museum can piggyback information about close-by products. Also, attendees of a large sports event may suffer from a congested LTE connection, but interesting game statistics can be broadcast during musical jingles and breaks. When entering a hotel room, a guest's phone will directly receive the Wi-Fi login and password, maybe even immediately display a slider to control the room temperature.

While a smartphone is able to receive the information carried by the song, a person should not notice any degradation in sound quality. We strive for achieving high bit rates and robust data transmission while preserving imperceptibility independent of the nature of the chosen audio file. Since the frequency range has to be shared between the data and the hearable music signal, psycho-acoustic phenomena are exploited to embed the data into the cover signal. Using the frequency masking effect, our system transmits data in OFDM subcarriers next to frequencies of high amplitude.

Our prototype achieves bit rates of over 900 bit/s for a variety of music styles. In a hallway, our system can transmit data up to 24 meters with bit error ratios (BERs) below 5 %. In a big auditorium, the BER can be kept at 10 % at a distance of 15 meters.

2 RELATED WORK

Several methods for hiding information in audio have been proposed, mostly in the context of *steganography*, aiming at data secrecy and robustness to compression and signal manipulation [4]. Several time domain methods are only applicable to file-based data transport and lead to high error rates when transmitting the audio over the air. These methods include least signification bit (LSB) encoding, echo hiding and hiding in silence intervals. In the frequency

---

[1]For a funny motivation, we refer to a recent xkcd comic: https://xkcd.com/2055/.

domain, LSB encoding in discrete wavelet transforms, phase coding and amplitude coding are employed.

Our focus is not on secrecy, but on embedding data in a way that does not disturb users, while achieving high data rates. Human auditory effects have been exploited before for data hiding using phase modulation, with simulation results achieving data rates up to 243 bit/s [9]. Our method transmits the data over the air, instead of hiding the information in a sound file and achieves data rates of up to 900 bit/s. While other approaches generate pleasant music from the information bits and may not achieve high data rates [8], we hide data in existing music.

Data can be transmitted hidden from listeners in ultrasound frequencies. This approach is only suitable for transmitting data over short distances [12], since the absorption of sound in air as well as the directivity of audio speakers increase with the frequency [5]. In the experiments with our system, which embeds data in lower frequencies, we show that data transmission is feasible over distances up to 24 m. Spread spectrum techniques focus on robustness while sacrificing data rate and achieve less than 100 bit/s [1]. Tone insertion is one approach which also uses the masking effect, like our technique, to maintain good audio quality. It has a better data capacity than spread spectrum methods, reaching for instance 250 bit/s [7]. Our method enables data transmissions with over 900 bit/s. An interesting technique is *modulated complex lapped transform (MCLT)*, which causes minimal distortions to the cover audio [17]. However, also this method achieves acceptable data rates only for short distances.

For this work, *orthogonal frequency-division multiplexing (OFDM)* is used. Other methods employing OFDM can transmit data either at several hundred bits per second over up to three meters [16] or send data at a lower data rate, but up to 5 or 7 meters [2, 11]. Using a high sound volume of 80 dB, the distance can be increased to 10 m [15]. Different from the existing work, our work takes into account the tonal harmonics of the used audio signal to find the most suitable frequencies for the OFDM subcarriers. This allows us to send data using lower sound volumes and still transmit over longer distances. Also, a non-data-aided time synchronization algorithm is implemented to increase the bit rate.

3 BACKGROUND
3.1 Human Auditory System

A so-called *psychoacoustic model* describes how audio frequencies are perceived by the *human auditory system (HAS)*. Acoustic waves are transformed into motion by the ear drum followed by ossicles in the middle ear. The spatial motion excites the fluids in the cochlea and thus the sensory cells of the basilar membrane which transfer the input to the nervous system. Excitations of similar frequencies or similar onset time instants are seen as one excitation by the basilar membrane. "Similar" frequencies are ones that fall into the same *critical bandwidth* which is a function of the frequency f and can be approximated by $BW_{cr}(f) = 0.2f$ for $f > 500$ Hz [6].

If a signal of high amplitude is present at a certain frequency f_m, a weak signal inside the critical bandwidth is imperceptible to a human. The signal at f_m is then called *masker* and the relation between its loudness and the one of the masked signal is described

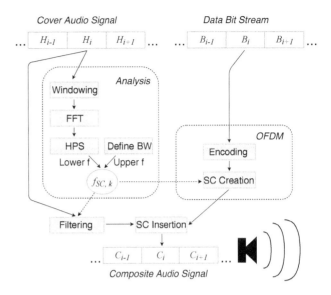

Figure 1: The processing steps to embed data into a cover audio file.

by a masking threshold which depends on their frequency difference [14].

3.2 OFDM

Orthogonal frequency-division multiplexing (OFDM) is a data modulation method where one OFDM symbol consists of a set of symbols sent on orthogonal subcarriers (SC) which are modulated with a method such as BPSK or QAM. The collection of subcarriers are transformed into a time domain OFDM symbol by an *inverse fast Fourier transform (IFFT)*.

4 SYSTEM DESCRIPTION

We propose a system for transmitting data hidden in music from a speaker to a smartphone microphone. Masking frequencies of a cover audio signal are detected and OFDM subcarriers are inserted close to them without humans being able to notice the modification. Still, a receiving smartphone can read out the information hidden in the music, – without knowing the music being transmitted – since microphones are not affected by the masking effect.

4.1 Transmission

The processing steps at the transmitting side are depicted in Figure 1. The cover audio signal is divided into segments H_i that are multiplied with a window function and then analyzed to find suitable frequencies for data insertion. OFDM subcarriers are inserted in a frequency range from 500 Hz to 10 kHz due to the sensitivity of smartphone microphones which decreases rapidly with higher frequencies.

The spectrum is split into an upper and a lower frequency region. For the first, a fixed bandwidth for data transmission is defined according to the properties of the HAS and smartphone microphones whereas for the latter, dominant frequencies of the cover signal are found with the method of the *harmonic product spectrum (HPS)* [3].

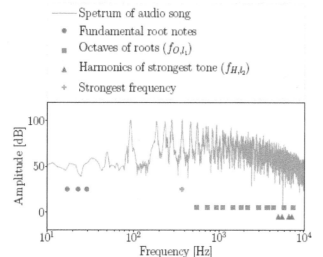

Figure 2: The higher octaves f_{O,l_1} of the fundamental root notes as well as the harmonics f_{H,l_2} of the strongest frequency represent the masking frequencies $f_{M,l}$.

The masking frequencies $f_{M,l}$ for the audio segment H_i are obtained by this analysis. From these, the frequencies $f_{SC,k}$ of the OFDM subcarriers are derived. A filter is used to clear the spectrum of the audio segment H_i at these frequencies. The subcarriers are then modulated with information bits to generate the composite segment C_i.

The length of one analyzed segment of the cover audio signal is set to $L = 8820$ samples $\hat{=}$ 200 ms. The length of an OFDM symbol is equal to L and contains a cyclic prefix of 2940 samples $\hat{=}$ 66.6 ms. Therefore, the difference in distance of the first and the last arriving echo can be up to 22.4 m without degrading the reception quality.

Upper Frequency Region. Frequencies just below 10 kHz carry information such as drum cymbals and voice consonants. They also contain higher harmonics of tonal instruments and therefore shape their tone. However, in [10] it was noticed that frequencies of music songs in a band from 5 kHz to 10 kHz can be replaced by OFDM subcarriers of the same amplitude without a severe degradation in sound quality. To reduce the sound degradation even more, our system only uses the frequency band of 8 kHz–10 kHz. The location and size of the upper frequency region is therefore a trade-off between bit rate and audio quality degradation.

The whole upper frequency region of the audio signal is filtered and replaced by OFDM subcarriers to obtain the same spectrum magnitude as the original signal.

Lower Frequency Region. The lower frequency region used for data insertion reaches from 500 Hz to 8 kHz. In this frequency range, the frequency masking is taken advantage of to hide data in subcarriers close to strong frequency components.

For the segment H_i, the fundamental *root notes* between the keys $C_0 = 16.35$ Hz and $B_0 = 30.87$ Hz of the three most dominant tones are found with the method of the harmonic product spectrum. From these three fundamental root notes which are too low to use

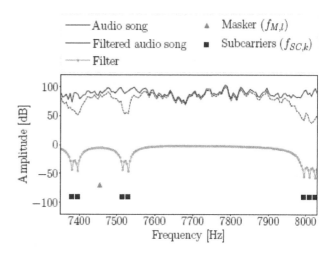

Figure 3: The cover song is filtered and subcarriers are inserted at those frequencies.

for data transmission, the higher octaves in the desired frequency range are taken as masking frequencies f_{O,l_1}.

Large gaps between these masking frequencies are filled with the frequencies f_{H,l_2} which are the harmonics of the strongest frequency. Figure 2 shows the lower frequency region. The frequencies f_{O,l_1} and f_{H,l_2} are used as the masking frequencies $f_{M,l}$ from which the subcarrier frequencies $f_{SC,k}$ of an OFDM symbol are derived: The locations in the spectrum just below and above these masking frequencies are used to insert the subcarriers to profit from the masking effect. Two subcarriers are inserted above and two below each masking frequency.

The information which three out of the twelve root notes are used gets transmitted to the receiver in the upper frequency region to allow calculation of the subcarrier frequencies at the receiver. As depicted in Figure 3, a filter is used to remove the audio data at the subcarrier frequencies $f_{SC,k}$.

The spectrum inside the critical bandwidth of each subcarrier frequency $f_{SC,k}$ in the lower frequency region is analyzed. The amplitude of each inserted subcarrier is chosen such that the subcarrier is detectable by the receiver and at the same time does not exceed the masking threshold level.

Since the amplitudes of the subcarriers are determined by the cover audio, the information bits are encoded in the phase difference of two consecutive subcarriers at the same frequency using differential BPSK.

4.2 Reception

After the audio signal with the hidden data has been played back by a loudspeaker, the microphone at the receiving side records the signal. The onset of the OFDM symbols can be detected using the cyclic prefix as described in [13], even in the presence of multipath signals. The information about the most dominant notes is then obtained by decoding the upper frequency region and the set of subcarriers in the lower frequency band can be reproduced.

In our prototype, the signal processing is carried out offline on a computer. However, the computational effort is low and can be

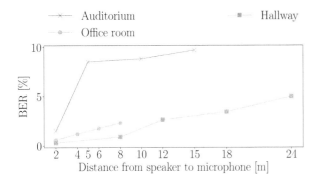

Figure 4: The BERs measured at different distances for the song *Viol* by *Gesaffelstein*.

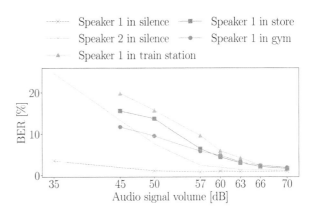

Figure 5: The BERs for varying audio signal volumes at a distance of 2 meters between the transmitter and the receiver.

done in real-time on smartphones. For the implementation in an app, *forward error correction (FEC)* algorithms will allow reliable transmission.

Note that the receiver does not need to know the music that is transmitted by the loudspeaker. If multiple music sources use our method, the unwanted signal is additional noise in the overlapping OFDM frequencies. Also, we would like to point out that keeping a smartphone's microphone continuously active consumes only little power, as services such as voice search with "Ok Google" already do this today.

5 DATA HIDING AND TRANSMISSION EXPERIMENTS

The data transmission robustness is tested with different cover songs and under several conditions including varying distances from the speaker to the microphone and different amplification levels. The modified audio signals are played back on a *KRK Rokit 8* speaker and a *Nexus 5X* smartphone serves as receiver.

BER vs. Distance. The BER is measured at different distances in three environments: A narrow hallway with carpet, an office without carpet and a large auditorium with a wooden floor. The office contains desks with computer screens and chairs, the auditorium is equipped with rows of bench seats. Figure 4 depicts the BERs with increasing distance for the song *Viol* by *Gesaffelstein*. In the hallway and the office, the BER increases linearly with the distance. Since the hallway is narrow, the direct sound waves and the reflections move more unidirectionally towards the microphone. The BER at a distance of 24 meters does not rise above 5 % in the hallway. In the auditorium, the BER rises abruptly at 4 meters. A possible explanation is the layout of the auditorium where the vertical walls of the wooden benches block the echoes from the floor at distances larger than 2 meters.

BER vs. Volume. We compare two different speakers in a silent environment as well as the system's performance under the influence of various noise sources. Speaker 1 is the same *KRK Rokit 8* speaker as in the previous section, whereas Speaker 2 is a *Logitech X-530* hi-fi speaker. These experiments are conducted in an office

room with carpet at a distance of 2 meters between the speaker and the smartphone. The BERs obtained in the different conditions are shown in Figure 5.

For high volumes, the BERs for both speakers are similar and remain at 1 % which seems to be a lower limit due to the residues of the filtered music signal which interfere with the OFDM subcarriers. At reduced volumes, the BER of Speaker 2 increases. Speaker 1 maintains an acceptable error ratio, probably since studio monitors are designed to show a flat frequency response independent of the volume.

To evaluate the impact of ambient noise on the system, noise has been recorded in three public areas: at a gym (53 dB), in a store (55 dB) and at a train station (60 dB). Again, Speaker 1 plays the audio with the hidden information at different volumes while Speaker 2, placed next to Speaker 1, simultaneously replays the recorded noise, such that at the smartphone the level of the noise alone matches the levels in the public areas. As expected, the BER increases in louder environments and with decreasing audio signal volume.

Different Cover Songs. To test the applicability to various music types, our method has been applied to 9 pieces of 5 different music genres.[2] Song snippets of 12 seconds are modified for which the achieved bit rates are listed in Table 1. Depending on the song, a data rate of nearly 1 kbit/s can be achieved. Table 1 also lists the error ratios measured in the auditorium with a level of 63 dB at a distance of 2 meters. The exact bit rate depends on the cover song since the chosen set of fundamental root notes decides on the number of valid subcarrier locations inside the lower frequency region.

The greatest challenge for the algorithm are songs with high dynamic range, for instance classical music. Since the magnitudes of the data-carrying subcarriers are adapted to the spectrum of the host audio signal, they can sink below the minimum level needed by the receiver for correct decoding.

---

[2]Song snippets are available at *https://doi.org/10.3929/ethz-b-000294476* - WAVE Files used in Audio Experiment for "Receiving Data Hidden in Music"

Table 1: List of analyzed songs sorted by the BERs.

Artist – Song	Bit Rate [bit/s]	BER [%]	Genre
J. S. Bach – Suite No. 2 in B minor BWV 1067: IV. Bourree I, II	971	14	Classical
Schola Romana Lucernensis & John Voirol – In Tempore Pacis	930	13	Classical
Bisco – Nothing's Left	922	4.3	Electronic
Fliptrix – Patterns Of Escapism	945	3.8	Hip Hop
Art Blakey – Moanin'	964	3.5	Jazz
Rümbold – Balcony	984	2.7	Hard Rock
John Coltrane – In A Sentimental Mood	953	2.5	Jazz
Sir Donkey's Revenge – Gawky Talky	982	2.1	Hard Rock
Gesaffelstein – Viol	964	1.5	Electronic

Continuously loud and busy Hard Rock or Electronic songs are optimal for hiding data as masking frequencies are strongly present over a wide frequency range.

5.1 Subjective Audio Quality Test

As objective metrics like the signal-to-distortion ratio do not necessarily correlate with the perceptibility of audio changes, we conducted our own experiments with test subjects.

Test Environment. To gather data about the degree of perceptibility of the modifications by our method, the same song snippets used for the experiments in the previous section (listed in Table 1) were published on a website designed for this audio quality test.

In the first experiment, a blind test, for each song snippet the participant is given either the modified or the original version to listen to. For each song the participant has to choose whether the original or the modified song snippet is present.

In the second experiment, the direct comparison, the participant can listen to both versions of each song snippet and compare them directly. The participant then has to decide which of the two versions is the original.

Results. Table 2 summarizes the test results. For Experiment 1 (E1), the amount of visitors who assume that the original version is present is described by two quantities: $p(O|O)$ indicates that the original version is actually present whereas $p(O|M)$ stands for the case of an erroneously labeled modified version.

Δp is the difference between $p(O|O)$ and $p(O|M)$ and represents the benefit of the original version over the modified version to be interpreted as original. A high percentage signifies that many people identify the modified versions while the originals are still recognized. If the percentage is low, a similar amount of both versions are labeled as originals so the modifications are not noticed.

The results of Experiment 2 (E2) are described by $p(E)$, which stand for the probability of an erroneous decision. In average over 30 % of the probands are not able to tell the difference between the two versions in the direct comparison. For the blind test, in only 18 % of the cases the modified versions appeared more suspicious than the original ones. However, the original versions are labeled as such

Table 2: Subjective audio quality test results: Experiment 1 (E1) is described using three columns $p(O|O)$, $p(O|M)$ and $p(E)$ (see Section 5.1) whereas the amount of errors in Experiment 2 is described by $p(E)$.

Artist – Song	$p(O|O)$, E1 [%]	$p(O|M)$, E1 [%]	Δp, E1 [%]	$p(E)$, E2 [%]
J. S. Bach – Suite No. 2 in B minor BWV 1067: IV. Bourree I, II	78.6	52.2	26.4	22.4
Schola Romana Lucernensis & John Voirol – In Tempore Pacis	56.2	36.8	19.4	28.6
Bisco – Nothing's Left	62.1	45.5	16.6	32.7
Fliptrix – Patterns Of Escapism	55.6	27.3	28.3	34.7
Art Blakey – Moanin'	79.2	55.6	23.6	42.9
Rümbold – Balcony	65.4	48.0	17.4	28.6
John Coltrane – In A Sentimental Mood	70.4	62.5	7.9	32.7
Sir Donkey's Revenge – Gawky Talky	84.6	68.0	16.6	38.8
Gesaffelstein – Viol	63.6	55.2	8.5	30.6
Average (50 Participants)	68.4	50.1	18.3	32.4

in 68 % of the test cases which indicates a bias towards the modified versions. Such a bias can occur since music pieces of common audio quality are chosen which possibly contain artifacts and noise arising from the recording or compression. Participants paying attention to any abnormalities perceive any unfamiliar sound elements as suspicious and therefore the original versions are often labeled as being modified.

Note that finding a bitrate level which results in $p(E) = 50$ % would require a huge number of experiments and participants, since $p(E)$ depends on the song and each participant can only judge one bitrate per song.

Similar to the findings when analyzing the BERs, the classical songs show a low performance in the direct comparison. A high dynamic range thus not only complicates a robust transmission but also the process of unobtrusive embedding.

6 CONCLUSION

In this paper, a novel system is proposed to hide data in music. The harmonic compositions of the cover songs are analyzed to exploit the masking effect. The system is evaluated under diverse circumstances. The BER measured at a distance of 15 meters in a big auditorium can be kept below 10 %. The method is applied to different cover songs and achieves bit rates of over 900 bit/s while being only slightly noticeable to the human ear. The computational effort for receiving the hidden data is low enough for real-time processing on smartphones. Through a standardized protocol, one universal app could be used in all situations without any user setup.

The next step in making our system accessible is a real-time implementation of the receiver in a smartphone app, maybe tailored for a specific use case. With additional user studies, the number and amplitude of the subcarriers can be optimized to allow higher data rates. Also, data rates might be increased by adapting the music, for instance by amplifying maskers.

REFERENCES

[1] Po-Wei Chen, Chun-Hsiang Huang, Yun-Chung Shen, and Ja-Ling Wu. 2009. Pushing information over acoustic channels. In *Proceedings of the IEEE International Conference on Acoustics, Speech, and Signal Processing, ICASSP 2009, 19-24 April 2009, Taipei, Taiwan.* 1421–1424.

[2] Kiho Cho, Jae Choi, and Nam Soo Kim. 2015. An acoustic data transmission system based on audio data hiding: method and performance evaluation. *EURASIP J. Audio, Speech and Music Processing* (2015), 10. https://doi.org/10.1186/s13636-015-0053-x

[3] Patricio de la Cuadra, Aaron S. Master, and Craig Sapp. 2001. Efficient Pitch Detection Techniques for Interactive Music. In *Proceedings of the 2001 International Computer Music Conference, ICMC 2001, Havana, Cuba, September 17-22, 2001.*

[4] Fatiha Djebbar, Beghdad Ayad, Karim Abed Meraim, and Habib Hamam. 2012. Comparative study of digital audio steganography techniques. *EURASIP Journal on Audio, Speech, and Music Processing* 2012, 1 (2012), 25.

[5] H E. Bass, Louis Sutherland, and A J. Zuckerwar. 1990. Atmospheric absorption of sound - Update. 88 (1990).

[6] Hugo Fastl and Eberhard Zwicker. 2006. *Psychoacoustics: Facts and Models* (3 ed.). Springer-Verlag, Berlin, Heidelberg.

[7] Kaliappan Gopalan and Stanley Wenndt. 2004. Audio steganography for covert data transmission by imperceptible tone insertion. In *Proc. The IASTED International Conference on Communication Systems And Applications (CSA 2004), Banff, Canada.*

[8] Anil Madhavapeddy, Richard Sharp, David Scott, and Alastair Tse. 2005. Audio Networking: The Forgotten Wireless Technology. *IEEE Pervasive Computing* 4, 3 (2005), 55–60.

[9] Hafiz MA Malik, Rashid Ansari, and Ashfaq A Khokhar. 2007. Robust Data Hiding in Audio Using Allpass Filters. *IEEE Transactions on Audio, Speech, and Language Processing* 15, 4 (2007), 1296–1304.

[10] Hosei Matsuoka, Yusuke Nakashima, and Takeshi Yoshimura. 2006. Acoustic Communication System Using Mobile Terminal Microphones. *NTT DoCoMo Technical Journal* 8 (2006). https://www.nttdocomo.co.jp

[11] Hosei Matsuoka, Yusuke Nakashima, Takeshi Yoshimura, and Toshiro Kawahara. 2008. Acoustic OFDM: Embedding high bit-rate data in audio. In *International Conference on Multimedia Modeling.* Springer, 498–507.

[12] Nirupam Roy, Haitham Hassanieh, and Romit Roy Choudhury. 2017. Backdoor: Making microphones hear inaudible sounds. In *Proceedings of the 15th Annual International Conference on Mobile Systems, Applications, and Services.* ACM, 2–14.

[13] Jan-Jaap van de Beek, Magnus Sandell, and Per Ola Börjesson. 1997. ML estimation of time and frequency offset in OFDM systems. *IEEE Trans. Signal Processing* 45, 7 (1997), 1800–1805.

[14] Jesko Lars Verhey. 1999. *Psychoacoustics of spectro-temporal effects in masking and loudness perception.* Bibliotheks- und Informationssystem der Carl von Ossietzky Universitaet Oldenburg.

[15] Qian Wang, Kui Ren, Man Zhou, Tao Lei, Dimitrios Koutsonikolas, and Lu Su. 2016. Messages behind the sound: real-time hidden acoustic signal capture with smartphones. In *Proceedings of the 22nd Annual International Conference on Mobile Computing and Networking (MobiCom) 2016.*

[16] Shuai Wang. 2011. Embedding data in an audio signal, using acoustic OFDM.

[17] Hwan Sik Yun, Kiho Cho, and Nam Soo Kim. 2010. Acoustic data transmission based on modulated complex lapped transform. *IEEE Signal Processing Letters* 17, 1 (2010), 67–70.

Nezha: Mobile OS Virtualization Framework for Multiple Clients on Single Computing Platform

Bin Yang, Shoumeng Yan*, Shuo Liu, Zhifang Long, Jie Yu
Hongyu Zhang, Yong Yao, Randy Xu, Fleming Feng, James Wu
Intel Asia-Pacific Research and Development Co.,Ltd, *Intel Labs
{bin.y.yang, shoumeng.yan, shuo.liu, zhifang.long, cynthia.yu, hongyu.zhang, yong.yao, randy.xu, fleming.feng,
james.y.wu}@intel.com

ABSTRACT

Mobile OSes, such as Android [1], have spread to non-smartphone use cases such as in-vehicle infotainment, electronic classrooms, and physical retail stores. These scenarios often require the installation of multiple standalone mobile devices to simultaneously serve different users. Meanwhile, computing capacity has increased quickly even on relatively low-cost computing platforms. To reduce the total cost of ownership, it is natural to ask: Is it possible to host multiple simultaneously interactive mobile **clients**[1] on a shared computing platform? Android multi-user or virtualization techniques allow running multiple Android profiles or instances on one device. However, they are only able to multiplex one set of peripherals such as one screen, one touch input, and one audio output between instances, which means only one instance at a time can be operated by the user. Therefore, Android virtualization techniques cannot meet the requirements of supporting multiple standalone screens for users with one computing platform.

This paper presents *Nezha*, a system to support multiple simultaneous interactive clients with an uncompromised user experience on a shared computing device. *Nezha* reduces total cost of ownership, lowers management overhead, and supports dynamic sharing of system resources. *Nezha* offers every client a full mobile OS instance that is virtualized based on container-like OS virtualization technology [2][3][4]. In our Android-based implementation, all clients utilize fully accelerated 3D graphics and standalone I/O peripherals such as touch, audio, and display. All clients share the computing capacity of a low cost but still powerful x86 platform. To our knowledge, *Nezha* is the first system that enables the full Android experience for multiple interactive clients backed by one computing platform. It is worth noting that *Nezha* employs a non-invasive design principle: *Nezha* extensions are made within the bounds of the hardware abstraction layer, with no modifications to the kernel and only minimal changes to the mobile OS framework. This makes *Nezha* easy to maintain against the quickly evolving upstream kernel and Android source tree. Our paper includes performance test results that demonstrate the scalability and low overhead of *Nezha*.

CCS CONCEPTS

• **Computer systems organization** → **Embedded systems**; *Redundancy*; Robotics; • **Networks** → Network reliability.

KEYWORDS

Multiple Clients, Container, Virtualization, Android

ACM Reference Format:
Bin Yang, Shoumeng Yan*, Shuo Liu, Zhifang Long, Jie Yu and Hongyu Zhang, Yong Yao, Randy Xu, Fleming Feng, James Wu. 2019. *Nezha*: Mobile OS Virtualization Framework for Multiple Clients on Single Computing Platform. In *The 20th International Workshop on Mobile Computing Systems and Applications (HotMobile '19), February 27–28, 2019, Santa Cruz, CA, USA.* ACM, New York, NY, USA, 6 pages. https://doi.org/10.1145/3301293.3302361

1 INTRODUCTION

Because of the rich app ecosystem, mobile OSes, including Android, have spread to non-smartphone use cases. One example is Android based devices that provide independent entertainment screens to all passengers in a car. In another example, many devices are installed in a physical retail store for consumers to check out orders. To simultaneously serve different users, existing solutions require multiple standalone mobile devices to be deployed.

Meanwhile, computing capacity has increased quickly even on relatively low-cost computing platforms. To take advantage of these cost savings, we designed a system architecture that consolidates multiple interactive clients onto a single System on a Chip (SoC), as illustrated in Figure 1.

- One SoC board is used as the computing platform that includes CPU, GPU, display controller, HDMI ports, USB ports, and other peripherals supported by a modern SoC platform. HDMI and USB cables connect client screens to the computing platform and offer input (touch pad) and output (screen display and audio output) channels for users to operate the screens. Signal splitter chips can also be used to extend the number of supported I/O channels.
- On the software side, we support multiple isolated Android instances running on the SoC platform at the same time, where each instance enables one interactive screen for one

---

[1]We use the term client to denote the hardware and software system of an interactive panel that is operable by a user. On hardware side, it has its own screen, touch input, and audio output while shares the computing platform (including CPU and shared peripherals) with other clients. On software side, its mobile OS runs on the shared computing platform.

user. These instances may run different Android customizations or even different Linux-based OSes to provide different functionality to customers. In an example scenario, three different OSes could run in three instances of a multi-client system: Android 7.0 runs in the first instance, Android 8.0 runs in the second instance, while Ubuntu Linux is running in the third instance.

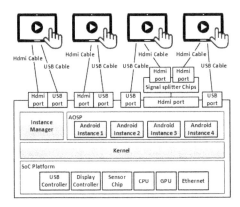

Figure 1: Abstract multi-screen system architecture

This architecture seems similar to the lightweight OS level virtualization technology [2][3][4], which is broadly used in the cloud with the popularization of Docker containers. However, the existing Docker solution only focuses on headless computing and does not support I/O peripheral sharing.

This paper presents *Nezha*, a system that hosts multiple interactive physical clients with uncompromised user experience on a single shared computing device. *Nezha* offers every client a full mobile OS experience by allocating an OS instance to each client with OS-level virtualization technology. *Nezha* distinguishes client-owned peripherals from shared ones, and manages them differently. Client-owned peripherals for HCI (human computer interaction), for example, USB-based touch pad and camera, HDMI-based screen and audio output, are exclusively assigned to a corresponding OS instance. *Nezha* also ensures that each client has virtualized but highly efficient access to the hardware and software assets that are integrated in the shared computing platform. The shared assets include accelerators (e.g. graphics and audio), controllers (e.g. display controller), sensors (e.g. humidity), network interfaces (e.g. Ethernet ports), trusted execution environment, and debugging capabilities, among others.

Nezha can reduce the total cost of ownership, support system resource sharing, and lessen management overhead. Let's take a closer look with an example. A physical retail store is equipped with many advertisement displays and POS machines to provide shopping guidance and checkout services to customers. Each machine is supported by a dedicated computing platform that runs Android OS. Typically, a computing platform that includes a Cortex-A SOC, 2G Memory, and 2G SSD, costs about 100 US dollars. A large physical retail store such as "Fresh HeMa" operated by Alibaba, can have 100 machines, which then require 100 computing platforms. If *Nezha* is used in a physical retail store to reduce the number of computing platforms, that money can be saved. The computing

power of a single computing platform can be dynamically allocated between different customers, providing resource sharing, so that quality of service can be met even if there is a heavy workload by one customer. Maintenance and management activities for the hardware and software are also reduced, due to the lower number of computing platforms.

Another example scenario showing the benefit of *Nezha* is Rear Seat Entertainment (RSE) in a car. A car is equipped with an RSE system for every seat, which is backed by dedicated computing platforms, but typically, only one driver and one passenger are in the car and only one RSE system is used. Using *Nezha*, independent entertainment services can be provided to all passengers with a single computing platform.

We have implemented a prototype of *Nezha* that supports multiple interactive Android clients on one x86 platform. To our knowledge, *Nezha* is the first system that enables the full Android experience on multiple interactive clients running on one computing platform. *Nezha* uses a non-invasive design principle: *Nezha* extensions are made within the bounds of the hardware abstraction layer (HAL), with no modifications to the kernel and only minimal changes to Android AOSP. The HAL is usually owned by SoC or device vendors, while the kernel and AOSP are maintained by the Linux Foundation and Google, respectively. A particular system feature (such as multiple client support) could be implemented by a vendor by changing a certain version of kernel or AOSP. However, for future versions of kernel and AOSP, the vendor must repeat the efforts of porting the changes. In some cases, if the kernel or AOSP has undergone major revision, the porting effort could be huge. Our HAL extension approach decouples *Nezha* from both kernel and AOSP updates, providing a huge maintenance savings for device vendors.

The rest of this paper is organized as follows: Section 2 describes *Nezha* from a user point of view. Section 3 provides a system overview from the implementation perspective. Section 4 introduces the implementation of each subsystem in detail. Section 5 evaluates *Nezha* performance against a series of benchmarks. Section 6 describes related works. Section 7 contains a summary and the plan of our future work.

2 *NEZHA* SYSTEM: USER PERSPECTIVE

Users can access multiple physical clients, each of which is composed of a dedicated set of HCI peripherals including a USB touch screen, a USB camera, an HDMI display panel, and an HDMI audio output. The onboard USB and HDMI ports corresponding to a client are regarded as dedicated ports for this client. All the clients share the CPU, the accelerators, the sensors, and the network interfaces on the computing board.

Each client is controlled with a stock Android environment instance which is isolated from all other instances. An end user controls a client in the same manner as using an Android tablet: running unmodified apps, watching videos, playing games, and surfing the internet. The user is not aware that the client is sharing computing resources with other clients. System-level user operations, such as network configuration or system shutdown, do not impact clients being used by other end users.

There is one special kind of user: the *Nezha* system administrator. The administrator creates and deploys Android images for clients. The Android images may be configured differently for individual clients, for example, the images may include different apps, settings, or access rights. It is even possible to deploy different versions of Android onto clients. The administrator also manages the lifecycle of the Android environments for the clients using a GUI application on a PC that has a USB/Ethernet link to the SoC board. ADB shell access is also available for administration purposes and also for testing or debugging.

3 IMPLEMENTATION OVERVIEW

As shown in Figure 1 , the Android-based implementation of *Nezha* offers every client a full user-level Android instance experience, taking advantage of certain OS level virtualization mechanisms in the Linux kernel, specifically namespace [18] and cgroup. Namespace allows *Nezha* to provide complete isolation of the applications view of the operating environment, including process trees, networking, user IDs, and mounted file systems. Cgroup allows limitation and prioritization of resources, such as CPU, memory, and network.

Upon power on, *Nezha* first boots up a minimal Linux environment, which is similar to the host environment in terms of Docker. All the Android instances can be regarded as children of the host, implying that the host can see into Android instances, but not viceversa. The host then spawns an always running instance manager. The instance manager is responsible for starting, stopping, and destroying the child Android instances. Sometimes, it can also be used as a convenient local utility to create and configure Android instances onsite, if a standalone *Nezha* management PC is not available. Our implementation of the instance manager is based on the Linux Container code, although we removed some complex logic that was not needed in our environment and added Android specific processing. Therefore, during lxc-start, it mounts proper Android data/system filesystems for a new instance, sets up new namespaces for the instance, and launches the Android init process towards the Android home screen. We also set up IPC channels between the instance manager and the instances.

Unlike headless servers where Docker containers work well, Android devices are expected to interact with a plethora of hardware modules, many of which are not originally designed to be multiplexed. Device virtualization does not exist for these peripherals. Cells [5] extends the kernel with a new device namespace and modifies all involved device drivers to properly respond to Android device accesses based on device namespace information. The Cells approach relies on a core assumption: only one foreground instance is visible and operable to the smartphone user. In the context of *Nezha*, because we have multiple screens, all the instances are simultaneously visible and usable by individual users. The shared onboard peripherals must be accessible for all the instances all the time, which is quite different from the exclusive device usage only by the foreground instance of Cells. Also, the Cells device namespace cannot support the dedicated devices of each client required by *Nezha*.

As a result, *Nezha* uses pure user-level methods to exclusively assign dedicated devices to the proper clients and efficiently multiplex the shared devices among all clients. In *Nezha*, the peripherals

are managed primarily at the HAL layer, and minor changes are made to the AOSP to connect it to the HAL peripheral management logic.

Nezha leverages the device discovery mechanism of Android (used by AOSP) to enforce the restriction or filtering policy to the device node creation process. This means that the peripherals that have been dedicated to a particular client are visible only to the Android instance that corresponds to that client. It also removes the capability of an Android instance to create device nodes in its environment, which prevents the instance from establishing a malicious access channel to the dedicated devices owned by other instances.

Nezha extends the HAL components of the shared peripherals to ensure that each client has virtualized but highly efficient access to the hardware and software assets that are integrated in the shared computing platform. The design pattern used to virtualize the peripherals is as follows: move the original HAL logic into a cross-instance daemon, and leave a virtual HAL in each instance, which forwards Android device accesses to the real HAL.

4 IMPLEMENTING DEVICE MANAGEMENT MECHANISMS

The following subsections describe how *Nezha* implements device dedication and multiplexing.

4.1 Virtualizing Binder without Code Modifications

Binder is an Android-specific IPC mechanism, which is comprised of three components: binder server, binder client, and binder driver. The binder driver is the cornerstone component for message delivery. In *Nezha*, we must prevent the IPC originating from one Android instance from being visible to other instances, for both correctness and isolation goals. The Android binder model employs a system-wide binder node, called context manager, to provide the naming and lookup system for binder services, which is managed by the binder driver. This default binder model does not work in our multi-instance system, because all services will be registered to this system wide context manager, without any isolation of binder IPCs among instances.

To virtualize the binder system to operate in our multi-instance scenario, our first idea was to change the binder driver to create a context manager for each instance. We added about 500 lines of code by creating a list containing the different context managers in single binder device node for Android versions before v8.0. However, this approach violates our principle of not changing kernel code, so we implemented a better solution.

We realized after v8.0, the Binder driver was improved to allow multiple binder device nodes to be created for different usages. A new kernel configuration controls the names of the device nodes which (by default) are binder. The binder driver loops over this name list and creates device nodes with these names. Each device node will be associated with a context manager. With this knowledge, it was simple for us to create a context manager for each instance. If we have N instances, we will configure this kernel option as a string, such as binder1, binder2, and binderN. The built-in logic of the binder driver will then create binder device nodes based on this configured string, and each of the nodes will have a context manager. Note that, given a kernel configuration file, it is trivial to automate the configuration process with a one-line sed script. To validate the functionality of this approach, we successfully backported the 8.0 binder driver to Android 7.0. In summary, although it seems counter-intuitive, *Nezha* successfully virtualizes the binder driver without one line of code change.

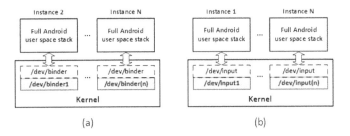

Figure 2: Binder and Uevent extension

The next step was to allocate the N binder device nodes to the instances one by one, as shown in Figure 2(a). These device nodes, although not backed by real peripherals, are similar to the client-dedicated peripherals. Therefore, we can use the same allocation method, which is described in the next section.

4.2 Allocating Client Dedicated Devices to Instances

When an Android instance is spawned, *Nezha* associates it with a particular client. In this process, *Nezha* allocates the client's dedicated peripherals (such as touch input, USB camera, etc.) to each instance. In our approach, we extended ueventd to assign device nodes to different instances, since Linux processes interact with the hardware peripherals through device nodes.

Ueventd is a process in every user-level Android environment. When an instance is started by the *Nezha* instance manager, the ueventd process is spawned by the Init process. It then runs a device node discovery method to populate device nodes into the /dev directory for kernel-discovered devices.

In *Nezha*, a configuration file is used to store a list of device nodes that are allocated to an instance. We extended ueventd so that its device discovery process checks every kernel-reported device discovery event against this configuration file. ueventd only creates a device node if the reported device has been found in the configuration file. After ueventd initialization is finished, the user space of an instance can only access the device nodes assigned to it; these are the nodes visible in the /dev directory of the current instance. Figure 3 explains the procedure. The gray boxes show process steps that were added by our approach.

Figure 2(b) shows that different /dev/inputX have been assigned to individual instances. The Android upper layer AOSP may still assume there is a /dev/input instead of /dev/inputX for it to operate. To fill this gap, the AOSP code could be changed so that it interacts with /dev/inputX, however, our principle is to make minimal changes to the AOSP and to keep the low-level changes transparent

to the upper layer. In *Nezha*, in addition to /dev/inputX, ueventd also creates a symbolic link between /dev/input and /dev/inputX.

Figure 3: Ueventd extension

In summary, using extensions to ueventd, we assigned different devices including camera, USB touch, and Binder into different instances. Also, a symbolic link enables us to avoid AOSP modifications.

4.3 Multiplexing Shared Devices via HAL Virtualization

Onboard devices, such as graphic engine, video engine, and security engine, will be shared among instances. We use the instance manager to host a global HAL for each shared device, and there is a virtual HAL in individual Android instances. The global HAL interacts with the device using the driver, while the virtual HAL talks with the global HAL. In addition to simple forwarding of operations from a virtual HAL, the global HAL takes advantage of its panoramic view to do advanced optimizations for some devices. We will explain our approach using display virtualization as an example.

Typical display drivers are not able to handle multiple requests from different users at the same time, assuming that the SoC only has one display controller. To avoid conflicts when multiple Android instances send display requests to the display driver at the same time, *Nezha* hosts the *Nezha* Display Composer (NDC) as a plugin of the instance manager. The NDC merges the display requests from different instances and sends the combined requests to the actual display controller via display driver interfaces.

As illustrated in Figure 4, for each Android instance, *Nezha* adds one virtual HAL layer for Android Gralloc and HWComposer HAL, called Gralloc vHAL and HWComposer vHAL, respectively. An Android instance calls the virtual HAL in the same way as calling a real HAL.

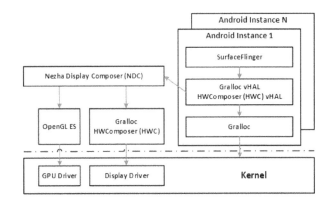

Figure 4: *Nezha* display architecture

For surface allocation/sharing operations in one Android instance, the Gralloc vHAL calls the real Gralloc HAL to complete the work within the instance. For each Android instance display request issued from the surface flinger to the HWComposer, the Gralloc vHAL and HWComposer vHAL first share the surfaces to NDC, and then redirect the display request to the NDC.

The NDC merges the display requests from each Android instance together, and calls the standard HWComposer HAL interface to send the display requests to the real display driver. In this way, there is only one actual display driver user, removing the conflicts caused by concurrent display requests from multiple Android instances.

The display surface sharing and display request redirection are transparent to each Android instance. There is no need to change the Android Gralloc and HWComposer HAL implementation. This greatly simplifies the *Nezha* implementation and makes it portable to platforms from different vendors.

5 EVALUATION

Nezha is designed to consolidate many independent client systems running simultaneously on a single hardware computing platform, enabling use cases such as multi-terminal Android retailer systems and Rear Seat Entertainment in cars. In both scenarios, the user experience in the context of concurrent usage and scalability are the key performance indicators to optimize and showcase. In our experimental multi-terminal retailer system shown in Table 1, multiple client OSes are running on single SoC centralized embedded system, rendering locally into multiple display panels connected to the main system, with 4 core CPUs, integrated GPU, and mid-size amount of memory.

Table 1: The experimental platform

	Multi-terminal Retailer System
CPU	I7-6770HQ 2.6 GHZ 4 core (4C8T)
GPU	Graphic Intel Skylake Integrated 950 MHz
MEMORY	DDR4 32 GB 2133 MHz

For this configuration, two types of test cases were designed, namely, OS instance/application launch, and game/video rendering. OS instance/application launch aimed to evaluate the user experience in terms of latency for starting new Android instances or starting a new application according to end user inputs. Game/video rendering aimed to evaluate the user experience in terms of frame rate for showing continuous contents in a client system, for example, gaming, 3D animation, and advertising.

For launch latency, the launch time of a new Android instance, and the cold launch time of Chrome (version: 54.0.2840.85) were measured when concurrent instances were running a compute-intensive game (Subway Surf). Figure 5 shows that the trend of instance startup time is approximately flat when the number of concurrent instances grows from 1 to 16. Notably, the startup time of the second instance is much shorter. We believe this is because the first instance has loaded the shared files into memory so that the second instance does not need to reload them. The reason for

the startup time increase of the 4th, 8th, and 16th instances is due to the increased contention of the shared kernel-critical sections.

The definition of cold launch for an application is to launch the application from a new process fork. Figure 6 shows the cold launch latency of the Chrome browser. In all figures, the y-axis shows the latency measurement and the x-axis marks the number of instances.

Figure 5: Android Startup Time (sec)

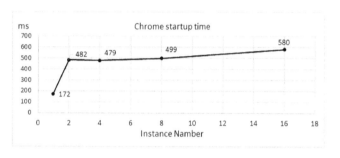

Figure 6: Chrome Application Startup Time (sec)

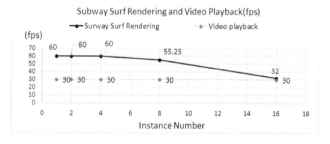

Figure 7: Subway Surf Rendering and Video Playback (fps)

Table 2: Subway Surf Resource Utilization

Concurrent Instances	1	2	4	8	16
fps	60	60	60	55.25	32
cpu%	2.7	3	11	22	34
gpu%	38	38	57	99	99
Mem%	6.86	9.72	15.9	26.67	48.48

To understand user experience under the worst case scenario, we measured the reached frame rate when all concurrent instances were running 3D games (Subway Surf) or playing videos (Android Photo App). Figure 7 shows the game frame rate starts to drop when the instance number grows bigger than 8. Our data (Table 2) shows that GPU reaches full utilization starting at 8 instances, indicating that the 3D gaming performance is bounded by the capability of the integrated GPU. It is worth noting that it still reaches 30 FPS even when the instance number grows to 16, which is good enough for a multi-terminal retailer system. Figure 7 also shows a smooth video playback performance which means the video engine of the tested computing platform is very powerful. In the figure, the y-axis shows the frame rate measurement and the x-axis marks the number of instances running concurrently.

5.1 Summary

Our evaluation of the performance data shows that the *Nezha* system could well support the scenario of a multi-terminal retailer system and similar use cases in embedded and IoT areas. Most significantly, *Nezha* shows characteristics of good performance scalability, enabling service providers to increase their service scale by simply upgrading hardware capabilities. The architectural advantage of deep resource sharing among OS instances, greatly reduces per instance deployment cost in different scenarios.

6 RELATED WORK

Mechanisms that can host multiple Android instances on one computing platform can be classified into three categories: virtualization, Android framework-level extension, and container-like OS level virtualization. Existing techniques target one-screen devices (such as a phone) where the screen is multiplexed among instances by device owners switching between applications, while our approach targets multiple simultaneously interactive screens for multiple users. Traditional virtualization is known to be ineffective on low-end devices [3][4][8][9][10][11][12][13][14][15][16][17]. Moreover, efficient virtualization of the many peripherals of client devices is also challenging. It is possible to extend the existing Android framework towards multi-client support, but that requires heavy modifications of the AOSP components (including Android managers of window, input, package, and activity, among others), leading to a huge maintenance burden. In addition, the isolation provided by a framework level solution is very weak and a bug in one client will crash the whole system.

6.1 OS-level solution

Cells [5] and Condroid [6] are both Android container solutions. Unlike *Nezha*, they focus on a single screen system. The modification in Cells are mostly in the kernel, which has challenges being accepted by the kernel community due to the loss of kernel uniformity. In contrast, most of the modifications in Condroid are in AOSP, which is difficult to upgrade and maintain since Google is not likely to accept these patches.

In contrast to Cells and Condroid, *Nezha* focuses on the scenario where multiple users use the devices from different panels at the same time. To improve the maintainability of our solution, all our changes are at the HAL level: there are no changes to the kernel, and only minimal changes to the AOSP (about 200 lines of code

in total). This means our solution can be ported to any kernel and Android dessert quickly.

7 CONCLUSIONS AND FUTURE WORK

This paper discussed *Nezha*, a lightweight solution to host multiple physical clients on a single computing platform. The key points in this paper are: 1) we designed a novel and simple approach to allocate client-dedicated devices to instances; 2) we used an original HAL virtualization technique to share devices; 3) we did not change kernel code and made minimal changes to AOSP; 4) we implemented a prototype for *Nezha* and provided detailed performance data to prove the minor overhead incurred by our solution.

Security is a concern in the *Nezha* solution because the common kernel is shared by different instances compared with a solution that uses VMs. We are investigating the possibility of enhancing security of every instance by using hardware virtualization technology.

8 ACKNOWLEDGMENTS

We would like to thank Camp, Mary and Tullis, Michael L for revising the paper. We would like to thank our shepherd Dr. Robert LiKamWa and the reviewers for their helpful comments.

REFERENCES

[1] Android https://en.wikipedia.org/wiki/Android
[2] Virtualization https://en.wikipedia.org/wiki/Virtualization
[3] King, Samuel T., G. W. Dunlap, and P. M. Chen. "Operating System Support for Virtual Machines." USENIX Ann. Technical Conf., General Track, pp. 71-84. 2003.
[4] Rose, Robert. "Survey of system virtualization techniques." (2004).
[5] J. Andrus, C. Dall, A. V. Hof et al., "Cells: a virtual mobile smartphone architecture", Proceedings of the 23rd ACM Symposium on Operating Systems Principles, pp. 173-187.
[6] Lei Xu Condroid: A Container-Based Virtualization Solution Adapted for Android Devices. http://ieeexplore.ieee.org/document/7130872/?reload=true
[7] Overlayfs https://en.wikipedia.org/wiki/OverlayFS
[8] Chen, X. Y., Smartphone virtualization: Status and Challenges, Proc. IEEE Intl Conf. Electronics, Communications and Control, 2011, pp. 2834-2839.
[9] Soltesz, Stephen, H. Ptzl, M. E. Fiuczynski, A. Bavier, and L. Peterson. "Container-based operating system virtualization: a scalable, High-performance alternative to hypervisors." ACM SIGOPS Operating Systems Review, vol. 41, no. 3, pp. 275-287. ACM, 2007.
[10] O. Eiferman, The Real Challenges of Mobile Virtualization, http://www.cellrox.com/blog/the-real-challenges-of-mobilevirtualization/.2014.
[11] Aguiar, Alexandra, and F. Hessel. "Embedded systems' virtualization: The next challenge?" Rapid System Prototyping (RSP), 2010 21st IEEE Intl Symp., pp. 1-7. IEEE, 2010.
[12] Barr, Ken, P. Bungale, S. Deasy, V. Gyuris, P. Hung, C. Newell, H. Tuch, and B. Zoppis. "The VMware mobile virtualization platform: is that a hypervisor in your pocket?" ACM SIGOPS Operating Systems Review 44, no. 4, 2010, pp. 124-135.
[13] Barham, Paul, B. Dragovic, K. Fraser, S. Hand, T. Harris, A. Ho, R. Neugebauer, I. Pratt, and A. Warfield. "Xen and the art of virtualization." ACM SIGOPS Operating Systems Review vol 37, no. 5, 2003, pp. 164-177.
[14] Brakensiek, Jrg, A. Drge, M. Botteck, H. Hrtig, and A. Lackorzynski. "Virtualization as an enabler for security in mobile devices." Proc. 1st workshop Isolation and integration in embedded systems, pp. 17-22. ACM, 2008.
[15] Enck, William. "Defending users against smartphone apps: Techniques and future directions." Information Systems Security, pp. 49-70. Springer Berlin Heidelberg, 2011.
[16] Laadan, Oren, and J. Nieh. "Operating system virtualization: practice and experience." Proc. ACM 3rd Ann. Haifa Experimental Systems Conf., pp. 17, 2010.
[17] Scott, S. L., G. Valle, T. Naughton, A. Tikotekar, C. Engelmann, and H. Ong. "System-level virtualization research at Oak Ridge National laboratory." Future Generation Computer Systems vol 26, no. 3, 2010, pp. 304-307.
[18] M. Kerrisk, Namespaces overview, http://lwn.net/Articles/531114/.2013.

The Computing Landscape of the 21st Century

Mahadev Satyanarayanan
Carnegie Mellon University
satya@cs.cmu.edu

Wei Gao
University of Pittsburgh
WEIGAO@pitt.edu

Brandon Lucia
Carnegie Mellon University
blucia@andrew.cmu.edu

ABSTRACT

This paper shows how today's complex computing landscape can be understood in simple terms through a 4-tier model. Each tier represents a distinct and stable set of design constraints that dominate attention at that tier. There are typically many alternative implementations of hardware and software at each tier, but all of them are subject to the same set of design constraints. We discuss how this simple and compact framework has explanatory power and predictive value in reasoning about system design.

ACM Reference Format:
Mahadev Satyanarayanan, Wei Gao, and Brandon Lucia. 2019. The Computing Landscape of the 21st Century. In *The 20th International Workshop on Mobile Computing Systems and Applications (HotMobile '19), February 27–28, 2019, Santa Cruz, CA, USA*. ACM, New York, NY, USA, 6 pages. https://doi.org/10.1145/3301293.3302357

1 Introduction

The creation of the Periodic Table in the late nineteenth and early twentieth centuries was an exquisite intellectual feat [36]. In a small and simple data structure, it organizes our knowledge about all the elements in our universe. The position of an element in the table immediately suggests its physical attributes and its chemical affinities to other elements. The presence of "holes" in early versions of the table led to the search and discovery of previously unknown elements with predicted properties. This simple data structure has withstood the test of time. As new man-made elements were created, they could all be accommodated within the existing framework. The quest to understand the basis of order in this table led to major discoveries in physics and chemistry. The history of the periodic table teaches us that there is high value in distilling and codifying taxonomical knowledge into a compact form.

Today, we face a computing landscape of high complexity that is reminiscent of the scientific landscape of the late 19th century. Is there a way to organize our computing universe into a simple and compact framework that has explanatory power and predictive value? What is our analog of the periodic table? In this paper, we describe our initial effort at such an intellectual distillation. The periodic table took multiple decades and the contributions of many researchers to evolve into the familiar form that we know today. We therefore recognize that this paper is only the beginning of an important conversation in the research community.

HotMobile '19, February 27–28, 2019, Santa Cruz, CA, USA
© 2019 Copyright held by the owner/author(s).
ACM ISBN 978-1-4503-6273-3/19/02.
https://doi.org/10.1145/3301293.3302357

2 A Tiered Model of Computing

Today's computing landscape is best understood by the *tiered model* shown in Figure 1. Each tier represents a distinct and stable set of design constraints that dominate attention at that tier. There are typically many alternative implementations of hardware and software at each tier, but all of them are subject to the same set of design constraints. There is no expectation of full interoperability across tiers — randomly choosing one component from each tier is unlikely to result in a functional system. Rather, there are many sets of compatible choices across tiers. For example, a single company will ensure that its products at each tier work well with its own products in other tiers, but not necessarily with products of other companies. The tiered model of Figure 1 is thus quite different from the well-known "hourglass" model of interoperability. Rather than defining functional boundaries or APIs, our model segments the end-to-end computing path and highlights design commonalities.

In each tier there is considerable churn at timescales of up to a few years, driven by technical progress as well as market-driven tactics and monetization efforts. The relationship between tiers, however, is stable over decade-long timescales. A major shift in computing typically involves the appearance, disappearance or re-purposing of a tier in Figure 1. We describe the four tiers of Figure 1 in the rest of this section. Section 3 then explains how the tiered model can be used as an aid to reasoning about the design of a distributed system. Section 4 examines energy relationships across tiers. Section 5 interprets the past six decades of computing in the context of Figure 1, and Section 6 speculates on the future.

2.1 Tier-1: Elasticity, Permanence and Consolidation

Tier-1 represents "the cloud" in today's parlance. Two dominant themes of Tier-1 are *compute elasticity* and *storage permanence*. Cloud computing has almost unlimited elasticity, as a Tier-1 data center can easily spin up servers to rapidly meet peak demand. Relative to Tier-1, all other tiers have very limited elasticity. In terms of archival preservation, the cloud is the safest place to store data with confidence that it can be retrieved far into the future. A combination of storage redundancy (e.g., RAID), infrastructure stability (i.e., data center engineering), and management practices (e.g., data backup and disaster recovery) together ensure the long-term integrity and accessibility of data entrusted to the cloud. Relative to the data permanence of Tier-1, all other tiers offer more tenuous safety. Getting important data captured at those tiers to the cloud is often an imperative. Tier-1 exploits economies of scale to offer very low total costs of computing. As hardware costs shrink relative to personnel costs, it becomes valuable to amortize IT personnel costs over many machines in a large data center. *Consolidation* is thus a third dominant theme of Tier-1. For large tasks without strict timing, data ingress volume, or data privacy requirements, Tier-1 is typically the optimal place to perform the task.

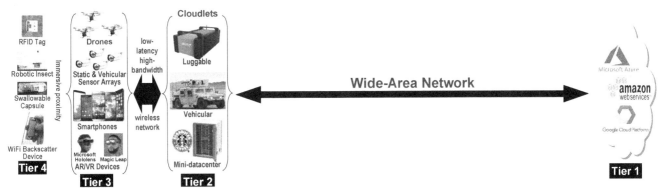

Figure 1: Four-tier Model of Computing

2.2 Tier-3: Mobility and Sensing

We consider Tier-3 next, because understanding its attributes helps to define Tier-2. *Mobility* is a defining attribute of Tier-3 because it places stringent constraints on weight, size, and heat dissipation of devices that a user carries or wears [29]. Such a device cannot be too large, too heavy or run too hot. Battery life is another crucial design constraint. Together, these constraints severely limit designs. Technological breakthroughs (e.g., a new battery technology or a new lightweight and flexible display material) may expand the envelope of designs, but the underlying constraints always remain.

Sensing is another defining attribute of Tier-3. Today's mobile devices are rich in sensors such as GPS, microphones, accelerometers, gyroscopes, and video cameras. Unfortunately, a mobile device may not be powerful enough to perform real-time analysis of data captured by its on-board sensors (e.g., video analytics). While mobile hardware continues to improve, there is always a large gap between what is feasible on a mobile device and what is feasible on a server of the same technological era. Figure 2 shows this large performance gap persisting over a 20-year period from 1997 to 2017. One can view this stubborn gap as a "mobility penalty" — i.e., the price one pays in performance foregone due to mobility constraints.

To overcome this penalty, a mobile device can offload computation over a wireless network to Tier-1. This was first described by Noble et al [25] in 1997, and has since been extensively explored by many others [8, 32]. For example, speech recognition and natural language processing in iOS and Android nowadays work by offloading their compute-intensive aspects to the cloud.

IoT devices can be viewed as Tier-3 devices. Although they may not be mobile, there is a strong incentive for them to be inexpensive. Since this typically implies meager processing capability, offloading computation to Tier-1 is again attractive.

2.3 Tier-2: Network Proximity

As mentioned in Section 2.1, economies of scale are achieved in Tier-1 by consolidation into a few very large data centers. Extreme consolidation has two negative consequences. First, it tends to lengthen network round-trip times (RTT) to Tier-1 from Tier-3 — if there are very few Tier-1 data centers, the closest one is likely to be far away. Second, the high fan-in from Tier-3 devices implies high cumulative ingress bandwidth demand into Tier-1 data centers. These negative consequences stifle the emergence of new classes of real-time, sensor-rich, compute-intensive applications [34].

| | Typical Tier-1 Server | | Typical Tier-3 Device | |
Year	Processor	Speed	Device	Speed
1997	Pentium II	266 MHz	Palm Pilot	16 MHz
2002	Itanium	1 GHz	Blackberry 5810	133 MHz
2007	Intel Core 2	9.6 GHz (4 cores)	Apple iPhone	412 MHz
2011	Intel Xeon X5	32 GHz (2x6 cores)	Samsung Galaxy S2	2.4 GHz (2 cores)
2013	Intel Xeon E5-2697v2	64 GHz (2x12 cores)	Samsung Galaxy S4	6.4 GHz (4 cores)
			Google Glass	2.4 GHz (2 cores)
2016	Intel Xeon E5-2698v4	88.0 GHz (2x20 cores)	Samsung Galaxy S7	7.5 GHz (4 cores)
			HoloLens	4.16 GHz (4 cores)
2017	Intel Xeon Gold 6148	96.0 GHz (2x20 cores)	Pixel 2	9.4 GHz (4 cores)

Source: Adapted from Chen [3] and Flinn [8]
"Speed" metric = number of cores times per-core clock speed.

Figure 2: The Mobility Penalty: Impact of Tier-3 Constraints

Tier-2 addresses these negative consequences by creating the illusion of bringing Tier-1 "closer." This achieves two things. First, it enables Tier-3 devices to offload compute-intensive operations at very low latency. This helps to preserve the tight response time bounds needed for immersive user experience (e.g., augmented reality (AR)) and cyber-physical systems (e.g., drone control). Proximity also results in a much smaller fan-in between Tiers-3 and -2 than is the case when Tier-3 devices connect directly to Tier-1. Consequently, Tier-2 processing of data captured at Tier-3 avoids excessive bandwidth demand anywhere in the system. Server hardware at Tier-2 is essentially the same as at Tier-1 (i.e., the second column of Figure 2), but engineered differently. Instead of extreme consolidation, servers in Tier-2 are organized into small, dispersed data centers called *cloudlets*. A cloudlet can be viewed as "a data center in a box." When a Tier-3 component such as a drone moves far from its current cloudlet, a mechanism analogous to cellular handoff is required to find and use a new optimal cloudlet [9]. The introduction of Tier-2 is the essence of *edge computing* [33].

Note that "proximity" here refers to *network proximity* rather than physical proximity. It is crucial that RTT be low and end-to-end bandwidth be high. This is achievable by using a fiber link between a wireless access point and a cloudlet that is many tens or even hundreds of kilometers away. Conversely, physical proximity does not guarantee network proximity. A highly congested WiFi network may have poor RTT, even if Tier-2 is physically near Tier-3.

2.4 Tier-4: Longevity and Opportunism

A key driver of Tier-3 is the vision of *embedded sensing*, in which tiny sensing-computing-communication platforms continuously report on their environment. "Smart dust" is the extreme limit of this vision. The challenge of cheaply maintaining Tier-3 devices in the field has proved elusive because replacing their batteries or charging them is time-consuming and/or difficult.

This has led to the emergence of devices that contain no chemical energy source (battery). Instead, they harvest incident EM energy (e.g., visible light or RF) to charge a capacitor, which then powers a brief episode of sensing, computation and wireless transmission. The device then remains passive until the next occasion when sufficient energy can be harvested to power another episode. This modality of operation, referred to as *intermittent computing* [17, 18, 21], eliminates the need for energy-related maintenance of devices in the field. This class of devices constitutes Tier-4 in the taxonomy of Figure 1. *Longevity* of deployment combined with *opportunism* in energy harvesting are the distinctive attributes of this tier.

The most successful Tier-4 devices today are RFID tags, which are projected to be a roughly $25 billion market by 2020 [27]. More sophisticated devices are being explored in research projects including, for example, a robotic flying insect powered solely by an incident laser beam [12]. A Tier-3 device (e.g., RFID reader) provides the energy that is harvested by a Tier-4 device. *Immersive proximity* is thus the defining relationship between Tier-4 and Tier-3 devices — they have to be physically close enough for the Tier-4 device to harvest sufficient energy for an episode of intermittent computation. Network proximity alone is not sufficient. RFID readers have a typical range of a few meters today. A Tier-4 device stops functioning when its energy source is misaimed or too far away.

3 Using the Model

The tiers of Figure 1 can be viewed as a canonical representation of components in a modern distributed system. Of course, not every distributed system will have all four tiers. For example, a team of users playing Pokemon Go will only use smartphones (Tier-3) and a server in the cloud (Tier-1). A worker in a warehouse who is taking inventory will use an RFID reader (Tier-3) and passive RFID tags that are embedded in the objects being inventoried (Tier-4). A more sophisticated design of this inventory control system may allow multiple users to work concurrently, and to use a cloudlet in the warehouse (Tier-2) or the cloud (Tier-1) to do aggregation and duplicate elimination of objects discovered by different workers. In general, one can deconstruct any complex distributed system and then examine the system from a tier viewpoint. Such an analysis can be a valuable aid to deeper understanding of the system.

As discussed in Section 2, each tier embodies a small set of salient properties that define the reason for the existence of that tier. Elasticity, permanence and consolidation are the salient attributes of Tier-1; mobility and sensing are those of Tier-3; network proximity to Tier-3 is the central purpose of Tier-2; and, longevity combined with opportunism represents the essence of Tier-4. These salient attributes shape both hardware and software designs that are relevant to each tier. For example, hardware at Tier-3 is expected to be mobile and sensor-rich. Specific instances (e.g., a static array of video cameras) may not embody some of these attributes (i.e., mobility), but the broader point is invariably true. The salient attributes of

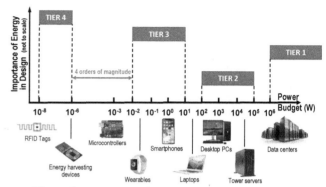

Figure 3: Importance of Energy as a Design Constraint

a tier severely constrain its range of acceptable designs. A mobile device, for example, has to be small, lightweight, energy-efficient and have a small thermal footprint. This imperative follows directly from the salient attribute of mobility. A product that does not meet this imperative will simply fail in the marketplace.

The same reasoning also applies to software at each tier. For example, Tier-3 to Tier-1 communication is (by definition) over a WAN and may involve a wireless first hop that is unreliable and/or congested. Successful Tier-3 software design for this context has to embody support for disconnected and weakly-connected operation. On the other hand, Tier-3 to Tier-2 communication is expected to be LAN or WLAN quality at all times. A system composed of just those tiers can afford to ignore support for network failure. Note that the server hardware in the two cases may be identical: located in a data center (Tier-1) or in a closet nearby (Tier-2). It is only the placement and communication assumptions that are different.

Constraints serve as valuable discipline in system design. Although implementation details of competing systems with comparable functionality may vary widely, their tier structure offers a common viewpoint from which to understand their differences. Some design choices are forced by the tier, while other design choices are made for business reasons, for compatibility reasons with products in other tiers, for efficiency, usability, aesthetics, and so on. Comparison of designs from a tier viewpoint helps to clarify and highlight the essential similarities versus incidental differences.

Like the periodic table mentioned in Section 1, Figure 1 distills a vast space of possibilities (i.e., design choices for distributed systems) into a compact intellectual framework. However, the analogy should not be over-drawn since the basis of order in the two worlds is very different. The periodic table exposes order in a "closed-source" system (i.e., nature). The tiered model reveals structure in an "open-source" world (i.e., man-made system components). The key insight of the tiered model is that, in spite of all the degrees of freedom available to designers, the actual designs that thrive in the real world have deep structural similarities.

4 The Central Role of Energy

A hidden message of Section 2 is that *energy* plays a central role in segmentation across tiers. As shown in Figure 3, the power concerns at different tiers span many orders of magnitude, from a few nanowatts (e.g., a passive RFID tag) to tens of megawatts (e.g., an exascale data center). Energy is also the most critical factor when making design choices in other aspects of a computing system. For example, the limited availability of energy could severely limit performance. The power budget of a system design could also be a major barrier to reductions of system cost and form factor. The relative heights of tiers in Figure 3 are meant to loosely convey the extent of energy's influence on design at that tier.

Tier-1 (Data Centers): Power is used in a data center for IT equipment (e.g., servers, networks, storage, etc) and infrastructure (e.g., cooling systems), adding up to as much as 30 MW at peak hours [6]. Current power saving techniques focus on load balancing and dynamically eliminating power peaks. Power oversubscription enables more servers to be hosted than theoretically possible, leveraging the fact that their peak demands rarely occur simultaneously.

Tier-2 (Cloudlets): Cloudlets can span a wide range of form factors, from high-end laptops and desktop PCs to tower or rack servers. Power consumption can therefore vary from <100W to several kilowatts. At this tier, well-known power saving techniques such as CPU frequency scaling [14] are applicable. Techniques have also been developed to reduce the power consumption of attached hardware (e.g., GPUs) [23], and to balance the power consumption among multiple interconnected cloudlets. As Figure 3 suggests, energy constraints are relatively easy to meet at this tier.

Tier-3 (Smartphones): Smartphones are the dominant type of computing device at Tier-3. Their power consumption is below 1000 mW when idle [22], but can peak at 3500-4000 mW. Techniques such as frequency scaling, display optimization, and application partitioning are used to reduce power consumption. Workload-specific techniques are also used in web browsing and mobile gaming.

Tier-3 (Wearables): Studies have shown that the energy consumption of smartwatches can be usually controlled to below 100 mW in stand-by mode with screen off [16]. When the screen is on or the device is wirelessly transmitting data, the energy consumption could surge to 150-200 mW. Various techniques have been proposed to further reduce smartwatch power consumption to <100 mW in active modes via energy-efficient storage or display management.

Tier-4: Energy-harvesting enables infrastructure-free, low-maintenance operation for tiny devices that sense, compute and communicate. Energy harvesting presents unique challenges: sporadic power is limited to 10^{-7} to 10^{-8} watts using, e.g., RF or biological sources. A passive RFID tag consumes hundreds of nA at 1.5V [26]. Emerging wireless backscatter networking enables communication at extremely low power [15]. Intermittent computing allows sensing and complex processing on scarce energy [5, 17]. Such capabilities enable a new breed of sensors and actuators deployed in the human body to monitor health signals, in civil infrastructure, and in adversarial environments like outer space [5]. RF beamforming extends the capability of batteryless, networked, in-vivo devices [19].

5 A Tiered View of the Past

In the beginning, there was only Tier-1. The batch-processing mainframes of the late 1950s and 1960s represented consolidation in its extreme form. In this primitive world, there were no representatives of Tier-2, Tier-3 or Tier-4. Those tiers could not emerge until the hardware cost of computing and its physical size had dropped by many orders of magnitude. The WAN shown in Figure 1 did not exist, but it was foreshadowed by remote punch card readers and line printers connected via point-to-point links to a mainframe.

The emergence of timesharing by the late 1960s introduced elasticity to Tier-1. In a batch-processing system, a job was queued,

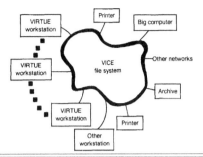

The figure at the top is from the 1986 description of the Andrew project by Morris et al [24]. The cloud-like Tier-1 entity ("VICE file system") offers storage permanence for the Tier-2 entities at the periphery ("VIRTUE workstations"). The verbatim comments above are from a 1990 paper [28] about this model of computing.

Figure 4: Limited Re-Creation of Tier-1 in a Tier-2 World

and eventually received exclusive use of the mainframe. Queueing delays increased as more jobs competed for the mainframe, thereby exposing the inelasticity of this computing resource. Timesharing multiplexed the mainframe at fine granularity, rather than serially reusing it. It leveraged human think times to provide the illusion that each user had exclusive access to Tier-1. This illusion broke down at very high load by the increase in queueing delays for user interactions. Until that breaking point, however, Tier-1 appeared elastic to varying numbers of users. The introduction of virtual machine (VM) technology by the late 1960s expanded this illusion. Now, elasticity applied to the entire vertical stack from low-level device drivers, through the (guest) operating system, to the top of the application stack. Many decades later, this encapsulating ability led to the resurgence of VMs in cloud computing.

Frustration with the queueing delays of timesharing led to the emergence of personal computing. In this major shift, Tier-1 was completely replaced by the brand-new Tier-2. An enterprise that switched from timesharing to personal computing was effectively disaggregating its consolidated Tier-1 infrastructure into a large number of dispersed Tier-2 devices. The co-location of a non-shared Tier-2 device with each user led to crisp interactive response. This, in turn, led to the emergence of a new class of latency-sensitive applications such as spreadsheets. A spreadsheet does not seem latency-sensitive today, but in the early 1980s its latency constraints could only be met at Tier-2.

An unintended consequence of the disaggregation of Tier-1 into dispersed Tier-2 elements was its negative impact on shared data. By the early 1980s, the archival data stored in its computing system was often of high value to an enterprise. Over the previous decade, business practices had been transformed by the easy sharing of data across timesharing users in an enterprise. The disaggregation of Tier-1 into dispersed Tier-2 devices destroyed the mechanisms for data sharing across users (e.g., a shared file system). It was at this juncture that the third important attribute of Tier-1, namely storage permanence, came to be recognized as crucial. How to preserve Tier-1's ability to share information easily, securely, and with appropriate access controls in a dispersed and fragmented Tier-2 world became a major challenge. The Andrew project [24] addressed this challenge by re-creating Tier-1 for the limited purpose of storage permanence, as shown in Figure 4. A distributed file system (AFS [10, 35]) created the illusion that all of Tier-1 storage was accessible via on-demand caching at Tier-2 devices. The resulting system provided users with the ease of data sharing characteristic of Tier-1, while preserving the crisp interactive response of Tier-2. Today, systems such as DropBox and Box are modern realizations of this concept.

As discussed in Section 2.1, a key attribute of a modern Tier-1 data center is its large pool of compute nodes that provide elasticity. This capability was pioneered by the Cambridge Processor Bank [1] in the 1979-1988 time period, and a few years later by Amoeba [40].

The emergence of Tier-3 coincided with the release of the earliest computers (circa 1983) that were small enough to be considered portable devices. The Radio Shack TRS-80 Model 100 (weighing roughly 1.5 kg and powered by 4 AA batteries) and the Compaq Portable (weighing 13 kg) were two early examples. There was explosive innovation in laptop hardware by the late 1980s. Once the Internet became widely used (mid-1990s), a key distinction between Tier-2 and Tier-3 was the stability and quality of Internet connectivity. In contrast to Tier-2 devices, Tier-3 devices typically had wireless connectivity with periods of disconnection and poor connectivity. The desire to preserve shared enterprise data access even when mobile led to the creation of Coda File System [31], which extended Figure 4 to Tier-3 devices.

By the mid-1990s handheld mobile devices referred to as *personal digital assistants (PDAs)* emerged. In the same timeframe, computing hardware had become small and light enough for *wearable computers* to be created [38]. These extreme optimizations of Tier-3 devices led to the mobility penalty discussed earlier (Section 2.2 and Figure 2). The need to process sensor streams in real time from these devices led to offloading (originally called "cyber foraging" [30]) from Tier-3 to Tier-1 or Tier-2.

6 Future Evolution

Our future computing landscape will include computing modalities that are not covered by Figure 1. We speculate on these modalities and their implications in this section.

Biological Computer Systems: Future computer systems will be inspired by, rendered in, and extensive of biology. Neuromorphic computing is seeing a resurgence with analog [11, 37] and delay-based [20, 39] architectures for neural machine learning. While analogies to biological behavior abound, spanning from circuits, to architectures, to software and algorithms, computer system behavior is rarely biological in its efficiency and capability. Other emerging systems leverage the efficiency of biological systems, rendering molecular-scale data storage [2] and processing [13] structures directly in biological substrates, such as engineered DNA. A key advantage of engineered biological computing systems is their extremely high degree of parallelism, distributing the responsibility for a task across vast numbers of molecular-scale components. A key challenge is the lack of reliability of individual components. This can be mitigated by using the extreme parallelism for redundancy. Future computing systems will extend biology with the mechanical capabilities of micro- and nano-robotics. This extension

can lead to an inversion of the relative costs of computing and actuation [7]. At macro-scale, the energy cost of actuation dominates that of computing; but at nano-scale, computing may dominate. Optimizing computing in such systems may lead to a new Tier-5.

Blurring boundaries between tiers: Tier boundaries in Figure 1 are likely to blur, leading to a continuum of devices with different power budgets, computing workloads and manufacturing costs. The major drivers of such blurring are advances in the manufacturing technologies. Such improvement not only allows a device to undertake more computing workloads with a lower power budget and a smaller form factor, but also fosters new computing models that fully integrate heterogeneous computing devices into a universal ecosystem. For example, significant chip-level convergence has occured across desktop PCs, laptops and smartphones in the past few years, leading to simpler task migration across these devices.

A consequence of such blurring boundaries is that the gap in capabilities between cloudlets at Tier 2 and battery-powered mobile devices at Tier 3 will diminish. In addition, today's requirement of chemical batteries at Tier-3 is likely to be gradually relaxed due to more advanced energy harvesting and wireless charging technologies. This allows significant reduction of device size and alleviates some design constraints of mobility. Energy harvesting will also be able to provide a much higher power budget, which then allows a richer set of computing tasks being executed at Tier-4 devices. Consequently, the transition between Tier 3 and Tier 4 will be much smoother. This smooth transition will simplify deployment of embedded computing objects, leading to new computing paradigms such as distributed AI in the future IoT.

Quantum Computing: In terms of physical size, energy demand and dependence on external cooling, quantum computers would seem to map naturally to Tier-1. However, their widespread adoption requires extensive rework of the entire computing landscape. This includes new programming languages to express probabilistic problems, new programmable quantum architectures, new compilers that target emerging quantum machines, and new debugging and verification tools that validate results [4]. We do not yet know how to incorporate such a disruptive change into the tiered model of Figure 1. For now, quantum computing is an outlier.

7 Closing Thoughts

We began with the question "Is there a way to organize our computing universe into a simple and compact framework that has explanatory power and predictive value?" In Sections 2 through 6 we have presented and discussed such a framework. Its essence is the segmentation of the computing landscape into tiers that embody a set of design constraints and architectural roles. Figure 1 illustrates the four tiers that constitute our computing landscape today. The discussion in Section 5 shows that these tiers are not pre-ordained. Rather, starting with a single tier, they have emerged over time in response to technical innovations and expanding goals.

Space, time and energy are the driving forces of this evolution. Networking, in general, and the Internet, in particular, grew out of our desire to transcend space. Mobility and proximity, which are both space-derived concepts, directly influence the designs of Tier-2, Tier-3 and Tier-4. Permanent storage aims to preserve precious data in spite of the ravages of time. As shown in Figure 4, it accounts for the enduring role of Tier-1. Energy plays a central role in shaping tiers, as shown in Figure 3 and discussed in Section 4. These fundamental themes of space, time and energy will continue to shape computing long after today's technology is obsolete.

We close by reiterating that this paper only represents a first step, not the last word, in the creation of a compact intellectual framework for reasoning about design choices in distributed systems. The periodic table, for example, is able to resolve its structure into orthogonal axes of periods and groups. If a comparable resolution of Figure 1 into fundamental axes were possible, that would enhance the analytical and predictive power of the model. A different extension would be to incorporate a taxonomy of communication that amplifies the computing-centric taxonomy that we have introduced here. Much work remains to be done.

Acknowledgements

We thank our shepherd, Aruna Balasubramanian, and the anonymous reviewers for helping us to improve this work. This research was supported by the Defense Advanced Research Projects Agency (DARPA) under Contract No. HR001117C0051 and by the National Science Foundation (NSF) under grant number CNS-1518865. Additional support was provided by Intel, Vodafone, Deutsche Telekom, Verizon, Crown Castle, NTT, and the Conklin Kistler family fund. Any opinions, findings, conclusions or recommendations expressed in this material are those of the authors and do not necessarily reflect the view(s) of their employers or the above funding sources.

REFERENCES

[1] Jean M. Bacon, Ian M. Leslie, and Roger M. Needham. 1989. *Distributed computing with a processor bank*. Technical Report UCAM-CL-TR-168. University of Cambridge.

[2] James Bornholt, Randolph Lopez, Douglas M. Carmean, Luis Ceze, Georg Seelig, and Karin Strauss. 2016. A DNA-Based Archival Storage System. In *Proc. of the 21st Intl. Conf. on Architectural Support for Programming Languages and Operating Systems*. Atlanta, GA.

[3] Zhuo Chen. 2018. *An Application Platform for Wearable Cognitive Assistance*. Ph.D. Dissertation. Computer Science Dept., Carnegie Mellon Univ.

[4] Frederic T. Chong, Diana Franklin, and Margaret Martonosi. 2017. Programming languages and compiler design for realistic quantum hardware. *Nature* 549 (September 2017), 180–187.

[5] Alexei Colin, Emily Ruppel, and Brandon Lucia. 2018. A Reconfigurable Energy Storage Architecture for Energy-harvesting Devices. In *Proceedings of the International Conference on Architectural Support for Programming Languages and Operating Systems*.

[6] Miyuru Dayarathna, Yonggang Wen, and Rui Fan. 2016. Data center energy consumption modeling: A survey. *IEEE Communications Surveys & Tutorials* 18, 1 (2016), 732–794.

[7] Eric Diller and Metin Sitti. 2013. Micro-Scale Mobile Robotics. *Found. Trends Robot* 2, 3 (Sept. 2013), 143–259. https://doi.org/10.1561/2300000023

[8] Jason Flinn. 2012. *Cyber Foraging: Bridging Mobile and Cloud Computing via Opportunistic Offload*. Morgan & Claypool Publishers.

[9] Kiryong Ha, Yoshihisa Abe, Tom Eiszler, Zhuo Chen, Wenlu Hu, Brandon Amos, Rohit Upadhyaya, Padmanabhan Pillai, and Mahadev Satyanarayanan. 2017. You Can Teach Elephants to Dance: Agile VM Handoff for Edge Computing. In *Proceedings of the Second ACM/IEEE Symposium on Edge Computing*.

[10] John H. Howard, Michael L. Kazar, Sherri G. Menees, David A. Nichols, Mahadev Satyanarayanan, Robert N. Sidebotham, and Michael J. West. 1988. Scale and Performance in a Distributed File System. *ACM Transactions on Computer Systems* 6, 1 (1988).

[11] Y. Huang, N. Guo, M. Seok, Y. Tsividis, and S. Sethumadhavan. 2016. Evaluation of an Analog Accelerator for Linear Algebra. In *ACM/IEEE Intl. Symp. on Computer Architecture (ISCA)*.

[12] Johannes James, Vikram Iyer, Yogesh Chukewad, Shyamnath Gollakota, and Sawyer B. Fuller. 2018. Liftoff of a 190 mg Laser-Powered Aerial Vehicle: The Lightest Wireless Robot to Fly. In *Proceedings of the IEEE Int'l Conference on Robotics and Automation*. Brisbane, Australia.

[13] Craig D. LaBoda, Alvin R. Lebeck, and Chris L. Dwyer. 2017. An Optically Modulated Self-Assembled Resonance Energy Transfer Pass Gate. *Nano Letters* 17, 6 (2017), 3775–3781. https://doi.org/10.1021/acs.nanolett.7b01112 arXiv:https://doi.org/10.1021/acs.nanolett.7b01112 PMID: 28488874.

[14] Etienne Le Sueur and Gernot Heiser. 2010. Dynamic voltage and frequency scaling: The laws of diminishing returns. In *Proceedings of Int'l conference on*

Power aware computing and systems.

[15] Vincent Liu, Aaron Parks, Vamsi Talla, Shyamnath Gollakota, David Wetherall, and Joshua R Smith. 2013. Ambient backscatter: wireless communication out of thin air. In *Proceedings of ACM SIGCOMM*, Vol. 43. 39–50.

[16] Xing Liu, Tianyu Chen, Feng Qian, Zhixiu Guo, Felix Xiaozhu Lin, Xiaofeng Wang, and Kai Chen. 2017. Characterizing smartwatch usage in the wild. In *Proceedings of ACM MobiSys*. 385–398.

[17] Brandon Lucia, Vignesh Balaji, Alexei Colin, Kiwan Maeng, and Emily Ruppel. 2017. Intermittent Computing: Challenges and Opportunities. In *Proceedings of the 2nd Summit on Advances in Programming Languages*.

[18] Brandon Lucia and Benjamin Ransford. 2015. A Simpler, Safer Programming and Execution Model for Intermittent Systems. In *Proc. of the 36th ACM SIGPLAN Conf. on Prog. Lang. Design and Implementation*. Portland, OR.

[19] Yunfei Ma, Zhihong Luo, Christoph Steiger, Giovanni Traverso, and Fadel Adib. 2018. Enabling deep-tissue networking for miniature medical devices. In *Proceedings of ACM SIGCOMM*. 417–431.

[20] Advait Madhavan, Timothy Sherwood, and Dmitri Strukov. 2016. Energy Efficient Computation with Asynchronous Races. In *Proc. of the 53rd Annual Design Automation Conf.* Austin, TX.

[21] Kiwan Maeng and Brandon Lucia. 2018. Adaptive Dynamic Checkpointing for Safe Efficient Intermittent Computing. In *13th USENIX Symposium on Operating Systems Design and Implementation (OSDI 18)*.

[22] Chulhong Min, Youngki Lee, Chungkuk Yoo, Seungwoo Kang, Sangwon Choi, Pillsoon Park, Inseok Hwang, Younghyun Ju, Seungpyo Choi, and Junehwa Song. 2015. PowerForecaster: Predicting smartphone power impact of continuous sensing applications at pre-installation time. In *Proceedings of ACM SenSys*. 31–44.

[23] Sparsh Mittal and Jeffrey S Vetter. 2015. A survey of methods for analyzing and improving GPU energy efficiency. *Comput. Surveys* 47, 2 (2015).

[24] James H. Morris, Mahadev Satyanarayanan, Michael H. Conner, John H. Howard, David S. Rosenthal, and F. Donelson Smith. 1986. Andrew: A Distributed Personal Computing Environment. *Communications of the ACM* 29, 3 (1986).

[25] Brian D. Noble, M. Satyanarayanan, Dushyanth Narayanan, J. Eric Tilton, Jason Flinn, and Kevin R. Walker. 1997. Agile Application-Aware Adaptation for Mobility. In *Proc. of the 16th ACM Symp. on Operating Systems Principles*.

[26] Vijay Pillai, Harley Heinrich, David Dieska, Pavel V Nikitin, Rene Martinez, and KV Seshagiri Rao. 2007. An ultra-low-power long range battery/passive RFID tag for UHF and microwave bands with a current consumption of 700 nA at 1.5 V. *IEEE Transactions on Circuits and Systems* 54, 7 (2007), 1500–1512.

[27] Statista: That Statistics Portal. 2016. Projected size of the global market for RFID tags from 2016 to 2020. https://www.statista.com/statistics/299966/size-of-the-global-rfid-market/. (2016).

[28] Mahadev Satyanarayanan. 1990. Scalable, Secure, and Highly Available Distributed File Access. *IEEE Computer* 23, 5 (1990).

[29] Mahadev Satyanarayanan. 1996. Fundamental Challenges in Mobile Computing. In *Proceedings of the ACM Symposium on Principles of Distributed Computing*.

[30] Mahadev Satyanarayanan. 2001. Pervasive Computing: Vision and Challenges. *IEEE Personal Communications* 8, 4 (2001).

[31] Mahadev Satyanarayanan. 2002. The Evolution of Coda. *ACM Transactions on Computer Systems* 20, 2 (2002).

[32] Mahadev Satyanarayanan. 2014. A Brief History of Cloud Offload. *ACM GetMobile* 18, 4 (2014).

[33] Mahadev Satyanarayanan. 2017. The Emergence of Edge Computing. *IEEE Computer* 50, 1 (2017).

[34] Mahadev Satyanarayanan, Paramvir Bahl, Ramón Caceres, and Nigel Davies. 2009. The Case for VM-Based Cloudlets in Mobile Computing. *IEEE Pervasive Computing* 8, 4 (2009).

[35] Mahadev Satyanarayanan, John H. Howard, David A. Nichols, Robert N. Sidebotham, Alfred Z. Spector, and Michael J. West. 1985. The ITC Distributed File System: Principles and Design. In *Proceedings of the 10th ACM Symposium on Operating System Principles*.

[36] Eric R. Scerri. 2007. *The Periodic Table: Its Story and Its Significance*. Oxford University Press.

[37] A. Shafiee, A. Nag, N. Muralimanohar, R. Balasubramanian, J. P. Strachan, M. Hu, R. S. Williams, and V. Srikumar. 2016. ISAAC: A Convolutional Neural Network Accelerator with In-Situ Analog Arithmetic in Crossbars. In *ACM/IEEE 43rd Annual Intl. Symp. on Computer Architecture*.

[38] Dan Siewiorek, Asim Smailagic, and Thad Starner. 2008. *Application Design for Wearable Computing*. Morgan & Claypool Publishers.

[39] James E. Smith. 2014. Efficient Digital Neurons for Large Scale Cortical Architectures. In *Proc. of the 41st Annual Intl. Symp. on Computer Architecuture (ISCA '14)*. Minneapolis, MN.

[40] Andrew S. Tanenbaum, M. Frans Kaashoek, Robbert Van Renesse, and Henri E. Bal. 1991. The Amoeba Distributed Operating System - A Status Report. *Computer Communications* 14 (1991), 324–335.

CryptoCurrency Mining on Mobile as an Alternative Monetization Approach

Sinh Huynh
Singapore Management University
npshuynh.2014@smu.edu.sg

Kenny Tsu Wei Choo
Singapore Management University
kenny.choo.2012@smu.edu.sg

Rajesh Krishna Balan
Singapore Management University
rajesh@smu.edu.sg

Youngki Lee
Seoul National University
youngkilee@snu.ac.kr

ABSTRACT

Can cryptocurrency mining (crypto-mining) be a practical ad-free monetization approach for mobile app developers? We conducted a lab experiment and a user study with 228 real Android users to investigate different aspects of mobile crypto-mining. In particular, we show that mobile devices have computational resources to spare and that these can be utilized for crypto-mining with minimal impact on the mobile user experience. We also examined the profitability of mobile crypto-mining and its stability as compared to mobile advertising. In many cases, the profit of mining can exceed mobile advertising's. Most importantly, our study shows that the majority (72%) of the participants are willing to allow crypto-mining as means to replace ads to trade-off for benefits such as a better user experience.

CCS CONCEPTS

• **Applied computing** → **Digital cash**; • **Human-centered computing** → **Empirical studies in ubiquitous and mobile computing**;

KEYWORDS

CryptoCurrency Mining, Mobile Monetization; Distributed Mobile Computing

ACM Reference Format:
Sinh Huynh, Kenny Tsu Wei Choo, Rajesh Krishna Balan, and Youngki Lee. 2019. CryptoCurrency Mining on Mobile as an Alternative Monetization Approach. In *The 20th International Workshop on Mobile Computing Systems and Applications (HotMobile '19), February 27–28, 2019, Santa Cruz, CA, USA.* ACM, New York, NY, USA, 6 pages. https://doi.org/10.1145/3301293.3302372

1 INTRODUCTION

As of the first quarter of 2018, 94% of all Android apps on Google Play and 88% of iOS apps on App Store were available for free [11].

The free-to-play pricing model with in-app advertising has remained the most popular and profitable monetization model for mobile app developers [2, 7].

However, many mobile users prefer an ad-free experience if given a choice because advertising has a negative impact on user experience. The mobile ad is usually in the form of a banner or full-screen image/video which obscures the phone screen. The appearance of ads could also disrupt user engagement. More importantly, mobile advertising is raising a privacy concern where user behavioral data in mobile contexts can be exploited for targeted advertising.

In this work, we explore the potential of an ad-free monetization model based on crypto-mining. The key idea is to leverage the opportunistic computing resources from smartphones to perform mining and distribute the reward to mobile developers. Mobile users can decide to pay for the mobile content by contributing either their computing resources (mining) or their time and attention (watching ads) depending on their personal preferences.

One interesting argument that motivated us to carry out this study is that a mobile device has limited computational resources, and is hence not suitable for energy-consuming and computation-intensive tasks. In fact, due to its compact physical size, the mobile device inherently has constrained resources, especially its limited battery capacity. However, mobile users do not run resource-hungry apps/games continually throughout the day. The mobile computing resources stay idle most of the time. Users have also adapted their phone usage behaviors to fit their devices' capability. For instance, people charge their mobile devices more frequently than before– multiple times a day and whenever a power source is available [5]. We argue that the resources of mobile devices can be leveraged to perform crypto-mining without noticeable interference with the user experience.

To evaluate our idea, we conducted a study with 228 Android users with their devices running crypto-mining under various conditions. We collected their CPU utilization, battery levels, and charging instances to examine the availability of mobile resources for mining and to see how mining may affect user experience. We also analyzed the profitability of mobile crypto-mining in comparison with advertising. Lastly, we surveyed users' *awareness* of the resource utilization for mining and their opinions on allowing the mining in exchange of being able to skip the ads in app/game. Our findings from the study are as follows:

- Mobile mining is as profitable as advertising under certain conditions. For example, average daily revenue from one mobile device performing mining only when it is plugged-in is equivalent to 3 to more than 50 full-screen ad impressions in some countries.

- Mining in the background at a low-intensity setting, would not cause any noticeable negative impact on battery life, charging speed or app performance.
- Users are open to crypto-mining on their mobile devices as an alternate means for developers to monetize. In our user study, 72% of participants are willing to allow (or would not mind) the mining if they can skip the ads and be well informed of the mining.

Our contributions are as follows:

- We empirically evaluated the crypto-mining on mobile as an ad-free monetization model for mobile app/game. In particular, we investigated the availability of mobile resources for mining, effects of mining on the resources and user experience, and the profitability of mining compared with advertising.
- We examined the feasibility of different strategies to use the opportunistic computing resources of mobile devices and minimize the negative effects of mining on the user experience.
- We studied the perceptions and attitudes of mobile users towards allowing mining in the background in exchange for an ad-free mobile experience.

2 BACKGROUND & RELATED WORK

Cryptocurrency mining: Blockchain systems often involve a cryptocurrency like Bitcoin that is created in exchange for the computational processing work performed by users in the distributed network. This distributed computational processing is known as *mining* and serves two purposes: (1) to verify the legitimacy of a transaction and to prevent double-spending; (2) to create more of the cryptocurrency to reward miners for performing the computational task. The cryptocurrency incentivizes transaction verifiers (miners) to use their computing power to verify the ledger.

The difficulty of mining also scales to keep the rate of block discovery (creating more of the currency) steady. The more computing power added to the network, the more computations required to create a new block. Conversely, if computational power is taken off the network, the difficulty adjusts downward to make mining easier. This adjustment of difficulty makes the mining outcome less volatile than the cryptocurrency itself.

Choosing a suitable algorithm for mobile mining: To evaluate mobile mining as a monetization model for developers, we chose the *CryptoNight* algorithm because it is specifically designed and maintained for mining using commodity CPUs. CryptoNight was originally developed in 2013, as the hash function of CryptoNote [3] and is designed to be inefficient on GPU, FPGA, and ASIC architectures, and mitigates *mining centralization*. This is opposed to other popular mining algorithms such as SHA-256 (Bitcoin) or Scrypt (Litecoin) [10] that can be mined using ASICs, which renders mining using normal PCs or mobile devices comparatively incompetent.

The resource utilization (main memory, CPU, and network) of CryptoNight on the desktop has been empirically studied [9], with the CPU being the most power-consuming component. In the same manner, mining on mobile devices could result in some negative

effects such as reduced battery life and app performance (e.g., lower frame rates). In this work, we proposed and evaluated suitable strategies to minimize these effects.

Cryptocurrency Mining on Mobile: Since the release of a JavaScript CryptoNight miner named CoinHive in September 2017 [4], an increasing number of Internet content providers have been trying to monetize their content using browser-based mining fully or along with ads. We adopt this approach into the mobile domain in which developers will be rewarded with cryptocurrency mined by users' mobile devices. As crypto-mining is a computation-intensive activity, the biggest problem facing mobile mining is that it could negatively affect user experience such as draining the battery and reducing app performance. However, by implementing the miner as a mobile background service, the mining process is independent of the app or game that users are playing. This is different from the traditional use case of a browser-based miner in which the mining process can only be triggered when users visit the website with the embedded miner. In other words, the duration and timing to run mobile mining process is independent and not limited to the running app. As a result, the mobile mining task can be *scheduled* to minimize the mining effects on user experience and optimize profit for developers. This enables crypto-mining to be a feasible monetization approach even in the resource-constrained condition of mobile devices.

3 PERFORMANCE CHARACTERISTICS OF MINING ON MOBILE DEVICES

We first conducted a micro lab experiment to understand how the CryptoNight miner performs on Android devices with different CPU specifications (Galaxy Note 4, Galaxy Tab S2, Galaxy S7, Galaxy S8). We measured the mining hash rate, CPU temperature, battery temperature and power consumption (battery discharge rate) corresponding to each mining intensity level.

We ran the Javascript CoinHive miner in the background with mining intensity levels from 10% to 50%. The intensity level indicates the percentage of time the CPU will be used to run the task. The number of mining threads was set equal to the device's number of CPU cores. For each intensity level, the mining task was performed for 20 minutes continuously. No other application ran during mining. The devices were unplugged and their screens were off. The room temperature was 26°C. At the beginning of each session, the battery temperature was approximately 27°C and the CPU temperature was around 30°C. We used Batterystats, a tool included in the Android framework, to collect the battery data. The CPU and battery temperature were logged every 5 seconds.

Table 1: Hash rate (hash/second) / Battery Discharge Rate (mAh) at different mining intensity levels.

Device	Mining Intensity Level		
	10%	30%	50%
Note 4	2.74 / 267.5	5.46 / 445.4	7.06 / 564.8
Tab S2	5.54 / 297.0	7.78 / 520.7	11.16 / 697.9
S7	6.52 / 326.7	13.38 / 523.5	16.08 / 780.9
S8	6.22 / 309.3	13.50 / 517.8	16.10 / 775.5

Table 1 shows the mining hash rate and battery discharge rate corresponding to each device and mining intensity level. More powerful devices with higher CPU clocks (Galaxy S7 and S8) can mine with higher hash rates. The mining task consumed more power and drained the battery more quickly at the higher intensity. For example, the discharge rate on Galaxy S7 is from 326.7 mAh (10.89%/hour) to 780.9 mAh (26.03%/hour) when the mining intensity increase from 10% to 50%. Android devices are also getting more energy-efficient. In particular, running the mining at the hash rate of 6 H/s, the discharge rate on Note 4 and Tablet S2 are around 400 mAh, while the corresponding discharge rate on Galaxy S7 and S8 is less than 300 mAh.

Table 2: Lab experiment: battery temperature / CPU temperature (°C) per mining intensity level.

Device	Mining Intensity Level				
	10%	20%	30%	40%	50%
Note 4	32/50	34/53	36/58	36/61	36/61
Tab S2	34/70	36/73	36/75	36/77	38/79
S7	33/51	35/63	36/71	37/74	38/77
S8	32/NA	34/NA	36/NA	36/NA	37/NA

Table 2 shows the temperature of battery and CPU after 20 minutes of mining per each intensity level. The mining has a significant heating effect on mobile devices. For instance, at an intensity level of 40%, the battery temperature across four devices all increased from 26°C to 36°C after the mining duration. We do not run the mining intensity level higher than 50% to avoid damaging the devices as the CPUs get close to 80°C at the intensity level 40% and 50%, and the mining hash rate is not stable after 10-15 minutes of mining. Overall, mining at higher intensity generates the same amount of profit faster, but it could cause significant negative impact on mobile devices such as heating and battery draining.

4 MOBILE MINING USER STUDY

We conducted an IRB-approved study with 228 Android users recruited from Amazon Mechanical Turk (ages from 18 to 62, M = 32.34, SD = 8.57; 85 females). 79% of the participants had used their current mobile device for less than 2 years. As for the gaming frequency on mobile, 49% of participants reported spending more than 3 hours each week playing.

4.1 Study Procedure

We first detail the study procedure and acquire consent from participants to take part in our study. The participants are then asked to install our experiment Android app. The app has two tasks that run in Android background service for 24 hours starting from the moment that the app is first opened:

- Crypto-mining using CPU: CryptoNight algorithm, Monero (XMR) coin [13], Coinhive JavaScript implementation. The number of threads of the mining task is set to the number of CPU cores on the device. Our intent is to run the mining task at low intensity for longer periods to prevent the battery from draining too quickly and moderate the device temperature. The mining intensity is set at 20%.
- Collecting mobile usage data: we register Broadcast Receivers to get updates of the device battery level, charging state and connectivity. We also collect the CPU utilization and CPU

temperature every 10 seconds. The CPU utilization is averaged across threads.

After 24 hours, participants are asked to answer a survey. The survey includes questions on user awareness of the effects of mining on battery life, charging speed, and processing speed (e.g., app responding, frame rate) for the past 24 hours. Additionally, we ask participants if they would allow their phone to run the background crypto-mining: '*Considering the background mining may cause some negative effects like you have experienced in the last 24 hours, would you allow it in exchange for the ability to skip ads? Please explain?*'.

4.2 Mining Modes

In the study, we included various experiment modes where the mining is triggered by different conditions. This is to study the mining performance and effects on user experience under different phone usage conditions. Each participating device was randomly assigned one of six modes in Table 3. Participants were not aware of their assigned mining modes.

Table 3: Experiment modes and mining conditions.

Mode	n	Mining Conditions			
		Network	Screen	Battery	Plug
Baseline	85				
Always	31	On		> 15%	
Plug	30	On		> 15%	In
Plug_FChar	31	On		100%	In
Unplug_ScrOff	28	On	Off	> 15%	Out
Unplug_ScrOn	23	On	On	> 15%	Out

In the Always mode, the app runs the mining as long as the Internet connection is available and the battery level is higher than 15%. These two conditions apply to all the mining modes. An Internet connection is required for all mining modes as a miner needs to periodically exchanges blockchain data and hash to avoid getting stale shares. We also set the minimal battery level as 15% to run mining to prevent the battery from getting entirely drained by the mining task. Plug_FChar is the least obtrusive mode in which the app only mines when the device is fully charged and still plugged in. We also include a baseline mode as the control group in this study.

5 RESULTS

In this section, we will first examine the profitability and stability of cryptocurrency mining on mobile to demonstrate its potential as a monetization model. We will also analyze the availability of mobile resources for mining, how the mining affects user experience and how users perceive it. Lastly, we discuss preference and opinions on allowing the background mining as a way to pay mobile developers.

5.1 Mining Profit

5.1.1 Profitability of mining as a mobile monetization model. Table 4 shows the average mining profit on one device estimated with the XMR price, the block reward and difficulty at the time we conducted our study (May 2018). For instance, Plug_FChar averaged 205.9 mins of mining in the 24 hours study duration and a hash rate of 5.15, giving an estimated profit of 0.11 cents.

Table 4: Average mining duration, hash rate and estimated profit of each mining mode .

Mining Mode	Duration (minute/day)	HashRate (hash/s)	Profit (cent/day)
Always	551.7	5.04	0.28
Plug	251.4	5.21	0.13
Plug_FChar	205.9	5.15	0.11
Unplug_ScrOff	326.3	5.80	0.19
Unplug_ScrOn	236.2	3.21	0.08

To give a perspective of how profitable mobile mining is as a monetization model for developers, we compare it with mobile advertising. In January 2017, the average full-screen ads eCPM (earnings per 1000 ad impressions) of Google Admob is $0.75, or 0.075 cent per one ad impression [1]. However, at the range lower than the first quartile of eCPM distribution, there were more than 40 countries with the eCPM ranging only from $0.02 to $0.4. In comparison with the mining profit shown in Table 4, it means that if user device performs mining at Plug mode, the daily mining reward is equivalent to the revenue from 3 to over 50 full-screen ad impressions in those countries.

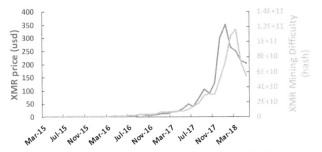

Figure 1: Monero (XMR) price and mining difficulty from May 2015 to May 2018.

5.1.2 Stability of mining as a mobile monetization model. Figure 1 shows the price and mining difficulty of Monero coin (XMR) in the last three years. As the difficulty level indicates the total computing power contributed to the network, we can see the miner responds quickly and accordingly to price changes. For instance, the mining difficulty started to increase significantly in November 2017 almost at the same time as the rise in price and then went down after the price decreased steeply in February and March 2018. This relationship between the price and the total computing power contributed to the XMR network results in the stability of the mining profit.

Figure 2 shows the comparison of average advertising and mining daily profit in the last three years. Note that the Admob eCPM data after January 2017 is not available. At the time of Oct 2016, the mining profit with our Plug configuration was equal to the average global eCPM ($0.75). In other words, daily mining profit per device at that time equaled the profit generated by one full-screen ad. However, mobile advertising revenue has a wide-spread distribution. The eCPM in many countries, especially in Asia, is much lower than the average (ranging from $0.02 to $0.4). For instance, Figure 2 shows the eCPM in China, India, and Russia are all approximately $0.3 in January 2017. The mining profit of Plug mode then was $1.50 per 1000 devices, meaning users in those countries can skip 5 ad impression daily by running the Plug mode. More importantly,

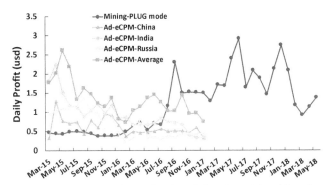

Figure 2: Average daily profit of mobile advertising (Google Admob, 1000 impressions of full-screen ad) and mining (XMR mining, 1000 devices, PLUG mode).

despite the fact the cryptocurrency has been very volatile with the price changing very fast (Figure 1), the mining profit is much more stable as a result of the adaptive mining difficulty level.

5.2 Mining Resources

5.2.1 Battery. Mobile users usually do not unplug the device right after it is fully charged (especially during the night) as there is no harm in keeping it plugged in. Figure 3 shows the distribution of time until participants in our study unplugged their phones after the battery was fully charged. 71% of the charging instances were of participants keeping the device plugged in for more than 30 minutes after the battery was fully charged. On average, each device was kept plugged in for 207 minutes after the charging has been completed for the 24 hours duration of the experiment. These are opportunistic time slots where we can run computation-intensive tasks like mining with minimal effect on the device's battery life.

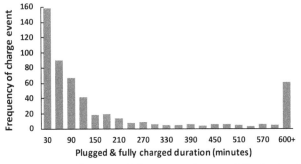

Figure 3: Distribution of duration when mobile device is fully charged and plugged in.

5.2.2 CPU. Our study shows that, in regular daily use (the baseline group), the CPU utilization is less than 20% more than half of the time. The CPU utilization is higher when the screen is on as the devices were in use. The CPU utilization when performing mining is 10-12% higher than the baseline. Although users' mobile CPUs still perform far below its full capacity, pushing the CPU utilization higher could drain the battery quickly and disrupt the user experience.

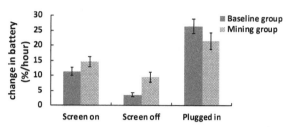

Figure 4: Mining effects on battery life.

5.3 Mining Effects and User Awareness

Figure 4 shows the effect of mining on the battery drain and charging speed. As expected, mining makes the battery drain faster. Running mining when the phone is not in use or not plugged in (Screen off), results in a battery drain of 0.16% per minute or around 9.5% per hour. This is significant as compared with the baseline–when the screen is off, the battery only drops 3-4% per hour. The average charging speed also decreased from 26.4% down to 21.5% per hour because of the mining. However, users may be unable to notice this effect on battery life.

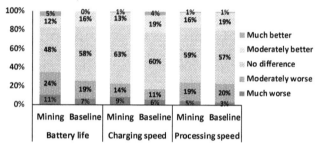

Figure 5: Survey: user perception of mining effects.

Figure 5 summarizes participants' perception regarding changes of battery charging speed, draining rate and CPU processing speed caused by the mining. We give a comparison of the perception between the baseline group and the mining group. Overall, 76% of the participants have not noticed any negative effects caused by the mining. There is no significant difference in the participants' perception of changes in processing speed and charging speed between the mining and baseline groups.

However, participants are more concerned about the battery life than the other two metrics. 35% of the participants in the mining group think that the battery drained faster during the study, the proportion is 12% higher compared to the baseline group. In other words, participants would notice that their user experience is negatively affected if the mining task runs constantly or runs when the device is unplugged (Always, Unplug_ScrOn and Unplug_ScrOff modes). On the other hand, mining when the device is plugged in (Plug or Plug_FChar) is less intrusive and would not cause any noticeable effects (with the configuration in our study).

5.4 User Preference

In the last part of the post-mining survey and after experiencing the background mining for 24 hours, we asked users if they consider mining to be a practical alternative to pay for the mobile content instead of watching ads.

Participants were open to the idea of their mobile computing resources being used to mine cryptocurrency in exchange for the

ability to skip the ads in apps/games. 47% of the participants indicated that they would allow the mining and 25% with a neutral opinion (i.e., choosing 'do not mind' option). Only 26% would not allow the background mining because of various reasons including privacy concern, negative impacts on phone usage, or not familiar with the concept of cryptocurrency. We also noticed that the acceptance rates of baseline modes are not better than those of the other mining modes, which is reasonable because most of the participants did not notice any different effects caused by the mining.

6 DISCUSSION

Privacy Concerns: The CryptoNight mining operation, itself, is highly anonymous as it just exchanges blockchain data with a cryptocurrency network or a mining pool – it does not collect any personal data at all. On the contrary, mobile ads, to improve their relevance, frequently collect user behavioral, location, and other contextual data [6]. Overall, we believe that cryptomining is fundamentally more privacy-preserving compared to mobile advertising.

User Consent: However, using computing resources without user knowledge and permission can be considered a malicious action on the part of developers. Unlike advertising which is usually easily identifiable, it is much harder for users to notice if a mining task is running in the background of their devices. Therefore, providing *user transparent* mining, with full user permission and understanding, is crucial before these types of techniques can be widely used by developers for monetization for developers.

User Preference: Both Mobile advertising and mining can be used as sources of income for developers; with each one "paid for" by users differently. For mining, the users "pay" by providing computing power that consumes both energy and and could lower the performance of users' devices. While smart scheduling can minimize the effects of mining on the user experience, the mining still incurs energy costs. On the other hand, users "pay" for mobile advertising by giving up their attention and privacy to various app-overlying frequently targeted ads. An opportunity this work provides is the feasibility for developers to inform users about the costs of each option and let them choose their preferred monetization approach.

Scaling for multiple apps: Our study was limited to only one app running a crypto miner in the background. In a full deployment, additional tooling would be required to handle the case of multiple apps competing with each other for the mining resources. In particular, we anticipate these functions to be: (1) monitoring the usage of all apps using a mining reward model, (2) scheduling the mining task with multiple competing processes, and (3) distributing the mined rewards to different app developers using a fair and efficient scheme.

Future of Crypto-mining: Despite the recent popularity of crypto mining, it has been criticized for being economically inefficient and / or consuming too much energy when running the miners. In addition, the legality of crypto mining is unclear in many countries. As such, it's possible that various markets and / or cell phone providers may block background mining. Those are major challenges that make the future of a crypto-mining monetization approach uncertain. However, even if crypto mining does not pan out, there are other cases where the spare resources of mobile devices can be leveraged for distributed applications with the goal of earning rewards. For example, mobile users can participate in a distributed cloud storage network like Filecoin[8] or Storj[12] in which their storage is used to host encrypted content for other clients in return for rewards. These potential distributed applications could be more economically productive and environmentally friendly.

7　CONCLUSION

In this study, we investigated the potential of crypto-mining as an ad-free monetization approach for mobile app developers. With the data collected from a lab experiment and a user study with 228 Android users, we demonstrate (1) the availability of opportunistic mobile resource that can be used for computation-intensive tasks such as crypto-mining; (2) the mining profit on mobile device is comparable to mobile advertising; (3) the mining task can be scheduled to minimize its negative effects on the mobile user experience; and (4) if being well informed, the majority of mobile users are willing to allow the crypto-mining in exchange for an ad-free experience. Hence, crypto-mining can indeed become a viable alternative source of income for mobile app developers.

REFERENCES

[1] Adtapsy. 2017. Mobile Ad Networks Interstitial eCPM Report. Available at: http://ecpm.adtapsy.com.
[2] Kati Alha, Elina Koskinen, Janne Paavilainen, Juho Hamari, and Jani Kinnunen. 2014. Free-to-play games: Professionals' perspectives. *Proceedings of nordic DiGRA* 2014 (2014).
[3] anonymous. 2014. Cryptonight. Available at: https://cryptonote.org/cns/cns008.txt.
[4] Coinhive. 2017. Monetize your business with your users' CPU power. Available at: https://coinhive.com/documentation/miner.
[5] Denzil Ferreira, Anind K Dey, and Vassilis Kostakos. 2011. Understanding human-smartphone concerns: a study of battery life. In *International Conference on Pervasive Computing*. Springer, 19–33.
[6] Mirza A Haq, Arsalan Mujahid Ghouri, et al. 2017. Distinctive Characteristics of Mobile Advertising in Measuring Consumers' Attitude: An Empirical Study. *Journal of Management Sciences* 4, 2 (2017), 199–216.
[7] J Tuomas Harviainen, Jukka Ojasalo, and Somasundaram Nanda Kumar. 2018. Customer preferences in mobile game pricing: a service design based case study. *Electronic Markets* (2018), 1–13.
[8] Protocol Labs. 2017. Filecoin. Available at: https://filecoin.io/filecoin.pdf.
[9] Panagiotis Papadopoulos, Panagiotis Ilia, and Evangelos P Markatos. 2018. Truth in Web Mining: Measuring the Profitability and Cost of Cryptominers as a Web Monetization Model. *arXiv preprint arXiv:1806.01994* (2018).
[10] COLIN PERCIVAL. 2012. Scrypt - Tarsnap. Available at: https://www.tarsnap.com/scrypt/scrypt.pdf.
[11] The Statistics Portal. 2018. Distribution of free and paid Android apps in the Apple App Store and Google Play as of 1st quarter 2018. Available at: https://www.statista.com/statistics/263797/number-of-applications-for-mobile-phones/.
[12] Storj. 2017. Storj. Available at: https://docs.storj.io/docs.
[13] Nicolas Van Saberhagen. 2013. CryptoNote v 2.0. Available at: https://cryptonote.org/whitepaper.pdf.

Earthquake Early Warning and Beyond: Systems Challenges in Smartphone-based Seismic Network

Qingkai Kong
University of California, Berkeley
Berkeley, CA
kongqk@berkeley.edu

Qin Lv
University of Colorado Boulder
Boulder, CO
qin.lv@colorado.edu

Richard M. Allen
University of California, Berkeley
Berkeley, CA
rallen@berkeley.edu

ABSTRACT

Earthquake Early Warning (EEW) systems can effectively reduce fatalities, injuries, and damages caused by earthquakes. Current EEW systems are mostly based on traditional seismic and geodetic networks, and exist only in a few countries due to the high cost of installing and maintaining such systems. The MyShake system takes a different approach and turns people's smartphones into portable seismic sensors to detect earthquake-like motions. However, to issue EEW messages with high accuracy and low latency in the real world, we need to address a number of challenges related to mobile computing. In this paper, we first summarize our experience building and deploying the MyShake system, then focus on two key challenges for smartphone-based EEW (sensing heterogeneity and user/system dynamics) and some preliminary exploration. We also discuss other challenges and new research directions associated with smartphone-based seismic network.

CCS CONCEPTS

• **Human-centered computing** → **Ubiquitous and mobile computing systems and tools**; • **Applied computing** → **Earth and atmospheric sciences**.

KEYWORDS

Earthquake Early Warning, Smartphone Seismic Network

ACM Reference Format:
Qingkai Kong, Qin Lv, and Richard M. Allen. 2019. Earthquake Early Warning and Beyond: Systems Challenges in Smartphone-based Seismic Network. In *The 20th International Workshop on Mobile Computing Systems and Applications (HotMobile '19), February 27–28, 2019, Santa Cruz, CA, USA*. ACM, New York, NY, USA, 6 pages. https://doi.org/10.1145/3301293.3302377

1 INTRODUCTION

Earthquakes are global hazards that frequently shake our nerves at various places on the Earth by killing people, interrupting normal life and work, and destroying cities. In order to record and understand earthquakes, instruments such as seismometers are installed globally to convert earthquake waves into digital time series including acceleration, velocity or displacement of the ground motion.

Although many scientists and engineers have devoted their lives to study earthquakes, it is still not feasible to predict earthquakes using today's science and technology. The recent development of Earthquake Early Warning (EEW) systems provides at least one way to identify the occurrence of an earthquake in near real-time and issue a warning to the public [1]. The effectiveness of EEW has been proved in various regions over the past decade by reducing fatalities, injuries, and damage caused by earthquakes, by alerting people to take cover, slowing down and stopping trains, opening elevator doors, and many other applications [22]. The concept of EEW is simple – seismic waves generated by earthquakes travel at the speed of sound, while electronic signals travel at the speed of light (analogous to seeing lightning before hearing the sound of thunder). If we can detect seismic waves quickly after the earthquake occur, we can leverage electronic signals travels much faster than the seismic waves to warn people at further distances before seismic waves arrive [13].

Traditional seismometers are high-quality research-grade sensors, which are costly to deploy and maintain. As such, only a limited number of seismic networks exist in the world to monitor earthquakes, and few places (will) have EEW systems (e.g., Japan, California, Taiwan, China, Mexico, Italy, Turkey, Romania, Switzerland). Many other regions with high earthquake hazards and dense populations (e.g., Nepal, Ecuador, New Zealand, Indonesia) do not have EEW systems [1]. Even for places with EEW systems, many of them are limited by low station density due to the lack of funding to increase the number of sensors.

To overcome the limitations of traditional seismic networks, the MyShake system takes a different approach – a smartphone-based seismic network that turns people's smartphones into portable seismic sensors [17]. Using sensors and communication units that are readily-available in consumer smartphone devices, we can achieve rapid detection of earthquakes and issue warnings to individual users in target regions. The advantages of building such a smartphone-based EEW system are multifold: (a) no need to deploy sensors and maintain them, (b) easily scale up to the global level, (c) increase public awareness and knowledge of earthquakes. This approach also allows us to bring EEW to any region where the local population is exposed to earthquake hazards, especially in areas where do not exist the traditional EEW system.

Such a high-gain system does come with a number of unique challenges in the real world. In this paper, we first summarize our experience building and deploying the MyShake system, then present the unique challenges of EEW and our initial exploration to address these challenges. While initiated as a seismology project, through this workshop paper, our goal is to introduce MyShake to the mobile computing community, so that we could seek expert

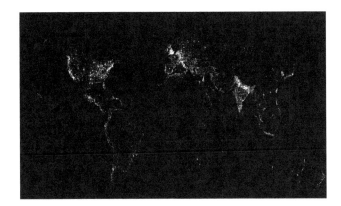

Figure 1: MyShake global user distribution. Brighter color indicates higher user density. Data used here are from all registered users with locations available during the period of 2016-02-12 to 2018-08-12.

feedback on possible solutions, potential improvements, and even new challenges/directions.

2 MYSHAKE SYSTEM

MyShake is a free Android app that has the ability to recognize earthquake shaking using the sensors in every smartphone. The app runs "silently" in the background, and when the shaking fits the vibrational profile of an earthquake, the app sends the anonymous information to a central server, which then confirms the location and magnitude of the quake by aggregating phones in a region. The whole system design is a collaboration between academia and industry, where seismologists at Berkeley Seismology Lab provided earthquake knowledge and designed the detection algorithms, while developers from Deutsche Telecom Silicone Valley Innovation Center implemented the whole system. An upgraded version of MyShake with new UIs and functionalities for both Android and iOS phones will be released in Spring 2019 to better engage participants and start issuing earthquake early warning to the public [20]. In this section, we give an overview of MyShake's current status and the overall system design.

2.1 MyShake Current Status

MyShake was released to the public on 2016-02-12 and grew rapidly into a global seismic network. It currently has more than 296K downloads, 40K active users, with 6K to 7K phones contributing data on a daily basis. Figure 1 shows the global distribution of MyShake users with available location information. We can see that the MyShake seismic network has already reached global coverage, and new users can join the network easily by downloading the MyShake app. Initial observations from the MyShake users show very promising results, indicating that the data collected from the phones are capable of supporting various seismological applications [16]. Within the first two and half years, the MyShake network has detected around 900 earthquakes globally with magnitudes ranging from M1.6 to M7.8. There are also initial results showing that the MyShake network could potentially provide structural health monitoring of buildings [15], or use the sensor array to detect smaller earthquakes.

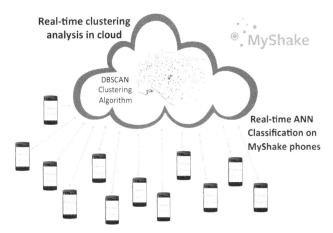

Figure 2: An overview of the MyShake system.

Table 1: Top 10 phone brands among 276,140 MyShake users.

Phone Brand	Percentage	Phone Brand	Percentage
Samsung	43.5%	Sony	4.4%
Motorola	6.1%	Google	4.2%
LG	5.6%	HTC	3.5%
Verizon	4.7%	Xiaomi	2.8%
Huawei	4.5%	Lenovo	2.7%

2.2 MyShake System Design

Figure 2 illustrates the current design of the MyShake system, which consists of two key components: (1) Each phone downloads MyShake application which has the capability of listening to the accelerometer and making decisions whether the experienced motion is due to earthquake by using an artificial neural network (ANN) model. The ANN model is trained by searching for the different characteristics between earthquake and human motions from various features [17, 19]. (2) The MyShake cloud server collects data from smartphones including state of health heartbeats, event triggers of the phones when they detect earthquake-like motions, and the corresponding time series of the phones' accelerometer data. A spatial and temporal clustering algorithm runs on the cloud server to aggregate information from multiple smartphones to identify earthquakes [18]. Whenever a phone detects an earthquake-like motion, it sends a trigger message including the time, location, and amplitude to the cloud server, where the clustering algorithm will confirm the earthquake and estimate earthquake parameters such as magnitude, location, and origin time. At the same time, the phone also records 5-minute (1 minute before and 4 minutes after the trigger) 3-component time series of acceleration and upload to the cloud server when the phone connects to WIFI and power. A detailed technical system architecture can be found in [17].

3 EEW CHALLENGES FOR MYSHAKE

While the current MyShake system is capable of detecting earthquakes on individual phones and collectively confirming earthquakes at the seismic network level, a number of unique challenges

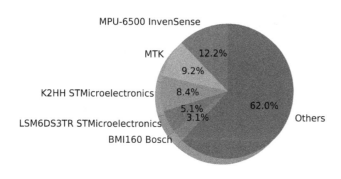

Figure 3: Top 5 accelerometer types in MyShake users' phones. Data are from 276,140 users.

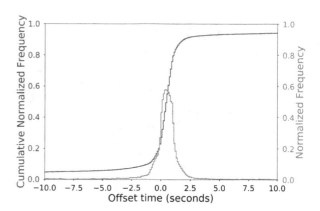

Figure 4: Distribution of MyShake phones' time offset based on 1 million randomly sampled NTP records using hourly synchronization.

need to be addressed in order to issue real-world EEW using such a smartphone-based seismic network. The key is to concurrently achieve highly accurate earthquake detection and highly efficient early warning, which requires pushing the boundaries of prior research. In this section, we highlight two key challenges that we have been working on, and discuss a few other challenges that are relevant to the mobile computing community.

3.1 Diversity of Sensing Hardware

Unlike traditional seismic networks, the MyShake network consists of individual users' smartphones. It is difficult to control the consistency of the sensing hardware. From the data collected by MyShake, it is clear that there exists a wide spectrum of brands/makes of the phones and sensors. As a result, these phones have different detection sensitivities due to the quality of the sensors, and even two different phones/sensors at the same location may or may not trigger on the same motion. A one-size-fits-all solution would not work well, and a comprehensive understanding of device diversity and sensitivity for earthquake detection is needed for the design of adaptive system strategies and parameters. The real-world data collected by MyShake include phone/sensor information as well as recorded waveforms from users' phones. An initial analysis using 276,140 MyShake users' data reveals a wide variety of phone brands and sensor types. The top 10 phone brands and their proportions are shown in Table 1. The top 5 accelerometer types account for about 40% of all the phones, as shown in Figure 3, and there are in total 367 different types of sensors in MyShake users' phones.

Inconsistent timing among commodity phones is particularly challenging for smartphone-based EEW. Seismic waves travel at about 3–6 km/s, and our clustering detection on the cloud server looks for coherent triggers from multiple phones. If there is a 5-sec offset on the phones with respect to the true time, seismic waves could have traveled for 30 km, which significantly impacts the effectiveness of earthquake detection and early warning. In the current MyShake system, each phone synchronizes via NTP (Network Time Protocol) every hour. Figure 4 shows the distribution of time offset between the phone clock and the true time at the time of NTP synchronization for 1 million randomly sampled records from our database. We can see that using hourly synchronization, most of the phones would have an offset time within 2.5 seconds.

3.2 Dynamics of Users and System

In the MyShake smartphone-based seismic network, the phones move with their users. As such, the seismic network changes constantly both in space and time, and the detection capability of the network varies by region and over time. For example, it is observed that more phones move to office (home) during the day (night), and during the night, more phones are stationary for longer periods of time. For example, Figure 5 shows the spatial distribution of MyShake users in the San Francisco Bay Area during day and night. We can see clear network distinctions between the two time periods, where the network is much denser and more spread out during the day vs. during the night. Figure 6 shows the percentage of phones which were steady for more than 30 minutes in the same area for two consecutive days. Again, we see a widefluctuation of the percentage over time. When phones are steady, they are in the best positions to detect earthquakes, while phones on the move cannot detect earthquakes reliably. Therefore, the percentage of steady phones in an area at any given time is actually a good indicator of the network's detection capability. Depending on the specific time and region when an earthquake occurs, the system may have different numbers of phones available at different locations, and different earthquake detection strategies and parameters may be needed for the system to detect the specific earthquake.

3.3 Other Challenges

Besides the two challenges mentioned above, there exist other challenges that are related to supporting EEW in the MyShake system. For instance, when an earthquake strikes, near real-time communication is crucial in terms of receiving trigger messages from individual phones and sending EEW messages to millions of users in one region (e.g., around 7 million people in the San Francisco Bay Area). Understanding the scalability and limitations of the current system and developing innovative techniques to reduce the notification latency could have a significant impact on saving lives and critical infrastructures. In addition, tradeoffs between the confidence and latency of earthquake detection should be carefully

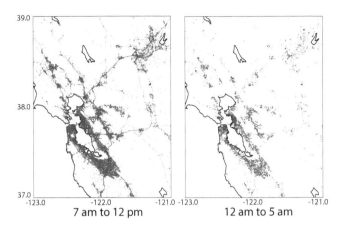

Figure 5: MyShake user distribution (sampled every 2 hours) in the San Francisco Bay Area. (Left) During the day from 7am to 12pm; (Right) During the night from 12am to 5am. Data used here are from 2017-07-01 to 2018-07-01.

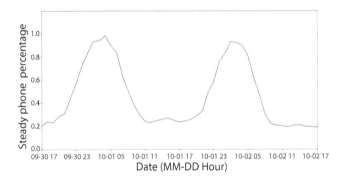

Figure 6: Percentage of steady MyShake phones (steady for more than 30 minutes) in the San Francisco Bay Area. Data plotted here are from 2017-09-30 5pm to 2017-10-02 5pm.

examined, and some multi-tiered EEW system design may be necessary. Furthermore, given the disruptive nature of EEW, system security is paramount to avoid incidental or targeted attacks. One particular aspect of system security is related to spoofed earthquake triggers, such as how easy it is to spoof earthquake triggers, and how robust the system is against spoofed earthquake triggers from individual phones, ad-hoc or coordinated groups of phones in a specific region and time period.

4 TACKLING THE EEW CHALLENGES

We have conducted some preliminary research in order to tackle the challenges of diverse sensing hardware and user/system dynamics. Specifically, we analyze the large-scale real-world data collected via MyShake, and have designed and developed a simulation platform to model different phone/user/system properties and evaluate their impact on the performance of EEW.

4.1 Tackling Diversity of Sensing Hardware

Given the heterogeneity of the sensing hardware in the MyShake network, it is important to link sensor/phone types to the quality

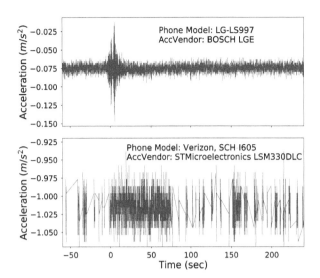

Figure 7: Waveform examples from 2 different users. The top waveform has good quality and records an earthquake, while the bottom waveform has lots of missing data.

of motion waveforms. As mentioned earlier, the brand/model of the phones and accelerometers are collected by the MyShake app. Meanwhile, time series of the acceleration recorded by these phones are also collected. Data quality information can be extracted from the collected waveforms. For example, using the 1-minute waveform before each earthquake trigger (background noise), the noise level of the phone can be estimated by calculating the standard deviation of the noise. The waveforms also contain data gaps which usually appear for some users, and the relative occurrence of these glitches could be monitored and used as an indicator of the sensor quality for different users. Besides, the sampling interval distribution can also tell us the recording stability of the sensor. Currently, we collect the 25th, 50th, 75th percentiles of the sampling intervals. Figure 7 shows two example waveforms from two different users. We can see that the first waveform has good quality and adequately captures a real-world earthquake event, while the second waveform has lots of missing data. For the first waveform, the standard deviation of the noise level is around 0.005 m/s^2, with no data gaps that are larger than 1s, and the 25th, 50th, 75th percentiles of the sampling interval are 39, 40, 41 msec. In contrast, the bottom waveform has a standard deviation of 0.03 m/s^2, 35 instances of data gaps that are larger than 1s (32 of them are larger than 2s), and 1, 59, 60 for the 25th, 50th, 75th percentiles. Based on these extracted metrics from the waveforms, we can model the sensing quality for different phones/sensors/users. The sensing quality can then be used as a weighting function of sensor importance/confidence in the detection algorithm to downgrade sensors with poor quality. Since the detection algorithm is based on collective intelligence of many smartphones, this quality measure can help make the algorithm more adaptive. For instance, in a given region, if only low-quality sensors are triggered, more triggered phones may be needed to declare an earthquake so as to decrease the chance of issuing a false warning, and vice versa.

With the current implementation of NTP synchronization every hour, most of the MyShake phones have a time accuracy within 2 seconds. We are investigating ways to further improve this accuracy. One approach is to increase the frequency of NTP synchronization, and the question is how smaller time intervals would improve time accuracy at the cost of increased overhead. Another approach is to utilize the time of arrival when the server receives heartbeats and triggers from individual phones, and the question is how location and neighboring phones may help augment existing time synchronization/calibration strategies.

4.2 Tackling Dynamics of Users and Systems

To tackle the challenge of user and system dynamics, we have developed a simulation platform to generate triggers caused by earthquakes in order to mimic actions in the MyShake seismic network and evaluate the performance of different design strategies. Our simulation platform works as follows. Given the information of a specific earthquake, we first use global population density within $1\ km^2$ to sample MyShake users in the region. Depending on the time of occurrence of the earthquake, different number of steady phones will be simulated. This sampling is based on the statistical relationship extracted from MyShake observations, which is shown in Figure 7b of [18]. Then, using both physical modeling (the spread of the P and S waves is based on a homogeneous medium, the Peak Ground Acceleration is based on an attenuation model developed by [4]) and statistical modeling (learned from MyShake observations, the distribution of the time errors on the phones are shown in Figure 4), we can determine each phone's triggering probability when different seismic waves pass by and the time of trigger for the specific earthquake with corresponding uncertainties. In addition, based on false positive triggers observed overtime (see Figure 2 in [18]), randomized false positive triggers and uncertainties in trigger time are added to the simulation. Finally, the triggers generated by the simulation platform can be evaluated by spatial-temporal clustering to confirm the earthquake and estimate its corresponding parameters. The current algorithm under testing is DBSCAN (Density-Based Spatial Clustering of Applications with Noise) [5], which is modified to accommodate the temporal information.

Using this simulation platform, we can easily generate multiple simulations for different network configurations to reflect spatial and temporal changes of MyShake users according to the occurrence time of the earthquake, and evaluate the effectiveness of different strategies and parameters for adaptive earthquake detection and early warning. Figure 8 shows the result of one example simulation. We can see the propagation of the seismic waves and the corresponding phones that are triggered in the network. The triggers outside the green seismic wave circle are random false positive triggers. In this simulation, our system is able to detect the earthquake within 5.2 seconds after the initial onset of the earthquake, and the green star in the figure shows the estimated location.

5 RELATED WORK

Besides MyShake, there are multiple efforts to develop EEW systems using smartphone sensors in the seismology community. [7]

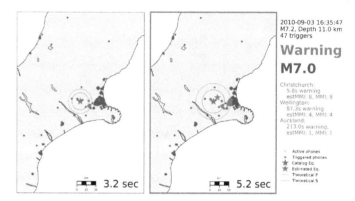

Figure 8: Simulation snapshots for the 2010 New Zealand M7.2 Darfield earthquake, obtained at 3.2 seconds (left) and 5.2 seconds after the earthquake, respectively. The origin of the earthquake is indicated by the purple star. The legend on the right shows the time when the MyShake system detected the event, and estimated the magnitude as M7.0 (blue fonts) at the location indicated by the green star. The blue dots are steady phones running MyShake at the moment of the earthquake, and the red dots are phones triggered by the earthquake. The green and red circles show the two types of seismic waves – P and S waves. The estimated intensity MMI (Modified Mercalli Intensity) and the warning time for 3 nearby cities are shown by the red text.

talked about a smartphone EEW system, but there was no public deployment. [8] also aims to build a global smartphone early warning system, but it lacks the capability of MyShake to separate earthquake signals from other human activities. There is also an app that detects earthquakes by monitoring when users launch the app and collecting users' reports [3], but it is much slower in terms of detection due to the added human reaction time. Our own prior MyShake publications were in the seismology domain and focused mostly on the functionalities and applications in geophysics. Specifically, [17, 19] described the initial development of the system and the design of the core ANN algorithm. [16] and [15] reported some seismological observations and the potential use of MyShake to monitor the health of buildings. [18] described the machine learning algorithms used in the MyShake system. In contrast, this paper focuses on new systems challenges related to issuing real-world EEW and aims to seek expert feedback from the mobile computing community.

Beyond the geophysics community, many efforts related to understanding sensing hardware heterogeneity including mobile devices and other low-cost sensors can provide insights to the MyShake project. [6] investigated performance of several low-cost accelerometers in terms of recording motions in the laboratory environment. [21] evaluated sensor biases, sampling rate heterogeneity and instability using 36 different devices, as well as their impact on the performance of human activity recognition. These studies used only a few models in controlled environments, and there was no corresponding evaluation in large-scale real-world applications. Researchers have also investigated sensor calibration in mobile devices, such as a time-varying Kalman filtering calibration technique to reduce sensor biases [2] and a machine learning based multi-position calibration scheme to address hardware heterogeneity in mobile devices [10]. In our work, using the large-scale real-world data collected via MyShake, we will evaluate sensing quality in terms of measuring ground motion, and further leverage/develop sensor calibration techniques to improve sensing quality and earthquake detection accuracy.

Characterizing human mobility dynamics using various datasets has received considerable attention. [14] extracted a human mobility model using 13-month wireless network traces collected from WiFi APs at Dartmouth College. [11] used WLAN traces to create a time-variant community mobility model. [9] derived a universal model to explain how individuals move using cellular network data in a European country. [12] proposed an approach to model how large populations move within different metropolitan areas using Call Detail Records. All these works aim to model human movement as a spatial-temporal relationship. Our work builds upon human mobility analysis, but further considers spatial-temporal availability and dynamics of steady phones for effective and efficient earthquake detection at both the individual phone level and overall seismic network level.

6 CONCLUSIONS AND FUTURE DIRECTIONS

Earthquakes are serious hazards globally, and MyShake has demonstrated the feasibility of building a smartphone-based seismic network for earthquake detection and early warning at the global scale. The initial deployment of MyShake has been successful, generating valuable data and new insights. In this paper, we have highlighted two key challenges for real-world EEW, namely, sensing heterogeneity and user/system dynamics, and potential solutions that we are exploring in terms of sensing quality measure and a simulation platform to model phone/user/system and adapt to different earthquake scenarios. Further improvements of our work include adaptive algorithms that take into account sensing quality and user/system dynamics, as well as simulations and real-world evaluations of those algorithms.

This paper is our first step towards connecting with the mobile computing community. Several EEW challenges remain for real-world deployment, such as EEW system scalability, latency and security, which can really benefit from the expertise of the mobile computing community. Furthermore, while our current focus is issuing earthquake early warning to the public, we envision much broader use of MyShake and smartphone-based seismic network from the hazard preparation and response aspects in smart cities. Specifically, a system like MyShake could be used before, during and after earthquake events, such as proactive structural surveillance, risk assessment, and context-aware earthquake education before earthquakes occur, EEW during an earthquake, as well as emergency response, rapid hazard information distribution, and long-term learning after an earthquake.

ACKNOWLEDGMENTS

We would like to thank the shepherd Xia Zhou and reviewers of our paper for their insightful and constructive feedback. MyShake is a joint collaboration between the Berkeley Seismology Laboratory and Deutsche Telecom Silicone Valley Innovation Center. The Gordon and Betty Moore Foundation funded this project through grant GBMF5230. This work was also supported in part by the National Science Foundation under grant number 1442971. Finally, we thank the MyShake team members and all the MyShake users!

REFERENCES

[1] R. M. Allen, P. Gasparini, O. Kamigaichi, and M. Böse. 2009. The Status of Earthquake Early Warning around the World: An Introductory Overview. *Seismological Research Letters* 80, 5 (2009), 682.

[2] P Batista, C Silvestre, P Oliveira, and B Cardeira. 2011. Accelerometer Calibration and Dynamic Bias and Gravity Estimation: Analysis, Design, and Experimental Evaluation. *IEEE Trans. Control Syst. Technol.* 19, 5 (Sept. 2011), 1128–1137.

[3] R. Bossu, F. Roussel, L. Fallou, M. Landès, R. Steed, G. Mazet-Roux, A. Dupont, L. Frobert, and L. Petersen. 2018. LastQuake: From Rapid Information to Global Seismic Risk Reduction. *International Journal of Disaster Risk Reduction* 28, November 2017 (2018), 32–42. https://doi.org/10.1016/j.ijdrr.2018.02.024

[4] G.B. Cua. 2005. *Creating the Virtual Seismologist: developments in ground motion characterization and seismic early warning.* Ph.D. Dissertation. California Institute of Technology.

[5] M. Ester, H.P. Kriegel, Jörg Sander, and X. Xu. 1996. Density-based spatial clustering of applications with noise. In *Int. Conf. Knowledge Discovery and Data Mining,* Vol. 240.

[6] J. R. Evans, R. M. Allen, A. I. Chung, E. S. Cochran, R. Guy, M. Hellweg, and J. F. Lawrence. 2014. Performance of Several Low-Cost Accelerometers. *Seismological Research Letters* 85, 1 (Jan. 2014), 147–158.

[7] M. Faulkner, M. Olson, R. Chandy, J. Krause, K. Mani Chandy, and A. Krause. 2011. The next big one: Detecting earthquakes and other rare events from community-based sensors. *IPSN '11* (2011), 13–24.

[8] F. Finazzi. 2016. The Earthquake Network Project: Toward a Crowdsourced Smartphone-Based Earthquake Early Warning System. *Bulletin of the Seismological Society of America* 106, 3 (may 2016).

[9] M. C González, C. A Hidalgo, and A.L. Barabási. 2008. Understanding individual human mobility patterns. *Nature* 453, 7196 (June 2008), 779–782.

[10] A. Grammenos, C. Mascolo, and J. Crowcroft. 2018. You Are Sensing, but Are You Biased?: A User Unaided Sensor Calibration Approach for Mobile Sensing. *Proc. ACM Interact. Mob. Wearable Ubiquitous Technol.* 2, 1 (March 2018), 11:1–11:26.

[11] W. Hsu, T. Spyropoulos, K. Psounis, and A. Helmy. 2007. Modeling Time-Variant User Mobility in Wireless Mobile Networks. In *IEEE INFOCOM 2007 - 26th IEEE International Conference on Computer Communications.* 758–766.

[12] S. Isaacman, R. Becker, R. Cáceres, M. Martonosi, J. Rowland, A. Varshavsky, and W. Willinger. 2012. Human Mobility Modeling at Metropolitan Scales. In *Proceedings of the 10th International Conference on Mobile Systems, Applications, and Services (MobiSys '12).* ACM, New York, NY, USA, 239–252.

[13] H. Kanamori. 2005. Real-Time Seismology and Earthquake Damage Mitigation. *Annu. Rev. of Earth & Planetary Sci.* 33, 1 (2005), 195–214.

[14] M. Kim, D. Kotz, and S. Kim. 2006. Extracting a Mobility Model from Real User Traces. In *Proceedings IEEE INFOCOM 2006. 25TH IEEE International Conference on Computer Communications.* 1–13.

[15] Q., Kong, R. M. Allen, M. D. Kohler, T. H. Heaton, and J. Bunn. 2018. Structural health monitoring of buildings using smartphone sensors. *Seismological Research Letters* 89, 2A (2018).

[16] Q. Kong, R. M. Allen, and L. Schreier. 2016. MyShake: Initial observations from a global smartphone seismic network. *Geophysical Research Letters* 43, 18 (sep 2016), 9588–9594.

[17] Q. Kong, R M Allen, L. Schreier, and Y.-W. Kwon. 2016. MyShake: A smartphone seismic network for earthquake early warning and beyond. *Science Advances* 2, 2 (feb 2016).

[18] Q. Kong, A. Inbal, R. M. Allen, Q. Lv., and A. Puder. 2019. Machine Learning Aspects of the MyShake Global Smartphone Seismic Network. *Seismological Research Letters* (2019). https://doi.org/10.1785/0220180309

[19] Q. Kong and M. Zhao. 2012. Evaluation of earthquake signal characteristics for early warning. *Earthquake Engineering and Engineering Vibration* 11, 3 (sep 2012), 435–443.

[20] K. Rochford, J. A. Strauss, Q. Kong, and R. M. Allen. 2018. MyShake: Using Human-Centered Design Methods to Promote Engagement in a Smartphone-Based Global Seismic Network. *Frontiers in Earth Science* 6 (2018), 237. https://doi.org/10.3389/feart.2018.00237

[21] A. Stisen, H. Blunck, S. Bhattacharya, T. S. Prentow, M. B. Kjærgaard, A. Dey, T. Sonne, and M. Jensen. 2015. Smart Devices Are Different: Assessing and Mitigating Mobile Sensing Heterogeneities for Activity Recognition. In *Proc. of the 13th ACM Conf. on Embedded Networked Sensor Systems (SenSys '15).* ACM, New York, NY, USA, 127–140.

[22] J. A. Strauss and R. M. Allen. 2016. Benefits and Costs of Earthquake Early Warning. *Seismological Research Letters* (2016). https://doi.org/10.1785/0220150149

Dejavu: Enhancing Videoconferencing with Prior Knowledge

Pan Hu
Stanford University
panhu@stanford.edu

Rakesh Misra
Uhana Inc.
rakesh@uhana.io

Sachin Katti
Stanford University
skatti@cs.stanford.edu

ABSTRACT

Videoconferencing over the Internet routinely suffers from poor quality as videoconferencing systems, in order to guarantee interactive delays which is critical to user experience, are commonly designed to stream at conservative qualities in the face of variable bandwidths. In this paper, we present Dejavu, a system that enables existing videoconferencing systems to alleviate this problem. The key insight that powers Dejavu is that recurring videoconferencing sessions, e.g., in the same conference room or by the same person, have a lot of visual similarities that can be encoded based on the sender's historical videoconferencing sessions, and shared with the receiver in advance. Accordingly, Dejavu first learns an offline mapping between low-quality and high-quality versions of frames in the sender's past videoconferencing sessions, and then applies this mapping in real time at the receiver to convert the low-quality frames into high-quality frames. As a result, a videoconferencing system equipped with Dejavu can continue to stream at conservative qualities to guarantee interactive delays like today, but can now additionally *enhance* the video quality at the receiver. Our evaluation shows that Dejavu can provide a 1.3 dB increase in PSNR for the same bandwidth consumption, or equivalently save up to 30% in bandwidth to deliver the same PSNR.

CCS CONCEPTS

• **Networks** → **Mobile networks**; • **Information systems** → *Multimedia streaming*.

KEYWORDS

Videoconferencing; Mobile networks; Deep neural networks

ACM Reference Format:
Pan Hu, Rakesh Misra, and Sachin Katti. 2019. Dejavu: Enhancing Videoconferencing with Prior Knowledge. In *The 20th International Workshop on Mobile Computing Systems and Applications (HotMobile '19), February 27–28, 2019, Santa Cruz, CA, USA.* ACM, New York, NY, USA, 6 pages. https://doi.org/10.1145/3301293.3302373

1 INTRODUCTION

Videoconferencing over the Internet routinely suffers from poor quality [16]. The reason is that videoconferencing systems need to deliver interactive end-to-end delays for the best user experience, so when network bandwidths are variable, in order to still

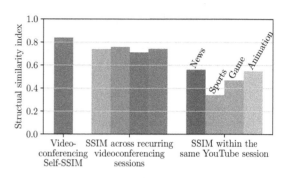

(a) Structural similarity (SSIM) index between different videos

(b) Sample frames from **different** videoconferencing sessions

(c) Sample frames from the **same** Youtube video stream

Figure 1: The key insight that powers Dejavu is that recurring videoconferencing sessions, e.g., in the same meeting room, are visually very similar. As (a) shows, the SSIM of frames *across* recurring videoconferencing sessions (0.70-0.75) is higher than the SSIM of even frames within the *same* video session involving news (0.56), sports (0.34), gaming (0.47) or animation (0.55). The sample frames in (b) and (c) illustrate this insight visually.

guarantee interactive delays, the common approach is to stream at very conservative qualities. As a result, in networks where user bandwidths are dynamic, e.g., in mobile networks, the video quality suffers. Most of the work in addressing this problem has focused on designing more-efficient video encoders [6, 7] and better real-time transport algorithms [4, 16] for videoconferencing.

In this paper, we adopt a different approach. Our guiding insight is that recurring videoconferencing sessions, i.e., sessions that happen in the same meeting room and/or involve the same person, have a lot of similarities in visual content *across* sessions. For example, many meeting rooms use a fixed camera, so the objects in the field of view like conference table, whiteboard etc. are largely the same in all sessions using that camera. Similarly, personal videoconferencing using a mobile or web camera always has the face and features of the same person. Note that this property of videoconferencing streams does not hold in general for any live or on-demand video stream. For example, as we show in Figure 1, frames *across* multiple videoconferencing sessions in a meeting room using a fixed camera had a significantly higher structural similarity index (0.70-0.75) than even frames *within* the same live/on-demand video streaming session involving news (0.56), sports (0.34), gaming (0.47) or animation (0.55).

The above insight led us to the following question: if there is so much similarity in the visual content *across* sessions involving the same sender, could we learn a mapping between the low-quality and the high-quality versions for a sender based on her past sessions, and share it with the receiver *before* a live session starts? If we could, then we could use this mapping at the receiver *during* a live session to up-convert the video quality in real time. As a result, existing videoconferencing systems could deliver the best of both worlds: they could continue to deliver interactive delays since the streaming over the network will continue to happen at the same qualities as today[1], but now they could also deliver better qualities as the receiver will *enhance* the video quality in real time. In effect, the spare computing power at the receivers could be employed to compensate for the conservative quality choices at the sender[2].

In order to realize the above vision, we present Dejavu, a system that can augment existing videoconferencing systems and enable them to deliver better video qualities while continuing to deliver the interactive delays that they do today. Dejavu shows that it is possible to learn a quality-enhancing *model* or mapping based on a sender's historical sessions that performs well in enhancing the video quality of future unseen sessions. Our initial evaluation shows that Dejavu can help videoconferencing systems improve their end-to-end PSNR by more than 1.3 dB while consuming the same bandwidth as today, or alternatively enable them to reduce their bandwidth consumption by 30% (thereby potentially leading to lower delays) while delivering the same PSNR as today.

2 DESIGN

In this section, we describe how Dejavu has been designed to realize the above vision. Dejavu operates in two stages, as shown in Figure 2.

In the offline stage, Dejavu uses videos from a sender's past videoconferencing sessions to: (i) generate training data by re-encoding the higher-quality frames at each resolution, e.g., 800 kbps at 540p, to lower qualities at the same resolution, e.g., 500 kbps at 540p, using the same encoding pipeline as the videoconferencing system, and (ii) train a deep neural network model using Dejavu's learning engine that learns the mapping between the lower-quality frames of a given resolution and their corresponding higher-quality frames, e.g., model to convert frames at 500 kbps at 540p to frames at 800 kbps at 540p. These models are shared with the Dejavu module at the receiver before the start of the next videoconferencing session.

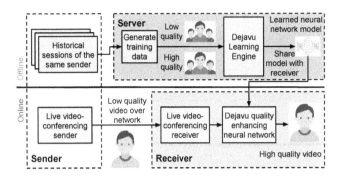

Figure 2: The Dejavu system consists of two components: an offline component that learns a quality-enhancing deep neural network, and an online component that enhances the quality of live videoconferencing at the receiver in real time.

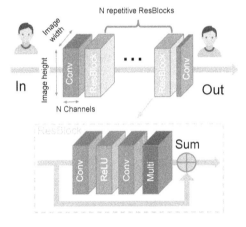

Figure 3: Dejavu's quality-enhancing neural network consists of convolutional layers and residual blocks [11]. It converts a low-quality image into a high-quality image at the same resolution.

In the online stage, the Dejavu module at the receiver applies the pre-trained neural network models on the conventional videoconferencing receiver output to up-convert the quality, e.g., from 500 kbps at 540p to 800 kbps at 540p, in real time.

2.1 Architecture of the quality-enhancing neural network

At the heart of Dejavu is the quality-enhancing neural network whose goal is to learn a mapping between the low-quality input frames and the corresponding high-quality output frames. We revised the neural network architecture proposed by EDSR [14] by removing bi-cubic upsampling layers so the output has the same dimension as input, which is also shown in Figure 3.

Dejavu's deep neural network consists of several repetitive ResNet [11] blocks sandwiched between two convolutional layers. Each ResBlock consists of a convolutional layer, a rectified linear unit (ReLU) layer, another convolutional layer and a multiply layer. There is a

---

[1] In reality, the additional processing at the receiver will add some delay, so for this to work, a requirement is that the additional delay has to be very minimal.

[2] This idea of using spare receiver compute resources to offset the loss in sending quality due to limited network bandwidths has been explored in a recent paper [18] but in the context of *on-demand* video streaming; as we describe in Section 6, learning an offline mapping for *on-demand* videos where the entire video content is known in advance is very different than that for *live* videos where the video content whose quality has to be enhanced is unseen and therefore not known in advance.

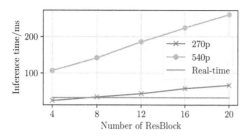

Figure 4: Comparison of the inference speeds of the quality-enhancing neural networks with different number of Res-Blocks for different input resolutions.

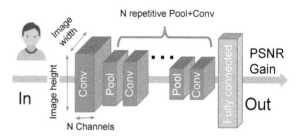

Figure 5: Patch-scoring neural network consists of shallow layers of max-pooling and convolutional blocks. It outputs a single floating number representing the PSNR gain if the quality-enhancing network were to be applied on the input patch.

Figure 6: Samples images from the training dataset for Dejavu: five colleagues participating in mock interviews in the same conference room.

skip connection from input to output of the ResBlock that helps in avoiding the vanishing gradient problem [11].

Instead of designing a neural network that works on the entire input image, we instead design it to work on smaller patches of the image. For example, instead of a neural network that works on a single 960×540 RGB image which would require 1.56M parameters, we instead design a neural network that can work on 144 80×45 patches; each neural network then has only 10.8k parameters. The reduced input size allows us to use deeper neural networks as well as more mini-batches for stable training.

2.2 Inference speed

A key challenge that Dejavu has to solve is in speeding up the inference of the deep neural network so it can be scored in real time, even with less powerful GPUs.

Figure 4 shows a comparison of inference speeds as a function of the number of ResBlocks at different input resolutions, using a high-end, NVIDIA Tesla P100 from Google Cloud. Assuming the video frame rate is 30 fps, we find that only very shallow networks can meet the real-time deadline of 33 ms, shown in red in the figure.

Dejavu applies two techniques to speed up inference:

Train/infer on Y (luminance) channel only: It is well known that human eyes are most sensitive to the luminance component of an image, and less sensitive to its colors. Therefore, we convert an RGB image into its equivalent YCbCr representation, where Y is the luminance component, and Cb and Cr are the two chrominance components. We found that by training/inferring a neural network on only the Y channel, while keeping Cb and Cr channels the same, we can still achieve significant gains in visual quality while taking only one third of the time for inference (the cost of converting RGB into YCbCr is minimal).

Patch scoring network: Dejavu's quality-enhancing neural network does not achieve the same improvement in visual quality on all patches. It is possible to improve the quality more on patches with a lot of edges or complex details, rather than patches with, for example, a white wall. So instead of scoring the quality-enhancing neural network on all patches, Dejavu has a patch-scoring network that predicts possible gains in quality, measured in peak SNR, as shown in Figure 5. During the inference process, the patch-scoring network ranks the patches according to their predicted gains in

quality. Dejavu selects the top k patches according to the available compute resources so as to meet the real-time requirement.

3 IMPLEMENTATION

We implement the neural network with TensorFlow [1] and Python 3. All the training and inference are done in Google Cloud for now. The trained neural network model is typically less than 870kB given 32 residual blocks and 32 features per each block, which can be sent to the receiver easily.

Video dataset. Since there is no widely-acknowledged dataset for videoconferencing, we created our own videoconferencing dataset by requesting five people to do mock interviews with us in our meeting room on the same day. Figure 6 shows some sample images from this data set. The camera was pointed towards a fixed direction to simulate conference room settings. We used a smartphone with mini-tripod to capture 1080p@60fps video.

Training dataset: Each video is about three minutes in length. All the videos were converted into VP9 format [1]. In videoconferencing, the video stream can be encoded at any bitrate ranging from between tens of kbps to several Mbps. We chose 7 representative bitrates in our experiment, including: 100, 200, 300, 500, 800, 1000, 2000 kbps. We compressed each video into different bitrate levels using FFmpeg, and used OpenCV [2] to extract compressed frames for training. To reduce the size of dataset, we reduced the frame rate from 60 fps to 2 fps. So the total number of frames is about 5 videos * 180 seconds * 2 fps * 8 levels = 12600. We then converted each frame into lossless png format to facilitate data loading.

The videos used to calculated similarity were downloaded from YouTube, including a CNN clip (news), a 2018 FIFA clip (sports), a

---

[1]We chose VP9 over H265 as VP9 is free and benchmarks show that VP9 has similar performance [9].

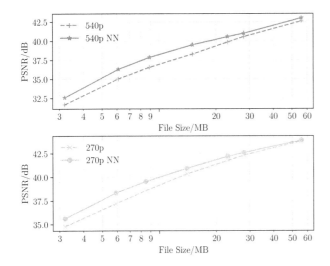

Figure 7: PSNR gain of Dejavu for inputs at two resolutions: 540p (blue) and 270p (orange). Each marker represents an encoding bitrate ranging from 100 kbps to 2000 kbps.

Dota v2 clip (gaming) and a Family Guys clip (animation), all of which are top-ranking 1080p HD videos.

4   EVALUATION

In this section we present some preliminary evaluation results for Dejavu. We aim to answer the following questions:

- What performance gains can Dejavu provide and how do we interpret the results?
- How does video similarity affect the performance of the quality-enhancing neural network?

We use PSNR [1] as the quality metric to quantify the performance gain of the quality-enhancing network. We train on four out of the five videos in the dataset and test on the fifth one. The results for 270p and 540p videoconferencing streams are shown in Figure 7, where x axis is the logarithm of the file size in MB and y axis is the PSNR in dB. Each marker indicates an encoding bitrate level in [100, 200, 300, 500, 800, 1000, 2000] kbps.

The file sizes grow monotonically as the encoding bitrates increase. As the figure shows, the quality-enhancing neural network is able to improve the PSNR by up to 1.3 dB for 540p and up to 1.1 dB for 270p videoconferencing streams at low to medium encoding bitrates. This gain is substantial as it is comparable to developing a new generation of video codec [8] which requires years of work. The gains diminish as the file sizes / encoding bitrates increase, as the room for improvement decreases.

Figure 8 shows sample pictures of the input/output of the neural network, and the corresponding ground truth. The PSNR and SSIM gains aside, we can see that the details are clearly refined in the output of the neural network with much less compression artifacts. The drawing on the white board is also much more readable. In Figure 9, we plot a differential error map that shows the boost in

---

[1] $PSNR = 48.13 - 10 \times \log_{10}(MSE)$ dB for 8 bits per sample image where MSE is mean squared error between the input and output image.

image quality due to Dejavu in different parts of the image [2]. The interesting observation is that most of the gain (shown in purple) occurs around edges.

We provide an alternative way to understand the performance gain by translating the result from Figure 7 into potential bandwidth savings, as shown in Figure 10. The figure shows that we can save more than 30% of the bandwidth to deliver video at the same quality as the original 540p@500kbps stream, while we can also achieve more than 25% bandwidth saving at 270p.

Another question we want to answer is: what is the performance gain if we train on a general video dataset and use the model to enhance videoconferencing sessions? The result is shown in Figure 11: the quality-enhancing neural network trained on a general video data set cannot bring significant PSNR gain (<0.1dB), and is significantly worse than the neural network trained on the videoconferencing dataset. The result is also in accordance with the similarity result shown in Figure 1 at the beginning of the paper, indicating that it is hard to improve the video quality if there is less similarity between the train and the test datasets.

5   FUTURE WORK

While the above results prove the potential of Dejavu in improving the visual quality of videoconferencing streams, a number of open items still need to be completed in order to make Dejavu ready for deploying in practical videoconferencing systems.

1. Evaluating the performance of Dejavu in the wild: The evaluation in this paper was performed for a simple, same-room different-person scenario. There is need for a larger-scale evaluation that collects data from more videoconferencing scenarios, including multiple persons in the same meeting room, same person but at different locations on different days, as well as scenarios that use front-facing camera on the go. Such data is necessary to better evaluate the real-world performance of Dejavu.

2. Integrating Dejavu into a videoconferencing application and measuring user experience: Our initial evaluation focused only on improving the video quality without taking into account the additional processing delay incurred at the receiver. However, optimizing delay and jitter are crucial for a good user experience with videoconferencing. Therefore, there might be a need to optimize the algorithm that selects video sending rates in videoconferencing frameworks like WebRTC in order to compensate for the additional processing at the receiver.

3. Supporting mobile / embedded devices with resource constraints: We used powerful GPUs in our current evaluation. However, not every videoconferencing device, especially mobile phones and embedded devices, can afford such a computational cost. Although sometimes it is possible to perform the computations in the cloud using a relay server if the receiver has a good downlink, relaying incurs additional delay as well as additional costs for the service provider. Therefore, there is a need to optimize Dejavu for devices with compute constraints. *Model compression* [10] and *knowledge distillation* [12] are two popular methods for reducing computation overhead: model compression compresses neural networks via pruning less important connections as well as quantizes

---

[2] We clip the data range from [-79, 61] to [-20, 20] for better color contrast.

(a) Top: input to Dejavu (**36.17** dB PSNR, 0.9445 SSIM);
middle: output of Dejavu (**37.53** dB PSNR, 0.9617 SSIM);
bottom: reference (ground-truth) frame.

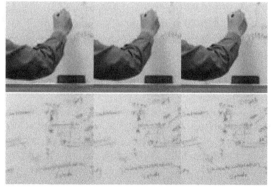

(b) Zoomed in versions of the blue and the purple boxes in (a).
Left to right: input, output, reference (ground truth).

Figure 8: Illustration of Dejavu's quality enhancement

weights so we can use less bits per weight; knowledge distillation involves training a smaller "student" model that mimics the behavior of the larger "teacher" model.

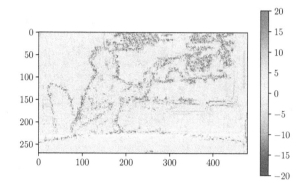

Figure 9: Error map showing how Dejavu improves quality over different areas of a frame, computed as a pixel-wise subtraction ($|I_{out} - I_{ref}| - |I_{in} - I_{ref}|$). Purple pixels indicate that Dejavu reduces the error at that pixel by 20 while red indicates Dejavu increases error by 20 (closer to purple means better performance). Notice that most of the improvement occurs around edges but red pixels could be very close to purple pixels.

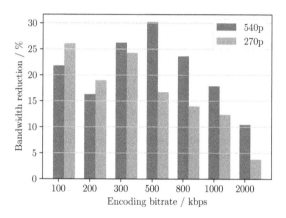

Figure 10: Equivalent bandwidth savings according to the PSNR gains of Dejavu for different encoding bitrates and input resolutions.

4. Exploiting inter-frame similarity: Dejavu currently processes every frame at the receiver using the same neural network; however there is an opportunity to design separate neural networks for key frames and predicted frames. Predicted frames are more common but carry less information, therefore it might be possible to enhance their quality using a smaller (shallower and less wide) neural network, whereas the current full-scale neural network could enhance only the key frames. As a result, the average run time of Dejavu at the receiver could be significantly reduced.

6 RELATED WORK

Dejavu's quality-enhancing neural network is built upon prior works in video super resolution [3, 15] and image super resolution [5, 13, 14]. Dejavu's novel contribution is to adapt these prior

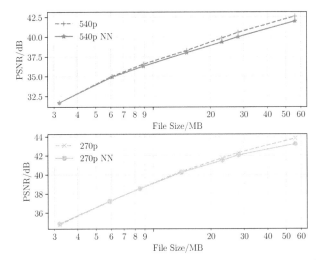

Figure 11: Comparison of PSNR gain when the quality-enhancing model is trained on general Youtube videos. The gains in PSNR are negligible (< 0.1 dB in most cases).

neural networks to exploit the unique properties of videoconferencing, and build a system that shows how such neural networks can be used in an end-to-end application like videoconferencing.

Dejavu shares similarities with NAS [17, 18] that explored a similar quality-enhancing problem but in the context of *on-demand video streaming*. Dejavu and NAS are similar in the sense that both aim to learn a mapping between the low-quality and the high-quality versions of video streams, and both aim to use the spare compute resources at the receiver to enhance the video quality at run time. However, Dejavu differs in two significant respects:

(i) While NAS needs to learn a *model that overfits* to this mapping for a *given and known* video stream, Dejavu needs to learn a *model that predicts* this mapping for *future unseen* video streams. This is because in on-demand video streaming, the video stream whose quality has to be enhanced is entirely known in advance, whereas in live videoconferencing, the quality enhancement has to be performed on video streams that are unseen until run time. Dejavu is therefore uniquely designed to solve a learning problem that is significantly different than the one solved by NAS.

(ii) While NAS aims to *increase the resolution* of a video stream, Dejavu aims to *increase the effective encoding rate while retaining the same resolution*. This is based on the insight that given a bandwidth target, in videoconferencing, it is usually better to send at a higher resolution using lesser bits per pixel than at a lower resolution using more bits per pixel. Therefore, in the context of videoconferencing, it is almost always more useful to be able to increase the effective bits per pixel, unlike in traditional live or on-demand video streaming where the choice largely depends on the nature of content in the video stream.

There have been works on jointly controlling video codec and transport protocols [6] that aim to improve the quality of real-time streaming. While Dejavu addresses the same problem, it adopts a different approach based on taking advantage of the similarities across recurring videoconferencing sessions.

7 CONCLUSION

In this paper, we discussed the design and evaluation of Dejavu, a system that enhances videoconferencing quality by extracting prior knowledge from historical sessions. We believe that Dejavu has great potential to improve existing videoconferencing systems as initial evaluation shows up to 1.3dB PSNR gain, or equivalently 30% savings in bandwidth. Our ongoing work is focused on addressing the open items in Section 5 to make Dejavu ready for deployment in practical large-scale videoconferencing systems.

Acknowledgements: We would like to thank our reviewers and our shepherd Eric Rozner for their valuable reviews. We would also like to thank Tianshu Chu, Keith Winstein and Samuel Joseph for their feedback on early drafts of this paper, and Stanford Platform Lab for supporting us.

REFERENCES

[1] Martín Abadi, Paul Barham, Jianmin Chen, Zhifeng Chen, Andy Davis, Jeffrey Dean, Matthieu Devin, Sanjay Ghemawat, Geoffrey Irving, Michael Isard, et al. 2016. Tensorflow: a system for large-scale machine learning.. In *OSDI*, Vol. 16. 265–283.
[2] Gary Bradski and Adrian Kaehler. 2000. OpenCV. *Dr. Dobbs journal of software tools* 3 (2000).
[3] Jose Caballero, Christian Ledig, Andrew P Aitken, Alejandro Acosta, Johannes Totz, Zehan Wang, and Wenzhe Shi. 2017. Real-Time Video Super-Resolution with Spatio-Temporal Networks and Motion Compensation.. In *CVPR*, Vol. 1. 7.
[4] Gaetano Carlucci, Luca De Cicco, Stefan Holmer, and Saverio Mascolo. 2016. Analysis and design of the google congestion control for web real-time communication (WebRTC). In *Proceedings of the 7th International Conference on Multimedia Systems*. ACM, 13.
[5] Chao Dong, Chen Change Loy, Kaiming He, and Xiaoou Tang. 2016. Image super-resolution using deep convolutional networks. *IEEE transactions on pattern analysis and machine intelligence* 38, 2 (2016), 295–307.
[6] Sadjad Fouladi, John Emmons, Emre Orbay, Catherine Wu, Riad S Wahby, and Keith Winstein. 2018. Salsify: Low-Latency Network Video through Tighter Integration between a Video Codec and a Transport Protocol. In *15th USENIX Symposium on Networked Systems Design and Implementation (NSDI 18)*. USENIX.
[7] A Grange and H Alvestrand. 2013. A VP9 Bitstream Overview, draft-grange-vp9-bitstream-00. (2013).
[8] Dan Grois, Detlev Marpe, Amit Mulayoff, Benaya Itzhaky, and Ofer Hadar. 2013. Performance comparison of h. 265/mpeg-hevc, vp9, and h. 264/mpeg-avc encoders. In *Picture Coding Symposium (PCS), 2013*. IEEE, 394–397.
[9] Dan Grois, Detlev Marpe, Tung Nguyen, and Ofer Hadar. 2014. Comparative assessment of H. 265/MPEG-HEVC, VP9, and H. 264/MPEG-AVC encoders for low-delay video applications. In *Applications of Digital Image Processing XXXVII*, Vol. 9217. International Society for Optics and Photonics, 92170Q.
[10] Song Han, Huizi Mao, and William J Dally. 2015. Deep compression: Compressing deep neural networks with pruning, trained quantization and huffman coding. *arXiv preprint arXiv:1510.00149* (2015).
[11] Kaiming He, Xiangyu Zhang, Shaoqing Ren, and Jian Sun. 2016. Deep residual learning for image recognition. In *Proceedings of the IEEE conference on computer vision and pattern recognition*. 770–778.
[12] Geoffrey Hinton, Oriol Vinyals, and Jeff Dean. 2015. Distilling the knowledge in a neural network. *arXiv preprint arXiv:1503.02531* (2015).
[13] Jiwon Kim, Jung Kwon Lee, and Kyoung Mu Lee. 2016. Accurate image super-resolution using very deep convolutional networks. In *Proceedings of the IEEE conference on computer vision and pattern recognition*. 1646–1654.
[14] Bee Lim, Sanghyun Son, Heewon Kim, Seungjun Nah, and Kyoung Mu Lee. 2017. Enhanced deep residual networks for single image super-resolution. In *The IEEE conference on computer vision and pattern recognition (CVPR) workshops*, Vol. 1. 4.
[15] Mehdi SM Sajjadi, Raviteja Vemulapalli, and Matthew Brown. 2018. Frame-Recurrent Video Super-Resolution. In *Proceedings of the IEEE Conference on Computer Vision and Pattern Recognition*. 6626–6634.
[16] Keith Winstein, Anirudh Sivaraman, Hari Balakrishnan, et al. 2013. Stochastic Forecasts Achieve High Throughput and Low Delay over Cellular Networks.. In *NSDI*, Vol. 1. 2–3.
[17] Hyunho Yeo, Sunghyun Do, and Dongsu Han. 2017. How will Deep Learning Change Internet Video Delivery?. In *Proceedings of the 16th ACM Workshop on Hot Topics in Networks*. ACM, 57–64.
[18] Hyunho Yeo, Youngmok Jung, Jaehong Kim, Jinwoo Shin, and Dongsu Han. 2018. Neural Adaptive Content-aware Internet Video Delivery. In *OSDI*. 645–661.

Towards Self-Driving Radios:
Physical-Layer Control using Deep Reinforcement Learning

Samuel Joseph[*]
Stanford University
josamuel@stanford.edu

Rakesh Misra[*]
Stanford University
rakeshmisra@alumni.stanford.edu

Sachin Katti
Stanford University
skatti@cs.stanford.edu

ABSTRACT

Modern radios, such as 5G New Radio, feature a large set of physical-layer control knobs in order to support an increasing number of communication scenarios spanning multiple use cases, device categories and wireless environments. The challenge however is that each scenario requires a different control algorithm to optimally determine how these knobs are adapted to the varying operating conditions. The traditional approach of manually designing different algorithms for different scenarios is increasingly becoming not just difficult to repeat but also suboptimal for new scenarios that previous-generation radios were not designed for.

In this paper, we ask: can we make a radio automatically learn the optimal physical-layer control algorithm for any scenario given only high-level design specifications for the scenario, i.e., can we design a *self-driving radio*? We describe how recent advances in deep reinforcement learning can be applied to train a self-driving radio for several illustrative scenarios, and show that such a learning-based approach not only is easily repeatable but also performs closer to optimal than the current state of the art.

CCS CONCEPTS

• **Networks** → **Wireless access points, base stations and infrastructure**; *Mobile networks*; • **Theory of computation** → **Reinforcement learning**.

KEYWORDS

Radios; Physical layer; Cellular networks; Reinforcement learning; Deep learning; LTE; 5G

ACM Reference Format:
Samuel Joseph, Rakesh Misra, and Sachin Katti. 2019. Towards Self-Driving Radios: Physical-Layer Control using Deep Reinforcement Learning. In *The 20th International Workshop on Mobile Computing Systems and Applications (HotMobile '19), February 27–28, 2019, Santa Cruz, CA, USA.* ACM, New York, NY, USA, 6 pages. https://doi.org/10.1145/3301293.3302374

[*]equal contribution.

1 INTRODUCTION

Modern radios[1], such as 5G New Radio (NR) [1], are expected to accommodate a wide variety of communication scenarios [6]. They are at once expected to be able to support high-bandwidth fixed wireless access, e.g., to provide fiber-like broadband connectivity to the home, very high-speed mobilities, e.g., trains moving at 300 km/h, and very low-power connectivity for IoT devices, among many others. No single physical-layer design can work well under all scenarios, hence the natural response of the standards bodies has been to specify designs with a large number of control knobs so that a radio can be tuned to the specific deployment scenario in the field. These control knobs range from modulation order and coding rate, to OFDM subcarrier spacing and cyclic prefix length, to reference signal (pilot) density, to transmit power scaling and so on. Each of these knobs has numerous settings leading to a combinatorially large number of choices, and radio designers need to design a control algorithm that chooses the right one dynamically at run time depending on the scenario and the varying operating conditions.

The current approach is to preprogram empirical control rules with configurable thresholds that can be adjusted by domain experts in an iterative trial-and-error manner on the field for each scenario. This approach has worked reasonably well for LTE but is under strain for 5G because of the much larger *number* and *complexity* of scenarios it is expected to support, e.g., LTE was not originally designed to support fixed wireless access or low-power IoT connectivity. Furthermore, 5G is expected to evolve to support network slicing where the wireless stack is adapted to future applications, e.g., peer-to-peer connectivity for autonomous vehicles, that are not fully defined yet, so an approach based on heuristic rules and thresholds is intrinsically limited in *how quickly* and *how optimally* it can be repeated to support new requirements.

In this paper, we argue for a learning-based approach to designing control algorithms for radios. Our vision is that radio designers should be able to provide only high-level specifications for a scenario, including the communication objective, the control knobs and measurements available, and a model for the wireless environment in that scenario, and the radio should be able to learn on its own an algorithm to adapt the control knobs in real time[2]; see Figure 1. In essence, the goal is to *learn*, rather than design, a near-optimal control algorithm that can be deployed on the field. We refer to such radios as *self-driving radios* (SDR). In doing so, we hope to repurpose the SDR acronym, originally used for a software-defined radio, to refer to a radio that has not only the flexibility to be configured in software (software-defined) but also the capability to build the right software to use in any given scenario (self-driving).

---

[1]In this paper, by *radio*, we refer to the radio baseband, not the front end.
[2]Note: this algorithm does not require access to user data, e.g., I/Q samples.

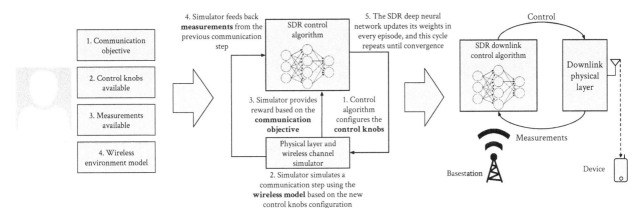

[Offline] A radio designer provides design specifications for a given communication scenario. The SDR learning engine converts the specifications into a physical-layer control algorithm encoded as a deep neural network (DNN) using reinforcement learning.

[Run time] A base station uses SDR DNN-based control algorithms to adapt the physical-layer control knobs in real time for both downlink (shown above) and uplink (not shown).

Figure 1: The self-driving approach to radio design. Unlike the traditional approach where radio designers manually design the physical-layer control algorithms, in this approach, they just manually specify the communication scenario and the radio learns a near-optimal control algorithm on its own using deep reinforcement learning.

We describe the SDR approach in more detail in Section 2, and contrast it with related work in Section 3. We illustrate the SDR approach in Section 4 by showing how to design control algorithms to jointly control the *modulation order* and *transmit power scaling* in several scenarios where a radio has to meet a throughput target while minimizing its average transmit power. We show in Section 5 that control algorithms using the SDR approach are able to meet their throughput targets 10-45% more often than the control algorithms in LTE, which is the industry state of the art, and only 7-26% less often than the offline-optimal control algorithms, while using similar transmit powers as LTE and 2-3 dB higher than optimal.

2 MOTIVATION FOR THE SDR APPROACH

In this section, we describe the two broad challenges in designing physical-layer control algorithms for modern radios using traditional approaches, and explain why a self-driving approach has the potential to overcome both challenges.

Challenge: should be quickly repeatable for new scenarios The physical-layer control algorithms for modern radios such as NR need to be easy to adapt to new, potentially unseen, scenarios in the future. These scenarios can be very diverse, and may span multiple use cases, device categories and wireless environments. Different use-case requirements, e.g., high throughput, low latency, high reliability etc., present different optimization objectives. Different device categories, e.g., low-power IoT, high-mobility IoT, fixed wireless etc., mean that the optimization must be performed under different device constraints. Different wireless environments, e.g., indoor vs outdoor, short range vs long range, stationary vs mobile etc., present different dynamics, which require different optimization strategies over time. As a result, every new combination of use case, device category and wireless environment requires a very different control algorithm. The traditional approach, which involves manually designing a control algorithm for every scenario using

empirical rules and thresholds, is tedious and inherently limited in how quickly it can be repeated for new scenarios.

SDR approach: learn rather than design The SDR approach aims to use machine learning to *learn* the optimal control algorithm. A learning-based approach is quickly repeatable for new scenarios because designing a new control algorithm just requires manually *specifying* the new scenario, see Figure 1, as opposed to manually *designing* a new algorithm, e.g., by fine tuning rules and thresholds.

Challenge: should sequentially optimize for a communication objective while controlling inter-dependent knobs In order to meet the needs of a wide variety of stressful scenarios, modern radios need to optimize for an explicit objective, e.g., an IoT radio may want to reliably upload a fixed-size packet under a total energy constraint, while controlling several control knobs that we had listed earlier. The challenge is two-fold. *First*, this optimization problem is sequential, i.e., a control decision in one time step affects the optimal decision in a subsequent step, e.g., the above IoT radio may choose to transmit at a higher power in the beginning to increase the reliability of the upload but will be left to work with a lesser energy budget subsequently. In traditional approaches, the decisions in one time step do not explicitly account for the consequences on future steps. *Second*, the set of control knobs is not just large but also inter-dependent, e.g., a drop in link quality can be handled by either reducing the modulation order or increasing the transmit power, among several other ways. The traditional approach uses separate algorithms to control these inter-dependent knobs, e.g., modulation and coding rate is chosen by a separate algorithm than the transmit power. As a result, as the scenarios become more complex, e.g., the wireless environment becomes more dynamic or the set of inter-dependent knobs becomes larger, the traditional approach becomes increasingly suboptimal.

SDR approach: learn by reinforcement using deep neural networks The SDR approach aims to learn the *joint* optimal control algorithm using *deep reinforcement learning* (RL). RL is a natural fit for sequential optimization and has been successfully applied in a number of problems [7, 9, 10] where a controller has to learn how to plan its actions with future consequences in mind. Deep neural networks (DNNs), owing to their large expressive power, are capable of encoding the complex strategies required for adapting the large inter-dependent set of control knobs. Therefore, a control algorithm expressed using a DNN and trained using RL has the potential to be near optimal, even in the most complex of scenarios.

3 RELATED WORK

Deep learning has been applied extensively in recent times to solve problems arising in mobile and wireless networking; see [15] for an excellent survey. Most of these works however relate to either (i) mobile data analysis, which involves using deep learning to solve *prediction* or *clustering* problems e.g., network prediction [11], traffic classification [12] etc., in contrast to SDR which uses deep learning for a *control* problem, or (ii) mobile network or link control, which involves using deep learning for mobile *network-layer* or *link-layer* control algorithms e.g., traffic scheduling [3], resource allocation [14], interference alignment [5] etc., in contrast to SDR which uses deep learning for *physical-layer* control.

Deep learning for wireless physical-layer control has been relatively much less explored. The closest we are aware of are works that used deep learning for building control algorithms for specific physical-layer knobs, e.g., closed-loop power control for VoLTE downlink [8], adaptive modulation and coding [4] etc. SDR is different from these works in two significant respects. First, SDR learns the *joint* optimal control algorithm, i.e., an algorithm to control all physical-layer knobs jointly for optimal performance, unlike these works that focus on individual control knobs independently. Second, SDR optimizes *explicitly* for the communication objective, unlike these works which focus on optimizing lower-level metrics like SINR which may not lead to the optimal communication performance, e.g., an energy-constrained IoT radio that wants to conserve battery does not care about maximizing SINR.

4 DESIGNING A SELF-DRIVING RADIO

Figure 1 illustrates the key steps in the design and deployment of a self-driving radio. We describe these key steps below.

A radio designer provides design specifications. First, a radio designer provides high-level design specifications for the physical-layer control algorithm, specifically: (i) the objective function that it must optimize, (ii) the control knobs that it must adapt, and their possible settings, (iii) the measurements that it can use to adapt the control knobs, and (iv) a channel model, or a set of channel traces, representing the characteristics of the wireless environment that it must optimize its strategy for.

A learning engine generates a physical-layer control algorithm. Next, a learning engine converts the above specifications into a physical-layer control algorithm, encoded typically as a DNN. This learning engine forms the core of the SDR capability. We will describe it in more detail in the rest of this section.

A radio uses the learned control algorithm at run time. Finally, DNNs that are learned using the above learning engine are used at run time to adapt the physical-layer control knobs for both downlink and uplink. In practice, we envision that any base station,

depending on its purpose and deployment, would typically need to support anywhere between 1-3 use cases, 2-4 device categories and 1-5 operating environments, so it might need to maintain on the order of a few such DNNs to tens of such DNNs[3]. At run time, before every transmission, a base station will first select the most relevant DNN for each of uplink and downlink, and then execute them to adapt the control knobs. The decisions of the DNNs will be enforced at the base stations for the downlink, and signaled via the control channel to the devices to enforce for the uplink.

In the rest of this section, we focus on the design of the SDR learning engine. To illustrate its working, we use the following scenarios as reference, in each of which a radio needs to meet an average throughput target in every 10-ms window while optimizing its average transmit power based on its energy sensitivity, and describe how to learn control algorithms for these scenarios.

Scenario 1: A radio on a phone needs to achieve 3-Mbps physical-layer throughput on the uplink in every 10-ms time window, to support, for example, HD (720p) real-time video conferencing.

Scenario 2: A radio on a connected autonomous vehicle (AV) has the same requirement as above; however, AVs are less battery constrained so they can afford to spend more energy per bit.

Scenario 3: A radio on an AV needs to achieve 5 Mbps instead of 3 Mbps on the uplink in every 10-ms time window, to support, for example, Full HD (1080p) real-time video conferencing.

4.1 SDR as a reinforcement learning problem

The SDR learning engine uses RL to learn a control algorithm. We start by describing how the design specifications for the above scenarios may look like, and how they map to the RL framework.

Reward function Radio designers need to specify the communication objective, based on the use case and the device category. In the RL framework, this defines the *reward function*. For example, in the above scenarios, a radio designer might want the control algorithm to optimize the following objective in every 10-ms window,

$$(NBS - NBS_{target}) - \epsilon \times EnergySpent$$

where NBS and $EnergySpent$ are the number of bits sent successfully and the corresponding energy spent, NBS_{target} is 30000 or 50000 bits corresponding to 10 ms times 3 or 5 Mbps respectively, and ϵ is a measure of the energy sensitivity of the device. As an illustration, ϵ may be 10 times lesser for AVs than for phones, e.g., 22.5 and 2.25 bits per energy unit for phones and AVs respectively[4]. The first component rewards the control algorithm for how much it exceeds the throughput target while the second component penalizes it for the energy spent, and ϵ controls the relative tradeoff between these two conflicting components.

Action space Radio designers need to specify the control knobs available, and their possible settings. In the RL framework, this defines the *action space*. For example, in the above scenarios, a radio designer might want the control algorithm to adapt two knobs every 1 ms - the *modulation order* and the *transmit power* (via baseband scaling) - while all other knobs are held fixed at their default settings. The modulation order controls the sending rate and therefore influences the throughput. The transmit power controls the

---

[3]Each DNN that we train in Section 4 is on the order of 10 kB, so we expect the combined memory footprint to be 1 MB or less.

[4]penalty for spending 1 energy unit = reward for exceeding target by 22.5 or 2.25 bits

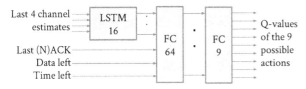

Figure 2: Architecture of the SDR Deep Q Network that we trained for each of the three reference scenarios in Section 4

energy spent, and also influences the reliability of the transmission, i.e., whether or not a transmission at a certain modulation order in a time step will experience a block error given the channel condition in that step. As an illustration, the possible settings may be 2 (QPSK), 4 (16-QAM) or 6 (64-QAM) for the modulation order[5], and 10, 15 or 20 dBm for the transmit power. The control algorithm's dilemma is that for a given transmit power, a higher modulation order in a time step can lead to a higher throughput *if* the transmission is successful, but also has a higher risk of a block error which would result in zero throughput in that step. On the other hand, for a given modulation order, a higher transmit power lowers the risk of a block error but also consumes more energy.

State space Radio designers need to specify the measurements available based on which the control knobs can be adapted. In the RL framework, this defines the *state space*. For example, the control algorithm could use the following measurements commonly available at a radio to adapt the modulation order and the transmit power: (i) *last* 4 *channel estimates*[6], (ii) *data left* to meet the throughput target in the 10-ms window, (iii) *time left* in the 10-ms window, and (iv) *ACK/NACK* of the transmission in the previous time step. While (i) and (iv) provide visibility into the link conditions, (ii) and (iii) help track the optimization state.

Learning environment Radio designers need to specify the wireless environment for which the control algorithm must be optimized. In the RL framework, this feeds into the *learning environment*. For example, a radio designer might choose the reference model in [13], and might want to optimize the control algorithm for mobility environments where speeds and path losses vary uniformly between 0-100 km/h and 70-90 dB respectively. Note that using such reference models is standard practice in the industry for designing and evaluating any new technology for mobile networks as it offers an easy, faithful and repeatable way for testing the technology in a wide variety of realistic and challenging deployment scenarios.

4.2 The SDR learning engine

In this section, we describe the working of the SDR learning engine, and explain how we converted the above specifications into a DNN-based physical-layer control algorithm for each scenario; see Figure 1 (central subfigure) for an illustration.

Physical-layer simulator We implemented a MATLAB simulator consisting of a physical layer that simulates an LTE- and NR-like OFDM-based transmitter and receiver, and a wireless layer that simulates the impact of wireless channels in baseband. In the wireless layer, we used 17600 of 22000 channel traces generated using the specified model above, each lasting 10 ms, for training the SDR control algorithm for each scenario; the rest were reserved for evaluation. In every step during training, the SDR control algorithm configured the modulation order and the transmit power of the physical layer, and the simulator fed back the updated state variables and the new reward.

RL method and DNN architecture We used deep Q-learning[7] to train the SDR control algorithm for each scenario. In this RL method, the control algorithm is represented using a Deep Q Network (DQN) [9] and it learns to estimate the *quality* of choosing each possible combination of actions from a given state. Figure 2 shows the architecture of the SDR DQN that we trained for each scenario. The last 4 channel estimates were fed into a Long Short-Term Memory (LSTM) layer, which is known to be good at time-series predictions, with 16 hidden units. The output of the LSTM layer was concatenated with the remaining inputs and fed through two fully-connected layers with 64 and 9 units each. The 9 outputs of the neural network correspond to the Q-values of the 3×3 possible combinations of actions.

Training We trained three SDR DNNs, one for each of the three reference scenarios. To make the training faster and more robust, we pre-cached the rewards and states from the simulator for all possible actions and time steps in the 17600 channel traces, and during training we only looked up a table for computing rewards and states. Exploration-exploitation tradeoff was annealed from 1 to 0.02 over 2 million time steps linearly, and learning rate was 0.01. Each DNN converged in around 20 million time steps, roughly corresponding to 2 million episodes, lasting about 32 hours[8] with a single Intel Xeon E5-2699 v3 CPU running at 2.30 GHz.

5 EVALUATION

In this section, we evaluate the SDR DNN-based physical-layer control algorithms that we trained in Section 4 for the three reference scenarios, in order to answer the following questions:

How does the SDR control algorithm perform compared to (i) LTE's uplink closed-loop power control and adaptive modulation algorithms, which represent the industry state of the art, and (ii) the offline-optimal control algorithm, which achieves the best possible performance in theory? (see Section 5.2)

What have the SDR DNNs actually learnt in terms of adapting to different scenarios and operating conditions? (see Section 5.3)

5.1 Evaluation method

Performance metrics The two metrics of interest to our reference problem are:

(i) the *target met (%)* which is the percentage of time windows in which the throughput target was met (higher is better), and

(ii) the *average transmit power* in a window (lower is better). Note that if the throughput target in a window is met in less than

---

[5]In the physical-layer setting that we use for our evaluation in Section 5, this translates to a sending rate of 2.1, 4.2 or 6.3 Mbps respectively.

[6]We arrived at the choice of 4 using trial and error, as adding more history did not provide any significant gain but made the training slower.

[7]There is scope to use more advanced learning algorithms, however as we show in Section 5, this learning algorithm already shows promising results.

[8]There is scope to make the training faster, however this is already a reasonable training cost given these models would be trained offline and would not usually need retraining for weeks or months.

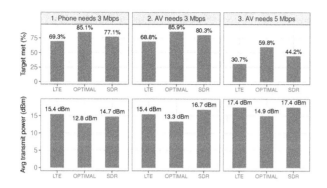

Figure 3: Benchmarking SDR's performance. In these scenarios, SDR meets its throughput targets 10-45% more often than LTE and 74-93% as often as the offline optimal solution, while using similar average transmit powers as LTE and 2-3 dB higher than offline optimal.

10 ms, the transmit power for the remaining time steps is assumed to be 0 while computing the average transmit power.

Benchmarks We evaluated three classes of control algorithms:

(1) *LTE*, specifically the adaptive modulation and power control algorithms defined in [2],

(2) *offline optimal*, obtained using dynamic programming assuming perfect knowledge of the future, and

(3) *SDR*, trained as described in Section 4.

Evaluation We evaluated the performance of the above control algorithms on 4400 traces, each lasting 10 ms, which were previously held back, and hence unseen, during the training of the SDR DNNs. Figure 3 summarizes the results.

5.2 Benchmarking SDR's performance

Note that the SDR approach is easily repeatable, as designing a control algorithm for a new scenario just requires us to provide the corresponding new specifications. In this section, we show that this repeatable approach is indeed able to adapt to new scenarios, and its performance is closer to optimal than traditional approaches.

SDR is able to adapt to different scenarios As one illustration, if we compare scenarios 1 and 2, we observe that SDR has been able to adapt to the lower energy sensitivity of AVs, as it uses a higher average transmit power for AVs (16.7 dBm) compared to phones (14.7 dBm) for the same throughput target (3 Mbps), to meet the target more often for AVs (80.3%) than for phones (77.1%). In contrast, since LTE does not adapt to the energy sensitivities of devices by design, its performance is similar (~69% target met using 15.4 dBm on average), and inferior to SDR[9], in both scenarios.

SDR's performance is closer to optimal than LTE In the three scenarios, SDR meets the throughput target 90.6%, 93.5% and 73.9% as often as the offline-optimal solution while using 1.9 dB, 3.4 dB and 2.5 dB higher transmit power respectively. In contrast, LTE meets the throughput target only 81.4%, 80.1% and 51.3% as often as offline optimal while using 2.6 dB, 2.1 dB and 2.5 dB higher transmit power respectively in the three scenarios.

5.3 Interpreting the behavior of SDR DNNs

In order to gain insights into what the SDR DNNs have actually learnt, we perform a *sensitivity analysis*. By this, we mean that we vary one input variable while holding the others fixed at different levels, and observe how each DNN changes its decisions in response. This allows us to both sanity check as well as interpret the behavior of the blackbox SDR DNN models.

In this section, due to lack of space, we restrict our attention to studying the sensitivity to the *last (most-recent) channel estimate* alone, which is the most important input for any adaptive modulation and transmit power selection algorithm. Figure 4 visualizes the results of this analysis in 6 different contexts. In each of the 6 subfigures, we sweep the most-recent channel estimate along the x-axis, from −95 dB to −70 dB, while the communication scenario and other input variables, indicated in the title and the subtitle respectively of each subfigure, are held fixed at different values.

Sanity check Qualitatively, we expect that as the link becomes stronger, the optimal behavior would be to transmit at higher modulation orders using lesser transmit powers. In each of the 6 subfigures, we observe that the SDR DNNs have been able to learn the expected qualitative behavior, i.e., as the most-recent channel estimate increases, the modulation order increases (monotonically) and the transmit power reduces (albeit non monotonically[10]).

Insights So what did the DNNs additionally learn that enabled them to outperform LTE? We observe that they have learnt to adapt the answers to three broad questions based on the context.

(1) What are the channel estimate thresholds for switching up the modulation order from 2 to 4, and from 4 to 6?

(2) Should the transmit power also be switched up when the modulation order switches up, and by how much?

(3) What are the channel estimate thresholds for switching down the transmit power?

We encourage the readers to study the subfigures in Figure 4 and observe how the answers to the above questions change depending on the context, specifically how they are different for different (i) devices (compare subfigures 1 and 2), (ii) throughput targets (compare 2 and 3), (iii) data left (compare 1 and 4), (iv) time left (compare 3 and 6), and (v) channel gradients (compare 2 and 5). These differences reveal why it is extremely hard for an algorithm based on manually-specified rules and thresholds, like the control algorithms used in LTE today, to capture the optimal solution, and why it is instead better to use a deep learning-based approach to design control algorithms for next-generation radios.

6 TAKING SDR TO PRACTICE

Where will the SDR learning engine operate in practice? We expect that the SDR learning engine will operate as a service, either locally at each base station or in the cloud, the latter being easier to scale and manage. Whenever a new scenario needs to be supported, a radio designer would submit the new design specifications to this service, which in turn will train an appropriate DNN and push it to the relevant base stations. Whenever the specifications change

---

[9]In scenario 2, even though SDR uses a slightly higher transmit power than LTE, it also meets the target more often; its overall reward is still higher.

[10]Whenever SDR increased the transmit power even as the link became stronger, it was always to support a corresponding increase in the modulation order so as to ensure the transmission is still reliable, which is a sensible behavior in hindsight.

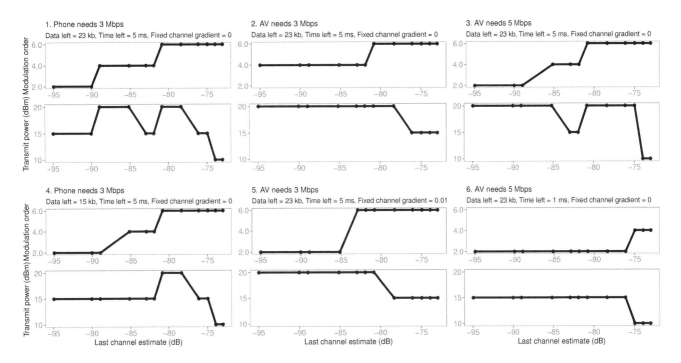

Figure 4: Sensitivity of the SDR deep neural networks to the most-recent channel estimate in different contexts. In all subfigures, the most-recent channel estimate is swept along the x-axis from −95 dB to −70 dB while the communication scenario and other input variables (indicated in the title and the subtitle of each subfigure respectively) are held fixed at different values.

or a base station detects a drift in the wireless environment, this service will be requested to retrain the affected DNNs.

What support is needed from the base stations? In order to use the SDR approach, base stations need to have (i) the flexibility to download and use new or upgraded control algorithms for different scenarios, and (ii) the ability to run the SDR DNNs in real time. The DNNs may need to run as often as every 1 ms in LTE, and possibly more often in NR; the DNNs that we trained in Section 4 took 0.8 ms on average to execute on a standard MacBook Pro with 2.9 GHz Intel Core i5. We envision that the base stations will use hardware accelerators to run these DNNs, which can reduce this by an order of magnitude and comfortably meet the real-time requirement.

How does the SDR approach work when a base station has to serve multiple devices simultaneously? This is a challenging open question and requires the SDR approach to be extended to the link layer, i.e., resource scheduler. This requires expanding both the state space (to handle states of a variable number of devices) and the action space (to also select resource schedule in addition to the physical-layer control knobs), incorporating fairness criteria in the objective function, and training the SDR DNNs using a simulator that also simulates the link-layer dynamics.

Acknowledgment We would like to thank our reviewers and our shepherd for their valuable reviews and feedback that helped bring this draft to its current state. We would also like to thank Manikanta Kotaru, Aaron Schulman and Kanthi Nagaraj for reviewing the draft, and Stanford Platform Lab for supporting this project.

REFERENCES

[1] 3GPP. NR: Physical channels and modulation. TS 38.211, Mar. 2018.

[2] 3GPP. NR: Physical layer procedures for control (Release 15). TS 38.213, Mar. 2018.

[3] S. Chinchali, P. Hu, T. Chu, M. Sharma, M. Bansal, R. Misra, M. Pavone, and S. Katti. Cellular network traffic scheduling with deep reinforcement learning. In *AAAI Conference on Artificial Intelligence*, 2018.

[4] R. Daniels and R. Heath. Online adaptive modulation and coding with support vector machines. In *IEEE European Wireless Conference 2010*, pages 718–724.

[5] Y. He, C. Liang, F. R. Yu, N. Zhao, and H. Yin. Optimization of cache-enabled opportunistic interference alignment wireless networks: A big data deep reinforcement learning approach. In *IEEE International Conference on Communications (ICC) 2017*, pages 1–6.

[6] ITU. IMT Vision: Framework and overall objectives of future development of IMT for 2020 and beyond. Technical report, Sept. 2015.

[7] H. Mao, R. Netravali, and M. Alizadeh. Neural adaptive video streaming with Pensieve. In *Proceedings of SIGCOMM '17*, pages 197–210, New York, NY, USA.

[8] F. Mismar and B. Evans. Q-Learning Algorithm for VoLTE Closed-Loop Power Control in Indoor Small Cells. *arXiv*, July 2017.

[9] V. Mnih, K. Kavukcuoglu, D. Silver, A. A. Rusu, J. Veness, M. G. Bellemare, A. Graves, M. Riedmiller, A. K. Fidjeland, G. Ostrovski, et al. Human-level control through deep reinforcement learning. *Nature*, 518(7540):529–533, Feb. 2015.

[10] D. Silver, A. Huang, C. J. Maddison, A. Guez, L. Sifre, G. Van Den Driessche, J. Schrittwieser, I. Antonoglou, V. Panneershelvam, M. Lanctot, et al. Mastering the game of go with deep neural networks and tree search. *Nature*, 529(7587):484, 2016.

[11] J. Wang, J. Tang, Z. Xu, Y. Wang, G. Xue, X. Zhang, and D. Yang. Spatiotemporal modeling and prediction in cellular networks: A big data enabled deep learning approach. In *IEEE Conference on Computer Communications, INFOCOM 2017*.

[12] Z. Wang. The applications of deep learning on traffic identification. *BlackHat USA*, 2015.

[13] C. Xiao, Y. Zheng, and N. Beaulieu. Novel sum-of-sinusoids simulation models for Rayleigh and Rician fading channels. *IEEE Transactions on Wireless Communications*, 5(12):3667–3679, December 2006.

[14] Z. Xu, Y. Wang, J. Tang, J. Wang, and M. C. Gursoy. A deep reinforcement learning based framework for power-efficient resource allocation in cloud RANs. In *IEEE International Conference on Communications (ICC) 2017*.

[15] C. Zhang, P. Patras, and H. Haddadi. Deep learning in mobile and wireless networking: A survey. *arXiv preprint arXiv:1803.04311*, 2018.

Hidden Figures: Comparative Latency Analysis of Cellular Networks with Fine-grained State Machine Models

Sangwook Bae*
KAIST
sangwook.bae@kaist.ac.kr

Mincheol Son*
KAIST
mcson@kaist.ac.kr

Sooel Son
KAIST
sl.son@kaist.ac.kr

Yongdae Kim
KAIST
yongdaek@kaist.ac.kr

ABSTRACT

Comparative latency analysis of cellular network control planes is an intuitive and effective method used to determine the superiority/inferiority of one cellular network over others. However, operational policies and network configurations vary across different networks, making it difficult to conduct fine-grained latency comparisons. We present a novel diagnostic method for the comparison of the latencies in processing control plane messages among cellular networks. For each cellular network, we automatically build a fine-grained state machine based on control plane signaling messages collected from user smartphones. From the state machines of multiple network operators, we identify common state transitions consisting of signaling messages. We then compare the latencies in the message intervals for each identified common transition. We discovered 38 bottleneck intervals from three representative control plane procedures by analyzing the state machines of five major operators. Our promising preliminary analysis deserves further research.

CCS CONCEPTS

• **Networks** → **Network performance analysis**; **Mobile networks**; • **Computing methodologies** → *Model development and analysis*.

KEYWORDS

Cellular network, State machine modeling, Comparative study, LTE Control plane

ACM Reference Format:
Sangwook Bae, Mincheol Son, Sooel Son, and Yongdae Kim. 2019. Hidden Figures: Comparative Latency Analysis of Cellular Networks with Fine-grained State Machine Models. In *The 20th International Workshop on Mobile Computing Systems and Applications (HotMobile '19), February 27–28, 2019, Santa Cruz, CA, USA*. ACM, New York, NY, USA, 6 pages. https://doi.org/10.1145/3301293.3302352

*Both authors contributed equally to the paper

1 INTRODUCTION

Cellular network operators strive to optimize their core network operations for the provision of high-quality services. A dominant factor in the performance of a cellular network is the control plane [11]. For instance, when a user's smartphone returns to its cellular network from the airplane mode, the control plane latency in an ATTACH procedure prolongs the waiting time. The latency in a ServiceRequest procedure also undermines the promptness of wireless Internet over LTE. Therefore, carriers focus on analyzing the latencies of the control plane of a target network as well as diagnosing the root causes of any possible bottlenecks.

A typical performance diagnosis involves measuring the latency of each control plane procedure with a local view and vetting whether the measurements satisfy an internal policy. This approach often fails to detect latency problems, thus disregarding the opportunity for performance improvements. Cellular network architectures, optimization logic, and configurations vary with different operators. Therefore, a bottleneck may exist only in one network operator. Taking local measurements without comparing the latency with other operators leads to failure in detecting such problems.

SCAT [6] showed promising results in a comparative study, which discovered six major problems of the control plane by using 17,710 circuit-switched fallback calls. It detected abnormal operations by comparison and then diagnosed the problem by manual inspection of signaling messages and standards. However, this study had two limitations: 1) the conducted analysis was coarse-grained, and 2) a significant portion of the analysis was manual. The first limitation is problematic because the study investigates abnormal control plane operations at the high level. For example, we observed that various operational scenarios performing the ATTACH procedure showed different latencies. Because SCAT ignored these individual operation scenarios, the root cause analysis had to be completely manual and speculative, inevitably causing the second limitation.

In this work, we present a novel approach for automatically constructing a fine-grained state machine and utilizing it for the comparative latency analysis of the cellular control plane. We start with automatically building a state machine from the control plane signaling messages from smartphones. We collect uplink/downlink messages as well as non-access stratum (NAS) state information from smartphone chipsets. For each network operator, we model the state machine so that a state becomes an observed NAS state, and a transition between two states becomes a sequence of the signaling messages that cause the change in state. We then compare the latencies between messages on common transition paths across

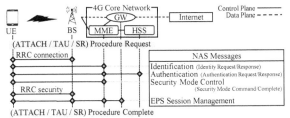

Figure 1: Control Plane Architecture

different state machines from multiple operators.

Our method is distinguished from SCAT by two design choices: **the automatic trace-driven modeling** and **the fine-grained comparative analysis considering various operation scenarios**. Building a full state machine according to multiple 3GPP specifications is a daunting task requiring enormous engineering effort. The proposed trace-driven modeling requires no effort in understanding the 3GPP specifications. By design, our state machine mirrors the operational model of each network operator that is already in service based on the signaling messages from smartphones. For the comparative analysis, we identify the same transition paths across different state machines and compare the latencies on the message intervals on them. That is, each transition path represents a common operation scenario between operators, which provides the ground for fair comparison.

Our state machine representation facilitates various comparative studies, from latency diagnosis to operating logic analysis. In this paper, we focus on a comparative study on the latency of three representative procedures: ATTACH, TrackingAreaUpdate, and ServiceRequest. We compare the shared transition path from the initial state to the normal state of each procedure at the message level. Our system then identifies problematic cases where the latency between two messages is higher than that in the shared transition path of the others' state machines. To demonstrate the effectiveness of our approach, we generate state machines using 390K signaling messages collected from five major carriers in two countries. Through this comparative study, we identified a total of 38 problematic cases. Each case is presented with a specific operation scenario constituted by actual signaling messages, which help us identify causes for latency. Our in-depth analysis discovered entities causing long latency, unnecessary encryption, and the absence of the authentication procedure, each of which is due to different operator-specific operation policies and configurations.

Pinpointing the bottlenecks is essential, but a difficult task without domain- and operator-specific knowledge. This paper highlights the promising results of a comparative analysis using fine-grained state machine representation of the cellular network via trace-driven modeling, thus requiring less effort for understanding of 3GPP standards.

2 CELLULAR CONTROL PLANE

A cellular network consists of user equipment (UE), a base station (BS), and a core network (Figure 1). The UE communicates with a BS using radio resource control (RRC) as well as exchange control plane messages with the LTE (4G) core network. The LTE core network has three entities: HSS (Home Subscriber Server), gateways (GWs), and MME (Mobility Management Entity). The HSS is a database containing subscriber information including phone numbers and service quality profiles. Also, the HSS provides the functionality of

user authentication and access authorization. It manages the security information of subscribers and generates their authentication vectors. The GWs provide connectivity between the UE and packet data networks (e.g., Internet). The GWs also assign IP addresses to the UE, and track usage records for billing. The MME provides the UE with EMM (Evolved Packet System (EPS) Mobility Management) and ESM (EPS Session Management) services through various entities (e.g., BS and HSS) and protocols (e.g., RRC and NAS). ESM procedures build a pipeline for data/voice services, called a bearer. EMM procedures control the mobility of users as well as establish user identity and data confidentiality over the bearers. In this paper, we focus on the three essential EMM procedures.

ATTACH: The ATTACH procedure is the first step for a UE to use any cellular service. It sends the unique identifier of the UE to an MME and establishes a secure channel between the UE and a BS after following the authentication procedure.

TrackingAreaUpdate: Cellular operators (in short, ISPs) divide the entire network into multiple tracking areas (TAs) for efficient mobility management. The core entities have the TA information of the UE. The UE updates its TA code through the TrackingAreaUpdate (TAU) procedure. The TAU procedure is conducted when moving to another TA or when switching between LTE and 3G cellular networks.

ServiceRequest: Any network demands the UE to establish a session for the data service. The UE sends an MME a ServiceRequest (SR) message for a user data session between the UE and a GW.

To complete the EMM abovementioned procedures, the MME performs the common procedures; identification, authentication and security mode control. In the identification procedure, the MME identifies a UE by exchanging IdentityRequest and IdentityResponse messages, and requesting its identification parameter. If necessary, the MME initiates an authentication procedure. The MME sends the UE an AuthenticationRequest message, derived from the UE's security key in the HSS. The UE then authenticates the network by validating the received message, and sends its response through the AuthenticationResponse message to the MME for mutual authentication. Also, if the security key is not present or the MME wants to use a new key, it initiates the security mode control (SMC) procedure by exchanging SecurityModeCommand and SecurityModeComplete messages. This procedure plays a key role in establishing the secrecy and integrity for the communication between the UE and the MME. Note that those operations are invoked *selectively* according to the status of the UE and the core networks, and the operating policies.

3 COARSE- VS. FINE-GRAINED ANALYSIS

Latency analysis on a cellular control plane is an essential process for analyzing the efficacy of deployed components (e.g., BS, MME) or new optimization configurations (e.g., S1-flex). Furthermore, designing a new core network requires identifying bottleneck points for scalable and robust cellular services [5, 11, 14, 15].

Coarse-grained Analysis. The common approach for this latency analysis is to run a naïve field test. A local tester with a smartphone measures the completion time of the NAS and RRC control plane procedures. The tester then compares the procedure completion times with their service-level standards, which only reflects the local view of the system. The operators measure their network only, without comparing and sharing the detailed results with the

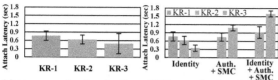

(a) Coarse-grained evaluation　(b) Fine-grained evaluation
Figure 2: Attach latency with two evaluation methods

other operators. We emphasize that such procedure-level performance analysis is rough. One procedure entails multiple operation scenarios, each of which involves a different set of NAS/RRC messages and participating entities, such as GWs or HSS. For instance, the TAU procedure covers 118 scenarios affected by the existence of pre-established RRC connections, expired identities, additional processes related to HSS or GWs (*i.e.*, authentication and session establishment), as well as failure recovery [1]. The tester usually knows little about the operation scenarios under testing, and focuses only on collecting the current measurement metrics.

We argue that current procedure-based latency analysis is unfit for comparative analysis. A blind comparison of the procedure completion time does not account for diverse operational scenarios. We observed that the relative order of the performance results of multiple operators differs in each scenario for ATTACH, TAU, and SR. For example, Figure 2 shows the completion times of ATTACH procedures among three ISPs in Korea. Solely based on a blind result comparison, one can conclude that KR-3 shows a better result than the others (Figure 2a). However, the performance of ATTACH varied in different scenarios. Figure 2b shows that KR-3 performs the worst when involving identity, authentication, and SMC messages. Thus, without considering each case, one can easily make the wrong assumption that a given ISP performs faster than the rest. Surprisingly, we observed that the previous works [6, 11] conducted this type of comparative analysis, ignoring diverse operation scenarios.

We also emphasize that local measurements without any comparison to other operators limits the detection of bottlenecks that stem from misconfiguration or unnecessary procedures. Moreover, deciding the bottleneck itself requires a lower bound value, which can be easily obtained from a comparative study. Thus, for an exact diagnosis of the control plane problem, a comparative analysis over multiple ISPs with a fine-grained comparison method is required.
Challenges in Fine-grained Analysis. There exist two technical challenges for an effective fine-grained comparative latency analysis: the difficulty in (1) analyzing the complicated control-plane operations and (2) considering the individual state information.

Identifying bottleneck points and the conditions that cause performance degradation requires an understanding of the standards (*i.e.*, RRC, or NAS) and operator-specific implementations. Note that the conformance-testing document has over 4,200 pages [4], while NAS and RRC standards are 500 and 700 pages, respectively [1, 3]. Therefore, examining the control plane messages and their diagnosis demands excessive engineering cost as well as domain-specific knowledge, which are arduous for the manual analysis process.

Comparative analysis requires exploiting state information including previous states, behaviors, and environmental conditions. An operator may have different latencies for performing the same control plane procedures because their previous procedures may

[1]These combinations result in 39 and 166 total cases in ATTACH and SR, respectively, in our dataset with our definition of the path in Section 4.2.

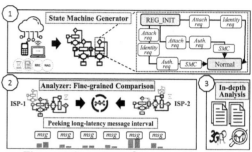

Figure 3: Overview of comparative study

affect the next procedure operations. Indeed, the ATTACH procedure following TAU failure shows different performance results when compared with ordinary ATTACH cases. Therefore, when comparing the two procedures, we should consider the previous state in order to avoid incorrect diagnosis results.

4 DESIGN

The goal of our analysis is two-fold: (1) conducting a fine-grained latency analysis on a target operator's control plane with minimum manual effort, and (2) comparing the latencies across different network operators while considering operator-specific policies and diverse operational scenarios.

To address this goal, we propose an **automated trace-driven modeling** technique. Figure 3 shows the overview of our analysis in three steps: (1) We start by building an operator-specific state machine based on control plane signaling messages. A transition between two states becomes a sequence of signaling messages. Instead of having custom states in the state machine, we leverage the 3GPP standard states. Thus, state machines from different ISPs share some same states and transitions. (2) We then identify the shared transition-paths across different state machines. Each path represents a distinct operation scenario shared across different ISPs. (3) Finally, for each message interval of such a shared transition path, we compute the latency between two messages and identify the long-latency message interval (LMI) whose value is relatively larger than those of other operators. The identified LMIs are valuable information for operators, who are in a dire need of pinpointing latent bottlenecks that may undermine the overall service latency.

4.1 Constructing the State Machine

Trace-driven modeling. We implement a state machine generator that builds a state machine from given control plane signaling messages. For each ISP, we feed its signaling messages collected from the UE to the generator to produce an operator-specific state machine. Therefore, the generated state machines are based on message traces; thus, the model naturally reflects operator-specific configurations and implementations in handling control plane messages. We use diagnostic message monitoring tools to extract the control plane signaling message [6, 13]. They connect to the UE via USB and expose the Diagnostic Message (DM) logs that the UE chipset produces. We selectively collect the DM logs that generate notifications regarding the reception/transmission of control plane signaling messages. Note that each of these messages contains a precise timestamp of the reception/transmission of the message.
States. We define a state as a combination of the EMM state and EMM substate. Note that we leverage the states defined in the 3GPP specification [1]. Such standard states serve as anchoring points

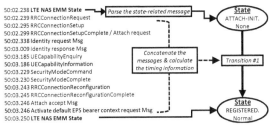

50:02.238 LTE NAS EMM State
50:02.239 RRCConnectionRequest
50:02.295 RRCConnectionSetup
50:02.299 RRCConnectionSetupComplete / Attach request
50:02.338 Identity request Msg
50:03.009 Identity response Msg
50:03.185 UECapabilityEnquiry
50:03.186 UECapabilityInformation
50:03.229 SecurityModeCommand
50:03.230 SecurityModeComplete
50:03.243 RRCConnectionReconfiguration
50:03.245 RRCConnectionReconfigurationComplete
50:03.246 Attach accept Msg
50:03.246 Activate default EPS bearer context request Msg
50:03.250 LTE NAS EMM State

Figure 4: Example of state machine construction

between different state machines, which contributes to identifying comparable transitions across state machines. This also makes the state machine analyzable, as the specification already describes the status and operation of each state. It also reduces the manual effort for building a state machine because the individual messages from the UE chipsets provide explicit state information.

Transitions. We define a transition as a sequence of RRC and NAS messages between two states except broadcasting messages (*i.e.*, Paging). When a sequence of observed RRC and NAS messages causes the state to change from a source to a sink state, the sequence of such message types becomes a transition. Because different operation scenarios involve different sequences of messages, each transition reflects a specific scenario that often involves 1) the existence of a radio connection, 2) the identification, authentication, or security requirements of the MMEs or BSs.

Figure 4 shows an example of building a state machine. The left-hand side shows the diagnostic messages extracted while conducting an ATTACH procedure. Based on the extracted logs, we define two states based on the LTE-NAS-EMM log messages, which the 3GPP standards define and the DM logs explicitly show. Further, we define the transition between two states to be the sequence of messages seen in the DM logs. We also store the timestamp information to compute the elapsed time to make the state transition. Note that the state machine construction process needs only a UE with a target ISP without any help from the BS or the core network equipment.

4.2 State Machine Comparison Strategy

With the generated state machine for each operator, the analyzer detects the LMIs through comparison. Comparing the state machine is an intuitive process, in which the states in the model are useful delimiters and the transitions represent a comparison target.

Pathwise comparison. From each state machine, we enumerate the list of paths, each of which is a transition sequence from a source to a sink state. For the source states [2], we use the initial states of ATTACH, TAU, and ServiceRequest operations. We set a sink state to be the REGISTERED.NORMAL state, where a UE is ready to use its call service. Thus, each path is an overall sequence of signaling messages and states until a target procedure is completed. A path represents how a target procedure is performed by an operator, which includes a service scenario or a failure recovery case.

Observing LMI over the shared path. Among the identified paths from each state machine, we find the shared paths that have the same transition sequence [3]. We then compare the latency of each message interval in the shared paths across different state machines. Latency is calculated by the difference between the timestamp of

---

[2]State format: [EMM state].[EMM substate] ATTACH: REGISTERED-INITIATED.None, TAU: TRACKING-AREA-UPDATING-INITIATED.None,
ServiceRequest: SERVICE-REQUEST-INITIATED.None
[3]Two transitions are the same if the order & type of messages are the same.

Table 1: Summary of our dataset

	KR-1	KR-2	KR-3	US-1	US-2
Signaling Msg #	20106	44445	39060	97103	193528
Procedures #	746	2212	1498	5549	9115

Table 2: Statistics of Generated State Machines

Operator	KR-1	KR-2	KR-3	US-1	US-2	Total
Total transitions	464	375	386	332	301	1,352
Shared transitions	161	218	229	99	97	297

(a) Generated Transitions in State Machines

Target Procedure	KR-1	KR-2	KR-3	US-1	US-2
ATTACH	15 (3)	11 (6)	16 (6)	8 (4)	3 (2)
TrackingAreaUpdate	35 (3)	20 (12)	33 (11)	37 (7)	14 (7)
ServiceRequest	11 (7)	38 (16)	51 (17)	65 (15)	44 (11)

(b) Diverse Cases of Target Procedures: *In each cell, A (B) denotes the following: A - # of transition paths; B - # of comparable cases*

an uplink message and the timestamp of its next downlink message. Note that the computed latency only measures the elapsed time in processing a control plane message at a target cellular network, not the latency caused by a UE. We further identify the long-latency message interval (LMI), if the latency of a certain message interval is relatively higher than those of other operators. Specifically, we define an LMI as occurring when (1) the latency of one operator exceeds twice that of another operator exhibiting minimum latency, and (2) the latency takes a more substantial portion than the sum of the latencies in the path divided by the total number of messages. We conservatively compared the latencies on the shared paths instead of defining the comparable paths between different state machines, which often demands operator-specific expertise. Comparing the non-shared path and devising a method to determine comparable paths will be performed in our future work.

5 COMPARATIVE ANALYSIS

We apply our analysis to five operators in order to demonstrate the effectiveness of our comparative analysis.

5.1 Dataset and Generated State Machine

Dataset. Table 1 provides a summary of our collected data, which includes 394,242 LTE signaling messages and 19,120 target procedures over five carriers. We collected the messages using diagnosis message monitoring tools [6, 13] and five types of UE (Galaxy S4/S5 and LG G2/G3/V10). We conducted various measures for collecting comprehensive signaling messages, such as turning on/off the airplane mode and data/voice service in stationary and mobility scenarios by physically visiting different cities in two countries. All data are either collected by us or extracted from the previous dataset [6]. For the KR dataset, we collect the traces from over 3,000 km movements via high-speed trains and cars between Seoul and Daejeon and driving all around South Korea. We also collected US dataset from several road trips [4] of visiting cities in US west as well as used the dataset from the prior work [6].

Generated state machine. We first demonstrate how the state machine effectively handles diverse scenarios for the fine-grained analysis. Table 2 shows the statistical results of the state machine for each operator. Our automated modeling differentiates 1,352 operational scenarios through transition representation. Surprisingly, only 297 transitions are shared between at least two operators (Table 2a), which implies that the remaining transitions are operated differently. We also observe that 323 scenarios exist across the three target procedures in all, through the pathwise comparison (Ta-

---

[4]We had to drive this far to collect signaling messages that generated from the scenarios such as moving another location or turning on the phone in a different region.

Table 3: Identified Long-latency Message Intervals (*An ISP with an LMIs is in bold*)

LMI-ID	Path	Uplink message	Downlink message	Appeared operator: ISP (average seconds)
LMI-1	ATTACH-1 [+]	ESM info. response	ueCapabilityEnquiry	**KR-2 (0.439)**, US-1 (0.171), KR-3 (0.124)
LMI-2	ATTACH-1	Attach request*	Auth. request	**US-1 (0.095)**, KR-2 (0.052), KR-3 (0.046)
LMI-3	ATTACH-2	Identity response	ESM info. request	**KR-1 (0.262)**, KR-3 (0.042), KR-2 (0.038)
LMI-4	ATTACH-3	NAS-SMC	ESM info. request	**US-2 (0.256)**, KR-3 (0.045), KR-2 (0.023)
LMI-5	ATTACH-3	ESM info. response	RRC-SMC	**US-2 (0.444)**, **KR-2 (0.259)**, KR-3 (0.110)
LMI-6	TAU-1	Identity response	EMM infomation	**KR-3 (0.130)**, KR-2 (0.065)

The message is piggybacked with RRC connection setup complete message [+]The path consists of following messages: Attach request - Auth. request -
Auth. response - SMC (NAS) - ESM info. request - ESM info. response - ueCapabilityEnquiry - ueCapabilityInfo. - SMC (RRC) - rrcConnectionReconfig. -
rrcConnectionReconfig.Complete - Attach accept - Activate default EPS bearer context request

ble 2b). Each operator has diverse yet unique operation scenarios. The results imply that each operator handles the procedures differently, and that this diversity stems from the operator-specific logic and configurations. These operator-specific logics are also reflected in the frequency of each path. For example, if an ISP turns on a re-authentication option, which always invokes an authentication procedure during the ATTACH procedure, the state machine contains the path containing the authentication request/response messages in the ATTACH procedure. In addition, the path appears more frequently in the state machine from the ISP than that of other ISPs who do not adopt the option [5]. We also compare each state machine from the trace with the one described in the 3GPP standard for completeness. Note that a direct comparison is difficult, because the state diagram of the 3GPP standard does not contain sub-states. Nevertheless, we confirm that all state machines generated from the trace hold the main states and sub-state for our targeted procedures except the states related to the failure states and transitions [6].

5.2 Lessons from Identified LMIs

We have observed 38 LMIs over the shared paths of three target procedures. Table 3 shows the selected LMIs in the shared paths [7]. The first column shows the list of message intervals; each exists in the shared path in the second column. The latency for each message interval is measured between the uplink and downlink messages. The last column shows operators with average latency over the collected observations. We find two implications from the identified LMIs, demonstrating the effectiveness of our approach.

First, every operator has an LMI, and no operator shows the lowest latency at every path. Also, each LMI occurs at different ISPs within the same control procedure according to the path. Table 3 shows that LMI-1 in ATTACH-1 is identified only at KR-2, whereas LMI-3 in ATTACH-2 is identified at KR-1. This implies that KR-2 is not optimized for the ATTACH-1 case, but exhibits low latencies for other cases. From those observations, we conclude that each operator is optimized differently and not fully optimized for all paths.

Second, an LMI exists even in paths having total latency lower than that of other operators. For example, the total latency of ATTACH-1 in US-1 is lower than that of KR-2, but US-1 contains LMI-2 (illustrated in Figure 5). This shows that comparing the total latency of a path alone across operators could result in failure to pinpoint long-latency intervals and their causes. Note that our prior work [6], which only considers the total latency of a target control plane procedure, fails to detect this case. Thus, the comparison requires: (a) consideration of diverse operation scenarios and (b) comparison of latency at the message-level. Our analysis achieves both of the requirements and effectively demystifies hidden perfor-

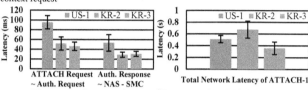

Figure 5: Comparison of Latency in ATTACH-1

mance degradation points.

5.3 Preliminary In-depth Study

In-depth study of LMIs. Table 3 shows that KR-2 has LMIs 1 and 5, both of which involve handling ESM information response messages. Considering that the ESM information response message in these paths (ATTACH-1,3) is handled by the operations between MMEs and GWs, we conclude that KR-2 has more room for optimization of the operations at two entities. For the remaining LMIs, we can adopt the same analysis approach, investigating the internal operation between the participating entities.

As Table 3 shows, US-1 has LMI-2 in ATTACH-1, performing the ATTACH procedure. Its latency is almost two-times larger than the others. First of all, we can conclude that the operation between MME and HSS of US-1 [8], handling the messages of the LMI, has more overhead than the others. Also, we further investigate all the uplink and downlink messages for LMI-2 by comparing them with those of other ISPs. We have found that only US-1 used encrypted messages for authentication in ATTACH-1, while the others do not cipher the authentication messages. Note that, ciphering the authentication messages is unnecessary in the context of the ATTACH procedure. The authentication procedure is designed to be performed without a security context, and a new security context is generated between the UE and MME after the authentication. We confirm that the encryption over these messages is unnecessary by checking the 3GPP standards [1, 2, 4] [9].

In-depth study of shared path. We have run the further analysis on the observed shared and non-shared paths. One interesting observation is that KR-1 has no shared paths which have the authentication logic. Authentication is a key step in generating a key (K_{ASME}), used for deriving the additional keys for ensuring the confidentiality and integrity of further control messages. This means that the key renewal policy of KR-1 is unique compared with the others, so that KR-1 reuses the pre-established session information aggressively by skipping the authentication procedure. This operational difference mainly stems from the ambiguity in the 3GPP standards, which do not specify the condition for the re-authentication procedure. Thus, it is highly dependent on the operating policy. Finally, this security implication of skipping the authentication deserves further study.

---

[5]We confirmed the existence of the option by interviewing one MME manufacturer.
[6]To identify these states, an active tester that transmits the manipulated control plane message to the cellular network is required. (We will discuss this in Section 6)
[7]Due to space limitations, we have shown only 6 LMIs in 4 paths.

[8]More specifically, the entities in charge of authentication vector.
[9]Clause 4.4.2.4 in the NAS spec mentions this case. However, it does not describe any underlying reasons for the encryption, and no conformance test case covers this issue.

6 DISCUSSION

Potential Directions: State machine representation facilitates the efficient analysis of the operating logic of the control plane on a cellular network. An interesting example involves analyzing the failure recovery logic, which is highly dependent on the operators and manufacturers, and its faulty design significantly affects the user experience. Promisingly, state machine representation makes it easy to extract and compare the failure recovery logic of each operator. Any path traversing the DEREGISTERED states represents a failure recovery operation scenario. We conducted the comparative latency analysis on such paths, which includes the failure recovery of TAU REJECT. A notable observation is that handling ATTACH REQUEST after TAU REJECT consistently takes 5 or 10s in US-1. Hong *et al.* observed the same issue with significant manual analysis [6], which demonstrates the effectiveness of our state machine representation.

Our approach still has room for improvement in the construction and use of the fine-grained state machine. We believe that the state machine representation considering more information such as the location of collected data, user action, and core equipment vendors, will aid in root cause analysis. Moreover, to improve the accuracy of the diagnosis, the pathwise comparison needs to select the paths exclusively by selecting the source state carefully. The analysis of the non-shared paths is also applicable to the identification of security problems. For example, a path heading toward failure states or time-consuming states could be an effective attack vector. Lastly, our approach, representing the operational scenarios as the path, could be applicable to the stateful fuzzing by executing dynamic testing at each path to discover the potential vulnerabilities.

Limitations of Trace-driven Approach: While the trace-driven approach is effective in reflecting the operating logic, the completeness of the model heavily depends on the collected traces. We believe that a larger dataset obtained through crowd-sourcing would address this limitation and reveal new findings. One solution would be to leverage an active data collector by exploiting the software-defined-radio and open source LTE stack [12]. Our approach relies on the observation of interacting control plane messages at the UE. Unfortunately, the UE has limited access to network-side operations, and finding the root cause of a problem demands a comprehensive understanding of cellular network specifications. Moreover, our approach may not identify an operator-specific configuration that does not produce the signaling messages. However, if such a configuration contains different contents in the signaling message, the fine-grained comparison of the content in the signaling messages may be able to resolve such cases. We emphasize that our work provides a starting point for investigations, which effectively reduces the effort for finding or understanding the cause of a bottleneck.

Related Work: Diagnosing the performance degradation problem in cellular networks has been extensively conducted in control plane [6, 7, 16], services [9], and radio access networks [8]. CNetVerifier [16] and LTEInspector [7] constructed models from the 3GPP specs, but these require extensive efforts to convert the natural language of the specs to the state machine and fails to reflect operating control plane logic. Similar to our work, RILAnalyzer [17] and MobileInsight [10] employ trace-driven modeling. However, RILAnalyzer exploits a probability of the state transitions, based only on the coarse-grained information from the 3G RRC protocol. Mo-

bileInsight presents a tool that provides fine-grained information on control plane messages, but it does not provide a way of (a) constructing a model of control plane operating logic, or (b) comparing the models in fine-grained fashion for the latency analysis.

7 CONCLUSION

We presented a novel diagnosis method for comparative analysis across multiple network operators, which is expected to be useful for network operators and manufacturers of cellular equipment. Our approach automates modeling from the trace to reflect the real operating logic, allowing for avoidance of the exhaustive process of standard document analysis. We also conducted a pathwise analysis for the fine-grained comparison over five major operators in two countries and identified 38 LMIs, which deserves further investigations. Our work is the first comparative latency analysis with fine-granularity information with promising results. Our state machine models are also applicable to the identification of problems in other domains including security and operation logic errors, which also deserves further research.

ACKNOWLEDGMENTS

We would like to thank the anonymous reviewers and our shepherd, Alastair Beresford, for their insightful comments and suggestions for improving the paper. This work was supported by Institute for Information & communications Technology Promotion (IITP) grant funded by the Korea government (MSIT) (2018-0-00831, A Study on Physical Layer Security for Heterogeneous Wireless Network). We would like to thank the authors of SCAT for the collection of data.

REFERENCES

[1] 3GPP. TS 24.301. Non-Access-Stratum (NAS) protocol for Evolved Packet System (EPS); Stage 3, 2017.

[2] 3GPP. TS 33.401. 3GPP System Architecture Evolution (SAE); Security architecture, 2018.

[3] 3GPP. TS 36.331. Evolved Universal Terrestrial Radio Access (E-UTRA); Radio Resource Control (RRC); Protocol specification, 2017.

[4] 3GPP. TS 36.523. Evolved Universal Terrestrial Radio Access (E-UTRA) and Evolved Packet Core (EPC); User Equipment (UE) conformance specification;, 2018.

[5] A. Banerjee, R. Mahindra, K. Sundaresan, S. Kasera, K. V. der Merwe, and S. Rangarajan. Scaling the LTE Control-plane for Future Mobile Access. In *CoNEXT*. ACM, 2015.

[6] B. Hong, S. Park, H. Kim, D. Kim, H. Hong, H. Choi, J. P. Seifert, S.-J. Lee, and Y. Kim. Peeking over the Cellular Walled Gardens-A Method for Closed Network Diagnosis. *IEEE TMC*, 17(10), 2018.

[7] S. R. Hussain, O. Chowdhury, S. Mehnaz, and E. Bertino. LTEInspector: A Systematic Approach for Adversarial Testing of 4G LTE. In *NDSS*, 2018.

[8] A. P. Iyer, L. E. Li, and I. Stoica. Automating Diagnosis of Cellular Radio Access Network Problems. In *MobiCom*. ACM, 2017.

[9] Y. J. Jia, Q. A. Chen, Z. M. Mao, J. Hui, K. Sontinei, A. Yoon, S. Kwong, and K. Lau. Performance Characterization and Call Reliability Diagnosis Support for Voice over LTE. In *MobiCom*. ACM, 2015.

[10] Y. Li, C. Peng, Z. Yuan, J. Li, H. Deng, and T. Wang. Mobileinsight: Extracting and Analyzing Cellular Network Information on Smartphones. In *MobiCom*. ACM, 2016.

[11] Y. Li, Z. Yuan, and C. Peng. A Control-Plane Perspective on Reducing Data Access Latency in LTE Networks. In *MobiCom*. ACM, 2017.

[12] openLTE. http://openlte.sourceforge.net.

[13] QXDM. qualcomm-extensible-diagnostic-monitor.

[14] A. S. Rajan, S. Gobriel, C. Maciocco, K. B. Ramia, S. Kapury, A. Singhy, J. Ermanz, V. Gopalakrishnanz, and R. Janaz. Understanding the bottlenecks in virtualizing cellular core network functions. In *LANMAN*. IEEE, 2015.

[15] M. T. Raza, D. Kim, K.-H. Kim, S. Lu, and M. Gerla. Rethinking LTE network functions virtualization. In *ICNP*. IEEE, 2017.

[16] G.-H. Tu, Y. Li, C. Peng, C.-Y. Li, H. Wang, and S. Lu. Control-plane Protocol Interactions in Cellular Networks. In *SIGCOMM*. ACM, 2014.

[17] N. Vallina-Rodriguez, A. Auçinas, M. Almeida, Y. Grunenberger, K. Papagiannaki, and J. Crowcroft. RILAnalyzer: A Comprehensive 3G Monitor on Your Phone. In *IMC*. ACM, 2013.

Enabling Multiple Applications to Simultaneously Augment Reality: Challenges and Directions

Kiron Lebeck, Tadayoshi Kohno, Franziska Roesner
University of Washington
{kklebeck,yoshi,franzi}@cs.washington.edu

ABSTRACT

Augmented reality (AR) platforms are evolving to support immersive 3D experiences. Most modern AR platforms support only a single immersive app at a time, but users may also benefit from the ability to engage with multiple apps at once. The ability of different apps to simultaneously augment a user's world raises critical questions: how might apps visually conflict with each other, and how can we design AR platforms to support rich behaviors while mediating conflicts? In this work, we pose and explore these questions, identifying means of visual conflict as well as platform design strategies to mediate conflicts. We then analyze state-of-the-art AR platforms (HoloLens, Magic Leap One, and Meta 2) to understand their trade-offs and identify unexplored gaps in the broader design space. Our exploration reveals key guidelines and lessons to inform future multi-app AR efforts.

ACM Reference Format:
Kiron Lebeck, Tadayoshi Kohno, Franziska Roesner. 2019. Enabling Multiple Applications to Simultaneously Augment Reality: Challenges and Directions. In *The 20th International Workshop on Mobile Computing Systems and Applications (HotMobile '19), February 27–28, 2019, Santa Cruz, CA, USA*. ACM, New York, NY, USA, 6 pages. https://doi.org/10.1145/3301293.3302362

1 INTRODUCTION

Augmented reality (AR) is ushering in a new era of immersive computing, with devices that can understand a user's physical world and blend 3D content into the user's view of the world. However, most modern AR platforms do not allow users to engage with multiple immersive apps simultaneously, and those that provide multi-app support still have significant limitations. Consider a user who wishes to engage with multiple apps while walking in a city, such as an AR navigation app [5], an AR game [11], and social apps that augment nearby people, e.g., by displaying their names above their heads or 3D masks over their faces. On a single-app platform, the user can only view and interact with one app at a time. By contrast, a multi-app platform could allow the user to shift their attention between apps — for example, periodically glancing at directions without closing their game, while still seeing social overlays on nearby people.

Realizing the vision of multi-app AR will require identifying and overcoming new challenges that stem from the unique capabilities of AR platforms. In particular, rather than sharing the blank canvas of a traditional computer screen and displaying content within isolated windows, the output of immersive AR apps will exist atop the backdrop of the user's ever-changing world. These apps may need to dynamically update their outputs in response to changes in the user's physical environment while simultaneously displaying content alongside each other, raising fundamental questions: how might immersive AR apps visually conflict with each other, and how can multi-app AR platforms allow different apps to simultaneously augment their shared world while mediating conflicts?

Prior AR-related efforts [1, 8, 9, 13] primarily focused on *individual* apps negatively influencing users' perceptions of the real world, rather than on visual conflicts between multiple apps. We currently lack a foundation for reasoning about these conflicts or understanding the design challenges involved with supporting multiple immersive apps. In this work, we provide such a foundation by conducting an intellectual investigation into the multi-app AR design space, deferring implementation and experimental evaluations to future work. Specifically, we contribute the following:

1. *Problem Identification*: We identify the need to view the design space of multi-app AR platforms with a critical eye towards visual conflicts that may occur between the output of different apps.

2. *Design Space Exploration*: We introduce a broad categorization of approaches for multi-app AR platforms to handle conflicts, and we uncover key trade-offs presented by different design strategies.

3. *AR Platform Analysis*: We analyze the multi-app capabilities of modern AR platforms to understand how they fit into the broader design space.

4. *Future Directions*: Through our exploration and analysis, we identify promising directions for future work. For example, we encourage future work to implement and evaluate key concepts set forth in this paper.

2 MOTIVATION

We begin with case study scenarios that highlight the possibilities of multi-app AR, including risks that users may face from visual interactions between apps.

Tourism. Alice uses Tour Guide while on vacation, which displays floating icons above landmarks that she can select to read more information. Restaurant Assistant displays food safety and customer ratings above nearby restaurants, which Alice can select to read detailed reviews and menu options. Navigation guides Alice as she walks to a new destination by displaying directional arrows on the ground, and for entertainment, an immersive POKÉMON game blends interactive 3D characters into Alice's physical environment.

Unfortunately, multiple POKÉMON characters inadvertently stand atop Alice's NAVIGATION arrows on the ground and prevent Alice from seeing her directions. At the same time, TOUR GUIDE has an endorsement contract with a local café, and to discourage Alice from eating elsewhere, it displays fake negative ratings above other eateries that block the true ratings of RESTAURANT ASSISTANT.

Social Gatherings. Bob is attending a festival with friends and wishes to connect with other attendees. SOCIAL MEDIA AR recognizes nearby people in Bob's extended network and displays their names, mutual friends, and common interests above their heads. Since Bob is interested in romantic connections, he also uses AR DATING, which computes compatibility scores of other users, highlights them, and displays the scores above their heads. Finally, Bob and his friends use IMMERSIVE SNAPCHAT FILTERS to modify each other's appearances in fun ways, such as overlaying humorous costumes.

Bob notices that a friend-of-a-friend is also identified as a potential romantic connection, with SOCIAL MEDIA AR and AR DATING both displaying information above their head. However, content from both apps appears jumbled atop each other, and Bob cannot disambiguate content from either app. AR DATING also identifies other potential partners near Bob, but since SNAPCHAT has already displayed full-body filters over them, AR DATING cannot highlight them.

The Workplace. Carol and her colleagues use AR to improve productivity at work, with COLLABORATIVE WORKSPACE allowing them to interact with shared 3D models and virtual whiteboards both in the office and remotely. COLLEAGUE ASSISTANT displays helpful reminders that float next to Carol's coworkers (such as upcoming meetings or recent emails), and AR CHAT allows Carol to stay connected with her team by displaying real-time messages that float next to her. Finally, AR ART lets Carol easily personalize her workspace with virtual paintings, sculptures, and other artwork.

Carol finds COLLEAGUE ASSISTANT helpful, but the app is compromised and intentionally positions its reminders to obscure AR CHAT messages. While AR ART improves Carol's workplace ambiance, the app is buggy and creates 3D objects that interfere with COLLABORATIVE WORKSPACE. Since there is no indication that AR ART created these objects, Carol believes COLLABORATIVE WORKSPACE to be malfunctioning and disables it. Additionally, when an AR CHAT message moves atop an AR ART piece on Carol's desk, the art is "knocked" to the ground.

A New Output Paradigm. The above scenarios raise a fundamental question: can a multi-app AR platform support the diverse needs of immersive apps while also mitigating negative interactions between them? As with apps on other computing platforms, immersive AR apps may compete for resources such as memory, CPU cycles, and network bandwidth. What sets these apps apart are their output needs.

Consider a traditional desktop app, such as a video game, text editor, or web browser. The outputs of these apps exist within independent windows, and the behavior of these apps does not depend upon the precise placement of their windows on the computer screen (i.e., the user could reposition any of the windows and the

apps would behave the same). However, in AR, the behavior of an app may depend directly on how its outputs are positioned in the context of the user's world. For example, the efficacy of Alice's NAVIGATION app depends upon the app's ability to precisely position directional arrows on the ground, and Bob's AR DATING and SOCIAL MEDIA AR apps must be able to place overlays above specific people's heads. Furthermore, on a traditional desktop display, all content shown on screen is controlled directly by either apps or the OS. By contrast, users will view AR apps atop the backdrop of the physical world rather than a blank screen. This external environment may change unpredictably, introducing variability that AR apps may need to contend with. For example, apps may need to dynamically update their outputs in response to changes in the user's world itself (e.g., AR DATING must update the locations of its overlays as people move throughout Bob's field of view), as well as changes in the user's own position within the world (e.g., NAVIGATION must appropriately place new arrows on the ground as Alice walks around and changes directions). AR presents a new output paradigm from traditional displays, creating new challenges that will require novel solutions.

Threat Model. In this work, we focus on the conflicts that stem from visual interactions between immersive AR apps, leaving a discussion of additional output modalities (e.g., audio) for Section 5. Furthermore, we focus on users' *perceptions* of AR content rather than their *interactions* with apps. Output conflicts may lead to harmful user interactions (e.g., AR "clickjacking"), but such issues depend on the specific input capabilities provided by an AR platform, which we consider out of scope.

Our threat model encompasses both apps that are malicious, as well as apps that are honest-but-buggy and do not intentionally seek conflict. We begin by considering a broad space of visual conflicts that may arise, including the following:

- *Occlusion.* The output of one app might block the user from seeing that of another. For example, Alice, Bob, and Carol all encounter occlusion above. We exclude situations where the user intentionally positions one app's content to occlude other apps, focusing on occlusion events that arise in the absence of user intent.

- *Placement Denial.* By occupying a particular space, one app might prevent another from generating content. For example, Bob's SNAPCHAT app prevents AR DATING from highlighting certain individuals, by occupying the space around them with full-body filters.

- *Eviction.* By moving content into a space occupied by another app, an offending app might cause the victim's content to be removed or displaced, as Carol experiences when AR CHAT knocks an AR ART object to the ground.

- *Masquerading.* One app might generate content that is mistaken for that of another. For example, Carol mistakenly perceives buggy output from AR ART as output from COLLABORATIVE WORKSPACE.

- *Content Modification.* As we will see in Section 3.2, certain conflict mediation mechanisms may modify the visual properties of app outputs, e.g., by adjusting transparency. Such approaches raise an additional threat: one app may be able to induce changes in the visual properties of another app's content.

3 DESIGN SPACE EXPLORATION

We now turn to our design exploration of multi-app AR platforms, asking: how can these platforms mediate visual conflicts between apps, and what are the trade-offs associated with different design alternatives? We consider the ability of an AR platform to meet the following criteria while remaining resilient to the above-mentioned conflicts:

- *Support for Multiple Applications.* Does the platform allow multiple apps to run simultaneously?
- *Full Output Autonomy.* Does the platform give apps full control over the placement of their outputs in 3D space?
- *Some Output Autonomy.* Does the platform give apps at least *some* positional control over their outputs?
- *Limited User Burden.* Does the platform require limited or no user involvement in managing output?
- *Limited Developer Burden.* Does the platform limit the need for app developers to handle unexpected interactions with other apps?

Figure 1 summarizes key trade-offs that characterize the design paths we discuss throughout this section.

3.1 Display Abstractions

The interface that an AR platform provides to apps for displaying content determines the space of available output behaviors. Consider the following:

Single-App. Inter-app conflicts cannot occur if only one app can display content at a time. While this approach is at odds with our goal of supporting multiple apps, it is the only design in Figure 1 to meet every other goal and may suffice for individual apps requiring the user's undivided attention.

Windows. One method for preventing output conflicts is to confine apps to separate regions of space — a 3D analogue of the window abstraction used by desktop PCs. We consider a model where windows are controlled by the user and cannot be created or repositioned autonomously by apps. These properties allow windows to visually isolate apps from each other, but in doing so, they trade-off the ability for apps to dynamically generate content throughout the user's world. While our prior work argued for the insufficiency of windows in AR due to such flexibility limitations [8], we find their viability actually depends upon the needs of specific apps. For example, Carol's AR CHAT, AR ART, and other apps naturally fit within bounded spaces, but Alice's POKÉMON and NAVIGATION apps require more dynamic output capabilities.

Shared World. The final model we consider is a shared world that allows multiple apps to simultaneously display content throughout the user's environment. This approach stands in contrast to windows, sacrificing visual isolation to give apps the flexibility to place AR content wherever they wish. As a result, one app may draw in the same space as another app or otherwise occlude that app's output. We explore strategies for addressing such conflicts below.

3.2 Managing Output in a Shared World

When considering how to manage output conflicts in a shared world, we must first determine *who* should shoulder this burden. Thus, we explore opportunities for the OS, apps themselves, or the user to take on this responsibility. While we present these design paths individually, we note that they may be combined to manage output in different ways.

3.2.1 OS-ENFORCED CONFLICT MEDIATION

As discussed above, giving apps the freedom to place content wherever they wish may lead to occlusion conflicts. We thus begin with two complementary design paths that enable the OS to prevent occlusion. These designs leverage the AR object abstraction proposed in our prior work [8]. AR objects are OS-managed primitives that encapsulate AR output — for example, a single POKÉMON character would be one AR object. The OS can modify the visual properties of AR objects (e.g., position or transparency) to prevent occlusion. Specifically, we introduce the following approaches:

1. *Runtime Policies.* The OS prevents occlusion by observing visual interactions between AR objects at runtime and enforcing policies that modify them in response. For example, the OS could observe when one of Alice's POKÉMON objects occludes a NAVIGATION arrow and turn the POKÉMON object partially or fully transparent to ensure that NAVIGATION's arrow remains visible.

2. *Declarative Output.* The OS provides apps with a language to abstractly indicate their output needs, but it controls *how* these needs are met to prevent occlusion. For example, Bob's AR DATING and SOCIAL MEDIA apps could request to display content above someone's head, and the OS would determine an appropriate layout. Similarly, Alice's RESTAURANT ASSISTANT app could place virtual signs in front of restaurants without controlling the precise 3D coordinates of these objects.

Trade-off: Intelligent Mediation vs. App Freedom. Runtime policies only allow the OS to identify occlusion after it has occurred, and they provide no contextual information about how the OS should respond to individual conflicts. By contrast, declarative output ensures that apps do not conflict in the first place, and by capturing the high-level needs of apps, it gives the OS the ability to intelligently respond to app requests. Consider AR DATING and SOCIAL MEDIA from above. If the OS understands that both apps are attempting to augment the same person's head, it could (for example) arrange content so that both apps are visible above the person's head, rather than making one app's objects invisible.

In providing more effective mediation capabilities, declarative output trades off the ability to support fine-grained object placement for apps. Declarative output naturally caters to apps that can specify their output needs in terms of high-level visual relationships to physical-world objects, such as AR DATING. However, this approach does not lend itself to apps such as Alice's POKÉMON game, which needs to create and move characters at precise 3D locations in Alice's world. For apps such as POKÉMON that cannot operate under a declarative model, runtime policies provide the OS with a potential fallback mechanism for mediating conflicts.

		Output Conflicts					Functionality Goals				
		Occlusion	Placement Denial	Eviction	Masquerading	Content Modification	Multi-App Support	Full Output Autonomy	Some Output Autonomy	Limited User Burden	Limited Dev Burden
Display Abstractions	Single App	✔	✔	✔	✔	✔	N	Y	Y	Y	Y
	Windows	✔	✔	✔	✕	✔	Y	N	N	N	Y
	Shared World	✕	✔	✔	✕	✔	Y	Y	Y	Y	Y
Output Management in a Shared World — Runtime Policies	Ex1: Modify Occluder	✔	✔	✔	✕	✕	Y	N	Y	Y	N
	Ex2: LRU	★	✔	✕	✕	✔	Y	N	Y	Y	N
Declarative Output	Ex1: Defined Layout	✔	✕	✔	✕	✔	Y	N	Y	Y	N
	Ex2: LRU	✔	✔	✕	✕	✔	Y	N	Y	Y	N
	Application Self-Management	★	✔	✔	✕	✔	Y	Y	Y	Y	N
	User-Managed Output	✔	✔	✔	✕	✔	Y	N	Y	N	N

Figure 1: Potential design paths for multi-app AR platforms. Check marks indicate that a design can prevent a conflict; stars indicate that the conflict is prevented when apps are trusted; and Xs indicate that a design cannot prevent the conflict.

Preventing Occlusion Can Enable New Conflicts. Preventing occlusion in a shared world fundamentally requires the OS to constrain the output behaviors of apps. In doing so, the OS may enable new forms of conflict. Recall the example runtime policy in which POKÉMON's object is made transparent when it occludes NAVIGATION's arrow. This policy allows NAVIGATION to *induce* visual modifications in POKÉMON's objects by placing arrows behind them. A declarative approach can also enable new conflicts — for example, the OS may deny an app's request to display content if it cannot determine an acceptable layout that would accommodate this request without causing occlusion.

As another cautionary example, consider a least-recently-used (LRU) mechanism that identifies overlapping objects and removes those that the user has interacted with least recently. When applied as a runtime policy or declarative output tool, an LRU mechanism enables even well-intentioned apps to inadvertently evict each other. Furthermore, a malicious app could leverage an LRU runtime policy to probe for the locations of other apps' objects by observing when its *own* objects are evicted, using this information to surround a victim app's objects and occlude them.

Limitation: Conflict Identification. A limitation of any OS-driven approach is that the OS may not be able to unilaterally decide which visual interactions are problematic. If the OS can determine a prioritization ordering for different apps, it can potentially decide which apps to act upon when mediating conflicts, whether it employs runtime policies, declarative output, or another strategy. However, the notion of what constitutes a conflict may not always be obvious, nor the decision of which app should receive priority. Note that we previously explored the idea of OS-enforced runtime policies in prior work [9]. However, that work focused primarily on visual conflicts between AR objects and real-world objects, where the real world was assumed to take priority, and it did not deeply consider the viability of runtime policies for resolving multi-app conflicts.

3.2.2 APPLICATION SELF-MANAGEMENT

We next consider the potential for apps to collaborate in avoiding conflicts by sharing information with one another and reacting to each other's requests. For example, if Alice's NAVIGATION app could provide the 3D locations of its directional arrows to POKÉMON and request that POKÉMON not occlude them, then POKÉMON could adjust its behavior while still providing the user with the same overall experience.

Application self-management allows apps to retain control over their outputs and respond to conflicts in predictable ways, in contrast to OS-enforced policies that impose external modifications on app content. The consequence of giving apps this level of control is that self-management is only viable under a threat model where apps are trusted to avoid interfering with each other given the information to do so (e.g., on a closed platform running well-vetted apps that are designed to cooperate). A malicious app could leverage any additional information given to it about other apps to attack them — for example, if POKÉMON was malicious and learned precisely where NAVIGATION's arrows were, it could strategically generate objects that occlude those arrows.

3.2.3 USER-MANAGED OUTPUT

Ultimately, the user may be best positioned to determine which conflicts are detrimental to their own AR experience. Thus, the final design path we explore is one that leaves mediation to the user's discretion. An AR platform could provide the user with different tools for this task — for example, to demote problematic apps to more restrictive states (e.g., confining them to windows), to delete

  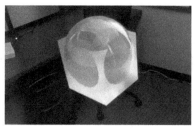

(a) Microsoft HoloLens   (b) Meta 2   (c) Magic Leap One

Figure 2: Multi-app photos from three AR headsets, taken with an iPhone 6 through the lens of each device.

individual AR objects, or to provide apps with behavioral cues (e.g., to instruct an app to avoid displaying content in specific spaces).

The OS also has an opportunity to inform the user's actions by enabling the user to easily discern potential conflicts. Recall Carol's COLLABORATIVE WORKSPACE app — Carol believed this app to be misbehaving, but the OS could inform her that the problematic object came from another app. Furthermore, the user may be unaware that certain conflicts have actually occurred. For example, unbeknownst to Alice, her TOUR GUIDE app displayed fake restaurant ratings that hid the overlays of RESTAURANT ASSISTANT. The OS could identify such visual interactions and provide Alice with this information so that she can act according to her wishes.

3.3 Summary

Identifying and mediating visual conflicts between AR apps is challenging, and different design strategies present varying trade-offs, as showcased in Figure 1. Our key insight is that any output mediation technique will infringe upon app functionality, and the precise nature of this infringement differs between design paths. Additionally, we observe that different techniques will be appropriate under different trust models, and our exploration highlights the potential for malicious apps to abuse well-intentioned capabilities.

4 AR PLATFORM ANALYSIS

In this section, we analyze the Microsoft HoloLens, Meta 2, and Magic Leap One AR headsets, asking: how do they fit into the broader design space above, and what unexplored directions may warrant further investigation? Each platform supports an immersive single-app mode that aligns with the first row of Figure 1, and we thus focus our analysis on the platforms' multi-app modes. Figure 2 depicts multi-app photos that we took through the lens of each device.

HoloLens. The HoloLens's multi-app mode supports Universal Windows Platform (UWP) apps, which run within 2D windows placed in 3D space by the user (Figure 2a). UWP apps run across different Microsoft platforms, providing a familiar interface for both users and developers. The window abstraction sacrifices support for immersive output to allow the HoloLens to enforce strong visual isolation between apps.

Meta 2. The Meta 2's multi-app mode is similar to that of the HoloLens, employing 2D windows placed in 3D space by the user (Figure 2b). The device tethers to a desktop PC and supports virtual "computer monitors" that enable the user to interact with their desktop's apps within AR windows.

Magic Leap One. By contrast, the Magic Leap One's multi-app mode supports multiple 3D apps at once. Apps may create "prisms" — bounded 3D regions in which they can display content. To probe the capabilities of prisms, we built multiple apps that display simple geometric shapes, and we ran two simultaneously. Figure 2c depicts two such apps: one displays a cube within a prism, and the other displays a sphere within a separate prism.

Prisms can be placed by the user, but we discovered that prisms from different apps are created atop each other by default. Apps can specify their prisms' sizes, but we could not determine if they can also control prism positions. If an app *can* control prism sizes and positions, then prisms act as a form of a shared world without conflict mediation mechanisms. As shown in Figure 2c, this design enables occlusion conflicts to occur. Furthermore, note that the cube and sphere are interleaved in 3D space, rather than one app receiving explicit rendering priority. Combining output from different apps in this way does not make intuitive sense from a user's perspective, suggesting that this occlusion is not intended behavior. We note that the Magic Leap developer guidelines suggest that prisms are *intended* to act as well-defined 3D windows, but this intention is not enforced by the platform.

5 DISCUSSION

Our design exploration and analysis establish a foundation for understanding and addressing key multi-app AR challenges. Here, we identify promising avenues for future work.

Output Management Techniques. Our analysis reveals a nascent multi-app landscape among today's AR platforms. Critically, no platform provides a shared world abstraction endowed with additional conflict mediation capabilities. Of the mediation strategies captured in Figure 1, we believe that declarative output is the most compelling path for further exploration. A declarative approach can prevent output conflicts even with malicious apps, and it strikes a balance between app flexibility and conflict mediation. The OS can handle app requests in a more predictable manner than runtime policies allow, and apps can exercise more immersive behaviors than a windowed display abstraction supports. Furthermore, this approach does not impose the burden of output management on users. Even though declarative output cannot support apps that require arbitrary 3D placement, it is well-suited for apps tasked with augmenting specific real-world objects (e.g., TOUR GUIDE and AR DATING).

Going forward, we propose that future work should validate the conceptual directions laid out in this work, by investigating the viability of declarative output (as well as the other above-mentioned output management techniques) in greater depth. One path would be to build a multi-application AR platform that supports different mediation strategies, and to evaluate these strategies along a number of axes — for example, the performance overheads that each technique imposes on applications; the ability of these techniques to effectively resolve output conflicts; the functionality limitations they place on application behaviors; and the burdens they place on both developers and users. Evaluating these criteria will better illuminate the trade-offs presented by different design paths, and will confirm (or contradict) our initial intuition regarding declarative output as the most promising path forward.

Non-Visual Output. While this work lays a foundation for addressing conflicts between AR applications in terms of visual output, AR platforms may provide additional output modalities as well, such as aural or haptic feedback. Future work should investigate conflicts that may arise between AR apps in terms of non-visual output, determine if and where design strategies for preventing visual conflicts can be adapted to non-visual settings, and identify areas where new approaches will be required. Additionally, future work should consider opportunities for AR platforms to leverage combinations of multiple output modalities to mediate conflicts (e.g., by incorporating both aural and visual cues to help users contend with visual conflicts between apps).

Understanding User Perceptions of Conflict. Determining the visual interactions that users find problematic can inform defensive efforts, particularly for conflicts that cannot be fully prevented. For example, as suggested in Figure 1, no design can truly prevent masquerading, which depends upon users' perceptions of AR content. An AR platform can *attempt* to prevent masquerading, just as early windowing systems employed labeling techniques to indicate the origins of different windows (e.g., [3]). However, a user may still incorrectly perceive the origin of AR content. Future work is thus needed to identify design strategies that effectively engage the user and minimize the impacts of such conflicts.

6   RELATED WORK

Our analysis reveals limited multi-app support on today's AR platforms. Researchers have previously proposed AR systems that support multiple apps, but they have not rigorously explored the design space or reasoned about conflicts that may arise. Argon [10] instantiates a shared world with overlapping full-screen, transparent windows for different apps, without conflict mediation. By contrast, Studierstube [15] confines app outputs to bounded 3D windows controlled by the user. Earlier non-AR efforts also considered secure windowing (e.g., [3]), but as discussed, AR raises new challenges.

Researchers have also studied security and privacy for AR more generally [2, 13]. Prior works consider output security (e.g., [1, 2, 8, 9, 13]), focusing on ways that AR apps could negatively impact users' views of the world. Our work instead explores visual conflicts *between* apps. Other efforts address input privacy, or preventing apps from accessing sensitive information in a user's environment (e.g., [4, 6, 7, 12, 14, 16, 17]) — our work is complementary.

7   CONCLUSION

Immersive multi-application AR platforms can enable users to interact with apps that simultaneously blend digital content into the physical world. However, AR apps may visually conflict with each other as they navigate the dynamically-changing environment of the user's world. In this work, we identify the challenges of mediating visual conflicts between apps without unduly infringing on their intended behaviors. We explore the design space of multi-app AR platforms and uncover key trade-offs presented by different design alternatives. We then analyze the design choices of current AR platforms and identify promising opportunities for future work. Our lessons lay a foundation to guide multi-application AR efforts, and we encourage future work to implement and evaluate the directions set forth in this paper.

ACKNOWLEDGMENTS

We thank Niel Lebeck and Earlence Fernandes for many helpful discussions and feedback on earlier drafts. We also thank our anonymous reviewers and our shepherd, Mahadev Satyanarayanan, for their valuable guidance and feedback. This work was supported in part by the National Science Foundation under Award CNS-1651230.

REFERENCES

[1] S. Ahn, M. Gorlatova, P. Naghizadeh, M. Chiang, and P. Mittal. Adaptive fog-based output security for augmented reality. In *Morning Workshop on Virtual Reality and Augmented Reality Network*, 2018.

[2] L. D'Antoni, A. Dunn, S. Jana, T. Kohno, B. Livshits, D. Molnar, A. Moshchuk, E. Ofek, F. Roesner, S. Saponas, M. Veanes, and H. J. Wang. Operating system support for augmented reality applications. In *HotOS*, 2013.

[3] J. Epstein, J. McHugh, R. Pascale, C. Martin, D. Rothnie, H. Orman, A. Marmor-Squires, M. Branstad, and B. Danner. Evolution of a trusted b3 window system prototype. In *IEEE Computer Society Symposium on Research in Security and Privacy*, 1992.

[4] L. S. Figueiredo, B. Livshits, D. Molnar, and M. Veanes. Prepose: Privacy, security, and reliability for gesture-based programming. In *IEEE Symposium on Security and Privacy*, 2016.

[5] https://www.theverge.com/2018/5/8/17332480/google-maps-augmented-reality-directions-walking-ar-street-view-personalized-recommendations-voting.

[6] S. Jana, D. Molnar, A. Moshchuk, A. M. Dunn, B. Livshits, H. J. Wang, and E. Ofek. Enabling fine-grained permissions for augmented reality applications with recognizers. In *USENIX Security Symposium*, 2013.

[7] S. Jana, A. Narayanan, and V. Shmatikov. A scanner darkly: Protecting user privacy from perceptual applications. In *IEEE Symposium on Security and Privacy*, 2013.

[8] K. Lebeck, T. Kohno, and F. Roesner. How to safely augment reality: Challenges and directions. In *HotMobile*, 2016.

[9] K. Lebeck, K. Ruth, T. Kohno, and F. Roesner. Securing augmented reality output. In *IEEE Symposium on Security and Privacy*, 2017.

[10] B. MacIntyre, A. Hill, H. Rouzati, M. Gandy, and B. Davidson. The argon AR web browser and standards-based AR application environment. In *ISMAR*, 2011.

[11] https://www.pokemongo.com/.

[12] N. Raval, A. Srivastava, A. Razeen, K. Lebeck, A. Machanavajjhala, and L. P. Cox. What you mark is what apps see. In *MobiSys*, 2016.

[13] F. Roesner, T. Kohno, and D. Molnar. Security and privacy for augmented reality systems. *Communications of the ACM*, 57(4), 2014.

[14] F. Roesner, D. Molnar, A. Moshchuk, T. Kohno, and H. J. Wang. World-driven access control for continuous sensing. In *ACM Conference on Computer & Communications Security*, 2014.

[15] D. Schmalstieg, A. Fuhrmann, G. Hesina, Z. Szalavári, L. M. Encarnaçao, M. Gervautz, and W. Purgathofer. The studierstube augmented reality project. *Presence: Teleoperators & Virtual Environments*, 11(1), 2002.

[16] R. Templeman, M. Korayem, D. J. Crandall, and A. Kapadia. Placeavoider: Steering first-person cameras away from sensitive spaces. In *Network and Distributed System Security Symposium*, 2014.

[17] J. Vilk, D. Molnar, B. Livshits, E. Ofek, C. Rossbach, A. Moshchuk, H. J. Wang, and R. Gal. Surroundweb: Mitigating privacy concerns in a 3D web browser. In *IEEE Symposium on Security and Privacy*. IEEE, 2015.

Scaling Up Your Web Experience, Everywhere

James Newman
Northwestern University

Robert H. Belson
Northwestern University

Fabián E. Bustamante
Northwestern University

ABSTRACT

We present an approach to improve users' web experience by dynamically reducing the complexity of websites rendered based on network conditions. Our approach is based on a simple insight – adjusting a browser window's scale (i.e., zooming in/out), changes the number of objects placed above-the-fold and thus hides the loading of objects pushed below the fold in the user scroll time.

We design *ScaleUp*, a browser extension that tracks network conditions and adjusts browser scale appropriately to improve user web Quality of Experience (QoE) while preserving the design integrity of websites. Through control experiments, we demonstrate the impact of *ScaleUp* on a number of key QoE metrics over a random sample of 50 from the top 500 Alexa websites. We show that a simple adjustment in scale can result in an over 19% improvement on Above-The-Fold (ATF) time in the median case. While adjusting a scale factor can improve metrics of QoE, it is unclear if that translates into an improved web experience for users. We summarize findings from a large, crowdsourced experiment with 1,000 users showing that, indeed, improvement to QoE metrics correlate with an enhanced user experience. We have released *ScaleUp* as a Chrome Extension that now counts with over 1,000 users worldwide, and report on some of the lessons learned from this deployment.

ACM Reference Format:
James Newman, Robert H. Belson, and Fabián E. Bustamante. 2019. Scaling Up Your Web Experience, Everywhere. In *The 20th International Workshop on Mobile Computing Systems and Applications (HotMobile '19), February 27–28, 2019, Santa Cruz, CA, USA.* ACM, New York, NY, USA, 6 pages. https://doi.org/10.1145/3301293.3302368

1 INTRODUCTION

Websites have become increasingly complex with hundreds of different objects — images, videos, scripts, and cascading stylesheet (CSS) files [9]. Besides creating the opportunity for more appealing websites, the additional complexity can slow down overall page loading time and negatively impact users and content providers alike. Changes in users' experiences have been linked to changes in revenue for content providers, especially for commerce websites [5, 8, 14].

For many users, the trend has gone mostly unnoticed with the concurrent growth in the capacity of Internet services. In the first quarter of 2017, the global average connection speed increased 15%

HotMobile '19, February 27–28, 2019, Santa Cruz, CA, USA
© 2019 Association for Computing Machinery.
ACM ISBN 978-1-4503-6273-3/19/02...$15.00
https://doi.org/10.1145/3301293.3302368

compared with the first quarter of 2016, and the top ten countries reported an average connection speed of 22.5 Mbps [2].

For others, however, either in regions with poor connectivity or temporarily accessing the web through low-end networks, this trend has resulted in significantly worsened web experiences. A common modern setting is in-flight connectivity (IFC), where latencies can be 10-100x higher than many residential networks, and packet loss ratios can reach up to 30%, resulting in page load times over 30 seconds even for the top 100 most popular sites [24].

While designing website for different devices (e.g., desktops and mobile) can help, this is done on a per content provider and website basis. Understanding how to improve the web experience of users everywhere and across websites, remains a open problem. Some efforts look to optimize pages based on dependency tracking [19, 22], others rewrite pages for better load times [10, 28], and some rely on proxy-based solutions [21, 25]. While promising, most of these projects require either dedicated infrastructure or prior runs of websites to affect positive change.

We present an approach to improve users' web experience by dynamically reducing the complexity of the websites rendered based on network conditions. Our approach is based on a simple insight – adjusting a browser window scale (i.e., zooming in/out), changes the number of objects in a website that are placed above the fold and thus a user's experience with the website. Importantly, we do not change the content on websites, rather, we simply force some of its placement to optimize user experience. As some of the content is pushed below the fold, the time it takes to load that content is hidden within the user's scroll time. This plays on the user's understanding of how webpages load, given the impression of a webpage loading faster by showing them a smaller portion of the webpage at a time.

We design *ScaleUp*, a browser extension that tracks network conditions to appropriately and dynamically adjust browser scale to improve user's web QoE without sacrificing the design integrity of websites. *ScaleUp* utilizes the Chrome *webRequest* API [11] – the same API used by popular web-based ad-blockers – to measure how quickly the server responds with the initial HTML page, and determines, at run-time, the most appropriate scale factor for the site (§2).

Through control experiments, we evaluated the impact of *ScaleUp* on two key QoE metrics using a random sample of 50 from the top 500 Alexa websites. We show that, a simple adjustment in scale factor can result in a 19% improvement on Above-the-Fold time [18] in the average case (§3).

While adjusting a scale factor can improve some metrics of QoE, it is unclear if that translates into an improved web experience for users. We present results from a large, crowdsourced experiment with 1,000 users showing that, indeed, these improvements are correlated with actual user experience (§4).

(a) Unscaled (b) Scaled

Figure 1: The visible impact of scale factors. A popular website rendered un-scaled, on the left, and at 1.5x scale on the right; the higher scale factor results in fewer objects loaded above-the-fold.

We have released *ScaleUp* as a Chrome Extension that now counts with over 1,000 users worldwide; we report on some of the lessons learned from this deployment.

2 SCALING UP WEB QOE

Addressing the impact of increasingly complex websites on users' experience over low-end connections is challenging. For starters, since users visit a wide range of sites during a day, an ideal solution should improve users experience across all sites. While blocking objects outright would seem to be a promising approach (e.g., [4]), a better solution would preserve the integrity of the website design. Finally, not all low-end connections are alike and users move between networks of different quality through their daily lives. Any solution should dynamically adapt to the capability of the current network.

Our approach is simple: dynamically adapt the complexity of the website rendered above the fold. We do this by adjusting a browser window scale (zooming in/out) based on measured network conditions. Effectively, by *zooming in* when network conditions worsen, we change the size of text and images, and thus the number of objects placed above-the-fold, hiding the loading of objects pushed below the fold in the user scroll time. As network conditions improve, *zooming out* lets the user enjoy the full content of a website.

Figure 1 illustrates this with a popular news website, loaded at two different scale factors, 100% and 150%. It is apparent that when the website is loaded with a larger scale factor there are fewer objects visible above-the-fold (ATF) and thus a lower ATF time and – potentially – a better user experience.

It may seem that the scaling mainly impacts images. While this is true, it doesn't fully cover the extent of the impact. Because the browser utilizes the viewport size in ordering resources to render, the zoom factor can impact which objects are rendered first, affecting how CSS rules are implemented and how iFrames (HTML) are loaded.

2.1 *ScaleUp* Design

We implemented our idea as a Chrome browser extension – *ScaleUp* – that tracks network conditions and dynamically adjusts browser scale to improve web QoE while preserving the design integrity of websites. *ScaleUp* relies on the Chrome webRequest API [11] to determine whether or not to scale a website. By utilizing a combination of callbacks revealed by the API, *ScaleUp* measures the time

Figure 2: User Interface of *ScaleUp*. The interface provides information on network conditions, such as latency and an approximation of time to first byte. In this example run (loaded over a slow 3G connection), the time to first byte is over 100ms and the website would have been scaled.

it takes to receive the headers of the initial HTML page. If that time is over certain thresholds, *ScaleUp* will adjust the scale factor of the browser. If latency measurements drop, perhaps after moving to a different network, the extension will adjust the scale again.[1]

To scale the website, *ScaleUp* uses the *chrome.tabs* API [12]. This API allows the extension to interact with and modify the tabs open in a user's browser. In particular, it reveals the *setZoom* function[2] to change the zoom of the tab by a certain scale factor.

Additionally, *ScaleUp* captures the ATF time of the website. To do this, it relies upon the ability of Chrome extensions to inject JavaScript onto websites that the user visits, coined *content scripts* [13]. We declare the script in the manifest file to be included on each new website that is loaded.

ScaleUp injects a modified Above-the-Fold (ATF) script [26] that measures the ATF time for the website on which it is included. ATF time refers to the time it takes for all content within the initial browser's viewport (i.e., no scrolling) to be loaded [18]. The script traverses the DOM tree of the page and records whether or not an object is above-the-fold based on the coordinates of the object and the viewport size. The script measures the load time of each object and then computes the time it takes for all the content ATF to load.

Finally, *ScaleUp* collects data on network conditions, scale factors, and QoE metrics for further analysis. For this it includes a JavaScript file to be executed when the page has completed loaded. We use the *chrome.runtime* API to communicate with *ScaleUp*'s background page. Once the ATF script has completed calculating the ATF time, we send the resulting times back to the background page which then reports it to our servers for storage. *No information is collected on the actual sites a user visits.*

In total, *ScaleUp* is 1,152 lines of original JavaScript code, and currently comprises 22MB of storage when counting other libraries it relies on, images, CSS, and HTML. *ScaleUp* was originally released

---

[1]We are exploring a combination of latency and website specific rules for the next version of the plugin.
[2]`chrome.tabs.setZoom(integer tabId, double zoomFactor, function callback)`

to the Chrome Web Store on February 15th 2017, and has since gone through 14 versions, reaching over 1,000 unique, persistent users.

Limitations. We designed and implemented *ScaleUp* as an extension to a desktop browser. As part of future work, we plan to explore ways to implements some of these ideas on mobile devices for which some websites may already be optimized, thus limiting the benefits of scaling, and where browsers typically lack support for extensions.

3 IMPACT OF SCALE FACTOR

In this section, we use control experiments to demonstrate the impact of adjusting the browser window scale on a number of key QoE metrics. For this, we focus on 50 random websites selected from the Alexa top 500.

To characterize the impact of scaling, we load each of these 50 websites for each of the scale factors considered: 90%, 100%, 110%, 125%, and 150%, multiple times. We use – as *ScaleUp* does – the *chrome.tabs* API to set up the scale, load the page, and collect several measurements using the extension Approximate ATF [3], including the number of different objects on a website, the number of those objects residing ATF, and the ATF time.

The machine running the experiments is a MacBook Pro with 16 GB of 1600MHz memory and an Intel Core i7 processor. It is connected to the Internet through a router that we controlled to minimize interference [15]. We use a TP-Link N750 Wireless Wi-Fi Dual Band router (TL-WDR4300) which we configure to run OpenWRT (Chaos Calmer 15.05.1, r48532) and the Linux's Traffic Control and Network Emulation tools, which we use to emulate the network conditions found in-flight. We configure the connection to mimic a cellular-based IFC connection as reported by Rula et al. [24]. This can be seen as a best-case for in-flight communications in terms of latency, found to be about 2x smaller than the alternative satellite connections.

Images Above-the-Fold. Figure 3 plots the changes in the number of images ATF as a function of the scale factor. As expected, even a small change in scale can result in a significant number of images being move bellow the fold (from 8 in the average case at the 90% scale factor to 4.6 at 150%). The ticks show the standard deviation on the number of images which also becomes smaller with larger scale factors.

Above-the-Fold Time. Our hypothesis is that as the average number of images drop at higher scales, the ATF time will also drop. Table 1 summarizes our results, showing the 50th, 90th and 95th percentile of both ATF and Page Loading Time (PLT) for different scale factors. While scaling has little to no impact on PLT, ATF times drops significantly with up to 25.2% in the average case and up to 44% at the 95% percentile.

In some respect, the lack of change noticed in PLT from scaling is the insight behind the *ScaleUp* approach. While no browser extension can improve the underlying network performance (e.g., latency, loss), it can improve the *perceived* performance as captured by the ATF time.

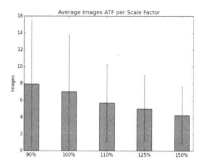

Figure 3: Average number of images that reside above-the-fold for different scale factors. As the scale factor increases, the corresponding number of images decreases as images are pushed below-the-fold.

Scale Factor	Percentile	ATF Time (ms)	PLT (s)
	Average	1,134.5	11.3
90%	90	1,536.8	20.5
	95	5,760.7	24.2
	Average	960.98	10.7
100%	90	939.53	20.4
	95	3,950.7	23.7
	Average	777.34	9.7
110%	90	964.2	16.9
	95	1,086.1	23.1
	Average	925.54	9.8
125%	90	1,537.0	18.0
	95	3,491.9	18.7
	Average	848.51	9.5
150%	90	1,317.4	18.8
	95	3,235.3	21.6

Table 1: Results from controlled experiment. We see that *ScaleUp* can improve ATF time 19% by increasing the scale factor from 100% to 110%. While there is not a significant impact on PLT, *ScaleUp* still improves the average load time by 1 second with only a 10% change in scale.

4 SCALE AND USER EXPERIENCE

The previous paragraphs demonstrate the impact of browser scale on key QoE metrics. In this section we present a crowdsourced user study exploring the effect of different scale factors on actual user quality of experience.

4.1 Methodology

We conducted a user study with a 1,000 participants in Amazon Mechanical Turk (AMT). The study focuses on capturing the impact of scaling on users' experience with the rendered website – including both how quickly the site loads as well as the potential impact of zooming on its aesthetics.

Each survey starts by collecting some basic demographic information, followed by the presentation of a series of websites at different scales. Participants are asked questions aimed at ranking the alternatives based on perceived load speed and appearance. The survey ends with some basic exit questions to understand what drove the user's selection of the fastest/slowest alternative and a free-text section on the factors determining what "looked best".

In more detail, the initial questionnaire includes gender, age range, and country, as well as their self-rated technical proficiency and the range of hours typically spent online. We use these to evaluate the role, if any, that such factors may have in their web browsing experience.

In the main part of the survey, we asked participants to view three simultaneous loads of the same website with different scales. We want to see how the changes measured in PLT and ATF, as a result of changes in scale, relate to user experience. We do this for 5 different sites randomly selected from the same set of top Alexa sites as in our control experiment. The versions were loaded with three scale factors — *90%*, *100%*, and *110%*. Although much larger scale factors are possible, we conservatively used the smallest possible scale factor;[3] changes in perception should be only more clear with large scales.

As in Varvello et al. [27], rather than using live sites during an experiment, we collect videos of the websites loading and use this to control for network and website variations between runs.

We provide users with three questions for each set of videos: *Which website loaded fastest?*, *Which website loaded slowest?*, and *Which website looked the best while loading?* The first two questions aim to capture perceived improvements on load time. The last one is used to determine how, if at all, the scale factor effects the aesthetics of the website.

Quality Control. When submitting a Human Intelligence Task (HIT), we limit it to users with >=95% lifetime approval rating and over 50 lifetime submitted tasks. We do this to ensure the reliability of our participants. Of the 5,000 ratings (1,000 HITs with 5 websites each) we received 4,597 (≈ 92%) results. Beyond the 5 websites, we also include one other website as a control case. The control case randomly places a "fast" website load against two identically slow ones. We use this as an additional form of quality control on all of the HITs. Of the 944 surveys who scored all the video sets, 850 of them passed the control test. We eliminated the 106 surveys from users who failed the test.

Ethical Considerations. Amazon's conditions of use explicitly prohibit tasks that gather personally identifiable information. The information we did collect is coarse enough that we have no reasonable way to map it to individuals. Our experiments collect data "about what", rather than "about whom", through the relatively innocuous task of selecting videos. Our institution's Institutional Review Board (IRB) determined our study to be *Not Human Research*.

4.2 Summary of Results

The following paragraphs summarize the results from our crowdsourced user experiment, starting with a characterization of participating users based on demographics and technical proficiency.

Demographics. We find that a majority of users are male (59.5%), and between between 25-31 years of age. The large majority comes

---

[3]Chrome does not allow for intermediate values, such as 99%.

Question	Scale Factor		
	90%	*100%*	*110%*
Loaded Fastest	30.1%	33%	**36%**
Loaded Slowest	**39.1%**	30.6%	30.3%
Looked the Best	33.2%	29.7%	**37.1%**

Table 2: Results from a crowdsourced study shows a clear correlation between scale factor and users' perceived loading time. Interestingly, the trend breaks when users are asked which website looks the best.

from the United States (77.4%) followed by India (18.1%); with the rest being from a variety of countries.

Focusing on the average number of hours spent online, we see a normal distribution with the majority of users, ≈36%, in the *4-8 hour* range. Meanwhile, few users selected either *<1 hour* or *>12 hours*, 0.5% and 8.8% respectively.

On the level of technical proficiency, 53.2% of users self-identified as *average* and 43.2% identified as *above average*. Only 3.6% of users selected the *below average* category.

Scale and QoE. Table 2 presents the percentage of users selecting, for different scale factors, the one that loaded the fastest, the slowest and that looked the best. Users selected *110%* scale as loading fastest 36% of the time and chose *90%* as loading the slowest 39.1% of the time. Even a small adjustment in scale can produce a 3% change of perceived quality of experience.

When users were asked which website "looked" the best, we notice an interestingly different trend from what we expected. The default, *100%* scale factor, was most commonly ranked at the bottom (29.7%). The option with highest scale factor, *110%*, was the most commonly selected as looking the best (37.1%). While the higher percentage of users for 110% could be explained by users looking for "larger" or "more clear" content, it is possible that the *90%* scale factor was popular because users could see more content. We leave the exploring of scale factors on users' perceived appearance as future work.

5 *SCALEUP* DEPLOYMENT

ScaleUp has been available in the Chrome Web Store for over a year. At the time of writing this, *ScaleUp* has 1,031 users actively checking for updates. Additionally, while this number is fairly consistent, there is some churn in our user base with an average of 8.7 installs and about 4.8 uninstalls per day. Figure 4 plots the changes in our user base over time (from February 2017 to June 2018), illustrating this.

Beyond improving users' web experience, *ScaleUp* serves as a crowdsource measurement tool for network performance and web quality of experience for in-flight WiFi users, its original customer base. As such, the extension collects bandwidth, latency, above-the-fold time, and page-load time, among other metrics. In addition, *ScaleUp* let users report their flight number in exchange for an update on their flight progress and an updated comparison of their network performance to that of other flights.

6 RELATED WORK

There have been numerous efforts to better characterize and improve web browsing performance and experience. Bocchi et al.

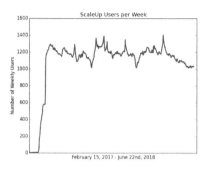

Figure 4: Number of users per week for the entirety of *ScaleUp***'s deployment. After the initial jump to over 1,000 users, the user base has remained relatively stable. This is encouraging and indicates that users enjoy browsing with** *ScaleUp*

published a comprehensive survey of the available perceived WebQoE measurement systems, including Google's SpeedIndexTest, Yahoo's YSlow, and dynaTrace, among others [7]. To improve web QoE, some recent work relies on proxies to aid with handling dependencies [19, 22] or precomputing the information needed for page loading by a mobile browser [20, 25], while others have examined how protocol usage can impact user experience [1, 6].

Some close related efforts have explored ways to improve the "perceived" performance of websites, by restructuring websites [28], re-prioritizing content on pages [10] and even using users' gaze to understand what to prioritize on a webpage [16]. Compared with some of the proposed ideas, our approach is easier to deploy and adopt as it does not require any additional infrastructure and works with any site.

While generally applicable to any high-latency network condition, our work was motivated by the challenging environment of in-flight communication. Recent efforts on characterizing IFC [23, 24] have shown some of these challenges and made the case that many of them would persist even with the promising technology advances in the space. Not surprisingly, there has been interest from IFC providers in improving web browsing experience. For example, ViaSat filed a patent on a method of progressive prefetching to help page load times while browsing on satellite connections [17].

7 CONCLUSION

We presented a lightweight approach to improve users' web experience by dynamically reducing the complexity of websites rendered. Through control experiments, we demonstrated the impact of *ScaleUp* on a number of key QoE metrics and random set of popular websites. We presented results from a crowdsourced experiment with 1,000 users showing that the measured improvement on metrics of QoE correlate with an enhanced user experience. *ScaleUp* has been available as a Chrome Extension for over a year and counts with over 1,000 consistent users worldwide.

There are a number of interesting directions for future work. In our design of *ScaleUp* we have intentionally avoided direct blocking of objects as not to compromise the website design. It may be worth

relaxing this constraint and consider the impact on user experience of limiting *font*, css or javascript objects. More generally, this work points to the need for better, deeper understanding of users' web QoE and the most reliable proxy metrics.

ACKNOWLEDGEMENTS

We thank our shepherd Ben Greenstein and the anonymous reviewers for their thoughtful feedback. This research was partially supported by NSF grant CNS-1619317 and a Google Faculty Research Award.

REFERENCES

[1] V. Agababov, M. Buettner, V. Chudnovsky, M. Cogan, B. Greenstein, S. McDaniel, M. Piatek, S. Colin, M. Welsh, and B. Yin. Flywheel: Google's data compression proxy for the mobile web. In *Proc. of USENIX NSDI*, 2015.
[2] Akamai. akamai's [state of the internet]: Q1 2017 report. https://www.akamai.com/us/en/multimedia/documents/state-of-the-internet/q1-2017-state-of-the-internet-connectivity-report.pdf, 2017. [Online; accessed 14-June-2018].
[3] A. Alemnew, V. Christophides, R. Teixeira, D. Rossi, et al. Narrowing the gap between qos metrics and web qoe using above-the-fold metrics. In *Proc. of PAM*, 2018.
[4] S. C. Apps. Images on/off. http://singleclickapps.com/images-on-off/, 2016. Accessed on 06.21.2018.
[5] N. Bhatti, A. Bouch, and A. Kuchinsky. Integrating user-perceived quality into web server design. *Computer Networks*, 33(1-6):1–16, 2000.
[6] E. Bocchi, L. D. Cicco, M. Mellia, and D. Rossi. The web, the users, and the mos: Influence of http/2 on user experience. In *Proc. of PAM*, 2017.
[7] E. Bocchi, L. D. Cicco, and D. Rossi. Measuring the quality of experience of web users. *SIGCOMM Comput. Commun. Rev.*, 4(4):8–13, 2016.
[8] A. Bouch, A. Kuchinsky, and N. Bhatti. Quality is in the eye of the beholder: meeting users' requirements for Internet quality of service. In *Proc. of SIGCHI*, 2000.
[9] M. Butkiewicz, H. V. Madhyastha, and V. Sekar. Understanding website complexity: Measurements, metrics and implications. In *Proc. of IMC*, 2011.
[10] M. Butkiewicz, D. Wang, Z. Wu, H. V. Madhyastha, and V. Sekar. KLOTSKI: reprioritizing web content to improve user experience on mobile devices. In *Proc. of USENIX NSDI*, 2015.
[11] Chrome. Chrome webrequest api. https://developer.chrome.com/extensions/webRequest. Accessed on 06.14.2018.
[12] Chrome. chrome.tabs. https://developer.chrome.com/extensions/tabs. Accessed on 06.14.2018.
[13] Chrome. Content scripts. https://developer.chrome.com/extensions/content_scripts. Accessed on 06.14.2018.
[14] K. Eaton. How one second could cost amazon 1.6 billion in sales. https://www.fastcompany.com/1825005/how-one-second-could-cost-amazon-16-billion-sales/, 2012. [Online; accessed 14-June-2018].
[15] A. M. Kakhki, S. Jero, D. Choffnes, C. Nita-Rotaru, and A. Mislove. Take a long look at quic. In *Proc. of IMC*, 2017.
[16] C. Kelton, J. Ryoo, A. Balasubramanian, and S. R. Das. Improving user perceived page load times using gaze. In *Proc. of USENIX NSDI*, 2017.
[17] P. Lepeska and W. B. Sebastian. Progressive prefetching, Mar. 6 2018. US Patent 9,912,718.
[18] P. Meenan. How fast is your website? *Commun. ACM*, 56(4):49–55, 2013.
[19] R. Netravali, A. Goyal, J. Mickens, and H. Balakrishnan. Polaris: Faster page loads using fine-grained dependency tracking. In *Proc. of USENIX NSDI*, 2016.
[20] R. Netravali and J. Mickens. Prophecy: Accelerating mobile page loads using final-state write logs. In *Proc. of USENIX NSDI*, 2018.
[21] R. Netravali, A. Sivaraman, S. Das, A. Goyal, K. Winstein, J. Mickens, and H. Balakrishnan. Mahimahi: Accurate record-and-replay for HTTP. In *Proc. USENIX ATC*, 2015.
[22] V. Ruamviboonsuk, R. Netravali, M. Uluyol, and H. V. Madhyastha. Vroom: Accelerating the mobile web with server-aided dependency resolution. In *Proc. of ACM SIGCOMM*, 2017.
[23] J. P. Rula, F. E. Bustamante, and D. R. Choffnes. When ips fly: A case for redefining airline communication. In *Proc. of HotMobile*, 2016.
[24] J. P. Rula, J. Newman, F. E. Bustamante, A. M. Kakhki, and D. R. Choffnes. Mile high wifi: A first look at in-flight internet connectivity. In *Proc. WWW*, 2018.
[25] A. Sivakumar, S. P. N., V. Gopalakrishnan, S. Lee, S. Rao, and S. Sen. Parcel: Proxy assisted browsing in cellular networks for energy and latency reduction. In *Proc. ACM CoNEXT*, 2014.

[26] Telecom. Atf-chrome-plugin. https://github.com/TeamRossi/ATF-chrome-plugin. Accessed on 06.14.2018.

[27] M. Varvello, J. Blackburn, D. Naylor, and K. Papagiannaki. Eyeorg: A platform for crowdsourcing web quality of experience measurements. In *Proc. ACM CoNEXT*, 2016.

[28] S. X. Wang, A. Krishnamurthy, and D. Wetherall. Speeding up web page loads with shandian. In *Proc. of USENIX NSDI*, 2016.

EdgeDroid: An Experimental Approach to Benchmarking Human-in-the-Loop Applications

Manuel Olguín
School of Electrical Engineering & Computer Science
KTH Royal Institute of Technology
Stockholm, Sweden
molguin@kth.se

Junjue Wang
School of Computer Science
Carnegie Mellon University
Pittsburgh, Pennsylvania
junjuew@cs.cmu.edu

Mahadev Satyanarayanan
School of Computer Science
Carnegie Mellon University
Pittsburgh, Pennsylvania
satya@cs.cmu.edu

James Gross
School of Electrical Engineering & Computer Science
KTH Royal Institute of Technology
Stockholm, Sweden
james.gross@ee.kth.se

ABSTRACT

Many emerging mobile applications, including augmented reality (AR) and wearable cognitive assistance (WCA), aim to provide seamless user interaction. However, the complexity of benchmarking these human-in-the-loop applications limits reproducibility and makes performance evaluation difficult. In this paper, we present EdgeDroid, a benchmarking suite designed to reproducibly evaluate these applications.

Our core idea rests on recording traces of user interaction, which are then replayed at benchmarking time in a controlled fashion based on an underlying model of human behavior. This allows for an automated system that greatly simplifies benchmarking large scale scenarios and stress testing the application. Our results show the benefits of EdgeDroid as a tool for both system designers and application developers.

ACM Reference Format:
Manuel Olguín, Junjue Wang, Mahadev Satyanarayanan, and James Gross. 2019. EdgeDroid: An Experimental Approach to Benchmarking Human-in-the-Loop Applications. In *The 20th International Workshop on Mobile Computing Systems and Applications (HotMobile '19), February 27–28, 2019, Santa Cruz, CA, USA*. ACM, New York, NY, USA, 6 pages. https://doi.org/10.1145/3301293.3302353

1 INTRODUCTION

There is increasing interest from academia and industry in novel applications such as immersive augmented reality (AR) or wearable cognitive assistance (WCA) [1, 2], also known as human-in-the-loop applications. These applications aim to seamlessly integrate into the lives of users to provide real-time, context-aware information by capturing user and environment information and leveraging compute-intensive algorithms to analyze the data in order to provide real-time feedback to the user. Sensory input, such as video,

audio, and other user-related data such as orientation and movement, are examples of what is typically captured, while the backend generally employs machine learning technologies such as Deep Neural Networks (DNN) [2]. Figure 1 depicts such a system. These applications are highly latency sensitive, measuring latency as the time from the capture of the sensory information until feedback is received. Delays above a certain threshold can hurt the user experience or even make the application unusable [3].

In literature, these challenging latency requirements have so far mainly been addressed through research on the optimal placement of the compute process. There is a broad understanding today that with the advent of edge computing, human-in-the-loop applications will become viable [3, 4, 5, 6]. However, with respect to end-to-end latency, there are many more trade-offs involved than merely the question of where the compute backend is placed. A human-in-the-loop application consists of various processing steps that can be influenced during the development of the application. What kind of compression to apply to the sensory input on the uplink; which backend algorithms to utilize; how to stage the backend; when to send feedback to the human users; and how to manage congestion on the loop, as well as wireless channel fluctuations — all these design choices impact the latency of the application. There are also many design choices in the infrastructure: how is the sensory input conveyed to the point of computation (i.e. by which wireless system; with which transmission/prioritization scheme); which hardware is running at the backend; which operating system; how is the feedback conveyed back to the human user? Finally, in production use these applications will most likely run concurrently with others. How does this, together with other best-effort applications, impact the latencies perceived by the human user? Existing studies [1, 2, 7, 8] of this class of applications have only lightly touched upon these issues [3]. On the other hand, recently published models for end-to-end latency of edge computing architectures [9, 10] are quite complex, while not accounting for the specifics of human-in-the-loop applications. We only have a coarse understanding of the many degrees of freedom upon which end-to-end latency depends.

The goal of this paper is to provide a methodological approach to studying these latency trade-offs, along with a tool, EdgeDroid

1.0*, that simplifies the benchmarking of human-in-the-loop applications. We view EdgeDroid 1.0 to be the very first, and simplest, of a family of tools that will embody increasingly sophisticated and accurate models of user behavior.

Due to the complex nature of the applications and the infrastructure, we opt for experimentally studying the trade-offs in a repeatable and controllable fashion. This is difficult mainly due to the unpredictable reaction of human users to the feedback from the backend — a user might very well misinterpret the feedback handed to them. EdgeDroid 1.0 mimics the operation of human-in-the-loop applications by replaying recorded traces of sensory input. This sensory information is then processed by the original compute process at the backend, generating feedback. However, this feedback is not processed by humans, but by a parameterizable model of human reaction. Through synchronized time tracking at the different processing points of the application, EdgeDroid 1.0 allows for accurate measurements of key performance metrics such as the distribution of delays across the application pipeline. Analysis of these metrics can be performed down to the individual input sample, allowing us to zoom into the internal model of the application under consideration. Thus, EdgeDroid 1.0 allows us to illuminate the many latency trade-offs existing at the level of the infrastructure, as well as the level of the application. It can also be used for debugging and validation, by comparing the expected execution flow of a particular trace with the actual flow during the benchmarking. To the best of our knowledge, this experimentally-driven benchmarking approach is the first one towards experimental performance characterization and potential optimization of human-in-the-loop applications

The rest of the paper is structured as follows: Section 2 presents some background on human-in-the-loop applications. Section 3 discusses the general approach taken with EdgeDroid, while Section 4 exposes the implementation details for EdgeDroid 1.0. We show the value of the tool through use case analysis in Sections 5 and 6, before discussing future work and concluding in Section 7.

2 BACKGROUND

Human-in-the-loop applications are novel applications aiming to seamlessly integrate into the lives of users and provide real-time, context-aware information.

Given the wide range of applications which fall under this concept, we have chosen to focus our initial efforts on one particular category: task-guidance wearable cognitive assistance (WCA) [2]. We have chosen this type of application for two reasons: one, their relative simplicity in terms of execution flow, and two, the already well-established existing body of work [2, 3, 7]. Task-guidance WCA applications aim to guide users in the execution of a task by monitoring user actions and providing real-time instructions, usually through wearable sensors and gadgets such as the Google Glass platform. They have many potential use cases including training and assistance for professionals performing complex tasks. Imagine for instance a specialized technician performing field repairs on a complex piece of machinery. A task-guidance WCA application

could offer real-time guidance in this task, by analyzing a real-time video feed from the technician's head-mounted camera and providing step-by-step repair instructions.

Broadly speaking, task-guidance WCA applications (and human-in-the-loop in general) process a multitude of inputs in parallel, which are also usually continuous, multidimensional and time-sensitive, e.g. video and audio feeds. These inputs are passed to the computation backend, where they are processed in the pipeline depicted in Figure 1. The first step of the backend processing is detection, which acts as a filter for irrelevant inputs. For example, this step could consist of a computer vision detector which discards all frames for which the relevant features were not detected or which were below a set threshold. The remaining inputs pass on to the symbolic representation stage, where features are extracted and parameterized for subsequent computation. For video frames, this parametrization would usually convert the visual data into a matrix representation of the relevant features. This representation of the inputs then continues on to the task model, where the actual application logic resides, before finally passing through the feedback generation stage at which point human-parseable feedback is generated; for instance, animations and voice commands.

The task model of a task-guidance WCA is a parameterized representation of the task in question and the steps required to complete it. It can be represented as a Finite State Machine (FSM) $M\{S, E\}$, where S is a set of states and E is a set of edges connecting these states. Each state $s_i \in S$ represents a configuration the application could potentially reach in an arbitrary execution, and each edge $e_{i,j} \in E$ corresponds to the ability of the application to switch from state i to state j based on some user input. We make a distinction between the set of *steps* required to complete the task, S_s, and S, since the latter may also contain states which represent user mistakes in the execution of the task. Thus, if we call the set of errors S_e, we can further define $S := S_s \cup S_e$.

These formalisms are exemplified in Figure 2, which represents an arbitrary segment of a linear task-guidance WCA application. $s_i, s_j \in S$ represent sequential states in the execution of the task, with the edge $e_{i,j}$ symbolizing the unique correct way of transitioning between them. While in s_i and in the absence of inputs, the task model continuously provides instructions to the user on how to move to s_j. We will refer to this type of output as *positive* feedback, since it guides the user forward in the execution of the task. On the other hand, in the case of an erroneous input by the user, the task model moves to s_k^e, where it will constantly provide instructions until the error is corrected and normal execution can resume. This type of output directs the user to move backwards in the task model, and thus we will refer to it as *negative* feedback.

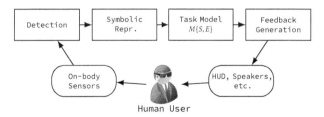

Figure 1: Pipeline of human-in-the-loop applications.

*We plan to make the EdgeDroid 1.0 benchmarking suite available as Free and Open Source Software and the recorded traces under a Creative Commons License.

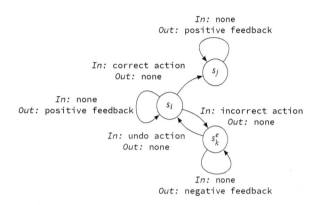

Figure 2: Segment of the internal task model of a linear task-guidance WCA.

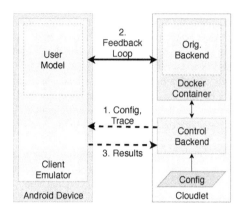

Figure 3: Architecture of the benchmarking suite.

3 APPROACH OF EDGEDROID

A system for benchmarking human-in-the-loop applications needs thus not only to be able to generate realistic, real-time inputs that follow the behavior of a real user but also be able to correctly react to feedback from the target application. The design of EdgeDroid 1.0 tackles these challenges from two angles. One, the generation of realistic inputs is delegated to a human user and provided to the suite in the form of a trace. This ensures that the raw sensory input data is realistic. Two, we propose the use of a *user model* to adapt the replay of the trace to the task model and current system conditions.

Concretely, our proposed approach works in the following way:

(1) A trace of the sensory inputs for an execution of the task is recorded. For example, for a video-based application, this trace could consist of a recording from the point of view of a user performing the task.

(2) This trace is *manually* segmented into the logical steps which lead to the completion of the task. In other words for the generation of the trace the task model must be known to the human operator.

(3) The benchmarking suite is then configured to use this trace and a certain number of virtual users. This is done through a TOML [11] configuration file on the backend.

(4) The benchmark is executed. Mobile devices are used to emulate users with wearable devices connecting to the *real cloudlet* over the *real network*. These devices replay the aforementioned trace, employing a *user model* to adapt the trace to changing system conditions and navigate the task model to reach the desired system state.

The extraction of metrics pertaining to the distribution of latencies across the application pipeline is the initial focus of EdgeDroid 1.0. We calculate latencies by synchronizing clocks across the system components and storing timestamps at key points in the feedback loop. These points include when input is sent and received, as well as when feedback is sent and received. We collect raw data about each input-feedback cycle between user and cloudlet, which includes metrics on all the major steps in the feedback loop: uplink, downlink and processing time, presence of feedback, payload size, and so on. This allows us to aggregate and obtain relevant statistics

in postprocessing, such as average delays per step or distribution of average delays across the feedback loop. We also store metadata regarding the task model with each measurement, for instance to link the state of the system with the current step being performed.

Note that this work does not directly target the *motion-to-photon* latency metric. This metric includes components such as sensing time and display time, which we do not consider. We also do not evaluate the accuracy of the applications themselves, as we consider them to be *black boxes*. The system *can* however be used to evaluate the trade-off between accuracy and performance, by comparing benchmarks performed using traces corresponding to different levels of accuracy.

4 IMPLEMENTATION OF EDGEDROID

The system architecture is composed of a *cloudlet*, where one or more instances of the target application run, and one or more client devices, as pictured in Figure 3. These correspond to completely unaltered instances of the target application, running inside containers [12]. This allows the suite to extract metrics from them while remaining transparent to the application. Here we also deploy the central component of EdgeDroid 1.0, the *control backend*.

The *control backend* is implemented in Python 3.6. Its main purpose is to act as a central point of control and configuration of the experiments, as well as to aggregate results. It controls the execution of the *application instances* and configures the experiment and client devices, while also collecting system metrics during the execution of the benchmarks. The experiments are configured in a centralized manner to simplify scaling. Backend and clients communicate over TCP, using a simple application-layer protocol which allows for remote configuration, transmission of the trace data and result data, and synchronization of clocks across the system. Note that although in the current implementation of the system the backend runs co-located with the *application instances* on the cloudlet, we plan on implementing functionality for distributed monitoring from a separate computer and/or across multiple cloudlets.

The *client emulators* correspond to Android applications with the main purpose of emulating a real user utilizing the target cognitive assistance application. The emulators achieve this by mimicking the operation of real clients, but instead of obtaining the input data from the on-board sensors, they extract it from the previously recorded

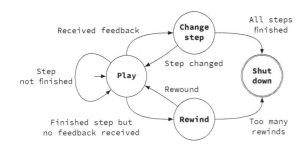

Figure 4: Preliminary user model.

Table 1: Hardware used in the experiments.

	CPU	Freq. [GHz]	Cores	RAM [GB]	Operating System
Cloudlet	Intel® Core™ i7–6700	3.4	4	32	Ubuntu 17.10, kernel v4.13.0
Clients	ARM® Cortex™–A53	1.3	4	2	Android 7.0

trace. They replay this data over the network to the *application instances* employing, as mentioned in Section 2, a *user model*, while simultaneously collecting client-side statistics and measurements.

The *client emulators* are remote-controlled — no interaction with a user is necessary once the application is initialized, simplifying large scale scenarios.

For our initial iteration of the EdgeDroid 1.0 benchmarking suite, we implement a preliminary user model, depicted in Figure 4, to run on the *client emulators*, designed with a linear task model in mind. In EdgeDroid 1.0, our model is that of a user who is totally impervious to poor system performance, and suffers no annoyance, fatigue, frustration, nausea or other shortcomings of real human users. This leads to a model of a user who responds in a precisely reproducible and deterministic manner to the same system stimulus every time. In the future, we envision building upon this approach with many more human-like user models that more accurately emulate attributes such as fatigue and annoyance.

Each *step* (i.e. segment) of the trace is played out to the backend until *feedback* is received. If no feedback is received before the end of the step, it is replayed a pre-configured numbered of times before completely aborting the task (i.e. giving up). Note that this model makes no distinction between positive and negative feedback, as both simply require the user to perform a specific action which is included in the trace.

5   USE CASES

In this section, we demonstrate the practical utility of EdgeDroid 1.0 through scalability measurements of real cognitive assistance application running on a cloudlet. The questions we aim to answer relate to the ability of EdgeDroid 1.0 to provide relevant and accurate metrics on the performance of human-in-the-loop applications running on edge computing infrastructure.

Of particular interest is the ability to provide information about scaling limits in terms of latencies at both micro and macro levels. We envision for instance a system designer performing the set of

experiments detailed in this section. The presented results would allow them to identify a bottleneck in performance. From that they could extrapolate to how they need to scale their system hardware to manage their expected load, or they might conclude that their wireless link is not good enough for the average case. They can also obtain real-time measurements to determine runtime measures to optimize performance, such as load balancing. On the other hand, imagine an application developer who wishes to optimize their application. EdgeDroid 1.0 would allow them to extract valuable information on where to focus their efforts.

We chose the open source *Gabriel* platform [2] running the LEGO assistance application [3] for our experimentation. This application guides a user through the assembly of a 2-dimensional LEGO model with visual and auditory instructions. This functionality can be observed online.[†] We chose it due to its maturity and stability compared to other applications which run on the *Gabriel* platform, as well as the relative simplicity of the task it performs. The application employs a straightforward, linear task model as the one described in Section 2. Each state only allows for one specific correct action by the user, and any other action triggers negative feedback until the application is reset to the previous state. The application has several different LEGO models to choose from, all of them roughly equal in complexity. The specific task chosen for the experiments detailed in this section consists of the assembly of a 7-piece LEGO model. The task has 7 distinct steps, and takes an average of approximately 2 minutes for a normal, untrained user to perform. The input to the task model consist of a video stream captured either by an Android phone or a Google Glass wearable.

It should be noted that the *Gabriel* platform by design always sends an acknowledgment for each input it receives, even when it is discarded, allowing us to measure latency for all inputs.

Table 1 shows the hardware and software specifications for the cloudlet and the clients. The components communicated through a single consumer-grade WiFi (IEEE 802.11n, 2.4 GHz) access point. We considered exclusively off-the-shelves hardware and software. To minimize interference during the measurements, we locked the wireless link to the least congested available channel.

To ensure statistical independence between each emulated user, the initialization of each client emulator was subject to a random delay within a predefined window of time at the beginning of each run. This way, the time between the start of any two clients in any repetition of the experiment is stochastic, leading to independent samples from each. We also only take into account metrics collected while *all* clients were concurrently running.

Our measurements were obtained from series of scenarios, repeated 100 times each. We performed three *optimal* scenarios with 1, 5 and 10 clients each, the signal strength of the WiFi link being an excellent −40 dBm. Next, a scenario where the 10 clients were moved to another room roughly 10 m away, thus degrading the network link to an average measured strength of −73 dBm. Finally, we studied an additional optimal single-client scenario focused on latency distributions and jitters within application execution path. This scenario is used to showcase the utility of EdgeDroid 1.0 for application developers.

[†]https://www.youtube.com/watch?v=7L9U-n29abg

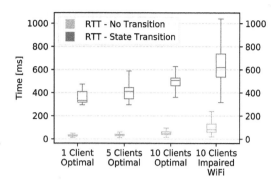

Figure 5: Comparison of round-trip-times for inputs that triggered a state transition in the task model versus inputs that did not.

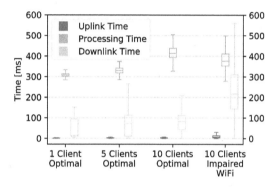

Figure 6: Distribution of latency across system components for inputs that triggered a state transition in the task model.

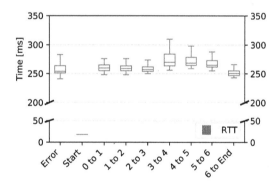

Figure 7: Round-trip-times for input-feedback cycles associated with state transitions in the internal task model for a single client connected over an optimal wireless link.

6 RESULTS

The results presented in this section provide valuable insights on both the system limits as well as on the application itself.

Figure 5 presents a comparison of the total measured round-trip-times (RTTs) both for inputs which caused a state transition and

inputs that did not. Next, Figure 6 shows a comparison of the distribution of latencies across system components for inputs that caused an internal state change in the task model of the application. We differentiate according to the three main components contributing to latency, namely *uplink* and *downlink transmissions*, and *backend processing*. Finally, Figure 7 depicts the distribution of RTTs for each transition in the internal task model for a single client connected over an optimal wireless link. These metrics were calculated by recording the measured input-feedback cycle delay corresponding to a change in state within the application. Thus, for instance, the measurements located at column "3 to 4" in the figure correspond to the aggregated round-trip-times for every input-feedback cycle corresponding to a change from state 3 to state 4 within the application task model, for the 100 repetitions of the scenario.

In the following discussion we will refer to inputs which triggered a transition in the task model as *feedback-rich inputs* and those that did not as *feedback-less inputs*.

For the analysis of these results, we will take into consideration the bound of 600 ms response time for step-by-step task-guidance derived by the authors of [3]. This bound marks the point after which further delays in the delivery of feedback to the user start to negatively affect user experience, and allows for a straightforward evaluation of the responsiveness of the system.

We will begin our analysis of the experiment results with Figure 5. These results present a stark contrast in the round-trip-times for inputs which cause a state transition versus inputs that do not, with RTTs for the former being up to an order of magnitude greater. It's worth mentioning though that responses to feedback-less inputs are invisible to the user, and are just included here as a sort of baseline to compare feedback-rich round-trip times with.

We can identify a pair of interesting effects in the scaling of the task-guidance WCA application. One, scaling behavior for the application seems to be linear with respect to the number of clients. Two, in the case of the impaired WiFi, the effect on the feedback-rich inputs is very pronounced, with the average of the RTTs for these inputs being over the previously discussed bound of 600 ms.

It is worth noting that already at just 10 clients the response times for feedback-rich inputs are very close to the bound. Looking at this through the lens of a an application developer, it could hint at a need for optimization of the later parts of the application pipeline, since RTTs for inputs which are discarded in the detection stage of the pipeline (i.e. feedback-less inputs) are still well below 200 ms.

EdgeDroid 1.0 allows researchers to zoom into specific components of the application feedback loop, as exemplified by Figure 6. From this figure it is clear that the main component which contributes to latency in the optimal case is the backend processing, further lending credibility to our previous comment on the need for optimization. Nevertheless, when the link quality decreases, the delays on the downlink start to overshadow the delays on the processing. Here, the downlink time sometimes almost reaches the ideal bound by itself. A system designer might then conclude from this that in order to be able to scale the application, their focus needs to be on improving the quality of the wireless link before increasing the processing power on the backend.

Finally, EdgeDroid 1.0 allows even more insights to be gained by homing in to individual steps in a task-guidance WCA. Consider

Figure 7. The figure shows clears spikes in latencies at the transitions from task state 3 to 4 and from task state 4 to 5, which could indicate to the application developer that these specific transitions are ripe for optimization.

7 CONCLUSIONS & FUTURE WORK

Benchmarking human-in-the-loop applications is hard, given their tight interaction with human users who complicate the scaling and repeatability of experiments. In this paper, we have presented a benchmarking suite for this type of applications, called Edge-Droid 1.0, capable of cutting out the need for users in performance evaluations. We achieve this by employing pre-recorded sensory input traces which we play over the network to the real application backend, employing a parameterized user model to react to feedback. We demonstrate its utility through a series of use case scenarios, from which we are able to extract metrics regarding latency both in regards to the application itself and the hardware stack. We believe the EdgeDroid 1.0 suite thus represents an important first step towards enabling inexpensive and low-complexity large-scale research on the scaling limits of this type of applications, a requirement for wide adoption of the technology.

Nonetheless, there is still future work to be done.

The user model presented in this paper is only preliminary, and we are currently conducting research in characterizing user behavior when interacting with WCA applications in order to present a more complete model in the future. As mentioned in Section 4, in EdgeDroid 1.0, our model is that of a user who does not suffer any of the shortcomings of real human users such as annoyance, fatigue, frustration, nausea. Rather, EdgeDroid 1.0 models a perfectly stoic user who is like an automaton and responds in a precisely reproducible and deterministic manner to the same system stimulus every time. Of course, no real human user is an automaton. In the future, we envision creating many versions of EdgeDroid (i.e., EdgeDroid 2.0, EdgeDroid 3.0, etc.) that embody more human-like user models that more accurately emulate attributes such as those mentioned above. Experimental validation of these human-like user models via user studies will be an important part of our future work.

We are also working on expanding the benchmarking suite to also work first with other types of Wearable Cognitive Assistance, and later with other categories of human-in-the-loop applications. Other types of WCA we will consider in future iterations of the tool include real-time task-assistance WCA applications (such as the Ping-Pong application described in [7]), which don't have a linear task model like task-guidance WCA and have tighter latency bounds and context- and information-providing WCA applications, for instance, applications which recognize faces and provide relevant social-media information related to that person. The latter also do not have a linear task model, but present more lax latency bounds.

ACKNOWLEDGMENTS

We thank Bobby Klatzky and Dan Siewiorek for many valuable technical discussions relating to this research. We also thank our shepherd, Wenjun Hu, and the anonymous reviewers for helping us improve the paper. This research was supported in part by the National Science Foundation (NSF), grant number CNS-1518865, the VINNOVA grant MERIT (2017–05232). Additional support was provided by Intel, Vodafone, Deutsche Telekom, Verizon, Crown Castle, NTT, and the Conklin Kistler family fund. Opinions, findings, conclusions or recommendations expressed in this material are those of the authors and do not necessarily reflect the view(s) of their employers or the mentioned funding sources.

REFERENCES

[1] D. Chatzopoulos, C. Bermejo, Z. Huang, A. Butabayeva, R. Zheng, M. Golkarifard, and P. Hui. 2017. Hyperion: a wearable augmented reality system for text extraction and manipulation in the air. In *Proceedings of the 8th ACM on Multimedia Systems Conference* (MMSys'17). ACM, Taipei, Taiwan.

[2] K. Ha, Z. Chen, W. Hu, W. Richter, P. Pillai, and M. Satyanarayanan. 2014. Towards wearable cognitive assistance. In *Proceedings of the 12th Annual International Conference on Mobile Systems, Applications, and Services* (MobiSys '14). ACM, Bretton Woods, New Hampshire, USA.

[3] Z. Chen, W. Hu, J. Wang, S. Zhao, B. Amos, G. Wu, K. Ha, K. Elgazzar, P. Pillai, R. Klatzky, D. Siewiorek, and M. Satyanarayanan. 2017. An empirical study of latency in an emerging class of edge computing applications for wearable cognitive assistance. In *Proceedings of the Second ACM/IEEE Symposium on Edge Computing* (SEC '17). ACM, San Jose, California.

[4] T. Bittmann. 2017. The edge will eat the cloud. *Gartner Research*.

[5] J. Flinn. 2012. Cyber foraging: bridging mobile and cloud computing. *Synthesis Lectures on Mobile and Pervasive Computing*.

[6] K. Ha, P. Pillai, W. Richter, Y. Abe, and M. Satyanarayanan. 2013. Just-in-time provisioning for cyber foraging. In *Proceeding of the 11th Annual International Conference on Mobile Systems, Applications, and Services* (MobiSys '13). ACM, Taipei, Taiwan.

[7] Z. Chen, L Jiang, W. Hu, K. Ha, B. Amos, P. Pillai, A. Hauptmann, and M. Satyanarayanan. 2015. Early implementation experience with wearable cognitive assistance applications. In *Proceedings of the 2015 Workshop on Wearable Systems and Applications* (WearSys '15). ACM, Florence, Italy.

[8] M. Satyanarayanan, P. Bahl, R. Caceres, and N. Davies. 2009. The case for vm-based cloudlets in mobile computing. *IEEE Pervasive Computing*.

[9] H. Al-Zubaidy, G. Dan, and V. Fodor. 2015. Performance of in-network processing for visual analysis in wireless sensor networks. In *Proceedings of the IFIP Networking Conference* (IFIP NETWORKING'15).

[10] S. Schiessl, H. Al-Zubaidy, M. Skoglund, and J. Gross. 2017. Finite-length coding in edge computing scenarios. In *Proceedings of the International Workshop on Smart Antennas* (ITG WSA '17).

[11] 2018. TOML. [Online; accessed 25. Sep. 2018]. https://github.com/toml-lang/tomll.

[12] 2018. Docker. [Online; accessed 14. Aug. 2018]. https://www.docker.com.

Paladin: Automated Generation of Reproducible Test Cases for Android Apps

Yun Ma[1,2], Yangyang Huang[2], Ziniu Hu[2], Xusheng Xiao[3], Xuanzhe Liu[2*]

[1]Tsinghua University [2]Peking University [3]Case Western Reserve University

yunma@tsinghua.edu.cn,{huangyangyang,bull}@pku.edu.cn,xusheng.xiao@case.edu,xzl@pku.edu.cn

ABSTRACT

Automated-test-generation tools generate test cases to enable dynamic analysis of Android apps, such as functional testing. These tools build a GUI model to describe the app states during the app execution, and generate a script that performs actions on UI widgets to form a test case. However, when the test cases are re-executed, the apps under analysis often do not behave consistently. The major reasons for such *limited reproducibility* are due to (1) backend-service dependencies that cause non-determinism in app behaviors and (2) the severe fragmentation of Android platform (i.e., the alarming number of different Android OS versions in vendor-customized devices). To address these challenges, we design and implement Paladin, a novel system that generates *reproducible test cases* for Android apps. The key insight of Paladin is to provide a GUI model that leverages the structure of the GUI view tree to identify equivalent app states, since the structure can tolerate the changes on the UI contents for an app behavior performed in different test executions. Based on the model, Paladin can search the view tree to locate the desired UI widgets to trigger events and drive the app exploration to reach the desired app states, making the test cases reproducible. Evaluation results on real apps show that Paladin could reach a much higher reproduction ratio than the state-of-the-art tools when the generated test cases are re-executed across different device configurations. In addition, benefiting from the reproducible capability, Paladin is able to cover more app behaviors compared with the existing tools.

KEYWORDS

Automated test generation; reproducible; Android app

ACM Reference Format:

Yun Ma, Yangyang Huang, Ziniu Hu, Xusheng Xiao, Xuanzhe Liu. 2019. Paladin: Automated Generation of Reproducible Test Cases for Android Apps. In *The 20th International Workshop on Mobile Computing Systems and Applications (HotMobile '19), February 27-28, 2019, Santa Cruz, CA, USA.* ACM, New York, NY, USA, 6 pages. https://doi.org/10.1145/3301293.3302363

1 INTRODUCTION

Recently, automated test generation has emerged as a promising approach to enabling various dynamic analyses of mobile apps, such as conducting functional testing, detecting security vulnerabilities, and checking compliance issues [7]. Researchers and practitioners have proposed many automated-test-generation (ATG) tools for Android apps [6] given the open-source nature and the high popularity of the Android platform. To generate a test case, these tools build a GUI model to represent the app states during the app execution, and generate a script that performs a sequence of interactions with the UI widgets and verifies outputs.

While the generated test cases can be used to explore the apps dynamically, the apps often do not behave consistently when the test cases are re-executed. That is, the test cases generated by the existing tools are limited in achieving **reproducibility**. Reproducibility of test cases is crucial in enabling various analyses of the app behaviors to improve app quality. For example, reproducibility enables developers to detect bugs and locate the causes as well as to conduct regression testing after fixing the bugs. But non-reproducible test cases will make it very difficult to re-trigger the bugs and perform regression testing since some behaviors may not be performed in some executions. Another application of reproducible test cases is to execute the same test cases on different device configurations to detect compatibility issues.

In this paper, to investigate the reproducibility of the test cases generated by ATG tools, we first conduct a characteristics study on the existing ATG tools as well as the record-and-replay tools. Our study shows that the test cases generated by the state-of-the-art tools are limited in achieving reproducibility even if the test cases can be used as the recorded scripts for replaying behaviors.

The major reasons are in two folds. On one hand, the dependencies of the backend services introduce non-determinism in app behaviors and outcomes. For example, a news app may randomly prompt ads on the news reading page, leading to slight changes in the page layout. As a result, the test cases generated when the page does not have ads may not be re-executed when the ads are prompted. On the other hand, the open nature of Android has led to a large number of devices with various configurations, which is known as the fragmentation issue [10]. For example, different devices have different sizes and resolutions of the screen, and different Android versions may render the same page in different ways. As a result, test cases generated on one device configuration may behave differently when they are re-executed on other device configurations.

To address the issues, we present Paladin[1], a novel system to generate reproducible test cases for Android apps. Our key insight is that for a specific app behavior, while service dependencies and device differences may cause differences on the UI contents, the structure of the view tree remains almost the same. Based on this insight, Paladin encodes the complete structure of the view tree in the model rather than just considering the UI contents. As such,

*Corresponding author.

HotMobile '19, February 27–28, 2019, Santa Cruz, CA, USA
© 2019 Association for Computing Machinery.
ACM ISBN 978-1-4503-6273-3/19/02...$15.00
https://doi.org/10.1145/3301293.3302363

[1]Paladin is publicly available at https://github.com/pkuoslab/Paladin

Table 1: Characteristics study of automated-test-generation and record-and-replay tools.

Tools	State Equivalence	UI Widget Location
Automated-Test-Generation (ATG) Tools		
AppDoctor	GUI Content	Coordinates
Collider	Event Handler	N/A
CrashScope	GUI Content	Coordinates
JPF-droid	Method Invocation	Resource ID, Name, Label
PUMA	GUI Feature Vector	Coordinates
Droidbot	GUI Content	Coordinates
Stoat	String Encoding of View Tree	Widget Indexes
Record-and-Replay Tools		
RERAN	N/A	Coordinates
VELERA	Visual Perception	Coordinates
Mosaic	N/A	Coordinates, Scale
Barista	Widget Existence	Resource ID, XPath
ODBR	N/A	Coordinates
SPAG-C	Image Comparison	Coordinates
MonkeyRunner	N/A	Coordinates
Culebra	GUI Content	Resource ID, Text, Content Description

our model can precisely identify equivalent app states and find the desired UI widgets, which can tolerate the differences of the UI contents. Additionally, since reproducing some behaviors may be required to trigger certain follow-up behaviors, the model enables test generation to reach higher coverage of app behaviors. In summary, Paladin has the following advantages:

- **Automated Test Generation.** Given an app under analysis, Paladin automatically explores it to build a GUI model, and generates a test case for each app state.
- **Reproducible Executions.** The generated test cases can be re-executed to ensure consistent app behaviors across different device configurations.
- **Better Behavior Exposures.** Paladin is able to run on complex commercial apps and cover more behaviors compared with existing ATG tools.

2 MOTIVATION & RELATED WORK

The execution of an Android app is driven by phone events, such as button clicks and SMS arriving. Thus, a test case for app analysis is represented as a sequence of phone events, where each phone event triggers a transition of app states. In this paper, we consider only the UI events such as click and scroll, which are triggered explicitly by user interactions. System events such as message notifications and network connections are left for future work. Besides, we take into account the GUI states, which focus on the UI layouts and widgets that are perceivable by users. We define that a test case of an app is reproducible if the app could perform consistent behaviors to reach the same states when the test case is re-executed in different device configurations, including the original device configuration where the test case is generated and other device configurations. Here, we regard the device configuration as the device model and Android version.

Based on the above definitions, reproducibility can be achieved if all the events in a test case are triggered in an expected order and produce the desired app states. This brings two problems to be solved, state equivalence and widget location. On one hand, how to identify equivalent app states should be designed carefully. Considering only the UI contents is likely to cause state space explosion, and considering only the page classes (i.e., activities on Android) is

not enough to reproduce the desired behaviors. More importantly, the changes caused by the backend-service dependencies and the Android fragmentation issue must be considered for driving the app to a desired UI state and interacting with the desired UI widgets such as buttons.

Before presenting our design, we first make a characteristic study to investigate the current support of generating reproducible test cases. Based on a recent survey on Android testing [9], we select 7 ATG tools of which the generated test cases are reported to be reproducible. We also select 8 record-and-replay tools from the same survey to study whether they can be integrated with the existing ATG tools to achieve reproducibility by using the generated test case as the recorded script. We focus on the state equivalence and the UI widget location adopted by these tools. Table 1 summarizes the analysis results.

2.1 State Equivalence

Most ATG tools consider two app states as equivalent ones if they have identical GUI contents. Obviously, such a strict definition would easily cause state explosion on today's complicated apps. For example, due to the non-deterministic behaviors caused by backend-service dependencies, the UI content varies slightly (e.g., pop-up ads on side bar) even when the same sequence of events are triggered, producing a daunting number of states for one page. Collider defines a state as a combination of registered event handlers and transitions as execution of event handlers. JPF-droid examines method invocations to verify states. Theoretically, method or handler invocations are more suitable than GUI changes to detect equivalent states for app exploration. But it requires instrumentation on the source code or byte-code level to emit events that indicate changes in the program state, which is difficult for complicated commercial apps. PUMA constructs a GUI feature vector and uses the cosine-similarity metric with a user-specified similarity threshold to identify equivalent states. Stoat encodes the string of the GUI view tree as a hash value to distinguish states. The problem is that the feature vector and the string encoding cannot easily adapt to different device configurations.

4 out of 8 record-and-replay tools do not specify state equivalence precisely. VELERA uses human visual perception to judge the test results, which is impractical for large-scale analysis. Culebra uses the GUI content to identify equivalent states, suffering from state explosion as discussed before. SPAG-C uses image comparison to identify equivalent states. However, image comparison is very susceptible to slight GUI changes such as different font styles and color settings.

2.2 UI Widget Location

There are 10 out of the total 15 examined tools that use the coordinates to locate widgets. However, considering only the absolute position of UI widgets is incapable of reusing test scripts on the devices with different screen resolutions. It is also error-prone for the GUI changes caused by different responses from backend services. Mosaic uses a series of scalings and normalizations to map coordinates between platforms. However, UI widgets do not simply scale linearly with screen dimensions. Some apps rearrange and even hide UI widgets based on the screen resolution. JPF-droid and Culebra take resource ID, label texts, and content descriptions into consideration. But UI widgets often share these properties, making it difficult to precisely locate the desired widgets. Barista uses XPath selector to locate UI widgets since the GUI view tree can be mapped to an XML document. But widget classes that constitute the XPath tags may differ in different Android versions. Stoat locates UI widgets by object indexes, which are likely to change under different device configurations.

In summary, test cases generated by the state-of-the-art tools are limited in achieving reproducibility even if the generated test cases can be used as the recorded scripts for record-and-replay tools.

3 APPROACH

The key insight of Paladin is that the structure of the GUI view tree of a specific app page remains almost the same regardless of the changes of the contents and layouts when a test case is re-executed in different device configurations. Therefore, we use the complete structure of the GUI view tree to build a structure-preserving model for identifying equivalent app states and locating UI widgets precisely. We next describe the details of the fundamental design of equivalent state identification and UI widget location.

3.1 State Equivalence

In Android, all the UI widgets of an app page are organized in a GUI view tree, similar to the DOM tree of a web page. After the app page is rendered, the view tree can be retrieved via UI Automator [5], which is a tool provided by the Android SDK. Figure 1(a) shows an app page which contains a text, a button, and an image button. Figure 1(b) shows an excerpt of the retrieved view tree. We can see that the text and the button are organized in a linear layout, and the linear layout together with the image button are organized in another linear layout. Formally, a view tree is represented by a tuple $VT = \langle N, E \rangle$. Here, N is the set of view nodes, of which some are directly exhibited on the page (the text node, button node, and image button node) and the others are used to organize the layout (the two linear layout nodes). $E \subset N \times N$ represents the parent-child relationship between nodes, where $e(n_1, n_2) \in E$ if n_1 is the parent node of n_2.

We propose to use the structure of the GUI view tree to identify equivalent app states. This design is inspired by the empirical fact that the view trees of GUIs produced by the same app behavior often share the similar structures, but different app behaviors typically result in different view trees. For example, the pages that show the details of different restaurants have the same structure, but the pages showing restaurant details and those showing a list of restaurant search results are obviously different in the structure of the view tree. Moreover, the rendered pages produced by a specific app behavior have similar view trees across different device configurations. Therefore, using the structure of the view tree to identify equivalent states can address the fragmentation issue.

In order to rapidly compare the view trees and identify the differences between two view trees, we encode each node of the view tree into a hash value and maintain a hash tree. The hash value of the root node can be used to distinguish app states. The hash function should meet two requirements. On one hand, the hash values should be different for view trees whose structures are different. On the other hand, given two view trees which have slightly

(a) An app page   (b) Excerpt of the GUI view tree

Figure 1: An example of a view tree.

differences, it should be efficient to find the differences in the structure based on the hash values. To meet these two requirements, we design a recursive bottom-up algorithm to compute the hash value of each node as shown in Algorithm 3.1. The algorithm accepts a view node r as input. If r has children nodes (Line 5), we use the algorithm to calculate all the hash values of its children recursively (Lines 7-9). Then, the algorithm sorts r's children based on their hash values to ensure the consistency of the structure hash value (Line 10), since a view's children do not keep the same order every time. Later, we concatenate the children's hash as $r.hashString$, and return the hash value of $r.hashString$ (Lines 11-15). If r does not have children nodes, the result is only the hash value of r's view tag and resource ID (Line 18). Given the root node of the view tree, the algorithm returns a hash value, which can be used to identify equivalent states.

```
Input: View r
Output: Structure Hash h
1 function TreeHash(r)
2   if r.InstanceOfWebview() then
3   |   r.setChildren ← r.parseHTML()
4   end
5   if r.hasChildren() then
6   |   children ← r.getChildren()
7   |   foreach c ∈ children do
8   |   |   c.hash ← TreeHash(c)
9   |   end
10  |   children ← SortByHash(r.getChildren())
11  |   r.hashString ← ""
12  |   foreach c ∈ children do
13  |   |   r.hashString ← r.hashString + c.hash
14  |   end
15  |   return hash(r.hashString)
16  end
17  else
18  |   return hash(r.viewTag + r.resourceId)
19  end
```

Algorithm 3.1: Computing the hash value of a view node.

This encoding method can be extended to Web elements as well. Since there is a plenty of hybrid apps which use HTML in WebView to display GUIs, we also incorporate the Web elements inside WebView component into the view tree (Line 3) rather than treating the WebView as a leaf node. So our model is applicable for hybrid apps.

Due to the non-determinism in app behaviors, the GUI may change in certain parts when the same sequence of events are triggered, and a trivial GUI change may result in a totally different hash value. For example, when a test case that explores the news page is re-executed, a notification about the news update may appear on the top of the screen. Since it is only a trivial GUI change and does not influence the majority of the other functionality, we should tolerate this difference and consider it to reach the expected state. Therefore, in order to make the model adaptive to changes, we design a structural similarity criteria. Given a computed GUI state triggered by an event, only when the similarity difference between the GUI's state and our stored state is above a threshold, we would regard it as a new state. Algorithm 3.2 shows how the similarity score is computed.

The algorithm accepts two view nodes and a threshold as inputs. If the two view nodes share the same hash value, their structures are the same, so the similarity equals 1 (Lines 2-4). Otherwise, there must be some differences between them. So we enumerate the children of these two nodes, and compute the similarities of the children nodes (Lines 9-17). To reduce the complexity, we will stop traversing if any pair of children nodes exceed the threshold (Lines 12-15). The similarity score is twice the number of nodes that are considered as the same divided by the total number of nodes including the two view nodes and all of their descendant nodes (Line 18).

Input: View s, View t, threshold τ
Output: Structural Similarity sim
1 **function** Similarity(s, t)
2 **if** $s.hash = t.hash$ **then**
3 | **return** 1
4 **end**
5 $hits \leftarrow 0$
6 **if** $s.tag = t.tag$ **then**
7 | $hits \leftarrow hits + 1$
8 **end**
9 **foreach** $sc \in s.getChildren()$ **do**
10 | **foreach** $tc \in t.getChildren()$ **do**
11 | | $tmp \leftarrow Similarity(sc, tc)$
12 | | **if** $tmp > \tau$ **then**
13 | | | $hits \leftarrow hits + tmp * tc.count$
14 | | | $break$
15 | | **end**
16 | **end**
17 **end**
18 **return** $2 * hits/(s.count + c.count)$

Algorithm 3.2: Structural similarity of two view trees.

3.2 Locating UI Widget

To ensure the reproducibility of test cases, we also need to precisely locate the UI widgets to trigger the desired events during test-case execution. Under such a condition, when a generated test case is re-executed, each event can be triggered at the same UI widget. Based on the GUI model designed above, a UI widget is represented using the hash values from the root node to the node of the UI widget. We summarize 3 cases in Figure 2 to illustrate the problems of locating UI widgets when the view tree of the same page is changed. Consider an example view tree shown in Figure 2(a). Assume that the leaf node with the dashed border line is to be located. Figure 2(b) shows Case 1, where there is a change on the black node (e.g. android.view.View in Android 5.1 is replaced by android.view.ViewGroup in Android 6.0+ instead). Figure 2(c) shows Case 2, where a widget is appended as a new leaf node (e.g. ads pop up in the current page). Figure 2(d) shows Case 3, where a deletion of irrelevant leaf node (e.g. settings to not display some UI widgets). In all these three cases, the view tree is changed. As a result, the recorded hash values could not be used to locate the corresponding UI widgets.

We design a heuristic search algorithm to locate a UI widget. As shown in Algorithm 3.3, it accepts a widget of the current view tree, a widget of the recorded view tree, the hash list of the target widget to be matched, and the current index in the hash list as input. When the index is equal to the size of the hash list, the algorithm returns

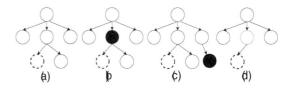

Figure 2: Cases of locating widgets.

(Line 3). Otherwise, it first checks whether the children of the current widget contains the next hash value. If yes, the algorithm will recursively go down to check the corresponding child widget (Line 9). If not, it would exclude the intersection of the children of current widget and the recorded widget to narrow down the search space, and try to recursively go down to check the unmatched child widgets (Line 12-18). For Case 1, since a substitution of a non-leaf node would not change the hash value of the node, we can still locate the recorded widget. However, for Case 2, the hash value of the root node changes after adding a new leaf node, which is equal to the hash of concatenation of all the children's hash value. The algorithm will detect that one child of the current node contains the next hash value (Line 7) and finally locate the widget. As for Case 3, all of the hash values change before reaching the target widget after deleting a leaf node. The algorithm will fail to check the next recorded hash value in Line 7 and jump to Line 12. Then, the algorithm will filter two children of current view that can be mapped to the recorded view and choose the middle child to explore, where it can precisely find the recorded widget.

Input: Current Widget cv, Recorded Widget rv, Hash List L, Index i
Output: Target Widget tw
1 **function** LocateWidget(cv, rv, L, i)
2 **if** $i = L.size()$ **then**
3 | **return** $cv.hash = L[i]?cv : null$
4 **end**
5 $children \leftarrow cv.children()$
6 $rv' \leftarrow rv.children().get(L[i + 1])$
7 **if** $children.has(L[i + 1])$ **then**
8 | $cv' \leftarrow children.get(L[i + 1])$
9 | $widget \leftarrow LocateWidget(cv', rv', L, i + 1)$
10 **end**
11 **else**
12 | $children' \leftarrow rv.children()$
13 | **foreach** $child \in (children - (children \cap children'))$ **do**
14 | | $widget \leftarrow LocateWidget(child, rv', L, i + 1)$
15 | | **if** $widget != null$ **then**
16 | | | $break$
17 | | **end**
18 | **end**
19 **end**
20 **return** $widget$

Algorithm 3.3: Locating a specific UI widget.

4 IMPLEMENTATION

We implement Paladin based on the standard Android SDK without requiring any instrumentation on the Android system or the app. Therefore, Paladin can be launched on any Android device and can work for commercial apps. Paladin consists of three main components: explorer, test generator, and executor interface. Given an app under analysis, the explorer first explores the app behaviors to construct the GUI model. Based on the model, the test generator is used to generate a test case for each state in the model. Each test case could be re-executed to reproduce the corresponding app state. The bottom layer of Paladin is the executor interface, which is responsible for connecting with the device to retrieve GUI information and execute commands. The details of each component are as follows.

Explorer exercises the app behaviors under a certain search strategy and builds the GUI model. Our current implementation adopts the most common search strategy, depth-first search. Nonetheless, Paladin can be easily integrated with other search strategies. For each state, we extract all the UI widgets that listen to events, and then systematically trigger the events of each widget. Next, we check whether the event brings the app to an equivalent state by comparing its structural hash value with all the other states in the model. If a new state is identified, we continue to apply the exploring algorithm on the new state. When the exploration on one state terminates, the app will backtrack to the previous state, continuing exploration.

Test Generator generates test cases for the states in the model. For each state, we try to find paths from the entry state of the model to the target state. This can be done by a standard breadth-first search. Starting from the target state, we enumerate every potential state path, and sorts them by their length. The shortest path is used to generate the test case.

Executor Interface communicates with the app execution environment to retrieve information and trigger events. We use UI Automator to retrieve the GUI view tree of app pages and execute ADB commands to trigger events. For web pages in WebView, we use Chrome Remote Debugging protocol to retrieve the DOM tree and trigger DOM events.

5 EVALUATION

In this section, we evaluate Paladin by answering two research questions: 1) How effective can Paladin ensure the app behaviors to be reproduced when the generated test cases are executed under different environments? 2) By encoding the view trees, could Paladin automatically generate test cases to cover more behaviors of real apps, especially complex commercial apps?

5.1 Reproducibility

According to our characteristics study in Section 2, the state-of-the-art ATG tools cannot generate reproducible test cases to run on different device configurations. As a result, to study the first research question, we compare Paladin with two record-and-replay tools, Monkeyrunner [4] which uses coordinate to locate widgets, and Culebra [2] which uses widget attributes to locate widgets.

We select five commercial apps from diverse categories but with the common feature of heavy dependencies on backend services so that the GUI contents and layouts are likely to change when the test cases are re-executed. Specifically, WeChat is one of the most popular instant messaging apps all over the world. QQreader is a reader app which often releases new novels on its home page. Picfolder is a tool app used to manage photos. EasyLoan is a financial app with frequently updated loan information. Missfresh is an electrical business app that regularly update recommended goods.

We run Paladin on each app for 15 minutes to explore app behaviors. Then we select one state from each app, representing a specific behavior, and generate a test case for the selected state. The selected state should be reached by performing at least 3 UI

interactions. Then we manually record the same UI interactions with Monkeyrunner and Culebra, generating the corresponding test scripts.

In order to investigate the reproducibility of generated test cases under different environments, we re-execute each test case in four scenarios. 1) Base line: each test case is executed on the same device where it is generated. We use the Nexus 6 with Android 7.1 OS, which has a 5.96-inch screen size and 2560x1440 resolution, to generate the test cases. 2) Across device models: each test case is executed on a Samsung S4 with Android 7.1 OS, which has a 5.0-inch screen size and 1920x1080 resolution. 3) Across Android OSes: each test case is executed on another Nexus 6 but with Android 5.0 OS. 4) Time evolving: each test case is executed on the same device where it is generated but after one day from the time when the test case was generated.

We use the reproduction ratio to measure the reproducibility, which is computed as the ratio of the correctly executed UI interactions over the number of recorded UI interactions during recording. Figure 3 shows the comparison results.

Under the same environment (Figure 3(a)). Both Paladin and Monkeyrunner can successfully execute all the test cases in selected apps. Culebra can only successfully execute cases in 2 apps (Wechat and QuickLoan) and totally fails to execute the test case of QQreader because Culebra highly relies on widget id and text descriptions. For example, the test case for QQreader is to open a novel and configure a different font. The home page of QQreader displays the reading percentage of each novel and thus changes from 0% to 2% after the initial record, resulting Culebra fails to identify the entry.

Across device models (Figure 3(b)). Monkeyrunner fails to perform correctly across device models because it considers only the coordinates of widgets. Culebra performs better than Monkeyrunner, but is still severely interfered by its dependencies on the widget id and the text descriptions. Paladin almost successfully executes all the test cases.

Across Android versions (Figure 3(c)). Paladin and Monkeyrunner perform equally well, but Paladin works much better in WeChat than Monkeyrunner. Culebra fails to replay most of the cases. The main reason is the minor differences of view structures found in different Android OSes.

Time evolving (Figure 3(d)). Paladin successfully executes all test cases, showing strong adaptive capacity to slight GUI changes. Monkeyrunner fails in QuickLoan, because a popup advertisement has changed the location of one widget slightly. Culebra behaves the worst due to extended changes in GUI.

5.2 Coverage

To study the second research question, we compare Paladin with three ATG tools in terms of coverage on app behaviors. Two tools are chosen from the study made by Choudhary et al. [6] where we tried all the surveyed tools but only Monkey [1] and PUMA [7] can work at the current commercial apps. We also choose a very recent tool Stoat designed by Su et al. [8], which is reported to be more effective than the state-of-the-art techniques.

We select two sets of Android apps for evaluation. One is from the open-source apps used in the study of Choudhary et al. [6]. We filter the apps with only one activity for which the ATG tools can easily reach very high coverage. After filtering, 22 apps are remained. The other set is from the most popular apps on Wandoujia, which is

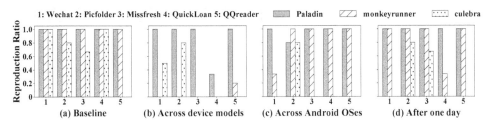

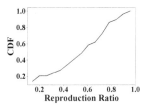

Figure 3: Comparison results of reproducibility.

Figure 5: Reproduction ratio of 72 apps.

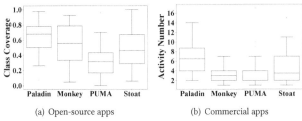

(a) Open-source apps   (b) Commercial apps

Figure 4: Comparison results of behaviors coverage.

a leading Android app marketplace in China. We tried 235 most popular apps to obtain 50 apps on which all the comparison tools can run. Actually, Paladin and Monkey can run all the 235 apps, but PUMA and Stoat can run only part of them. Such a result indicates the better compatibility of Paladin for complex commercial apps.

To quantify the behaviors coverage, we use the class coverage reported by Emma [3] for open-source apps. For commercial apps, we use the activity number counted from the logcat utility, which is a log tool provided by Android SDK. We deploy each tool on a dedicated Nexus 6 smartphone (4-core 2.7GHz CPU and 3GB LPDDR3 memory), and run all the four tools simultaneously on each app. We set one hour as the timeout for exploring an app.

Figure 4 shows the comparison results of behaviors coverage. For open-source apps, Figure 4(a) shows that Paladin reaches a higher coverage (68% in the median case) than the other ATG tools (56% of Monkey). Meanwhile, Paladin's structure-preserving model helps to eliminate the extreme deviations, resulting in a smaller standard error of the coverage distribution. Figure 4(b) shows that Paladin performs much better in commercial apps than the other tools. Paladin can explore 6.5 activities in the median case while the median number of explored activities of the other tools are below 4. Such a result can be attributed to the higher complexity of commercial apps and thus demonstrate the practical usage of Paladin. In fact, due to complex app behaviors, it is hard to judge whether such a coverage result is better enough, especially for commercial apps. We plan to manually explore the apps and compare the coverage in our future work.

Finally, we study how high percentage the generated test cases are reproducible on the same device. Since Monkey uses GUI content to distinguish states, one-hour exploration generates too many test cases which are impossible to enumerate. PUMA and Stoat has not provided interfaces to re-execute test cases so far. As a result, we study only Paladin. We execute the test cases generated for the 72 apps, and manually check whether the app reaches the same state as the one when the test case is generated. Assume that a GUI model consisting of n states is constructed by exploring an app, and the generated test cases can reproduce m states. Then the reproduction ratio is calculated by $\frac{m}{n}$. Figure 5 shows the distribution of the reproduction ratio among the 72 apps. The median reproduction ratio is 56.9%, meaning that 56.9% of test cases generated for an app can be re-executed to reproduce the same app behaviors.

6 CONCLUSION

This paper makes a first-step effort to automatically generate reproducible test cases for Android apps. We design and implement Paladin to achieve the goals of automated test generation, reproducible executions, and better behavior exposures. The key design of Paladin is to leverage the complete structure of the view tree to identify equivalent app states and locate UI widgets. Compared with the state-of-the-art tools, test cases generated by Paladin can be executed across different device configurations. In future work, since mobile devices are now supporting more pervasive tasks [11] leading to more origins of non-determinism in app behaviors, we plan to comprehensively study the non-deterministic app behaviors and enable the analysis of them.

ACKNOWLEDGMENTS

We thank our shepherd Alastair Beresford and anonymous reviewers for their feedback and suggestions. This work was supported by the National Key R&D Program under the grant number 2018YFB1004800, the National Natural Science Foundation of China under grant numbers 61725201, 61528201, 61529201, the Beijing Municipal Science and Technology Project under the grant number Z171100005117002, and China Postdoctoral Science Foundation.

REFERENCES

[1] 2018. Application Exerciser Monkey. https://developer.android.com/studio/test/monkey.html.
[2] 2018. Culebra. https://github.com/dtmilano/AndroidViewClient/wiki/culebra.
[3] 2018. EMMA code coverage. https://sourceforge.net/projects/emma/.
[4] 2018. Monkeyrunner. https://developer.android.com/studio/test/monkeyrunner/index.html.
[5] 2018. UI Automator. https://developer.android.com/training/testing/ui-automator.
[6] Shauvik Roy Choudhary, Alessandra Gorla, and Alessandro Orso. 2015. Automated Test Input Generation for Android: Are We There Yet?. In *Proc. of ASE 2015*. 429–440.
[7] Shuai Hao, Bin Liu, Suman Nath, William G. J Halfond, and Ramesh Govindan. 2014. PUMA: programmable UI-automation for large-scale dynamic analysis of mobile apps. In *Proc. of MobiSys 2014*. 204–217.
[8] Ting Su, Guozhu Meng, Yuting Chen, Ke Wu, Weiming Yang, Yao Yao, Geguang Pu, Yang Liu, and Zhendong Su. 2017. Guided, stochastic model-based GUI testing of Android apps. In *Proc. of ESEC/FSE 2017*. 245–256.
[9] Mario Linares Vásquez, Kevin Moran, and Denys Poshyvanyk. 2017. Continuous, Evolutionary and Large-Scale: A New Perspective for Automated Mobile App Testing. In *Proc. of ICSME 2017*. 399–410.
[10] Lili Wei, Yepang Liu, and Shing-Chi Cheung. 2016. Taming Android fragmentation: characterizing and detecting compatibility issues for Android apps. In *Proc. of ASE 2016*. 226–237.
[11] Zuwei Yin, Chenshu Wu, Zheng Yang, and Yunhao Liu. 2017. Peer-to-Peer Indoor Navigation Using Smartphones. *IEEE Journal on Selected Areas in Communications* 35, 5 (2017), 1141–1153.

IoT Maps: Charting the Internet of Things

Peter Shaw
School of Computing and Communications
Lancaster University
Lancaster, U.K.
p.shaw@lancaster.ac.uk

Mateusz Mikusz
School of Computing and Communications
Lancaster University
Lancaster, U.K.
m.mikusz@lancaster.ac.uk

Petteri Nurmi
University of Helsinki &
Lancaster University
Lancaster, U.K.
p.nurmi@lancaster.ac.uk

Nigel Davies
School of Computing and Communications
Lancaster University
Lancaster, U.K.
n.a.davies@lancaster.ac.uk

ABSTRACT

Internet of Things (IoT) devices are becoming increasingly ubiquitous in our everyday environments. While the number of devices and the degree of connectivity is growing, it is striking that as a society we are increasingly unaware of the *locations and purposes* of such devices. Indeed, much of the IoT technology being deployed is invisible and does not communicate its presence or purpose to the inhabitants of the spaces within which it is deployed. In this paper, we explore the potential benefits and challenges of constructing *IoT maps* that record the location of IoT devices. To illustrate the need for such maps, we draw on our experiences from multiple deployments of IoT systems.

CCS CONCEPTS

• **Human-centered computing** → **Ubiquitous and mobile computing**.

KEYWORDS

mobile computing; internet of things; map schemas

ACM Reference Format:
Peter Shaw, Mateusz Mikusz, Petteri Nurmi, and Nigel Davies. 2019. IoT Maps: Charting the Internet of Things. In *The 20th International Workshop on Mobile Computing Systems and Applications (HotMobile '19), February 27–28, 2019, Santa Cruz, CA, USA.* ACM, New York, NY, USA, 6 pages. https://doi.org/10.1145/3301293.3302375

1 INTRODUCTION

The Internet of Things (IoT) is growing rapidly with an estimated 23 billion connected devices deployed worldwide in 2018 [28]. These devices range from expensive infrastructure components, such as actuators in smart cities, through to low-cost commodity devices such as radio frequency beacons (e.g. iBeacons). Deployment strategies for such IoT devices range from carefully controlled large-scale

rollouts with significant organisational support through to ad-hoc deployments by individuals. While the number of devices, and the degree of connectivity is growing, it is striking that as a society we are increasingly unaware of the *locations and purposes* of such devices. In keeping with Weiser's vision of technology that fades into the background, much of the IoT technology being deployed is essentially designed to be invisible. This lack of awareness both limits the services that can be provided and raises concerns for users and system owners.

Fully harnessing the capabilities of IoT deployments while avoiding potential disadvantages, e.g. related to privacy and security concerns, requires knowledge about available devices, their locations, and capabilities. In other words, IoT devices should be *mapped*. While there have been previous attempts at cataloguing IoT devices (e.g. [14]) these have mostly focused on registering networked devices without providing detailed information about the locations and capabilities of devices. In this paper, we explore the potential benefits of constructing comprehensive maps of IoT devices, identifying key research challenges and describing partial solutions to these issues. To illustrate the need for such maps, we draw on our experiences of deploying multiple IoT systems. We make three contributions:

(1) We highlight the importance of producing and maintaining maps of the IoT using illustrative examples drawn from real-world case-studies.
(2) We present an example map schema designed to capture data on a broad class of IoT devices, and highlight some remaining challenges.
(3) We discuss the challenges in populating and maintaining maps of the IoT.

Overall, we aim to stimulate new work by the mobile computing community to begin to create general purpose IoT maps.

2 USE CASES FOR IOT MAPS

2.1 Overview of Case Studies

We motivate the need for IoT maps by highlighting three case studies drawn from our previous research.

Using Maps for Personalisation of Smart Spaces. Personalisation in the context of the IoT and smart spaces evokes privacy concerns. For the digital signage personalisation system 'Tacita', a deployment which has motivated our work, privacy was a primary focus at an architectural level [5]. Typical display personalisation systems require viewers to install applications that transmit their preferences to personalisable displays [16] – enabling displays to observe and track viewers and therefore imposing a significant privacy risk. In contrast, Tacita relies on users downloading maps of nearby displays. The detection of user proximity to displays is determined on the user's device, and requests to personalise content on nearby displays are issued accordingly.

Supporting Privacy Awareness. Future pervasive computing environments are likely to include large numbers of sensors such as cameras and microphones embedded in the physical environment and capable of capturing personal data. Such data can be used for a wide range of applications ranging from augmented cognition through entertainment to personalised advertising. In previous work, we found indications that user attitudes to sensing and data collection in smart environments depends highly on the intended purpose [27] – security was deemed the most acceptable while applications that appeared to only benefit the collector (e.g. for personalised ads) were widely disliked. Interestingly, participants were strongly opposed to any form of covert data collection and highlighted the importance of the ability to determine the nature of data collection taking place in any given space. Maps can be used as a technique that allows users (and applications) to identify instrumented spaces.

While using maps requires manual effort and does not protect users against deliberate covert surveillance it does provide a mechanism for owners of physical spaces to inform occupants of the data capture. We created a prototype application in which maps could be downloaded to a smartphone, using regions to represent areas of surveillance with an associated list of devices (e.g. cameras). Additional data about regions can also be included such as: size of regions, legal agreements and their time validity periods, devices in use, and the owner of the data collected. Upon approaching a region, users were presented with a notification listing devices in use and offering an option to accept the data collection (suppressing future notifications for the same region) or decline (providing an opportunity for future work on surveillance consent).

Instantiating Cloudlets for Privacy Preservation. Spaces are increasingly often equipped with IoT sensing and processing capabilities, potentially capturing sensitive data about individuals present in the space. Privacy mediation is an approach allowing individuals to control and mediate the captured data using Cloudlets before it is released beyond the immediate physical area [26]. For example, in the context of smart meeting rooms that consist of microphones and video cameras capturing events taking place in the space, users can configure privacy mediators to prevent or limit the amount of data collected. In order to ensure that privacy mediation takes place at the point at which the users enter the space, the corresponding Cloudlets need to be ready – imposing the requirement for detecting users before entering the space. This can be achieved through the specification of 'trigger zones', a separately monitored region purely serving the purpose of instantiating appropriate processes prior to the user entering smart space. In maps, active regions of data capture, locations of individual sensors, and trigger zones can be defined separately in the form of geo-fences or

proximity-based location descriptions, in addition to configuration parameters to support privacy mediation.

2.2   Example Implementation

We implemented all of the use cases as part of a common demonstrator system consisting of three core components: a map generator, a map repository, and mobile clients. The map generator is a simple tool that creates a map of IoT devices using a common schema based on a set of source lists that hold information on the devices available, their locations (in the form of proximity-based locations using iBeacon identifiers and their absolute locations in latitude/-longitude) and capabilities. The maps created are stored within the map repository that serves as a centralised storage and distribution space. Within the map repository, we support the storage of multiple versions of a single map supporting different scenarios and deployment stages. Mobile clients can access the map repository to retrieve specific maps and use the information within the map to instantiate functionalities. For example, we developed a mobile phone application that utilises 'trigger zones' to prepare geo-fences and track the user's location in order to instantiate appropriate cloudlets for privacy preservation, or in order to request personalised content on displays nearby.

3   MAP SCHEMAS

Currently no standardised solution for IoT maps exists. In this section we present an example of a partial solution that we adopted to support the privacy mediator use case.

3.1   Example of IoT Mapping

We designed a map schema to support privacy mediation using cloudlets (fig. 1). The schema consists of three high-level entities: *unique identifier*, *meta*, and *domains*. The meta objects consist of the global description of the map including its temporal validity (in the form of start and expiration dates), the publication date of the map and its version. The domains object consists of a list of active areas of data capture that are owned by the same entity (e.g. a commercial organisation). Domains provide the name of the organisation, the API end-point for privacy mediation requests at the organisational level, and a list of data capture zones in which sensors and devices can capture potentially privacy invasive data. Each data capture zone consists of lists of regions, trigger zones and capabilities. Regions specify the geographical locations or boundaries of the space in which data capture is taking place. Such locations can be described, for example, by specifying circular regions (latitude, longitude and radius) or proximity-based locations (based on Bluetooth Low Energy beacons). Trigger zones represent descriptions of monitored areas which, when entered by the user, trigger an immediate notification to the backend system. Similar to regions, trigger zones can be described using geo-fences or proximity-based location descriptions. Capability objects define the available mediation services of the data capture zone, such as audio and video processors in the context of smart meeting rooms. Each capability is described by a universally unique identifier object, a human-readable name, and a list of supported cloudlet applications – in this case representing privacy mediators. Each cloudlet application consists of an object that defines the application programming interfaces used to notify the service of the user's presence in the data capture area (callback_url), a URL to the user-facing configuration interface, and a set of additional metadata objects including the name of the cloudlet application, an icon and a URL to the homepage.

3.2 Further Considerations

We note that whilst we aimed that our proposed map schema can be reused in different domains, a generalised schema that goes beyond the support of privacy mediation leads to a number of challenges that need to be considered.

2D vs 3D. Maps have traditionally represented two dimensional top down perspectives of the world with some extensions in recent years to support the three-dimensional modelling of structures in prominent cities. With the increased popularity of indoor mapping and tracking, we will likely see a growing demand to model more complex structures. In our proposed map schema, we currently follow a two-dimensional approach, ignoring the altitude of active regions and trigger zones. Supporting three-dimensional models of the world introduces challenges regarding representation, visualisation and interaction. We note that some of these challenges, however, have been addressed with systems such as Building Information Modelling (BIM) that are designed to provide digital representations of places and structures for planning and construction purposes [7].

Access Control. Our map schema assumes that users have full access to the data stored within the map. However, in some cases certain sections of a map may be considered confidential and may require access restrictions. Supporting such access control will likely add a new layer of complexity to the map schema definition in order to supply detailed information on access permissions for individual users or groups. We note that initial work has been carried out to incorporate security features (e.g. access control lists) in the context of BIM [18].

Moving Objects. Traditionally, mapping has been used to represent stationary devices and structures such as buildings and sensors embedded in the environment. However, modern IoT devices are often mobile and move frequently within and across spaces (e.g. wearable IoT sensors). The challenges for representing moving objects within a map lie particularly in the processes to maintain and report frequent location updates (e.g. at the level of seconds, minutes or hours) – and are highly depended on the location technique that has been chosen to describe the location of moving objects.

Indoor vs. Outdoor. While outdoor mapping and location tracking is well established, indoor location tracking is an active area of research and imposes a number of challenges regarding reliability and accuracy of location tracking techniques [4]. Researchers have already worked on utilising existing Wi-Fi infrastructure to support indoor location tracking and on improving the accuracy of such tracking techniques [15, 19]. However, in order to support commercial-grade applications, the wide deployment and adoption of accurate indoor location tracking techniques and appropriate maps of IoT devices that are situated indoors will become an important challenge in future.

Single Common Map vs. Bespoke Maps. Our example schema was mostly bespoke to our systems with attempts at generalisation

```
{
  "id":"0db4c16a-f225-4a71-8e05-fbb7d4619c99",
  "meta":{
    "description":"Cloudlets",
    "start_date":"01/10/2018",
    "expiration_date":"02/10/2019",
    "publication_date":"01/10/2018",
    "map_version":"1.2",
    "agreement":"n/a"
  },
  "domains":[
    {
      "name":"Company Office",
      "server":"https://example.com/
          privacy_mediator_request",
      "data_capture_zones":[
        "use_capturezone_as_triggerzone":false,
        "regions":{
          "circular_regions":[
            {
              "lat":"41.367149",
              "long":"-37.580631",
              "radius":"30m"
            }
          ]
        },
        "trigger_zones":{
          "circular_regions":[
            {
              "lat":"41.367149",
              "long":"-37.580631",
              "radius":"50m"
            }
          ],
          "proximity_beacons":[
            {
              "beacon_major":"10",
              "beacon_minor":"5",
              "beacon_type":"iBeacon",
              "beacon_uuid":"41fbe746-8e66-46a2
                  -95bd-a1e1fb2b0783"
            }
          ]
        },
        "capabilities":{
          "uuid":{
            "cloudlet_id":"company-meeting-room
                -5",
            "cloudlet_name":"Meeting Room 5"
          },
          "cloudlet_apps":[
            {
              "name":"Privacy Mediator",
              "callback_url":"https://example.
                  com/tacita_callback",
              "description":"Mediates sensors on
                  behalf of the user.",
              "icon_url":"https://example.com/
                  privacy_mediator_logo.png",
              "homepage":"https://example.com",
              "config_url":"https://example.com/
                  config"
            }
          ]
        }
      }
    ]
  }
}
```

Figure 1: Example JSON map used for proximity triggered cloudlet provisioning.

(e.g. supporting generic 'capabilities' that can represent privacy mediation and personalisable display applications at the same time). It is unclear if a 'one map fits all' approach is desirable, or even possible in the context of mapping 'the IoT'. However, designing bespoke map schemas would likely lead to a large number of heterogenous maps that become unusable beyond their original context – or incur a heavy cost to be integrated into other contexts.

We note that the set of challenges presented is not exhaustive and that a number of other challenges are likely to emerge as more research is conducted regarding the design and implementation of generalisable mapping schemas – potentially leading to new IoT mapping standards.

4 POPULATING MAPS

The population and maintenance of maps is a further challenge in our proposed approach. Maps can be populated from three key sources: (i) authorities, (ii) ordinary users, and (iii) data provided by infrastructures. Based on these available sources, we provide a set of example population techniques that can be applied in order to create and maintain maps of the IoT.

Authoritative. The obvious solution is to employ an authority (e.g. system administrator or owners of spaces) that collects and supplies information about available IoT devices. The main advantage is that the map is likely to have a high accuracy, and capabilities of the devices can be easily identified. The main drawback is that the collection of required information can be laborious, particularly if large IoT deployments have to be mapped from scratch. Additionally, IoT devices present in the same space may be owned by distinct authorities, leading to only partially complete IoT maps of spaces. Nevertheless, authoritative maps are likely to serve as starting points for IoT maps, but should not be interpreted as absolute ground truths.

An example application for the authoritative approach is the 'Using Maps for the Personalisation of Smart Spaces' use case in which the locations, capabilities and interfaces of personalisable displays (and other devices) are populated by a trusted entity that controls the deployment, and made accessible in the form of a centrally hosted map.

Crowdsourcing. In the crowdsourcing approach, a number of regular users provide the necessary data to create maps, akin to OpenStreetMap. This reduces the burden of a dedicated party responsible for populating a map. However, information quality is likely to decrease as users may not be aware of the device capabilities and exact locations. Similarly, coverage may suffer as users fail to identify all relevant devices. The usefulness of crowdsourced information can be potentially increased using a two-phased approach where the information provided by users is verified in a second phase conducted by domain experts or through automated analysis (e.g. by comparing multiple reports of the same device, or based on computer vision techniques whereby images taken by users are matched against a device database to populate the relevant parts of the map schema).

Crowdsourcing may be the most appropriate population technique for the 'Supporting Privacy Awareness' use case. Users could collectively report IoT sensors that are visible in the environment and, for example, collect sensitive information about individuals (e.g. cameras and Bluetooth Low Energy beacons used to support indoor location tracking). The crowdsourced map then serves as a foundation to make other individuals aware of the potential data collection taking place in the space.

Infrastructure Sensing. The population of a map can also be delegated to the infrastructure itself. For example, analysis of electric signals has been used to identify home appliances [10] and network traffic signatures have been used to identify IoT devices in a specific administrative network [22] removing the need for human effort. However, the underlying sensing techniques may not generalise sufficiently across diverse environments and provide only limited device information.

The 'Instantiating Cloudlets for Privacy Preservation' use case is an example in which cloudlet components (e.g. cameras and microphones that can be found in smart meeting rooms) can automatically report their capabilities (e.g. the support of video and audio recordings) and their location to a centralised map generator – reducing the need for manual updates and enabling the support of larger-scaled deployments.

Opportunistic Crowdsensing. Opportunistic crowdsensing can be seen as a halfway point between user- and system-generated maps. The idea is to use sensors available on mobile devices to identify IoT devices as users navigate across spaces. For example, magnetometers are capable to identify signatures of specific displays [23] and could be used to detect other IoT sensing devices [8]. However, this approach would also identify non-IoT devices, such as elevators or ticketing machines [9], i.e. leading to noisy results. Additionally, the signatures of devices would depend on the orientation of the magnetometer relative to the device [3]. Discovered devices can then be associated with locations either by the user manually supplying the location (suffering from the need to label locations) or automatically using appropriate localisation techniques (potentially resulting in biases in estimated locations [17]).

Similarly to crowdsourcing, the use of opportunistic crowdsensing can be an appropriate technique to gather information on IoT devices for privacy awareness purposes (as described as part of the 'Crowdsourcing' approach).

We note that in our demonstrators we adopted the authoritative approach as system and available client components are owned and managed by a single entity. Of course, the choice of the map population technique is highly dependent on use cases and requirements. In some cases, for example, the use of multiple techniques can provide a number of benefits including the ability to verify and validate existing maps.

5 DISCUSSION

In addition to populating IoT maps there are a number of additional challenges that can be identified:

IoT Maps for Connected Devices. Existing research on mapping IoT devices has predominantly focused on identifying connected devices such as networked IoT temperature and air quality sensors. While useful, these systems only provide a partial solution as they do not consider the full spectrum of sensing capabilities, actuators, and interfaces connected IoT devices incorporate. The use cases presented are examples of applications where full-fledged maps are required.

Maintenance. IoT maps are only useful if they accurately capture the devices that are currently available in the environment. This requires active maintenance, particularly within larger administrative regions. Infrastructure sensing could potentially be used to identify "anomalies" that serve as starting points to investigate changes in the environment. Note that this covers both the appearance of new devices, and disappearance of existing ones.

Global or local scale. Existing initiatives to catalogue IoT devices tend to focus on providing a *global* index of IoT devices. While having such a map would certainly be desirable, for many applications it is sufficient to have a *local* view that captures all available devices and their capabilities within a specific administrative region (e.g. a building or a room). Attempting to construct global-scale maps introduces unnecessary overhead – both regarding access and maintenance of such maps. Local solutions that describe IoT sensors and capabilities of instrumented environments in which users are currently present can be made more dynamic (making it easier for administrators and developers to provide updates) and therefore of higher quality to the user.

Proximity vs. Absolute Location. We recognise that locations (e.g. to describe regions, trigger zones and the actual location of sensor deployments) can be captured through a range of techniques – using relative or absolute descriptions. Depending on the location of sensors and actuators (e.g. indoor vs. outdoor), certain location techniques may be not sufficient or appropriate. We specifically proposed a map schema that is flexible to accommodate different location tracking technologies depending on the use case of the IoT device or service that is defined. Additionally, the flexibility allows us to model both stationary and portable IoT devices without the limitations of a specific localisation technology.

Not just points. While knowing the exact location is useful for some sensors and other objects, it is not always the only piece of geographical data that is useful. For example, the locations of the effective range of devices within an environment may also be of importance such as the field of vision of a video camera, or the maximum capture distance of microphones. We note that including additional regions and metadata is not a novel concept but often overlooked in current IoT maps.

Evaluation. The quality of mapping approaches are commonly assessed using measures such as freshness (or timeliness), coverage (or recall), and accuracy. However, these measures provide only a partial solution for IoT maps due to each device having multiple pieces of information that need to be captured. Indeed, coverage can refer to the fraction of devices or the total set of capabilities of devices. Similarly, freshness depends on whether the unit of assessment is a device or specific functionality. This suggests that new metrics for evaluating the quality of IoT maps will be required.

6 RELATED WORK

Many platforms have been proposed for solving the challenge of describing and cataloguing IoT devices, sensors, and services [6, 13, 20]. While having this data is clearly important, with no commonly

adopted standard many of these systems appear not to be used beyond the initial period of research. 'Thingful.net' is an example of a service that aimed to become the "Google of the IoT" [2], i.e. providing a search engine for IoT devices – yet at the time of writing objects listed appear to have not been updated in over a year. Many platforms tend to feature simplistic approaches to describe locations (longitude, latitude, and sometimes altitude) suitable for overlaying data layers on top of base maps. However, using different frames of reference (e.g. metric measurements in relation to an origin point) is not supported by these platforms. This limitation highlights that although the issue of mapping the IoT is not a new problem, additional work is required to converge on a standard and to ensure correct scoping of attempts to cataloguing the IoT.

User contributed data for maps is also an area that has seen much interest. An early example of this is 'War driving', the act of locating and recording geo-locations of Wi-Fi networks from a moving vehicle [1, 17]. More recently, OpenStreetMaps [11] is an example of a successful attempt to crowd source a base map and additional data layers of objects and places. Some weaknesses are still present when trying to employ this strategy. For example, it is unrealistic for users to report very frequent location changes of devices (e.g. every minute). In addition, a critical mass of users is required – the WikiBeacon service [25] appears to lack sufficient engagement to be considered a viable source of an up-to-date map of beacons around the world.

If user contributed data is not sufficient to build a map of the IoT strategies for automating the process will be required. While mapping of the outside world has recently reached a level of detail sufficient to support a wide range of applications, the mapping of indoor spaces are still lacking the higher level of accuracy these smaller scale areas require. Automated solutions infer indoor maps from the use of wearables that report movement traces [24] or in combination with accelerometer and magnetometers [29]. Another approach is to have a robot perform the mapping [21]. If indoor mapping and location tracking reaches sufficient accuracy for common commercial devices, we are likely to see a significant increase in applications and usage.

The value of maps of IoT devices in pervasive environments was perhaps best illustrated in the Active Bat project [12] that created models of smart spaces and tracked the movement of people and objects within these spaces. The Active Bat system even provided an API to enable applications to be developed that utilise the ability of spatial triggers.

7 CONCLUSIONS

In this paper we have highlighted reasons why mapping the IoT is an important area of research with potential benefits for multiple stakeholders. Despite its importance and significant prior work in the field of IoT, there are no standardised or widely adopted solutions to achieve such mapping. Developing appropriate solutions will require a coordinated effort from the research community – the challenges are diverse and we would anticipate a federated solution in order to accommodate the full range of mapping scenarios. It is also vitally important that any mapping technologies or repositories are open and not owned by any single entity.

Our concrete proposal for the way forward is that the community begins to develop a comprehensive set of requirements derived from a broad collection of use cases. These requirements can drive the selection of an appropriate set of open mapping technologies that can, initially, be tested in the context of a single use case or technology, e.g. mapping Bluetooth Low Energy beacons.

Drawing on our experience of deploying multiple IoT systems we hope to continue exploring the challenges in future works and encourage 'mapping the IoT' to be considered for its value and potential in future systems and services.

ACKNOWLEDGMENTS

This work is part funded by the UK EPSRC under grants EP/N028228/1 (PACTMAN) and EP/N023234/1 (PETRAS IoT Research Hub – Cybersecurity of the Internet of Things).

REFERENCES

[1] Hal Berghel. 2004. Wireless infidelity I: War driving. *Commun. ACM* 47, 9 (2004), 21–26.
[2] Jonathan Brandon. 2018. Thingful aims to be the Google of the Internet of Things. http://telecoms.com/206211/thingul-aims-to-be-the-google-of-the-internet-of-things/. (2018). Accessed: 2018-10-17.
[3] Jaewoo Chung, Matt Donahoe, Chris Schmandt, Ig-Jae Kim, Pedram Razavai, and Micaela Wiseman. 2011. Indoor location sensing using geo-magnetism. In *Proceedings of the 9th international conference on Mobile systems, applications, and services*. ACM, 141–154.
[4] Davide Dardari, Pau Closas, and Petar M Djuric. 2015. Indoor Tracking: Theory, Methods, and Technologies. *IEEE Trans. Vehicular Technology* 64, 4 (2015), 1263–1278.
[5] Nigel Davies, Marc Langheinrich, Sarah Clinch, Ivan Elhart, Adrian Friday, Thomas Kubitza, and Bholanathsingh Surajbali. 2014. Personalisation and privacy in future pervasive display networks. In *Proceedings of the SIGCHI Conference on Human Factors in Computing Systems*. ACM, 2357–2366.
[6] Suparna De, Tarek Elsaleh, Payam Barnaghi, and Stefan Meissner. 2012. An internet of things platform for real-world and digital objects. *Scalable Computing: Practice and Experience* 13, 1 (2012), 45–58.
[7] Chuck Eastman, Paul Teicholz, Rafael Sacks, and Kathleen Liston. 2011. *BIM handbook: A guide to building information modeling for owners, managers, designers, engineers and contractors*. John Wiley & Sons.
[8] Shane B. Eisenman, Emiliano Miluzzo, Nicholas D. Lane, Ronald A. Peterson, Gahng-Seop Ahn, and Andrew T. Campbell. 2010. BikeNet: A Mobile Sensing System for Cyclist Experience Mapping. *ACM Trans. Sen. Netw.* 6, 1, Article 6 (Jan. 2010), 39 pages.
[9] Moustafa Elhamshary, Moustafa Youssef, Akira Uchiyama, Hirozumi Yamaguchi, and Teruo Higashino. 2016. TransitLabel: A crowd-sensing system for automatic labeling of transit stations semantics. In *Proceedings of the 14th Annual International Conference on Mobile Systems, Applications, and Services*. ACM, 193–206.
[10] Sidhant Gupta, Matthew S. Reynolds, and Shwetak N. Patel. 2010. ElectriSense: Single-point Sensing Using EMI for Electrical Event Detection and Classification in the Home. In *Proceedings of the 12th ACM International Conference on Ubiquitous Computing (UbiComp '10)*. ACM, New York, NY, USA, 139–148.
[11] Mordechai Haklay and Patrick Weber. 2008. Openstreetmap: User-generated street maps. *Ieee Pervas Comput* 7, 4 (2008), 12–18.
[12] Andy Harter, Andy Hopper, Pete Steggles, Andy Ward, and Paul Webster. 1999. The Anatomy of a Context-aware Application. In *Proceedings of the 5th Annual ACM/IEEE International Conference on Mobile Computing and Networking (MobiCom '99)*. ACM, New York, NY, USA, 59–68.
[13] Sehyeon Heo, Sungpil Woo, Janggwan Im, and Daeyoung Kim. 2015. IoT-MAP: IoT mashup application platform for the flexible IoT ecosystem. In *Internet of Things (IOT), 2015 5th International Conference on the*. IEEE, 163–170.
[14] IoT Ecosystem Demonstrator Interoperability Working Group and Rodger Lea. 2013. *HyperCat: an IoT interoperability specification*. IoT ecosystem demonstrator interoperability working group.
[15] Kasthuri Jayarajah, Rajesh Krishna Balan, Meera Radhakrishnan, Archan Misra, and Youngki Lee. 2016. LiveLabs: Building In-Situ Mobile Sensing & Behavioural Experimentation TestBeds. In *Proceedings of the 14th Annual International Conference on Mobile Systems, Applications, and Services (MobiSys '16)*. ACM, New York, NY, USA, 1–15. https://doi.org/10.1145/2906388.2906400
[16] Rui José, Nuno Otero, Shahram Izadi, and Richard Harper. 2008. Instant places: Using bluetooth for situated interaction in public displays. *IEEE Pervasive Computing* 7, 4 (2008).
[17] Minkyong Kim, Jeffrey J Fielding, and David Kotz. 2006. Risks of using AP locations discovered through war driving. In *International Conference on Pervasive Computing*. Springer, 67–82.
[18] P. T. Kirstein and A. Ruiz-Zafra. 2018. Use of templates and the handle for large-scale provision of security and IoT in the built environment. (March 2018), 10 pages.
[19] Manikanta Kotaru, Kiran Joshi, Dinesh Bharadia, and Sachin Katti. 2015. SpotFi: Decimeter Level Localization Using WiFi. In *Proceedings of the 2015 ACM Conference on Special Interest Group on Data Communication (SIGCOMM '15)*. ACM, New York, NY, USA, 269–282. https://doi.org/10.1145/2785956.2787487
[20] Fei Li, Michael Vögler, Markus Claeßens, and Schahram Dustdar. 2013. Efficient and scalable IoT service delivery on cloud. In *Cloud Computing (CLOUD), 2013 IEEE Sixth International Conference on*. IEEE, 740–747.
[21] Ren C Luo and Chun C Lai. 2012. Enriched indoor map construction based on multisensor fusion approach for intelligent service robot. *IEEE Transactions on Industrial Electronics* 59, 8 (2012), 3135–3145.
[22] Markus Miettinen, Samuel Marchal, Ibbad Hafeez, N Asokan, Ahmad-Reza Sadeghi, and Sasu Tarkoma. 2017. IoT Sentinel: Automated device-type identification for security enforcement in IoT. In *Distributed Computing Systems (ICDCS), 2017 IEEE 37th International Conference on*. IEEE, 2177–2184.
[23] Rui Ning, Cong Wang, Chunsheng Xin, Jiang Li, and Hongyi Wu. 2018. DeepMag: Sniffing Mobile Apps in Magnetic Field through Deep Convolutional Neural Networks. In *2018 IEEE International Conference on Pervasive Computing and Communications, PerCom 2018, Athens, Greece, March 19-23, 2018*. 1–10.
[24] Damian Philipp, Patrick Baier, Christoph Dibak, Frank Durr, Kurt Rothermel, Susanne Becker, Michael Peter, and Dieter Fritsch. 2014. Mapgenie: Grammar-enhanced indoor map construction from crowd-sourced data. In *2014 IEEE International Conference on Pervasive Computing and Communications (PerCom)*. IEEE, 139–147.
[25] Radius Networks. 2018. WikiBeacon by Radius Networks. http://www.wikibeacon.org/. (2018). Accessed: 2018-10-18.
[26] Mahadev Satyanarayanan, Victor Bahl, Ramón Caceres, and Nigel Davies. 2009. The case for vm-based cloudlets in mobile computing. *IEEE pervasive Computing* (2009).
[27] Peter Shaw, Mateusz Mikusz, Nigel Davies, and Sarah Clinch. 2017. Using Smartwatches for Privacy Awareness in Pervasive Environments. *HotMobile 2017* (2017).
[28] statista. 2018. Internet of Things - number of connected devices worldwide 2015-2025). https://www.statista.com/statistics/471264/iot-number-of-connected-devices-worldwide/. (2018). Accessed: 2018-10-18.
[29] Yiguang Xuan, Raja Sengupta, and Yaser Fallah. 2010. Crowd sourcing indoor maps with mobile sensors. In *International Conference on Mobile and Ubiquitous Systems: Computing, Networking, and Services*. Springer, 125–136.

Freeloader's Guide Through the Google Galaxy

Joshua Adkins
University of California, Berkeley
Berkeley, California
adkins@berkeley.edu

Branden Ghena
University of California, Berkeley
Berkeley, California
brghena@berkeley.edu

Prabal Dutta
University of California, Berkeley
Berkeley, California
prabal@berkeley.edu

ABSTRACT

One of the largest impediments to pervasive sensing is ensuring equally pervasive network access. While we can create wireless sensors that last for years without human intervention, the network infrastructure to support their deployment requires planning, power, and maintenance. The potential for a crowd-based solution to this problem is ripe—ever pervasive smart phones have the hardware and connectivity to serve as ubiquitous mobile gateways—however the fragmentation of low power wireless protocols combined with the lack of incentive for users to sacrifice their own resources transporting others' data has made this approach untenable.

Through an "off label" use of Google's Physical Web and Nearby Notifications, it was possible to ignore these problems and exploit nearly the entire global population of Android phones to slowly transport sensor data to an arbitrary web server. This mechanism was enabled by default and transparent to the phone's user. On one hand, it served as an exciting opportunity to explore infrastructure-free wireless networking. In a one week deployment of five devices transmitting at 1 Hz, we were able to successfully transport 326 kB of data with an average data rate of 0.1–2.6 bps. This is slow, but sufficient for many applications such as environmental monitoring and sensor status reporting. On the other hand, a mobile operating system probably should not have enabled exfiltration of arbitrary data without a user's knowledge or consent. While Nearby Notifications has now been decommissioned, we examine security policy requirements for future systems that interact with nearby devices, and we envision a similar, intentional mechanism to allow data hitchhiking for the Internet of Things.

CCS CONCEPTS

• **Networks** → **Network experimentation**; *Mobile and wireless security*; *Mobile ad hoc networks*.

KEYWORDS

Physical Web, Gateway, Android, Data transport

ACM Reference Format:
Joshua Adkins, Branden Ghena, and Prabal Dutta. 2019. Freeloader's Guide Through the Google Galaxy. In *The 20th International Workshop on Mobile Computing Systems and Applications (HotMobile '19), February 27–28, 2019, Santa Cruz, CA, USA*. ACM, New York, NY, USA, 6 pages. https://doi.org/10.1145/3301293.3302376

HotMobile '19, February 27–28, 2019, Santa Cruz, CA, USA
© 2019 Copyright held by the owner/author(s).
ACM ISBN 978-1-4503-6273-3/19/02.
https://doi.org/10.1145/3301293.3302376

1 INTRODUCTION

Google deployed the largest standardized and widely available network for freely transporting extremely low-rate data from resource-constrained devices, realizing coverage of as much as 20% of the land area of the globe [10]. Interestingly, it is not clear whether they are aware of their accomplishment. The Nearby notification service [9], part of Google's Physical Web [6], aimed to facilitate interactions with physically close devices. However, it turns out that this same service, installed and automatically running on every Android smartphone between June 2016 and December 2018, could be used to ferry sensor data.

The desire for ubiquitous, seamless connectivity for sensor networks has remained unfulfilled for some time now. The research and industrial community has long explored a plethora of techniques for enabling low-cost data transport for deployed sensors, but while there are numerous MAC protocols and standards targeting resource-constrained devices, the reality is that no single leading standard has emerged. On top of this, reliable network deployments require system administrators to install and maintain gateways to provide coverage, an infrastructure requirement adding unwanted overhead to real-world applications.

One enticing solution to this infrastructure challenge is the smartphone, and there have been several proposals suggesting their use as gateways for pervasive sensors [5, 15, 18]. Phones go everywhere people go, contain low-power networking hardware, maintain near constant connectivity to the cloud through cellular infrastructure, and have human oversight to maintain their functionality. Unfortunately, we have never figured out how smartphone gateways would work in practice. Just using smartphones does not fix the problems with standardization, and users are hesitant to waste their precious battery and data limits to transport others' data. Furthermore, there is an underlying concern of transporting malicious data or leaking private information by acting as a gateway.

While these concerns have rightfully slowed the explicit adoption of personal smartphones for generic data transport, we leverage what was arguably an architectural bug in Google's Physical Web to explore the possibility of ubiquitous smartphone data transport. The mechanism relied on Nearby Notifications, a service which transported URL data contained in Bluetooth Low Energy (BLE) [2] beacons through HTTP GET requests to populate summary information about each device. Until December 2018, Nearby ran by default on nearly all Android phones with Bluetooth enabled. The amount of data transported was small, only 10 bytes at a time; and slow, only transmitting data when a phone transitioned from idle to active. But it resulted in a pervasive mechanism by which sensors could send arbitrary data through smartphones carried by over half of the population. This possibility allows us to explore 1) how well this data channel worked in practice, 2) the security implications of its existence, and 3) the opportunity to use smartphones as universal gateways moving forward.

In a one-week deployment of five devices around UC Berkeley's campus, we were able to transmit a total of 326 kB of data with an average data rate ranging from 0.1–2.6 bps. The channel had very low packet reception rates (PRR) ranging from 0 to 16%, and equivalently poor energy efficiency, but we were still able to receive data from sensors without any network deployment or management outside of a web server that was created to receive the HTTP GET requests. This transport mechanism would not have been a good choice for applications which need reliable, timely, or data intensive transport, but it may have been perfectly suited to many other applications such as low-rate environmental sensing, collecting metrics about the usage of buildings or trails, and reporting the status of sensors which are not currently networked.

In general, the only way to detect that a device was using your phone for data transport was by actively scanning for BLE packets that meet the Physical Web beacon specification. Furthermore, this service was enabled by default on Android phones, and the only way to stop your phone from being used was to turn off Bluetooth or explicitly disable the Nearby notification service. If viewed as a side channel for data exfiltration, this mechanism offers plenty of bandwidth to offload a key or password, and it would be particularly applicable for this use case given that a malformed BLE packet could be transported without any notification to the user. While architectural changes to the Physical Web could have significantly slowed down this method of data transport, and the notification service should not have performed HTTP GET requests without displaying them to the phone's user, it would be difficult to entirely stop the leakage of information from a beaconing sensor to its associated web server and still achieve the original goals of the Nearby notification service.

Between the original writing of this paper and its publication, Google announced the shutdown of Nearby Notifications due to the increasingly spammy nature of messages being received by users [1], and on December 6, 2018, the service was discontinued. Therefore, the transport mechanism reported in this paper is no longer functional. We do not believe, however, that this nullifies the findings of the work. Google still deployed the largest ad-hoc network for resource-constrained devices to date. Using this network was incredibly easy because it required only knowledge of BLE and HTTP, ubiquitous technologies in sensor networks and the web respectively. Finally, we were able to successfully transport a relatively large amount of data without over-utilizing the resources of any one phone individually. Looking forward, this leads us to imagine a world in which a data transport mechanism like this one is encouraged and nurtured, and explore solutions to the economic, standardization, and privacy concerns that might otherwise prevent a wide-scale crowd-based data backhaul.

2 BACKGROUND & RELATED WORK

First, we explore the background that lead to the Physical Web as it exists today. Then we explore the works that inspire and are benefited from opportunistic smartphone data transfer.

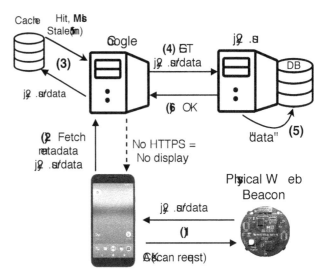

Figure 1: Architecture of Google's Physical Web and our transport mechanism. (1) In the Physical Web smartphones scan for Eddystone-compliant beacons using BLE and respond with a scan request when a beacon is received. **(2)** The phone requests that a Google server fetch metadata about the URL in that beacon. **(3)** If the server has the metadata for that URL cached, it will respond from its cache, **(4)** otherwise it will GET the URL from the remote server. **(5)** If that server is under control of a third-party, they can store the URL path as data and **(6)** respond with an OK. If the beacon and server do not use HTTPS none of this is displayed on a user's phone. To prevent caching of repeat data, some randomness 'r' can be appended into the URL path. This process was enabled by default on phones running Android 4.4 and newer through the Nearby notification service and occurs for a few seconds every time the phone transitions from idle to active.

Eddystone, Physical Web, and Nearby. For the last four years Apple and Google have been pushing to make the distributed set of devices and sensors that comprise the Internet of Things more scalable and interactive, and they have attempted to accomplish this goal by binding physical devices to web-based resources. In 2014, Google released the UriBeacon protocol, which enables BLE beacons to point to URLs [7]. UriBeacon was replaced by the Eddystone standard, which adds the ability to beacon unique IDs and telemetry data in addition to URLs [8]. In an Eddystone packet, which is what we use for this work, URLs can be up to 17 bytes, not including the protocol specification (e.g., http://).

The Physical Web project is a browser for physical devices which uses Eddystone beacons (along with other discovery protocols) to find and display relevant web content [6]. The architecture for the Physical Web is shown in Figure 1. In the Physical Web, the smartphone listens for Eddystone URL beacons, the contents of which are fetched from a Google server when the user requests. If the page is in the server's cache, it is sent to the user, otherwise it is fetched from the remote location then served to the smartphone and cached on the server for some period of time.

Nearby Notifications is a service which by default ran in the background on all phones running Android 4.4 or newer [9] starting in June 2016. If the user's Bluetooth was turned on, and Nearby was not manually disabled, it would perform a BLE scan every time the phone transitioned from an idle to active state (such as when the user wakes up their screen). Upon receiving an Eddystone beacon, it would fetch the metadata for the advertised URL using an HTTP GET request, displaying a notification which the user could click to open the website. If the Eddystone beacon did not conform to the Physical Web and Nearby security standards, the metadata would still be fetched from the remote server, but the beacon would not be displayed to the user. Other phones, such as iPhones, could still receive and use Eddystone beacons to find nearby devices, but they did not run Nearby Notifications.

In October, 2018 Google announced that it would shut down the Nearby Notification service due to spammy notifications appearing on users' phones, and in December, 2018 the service was stopped [1]. This means that notifications are no longer being pushed to users' smartphones about nearby devices and the fetching of metadata about nearby devices is no longer operating as a background service.

Mobile Phones as Gateways. The ubiquity of smartphones makes them a prime target for providing opportunistic connectivity to devices. Fürst et al. investigate the use of smartphones as access points for home appliances [5], guaranteeing that a user is present when communication occurs and alleviating some security concerns. Classic Bluetooth has been used to provide communication for devices in oilfields and offices [15]. The authors find that intentional visitation of sensors is often required given the limited range of Bluetooth. While some applications exist, a large area of research remains in determining what services smartphone gateways should provide to sensors, in creating policies for handling data flows, and in providing incentives to users that are providing this access [18]. Furthermore, little research has performed any at-scale evaluation of smartphones as gateways.

Applications of Ubiquitous Intermittent Networking. For low power sensors, getting internet connectivity is a difficult process. Maybe they are deployed along hiking trails with no WiFi to be found for miles [11, 17]. Maybe they are deployed throughout cities [3, 16], where networks are everywhere, but none of them are available for transporting your data. All of these locations are short on low-power connectivity but high on foot traffic. Data transfer through Physical Web beacons could breathe life into these applications by ubiquitously and cheaply communicating measurements. These ideas also connect strongly to delay tolerant networking [4]. While beacons may be unattended for long stretches, the eventual presence of a smartphone enables application data to be transmitted. While the explored networking channel is not delay tolerant, it may be possible to include delay tolerance as a feature of future smartphone gateways.

3 HOW DATA CAN HITCHHIKE

To transfer data through the Physical Web, we encode it into the Eddystone beacon URL. When an Android user wakes up their phone, the phone receives these beacons and requests the metadata for that URL from a Google server. If the metadata associated with that URL is not already cached, the server calls HTTP GET on the URL. The remote server can then extract data encoded in the path

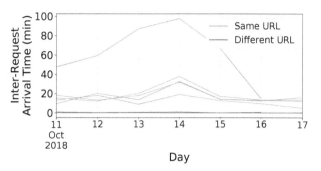

Figure 2: The daily average inter-request arrival time in minutes for devices beaconing the same URL vs rotating URLs. From this plot we see that nearly all beacons from rotating URLS result in requests to our server and we can estimate the amount of time until Google's servers considered a cached URL stale and fetched the page again from the remote server. We estimate this time to average around 15 minutes, but as high as 30 minutes on some days such as October 14th. We believe the beacon with very high inter-request arrival times to be an outlier due to a combination of caching and very low reception rate, not indicative of the actual cache refresh rate. To ensure repeated data gets to the remote server, beacons transmitting at 1 Hz with a 30 minute cache refresh rate, must include an 11 bit nonce with their data.

of the requested URL and respond to the request with arbitrary data. This process is shown in Figure 1. Notably, if the URL specified is not using the HTTPS protocol, then the metadata for this beacon/URL will not be displayed on the user's phone as it would have been for a valid Nearby Notification.

Therefore, to receive data through this mechanism all you need to do is set up a web server with a short domain name and record the paths of each request to this web server. Eddystone beacons can contain up to 17 bytes of URL data, and the shortest domain name we could reasonably purchase was j2y.us, leaving every beacon up to 11 bytes of payload.

Cache Prevention. To ensure that every beacon has the opportunity to hit our server, we must prevent Google's server from caching the URL. We were unable to find any way to do this from the server side, so instead we introduce a nonce to the URL.

To calculate the minimum length of this nonce, we first need to establish the cache refresh rate of Google's servers, as demonstrated in Figure 2. In the experiment we find that the inter-request arrival time for beacons sending the same URL is around 15 minutes, and confirm that it is significantly lower for URLs that are not repeated. At a 1 Hz transmission rate and a nonce overflow of 30 minutes to be conservative, 11 bits of nonce is required to prevent caching of repeated data. Subtracting this from our available payload, each beacon is capable of transmitting a little more than 9 bytes of data.

Acknowledgements and Adaptation. One of the largest downsides to this data channel is that it is unidirectional. Because data transport is largely based on foot traffic, this means that beacons spend significant periods of time transmitting with no smartphone present to transport their data.

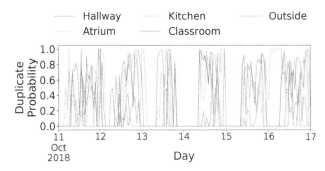

Figure 3: The probability of the same packet being received more than once by the server, every hour. High duplication probabilities indicate that the network could carry more capacity, and that beacons could take advantage of that capacity by transmitting faster than our 1 Hz transmission rate. Transmitting faster should lower the probability that two phones receive the same beacon. For our packet reception rate and throughput calculations we deduplicate the data, underestimating the maximum throughput.

To alleviate this, we propose using the "scan request" mechanism of BLE. Scan requests are responses to beacons that scanners transmit to request additional information from the device. While searching for Physical Web devices, Android phones automatically transmit a scan request for each beacon they discover. Beacons can use this scan request to accomplish two goals: 1) have some confidence that transmitted data will reach the remote server, and 2) adapt their transmission rate to better reflect the current phone density in an attempt to save energy.

Unfortunately, because scan requests from multiple scanners often conflict [12], waiting for a scan request to confirm data transmission may significantly reduce a beacon's data rate. To save energy, nodes could back off their transmission rate the longer they go without a scan request, then beacon very quickly on the first scan request they receive. For example, in an indoor, commercial setting, as long as the beacon does not slow its transmission so much they that it fails to detect a scan request early in the morning, this would allow it to save energy throughout the night and have higher data throughput during the day when phones are present.

4 EXPERIMENTAL RESULTS

To evaluate the channel capacity and packet reception rate we deploy 10 beacons around UC Berkeley's campus for one week. Deployments occurred in pairs, where one beacon in each pair is transmitting the same URL, and the other is transmitting an incrementing URL. Both of these beacons transmit at 1 Hz, and we log all requests received by the web server. Data analysis is only performed on the five beacons with incrementing URLs because the transmissions from the other beacons are often cached as explained in Section 3. Nodes are deployed in variety of locations, including a kitchenette, a heavily-used classroom, a hallway between offices, a small atrium, and an outdoor garden near a sparsely traveled path.

Duplicate packets. Because each incrementing URL is only transmitted once, we did not expect to receive a significant number of duplicate packets. Upon analysis we find that during periods of high

foot traffic there is a high probability that packets are duplicated. This was most likely caused by two phones receiving a packet at the same time and triggering a request from a google server before the URL from either request could be cached. This is effectively wasted network capacity; if the beacons were transmitting faster, then the probability that two phones receive the same beacon should be lower. The probability of duplicate packets over time is shown in Figure 3. We see that there are periods where nearly all packets are duplicated at least once, and often packets are duplicated multiple times. We would certainly see higher total throughput if we increased transmission rate, but because it is difficult to quantify the degree of increase, we remove all duplicate packets in the remainder of our analysis.

Packet reception rate. To measure the packet reception rate, we deduplicate the received packets as mentioned above. In Figure 4, we see packet reception rates that correlate with times that the respective spaces are occupied. The burstiness of packet reception rate indicates that back-off mechanisms based on scan requests could be highly effective, however we did not evaluate the impact of this policy experimentally.

Throughput. Because every packet carries the same amount of data and beacons are transmitting at a uniform rate, network throughput is a scalar multiple of the packet reception rate. We find average network throughput to range from 0.1 bps for the outdoor node to 2.6 bps for the heavily trafficked classroom, with other nodes averaging around 0.5 bps. This throughput does not reflect the reliable network throughput. In many applications, data redundancy or the scan request acknowledgment mechanism discussed in Section 3 would have to be introduced to ensure data reception, and this would reduce final data throughput for a network of this type.

5 DISCUSSION

Never before have we been able to crowd-source data transport through such a large percentage of the population. The idea that we could stick a random sensor nearly anywhere and eventually receive data from it is unprecedented. At the same time, the use of this service did present a security vulnerability, and similar vulnerabilities could easily be present in future services that interact with nearby devices, especially if they are enabled on a large number of smartphones by default. We therefore use this section both as an opportunity to examine potential lessons learned about security from this experiment, and to imagine a service such as this one with the necessary oversight and capabilities such that the benefits of universal data transport outweigh the security risks.

5.1 Safely Interacting with Nearby Devices

With the Nearby notification service now discontinued, we do not feel it necessary to explore the specific methods by which Google may fix the service, however we do believe analyzing the primary reasons why this could be used for data exfiltration is useful for future services interacting with proximal devices. At its core the Nearby notification service could be used for data exfiltration because 1) it was running en masse on smartphones without the knowledge of many users and 2) it was interacting with devices without clearly notifying the user of these interactions.

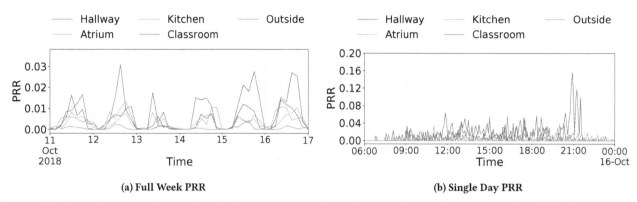

(a) Full Week PRR   (b) Single Day PRR

Figure 4: (a) The packet reception rate (PRR) plotted across a full week averaged over 3 hour intervals, and (b) the PRR plotted for a single day averaged over 5 minute intervals. From the PRR we can see that, as we expect, more highly trafficked areas successfully transmit more packets. In (a), the highest PRR is in the classroom during a homework/office hours session that fills up the room, and we see the sparsely traveled walkway consistently has the lowest PRR. While these are low packet reception rates, falling to zero during the middle of the night, all nodes successfully transmitted some packets each day, even during the weekend.

Even with the brief Bluetooth listening window on each phone and the caching implemented to limit the number of requests received by each device's web server, the sheer scale of all Android devices performing a specific task is powerful enough to result in significant data transport. This leads us to believe that Google should have used much stronger caching policies when implementing Nearby Notifications and more generally that the side effects of background services operating at this scale need to be more carefully considered. Other research has discussed the need to make peripheral interactions more apparent to a device's user [13, 14], and we believe this argument should extend to external devices, especially for interactions not explicitly initiated by the user.

On a more positive note, this experiment exposes the benefits of MAC address randomization. We at first hypothesized that this mechanism could have been used for low-infrastructure people-tracking by recording the MAC addresses of scan requests and then sending them through that same persons's smartphone. However, the BLE MAC address randomization present in newer versions of Android, rotates addresses quickly enough that this is not possible. It may have still been possible to scan for more permanent MAC addresses on another networking interfaces (such as the MAC addresses associated with a WiFi connection) and transport them over the proposed mechanism, but this would greatly increase the complexity of the system.

5.2   Envisioning a Crowd-Sourced Gateway

An important path forward is to address the core problems holding back the vision of a global, crowd-sourced gateway: compensation for used resources, security and privacy concerns, and a minimal but sufficient set of services for universal data transport.

Compensation. To compensate for used resources we imagine a global clearinghouse for transferred data. Data is shuttled from a user's phone, to their mobile service provider, then from their mobile service provider to the clearinghouse. To retrieve the data, entities must both verify their identity (most likely using existing PKI) and pay the going rate for data transfer, which can then be applied to directly to the bill of the user who transferred the data.

While rather complicated, a solution like this one could be almost entirely facilitated a large company like Google, Samsung, or Verizon. Also important, users need to be able to set limits as to how much data they transfer, and how much battery this can consume. Given the utility of even small amounts of sensor data, we do not expect either of these be technically limiting so much as necessary for providing users with the agency to enforce security and privacy constraints. Additionally, the amount of data transferred by these devices is small relative to the image and video heavy mobile browsing users do on a daily basis. Even if all 326 kB collected during this study had been transferred by a single phone, that user's costs would have been affected imperceptibly.

Security and Privacy. If users are transferring others' data, there will always be a chance for data exfiltration. Solutions to prevent it border on contradictory to the goal, however allowing users to audit the list of owners or domains for the data they have transferred is at least a step in the right direction. We also imagine encouraging users to create geofenced zones in which data should not be transported except from approved devices to prevent easy tracking of users in and around their homes. Secure facilities and corporate campuses would need to continue down the path of both active network scanning to eliminate threats and policies to turn off network interfaces or remove phones entirely. From a privacy perspective, any global service, through Google or otherwise, should continue operating as a proxy for requests so that owners of beacons can not identify the IP address or MAC address of a courier phone.

Architecture of Smartphone Gateway. A universal smartphone gateway could provide a full and capable networking solution for resource constrained sensors including reliable and bidirectional data transport, delay tolerance, time updates, and even phone-collected information such as location to help contextualize the data being transported. We explore the possibilities for these extra services in our prior work [18]. However, one of the largest impediments to realizing these services in practice is standardization, and the reason that this transport mechanism was so easy to implement was its use of well-understood interfaces such as BLE advertising and HTTP to transport the data. Even though this architecture only provided unreliable, unidirectional communication, it still can support a sufficient number of applications that a more intentional version may gain traction given a proper compensation scheme and transparency policy.

Moving forward, the use of a specific scan request packet or a BLE connection could be formalized to acknowledge successful custody transfer, and delay tolerance could be supported by simply waiting to forward data until a cellular signal is available. These two additions would add significant functionality and enable applications such as off-the-grid environmental monitoring without adding significant complexity. To enable bidirectional communication and end-to-end acknowledgment of data transport, we imagine an HTTP proxy service which utilizes BLE connections to send HTTP requests and return HTTP responses similar to that proposed in our prior work [18]. We again stress, however, that we believe the expansion of gateway services to support all or even a large portion of IoT applications is likely to make standardizing these services more difficult. Further, applications which need reliable or bidirectional communication are much more likely to find the opportunistic nature of a smartphone gateway lacking.

5.3 Ethics

As a final aside, we would like to briefly discuss our ethics in running this experiment. To start, we collected no human data or personally identifiable information; all requests to our server came directly from a Google server. Because we do not have identifiable human subjects, we are outside the scope of an IRB. We also note that the potential harms of our experiment are incredibly low, potentially non-existent. All Android phones were already running this feature, and there are already many beacons deployed around campus, so the traffic generated by our beacons is a fraction of the existing beacon traffic and should not impact battery life or data use of nearby phones. Finally, the ability of any entity to immediately use this feature upon submission was limited because it requires physically deploying new beacons or performing a firmware update on existing beacons, neither of which seem plausible at scale. Of course now the ability of someone to use this service maliciously does not exist due to its discontinuation.

6 CONCLUSIONS

The Physcial Web is envisioned and intentioned to support nearby intelligent spaces, bridging the gap between users and the devices around them. In practice, the Physical Web and Nearby Notifications was also the single largest network backhaul for low-power devices ever deployed, literally affording coverage everywhere people go. Now that Nearby Notifications has been discontinued, where do we go from here? We could view this as a now-patched security vulnerability, for both persons and property owners, noting that unwitting individuals may have been inadvertently supporting the exfiltration of data. Or, we could could choose to recognize this as a missed opportunity. By characterizing the impact of the current system and adding just enough capability for a wider set of applications, we could finally enable the dream of pervasive, low-power data backhaul.

7 ACKNOWLEDGMENTS

This work was supported in part by the CONIX Research Center, one of six centers in JUMP, a Semiconductor Research Corporation (SRC) program sponsored by DARPA. Additionally, this material is based upon work supported by the National Science Foundation under grant numbers CNS-1824277, DGE-1256260, and DGE-1106400, and NSF/Intel CPS Security under grant CNS-1822332.

REFERENCES

[1] Android Developers Blog. 2018. Discontinuing support for Android Nearby Notifications. https://android-developers.googleblog.com/2018/10/discontinuing-support-for-android.html. (25 Oct 2018).
[2] Bluetooth Special Interest Group. 2018. Bluetooth SIG. https://www.bluetooth.com/. (Mar 2018).
[3] Yun Cheng, Xiucheng Li, Zhijun Li, Shouxu Jiang, Yilong Li, Ji Jia, and Xiaofan Jiang. 2014. AirCloud: a cloud-based air-quality monitoring system for everyone. In *Proceedings of the 12th ACM Conference on Embedded Network Sensor Systems (SenSys'14)*. ACM.
[4] Kevin Fall. 2003. A delay-tolerant network architecture for challenged internets. In *Proceedings of the 2003 conference on Applications, technologies, architectures, and protocols for computer communications (SIGCOMM'03)*. ACM.
[5] Jonathan Fürst, Kaifei Chen, Mohammed Aljarrah, and Philippe Bonnet. 2016. Leveraging physical locality to integrate smart appliances in non-residential buildings with ultrasound and Bluetooth Low Energy. In *2016 IEEE First International Conference on Internet-of-Things Design and Implementation (IoTDI'16)*. IEEE.
[6] Google. 2017. The Physical Web. https://google.github.io/physical-web/. (Jun 2017).
[7] Google Inc. 2015. UriBeacon Open Source Project. https://github.com/google/uribeacon. (July 2015).
[8] Google Inc. 2017. Eddystone. https://github.com/google/eddystone. (Apr 2017).
[9] Google Inc. 2018. Nearby. https://developers.google.com/nearby/. (Oct 2018).
[10] GSM Association. 2012. Universal Access – How Mobile can Bring Communications to All. https://www.gsma.com/publicpolicy/wp-content/uploads/2012/03/universalaccessfullreport.pdf. (2012).
[11] Jyh-How Huang, Saqib Amjad, and Shivakant Mishra. 2005. Cenwits: a sensor-based loosely coupled search and rescue system using witnesses. In *Proceedings of the 3rd international conference on Embedded networked sensor systems (SenSys'05)*. ACM.
[12] Robin Kravets, Albert F Harris, III, and Roy Want. 2016. Beacon trains: blazing a trail through dense BLE environments. In *Proceedings of the Eleventh ACM Workshop on Challenged Networks (CHANTS'16)*. ACM.
[13] Zongheng Ma, Saeed Mirzamohammadi, and Ardalan Amiri Sani. 2017. Understanding sensor notifications on mobile devices. In *Proceedings of the 18th International Workshop on Mobile Computing Systems and Applications (HotMobile '17)*. ACM.
[14] Saeed Mirzamohammadi and Ardalan Amiri Sani. 2018. Viola: trustworthy sensor notifications for enhanced privacy on mobile systems. *IEEE Transactions on Mobile Computing* (2018).
[15] Unkyu Park and John Heidemann. 2011. Data muling with mobile phones for sensornets. In *Proceedings of the 9th ACM Conference on Embedded Networked Sensor Systems (SenSys'11)*. ACM.
[16] Rijurekha Sen, Abhinav Maurya, Bhaskaran Raman, Rupesh Mehta, Ramakrishnan Kalyanaraman, Nagamanoj Vankadhara, Swaroop Roy, and Prashima Sharma. 2012. Kyun queue: a sensor network system to monitor road traffic queues. In *Proceedings of the 10th ACM Conference on Embedded Network Sensor Systems (SenSys'12)*. ACM.
[17] Gilman Tolle, Joseph Polastre, Robert Szewczyk, David Culler, Neil Turner, Kevin Tu, Stephen Burgess, Todd Dawson, Phil Buonadonna, David Gay, and others. 2005. A macroscope in the redwoods. In *Proceedings of the 3rd international conference on Embedded networked sensor systems (SenSys'05)*. ACM.
[18] Thomas Zachariah, Noah Klugman, Bradford Campbell, Joshua Adkins, Neal Jackson, and Prabal Dutta. 2015. The Internet of Things has a gateway problem. In *Proceedings of the 16th International Workshop on Mobile Computing Systems and Applications (HotMobile'15)*. ACM.

Consumer Smart Homes: Where We Are and Where We Need to Go

Shrirang Mare, Logan Girvin, Franziska Roesner, Tadayoshi Kohno

Allen School of Computer Science & Engineering

University of Washington

Seattle, USA

{shri,lsgirvin,franzi,yoshi}@cs.washington.edu

ABSTRACT

Currently a variety of smart home systems are available from different vendors, who made different designs choices in how these systems operate, which in turn affect end users. A key question that we consider in this work is how these commercially available smart home systems differ in practice, what are the implications of those differences, and whether other design alternatives might be better. To answer these questions, we systematically evaluate seven popular smart homes and identify their underlying design choices around access control, privacy, and automation, and highlight the implications of those design choices for end users. We surface challenges and tensions for design choices around topics like security, privacy, usability, automation, and reliability, and we make design recommendations where possible. Our findings lay the groundwork for future research in this area.

KEYWORDS

Automation, Internet of Things, Privacy, Security, Smart Home

ACM Reference Format:

Shrirang Mare, Logan Girvin, Franziska Roesner, Tadayoshi Kohno. 2019. Consumer Smart Homes: Where We Are and Where We Need to Go. In *The 20th International Workshop on Mobile Computing Systems and Applications (HotMobile '19), February 27–28, 2019, Santa Cruz, CA, USA*. ACM, New York, NY, USA, 6 pages. https://doi.org/10.1145/3301293.3302371

1 INTRODUCTION

In recent years, the number and variety of consumer smart home devices has increased rapidly. The mobile and transient nature of smart home computing (e.g., occupants come and go in a home, devices can be controlled via mobile phones when a user is at home or away, guest users come and go but may wish to control the devices when they are home) raises several design challenges around topics such as access control, automation, and privacy [1, 5, 6]. It is unclear what design practices current smart homes follow, how they address the tensions and challenges raised by past research, and what new (if any) challenges and implications (for end users)

these modern smart homes introduce. In this paper we attempt to fill this gap by evaluating seven modern consumer smart homes.

Our intent is not to cast stones at any particular smart home vendor. We seek to illuminate the current design choices in consumer smart homes and surface the many tensions. We hope our findings will be useful to product developers to refine their products, and the tensions that we identify will help guide future research in this space.

Much of the prior work on modern smart home devices has been focused on a particular device, a particular smart home, or a particular component of a smart home (e.g., [7, 15, 22, 23]). In contrast to studying a specific smart home product, we take a broader view and collectively evaluate seven different smart homes to understand the different design alternatives and their implications on end users. We based our evaluation on three prominent themes in smart home computing: access control, privacy, and automation. Along these themes, we seek to answer questions such as: How do different smart homes address access control, accounting for changes in users' mobility and context? How do different smart homes handle privacy within a home? How do different smart homes handle automations?

Contributions. We make three contributions.

(1) We experimentally evaluate seven different, commercially available consumer smart home platforms, to assess design similarities and differences, and gauge the impact of common and different design decisions on end users.

(2) Our research surfaces a number of fundamental tensions between different stakeholder values – including security and privacy, usability, and reliability.

(3) Driven by these findings, we propose technical directions for both industry and the academic community – directions that, if pursued, can help provide a foundation for navigating stakeholder values in the future.

2 EVALUATION METHOD

In our evaluation, we focused on smart home hubs and not on individual smart devices, because hubs serve as platforms on which smart homes are built and they also provide an interface through which users interact and control their smart home. We chose seven smart home hubs to evaluate: Amazon Echo, Apple Home, Google Home, Phillips Hue, SmartThing, Vera, and Wink. To evaluate each smart home hub, we created separate testbeds that included the smart home hub, two sensors (a motion sensor and a door sensor), an actuator (smart power outlet), and a router. We wanted to study each smart home from the perspectives of three types of users: the primary user, occupant user who first sets up the smart home; the secondary user, other occupant users of the smart home; and the guest user, non-occupant users who may visit the home just for a few hours or for days. So with each home, we set up three mobile phones, one for each type of user.

We evaluated the smart homes in a lab setting for a week as expert end users. Leveraging prior work on how end users use smart homes [22], we systematically designed our evaluation to mimic the different stages of smart home usage, and we created a rubric with instructions for each stage. Specifically, the rubric included instructions for setting up smart home hub, adding and removing devices, adding and removing users, editing the home configuration (e.g., automations to create), and finally, dismantling the home. The rubric also included instructions to evaluate access control mechanisms, test automations, and observe privacy controls available to end users.

Using the rubric, one researcher conducted the experiments with all the seven smart homes, and took detailed notes on the output and state of each smart home during each step in the rubric. Two researchers analyzed these detailed notes to understand the design choices and mechanisms around access control, privacy, and automation in each of the smart homes. We conducted our experiments in May 2017 and again in September 2018 to check whether our initial findings were still valid after one year (we found they were).

Threat model. Any malicious actor in the smart home ecosystem may pose a threat to a smart home user's security, privacy, or safety. For example, a malicious device manufacturer or a malicious smart home app may monitor or control a smart home without the smart home user's consent, or in a multi-occupant home a malicious occupant may spy on other occupants. Some actors outside the smart home ecosystem (e.g., neighbors, guests, remote online adversary) may also compromise a smart home by gaining physical access or remote access to one or more devices in the smart home. In this paper we mainly focus on the security and privacy threats from a malicious smart home occupant to other occupants and guests in the smart home.

3 FINDINGS

We group our findings into the three main themes in smart home computing: access control, privacy, and automation. Table 1 gives a visual summary of our findings.

3.1 Access Control in Smart Homes

Access control is fundamental to any multi-user OS or platform, including smart homes, and so we studied how different smart homes handle access control. Overall, we found that different smart homes have different access control models, which they use to control occupants' access to different types of data and resources in the home; some smart homes attempt to improve usability by offering multiple interfaces to control devices, but this feature can undermine access control in the smart home.

Different access levels. One prominent difference in the smart homes we studied is the types of users (and the granularity of access controls) that they support. For example, on one end of this spectrum is SmartThings, which supports only one type of user as it treats all users in a home equally, giving them the same level

of access and the same view of the smart home, and on the other end is Vera, which supports four types of users, each with varying levels of access: *administrator* (owner privilege), *advance* (administrator user privileges but cannot add/remove users), *basic* (advance user privileges but cannot add/remove automations or scenes), and *notification-only* (can only view notifications). The other smart homes we studied fall somewhere on this spectrum. Wink and Apple Home have two levels of access: *primary user* (who has owner privileges) and *secondary user* (who, by default, can operate devices but cannot add or remove devices or users). Furthermore, in Apple Home and Wink, the primary user can increase the privileges of a secondary user, allowing that user to manage devices and users. Amazon Echo, Google Home, and Philips Hue do not support multiple users. Thus, different smart homes have different approaches for access control.

Different use of access policies. Smart homes use policies to control access to use (or operate) devices, add or remove users and devices, organize devices in scenes or rooms, and add or remove automations. Generally, in all smart homes, the primary user has the highest (owner) privileges, but the privileges of the secondary user differ among smart homes. In Vera and Wink, the secondary user cannot add or remove other users but can add or remove devices and create automations. In SmartThings all users have the same privileges.

Risk of undermining access policies. To improve usability and reliability, some smart devices can be configured such that they can be controlled via multiple interfaces. For example, an outdoor smart camera can be integrated with a voice assistant like Amazon Echo, such that it can be controlled through the smart home hub (the default interface) as well as through the voice assistant (an alternate interface). However, alternate interfaces can undermine a device's access control policy (set by the user) if the alternate interface cannot enforce access control. For instance, in the previous example, if the voice assistant cannot recognize the user issuing voice commands, anyone near the voice assistant can control the outdoor camera, irrespective of the access control policies set for the camera.

Guest access. The transient nature of guests presents a unique access control challenge in smart homes – how to easily grant and control access for guests? As shown in Table 1, different smart homes have different strategies for guest users. In Wink and Apple Home, a guest user can be given access to *certain* devices, whereas in Vera, a guest user can be given *limited* access to *all* the devices. In Apple Home, guest access can be restricted (based on location) to only when the guest is at home. In the other smart homes we tested, once a guest is given access to a smart home device, the guest can control the device remotely and retains access until it is revoked. This approach of managing guest access (where the owner has to grant explicit access and then revoke it) is burdensome for smart home users.

3.2 Privacy

We consider threat to occupants' privacy from external entities and from other occupants in the home.

Privacy from external entities: lack of transparency. A smart home *continuously* collects data about *all* its occupants when they

Property	Ref.	SmartThing	Wink	Apple Home	Vera	Phillips Hue	Amazon Echo	Google Home
Hub category		Multi vendor	Multi vendor	Multi vendor	Multi vendor	Single vendor	Cloud only	Cloud only
Supports multiple users	[18, 24]	●	●	●	●	●	○	○
Access control								
Number of user types		2	2	2	4	1	1	1
Supports guest mode	[10]	○	○	●	○	○	○	○
Supports device level access	[12]	○	●	○	○	○	○	○
Time-based policies	[12]	○	○	○	○	○	○	○
Location-based policies	[3]	○	○	●	○	○	○	○
Privacy								
Detects user presence		●	●	●	●	○	N/A	N/A
User owns the data	[17]	Unclear	Unclear	●	Unclear	Unclear	Unclear	●
User can delete data	[14, 17]	Unclear	Unclear	●	Unclear	Unclear	●	●
Data shared between users	[4, 19]	All	Some	None	Some	None	N/A	N/A
Location where data is stored	[9]	Cloud	Cloud	Cloud	Cloud	Cloud	Cloud	Cloud
Automation								
Communication model		Mixed	Mixed	Mixed	Mixed	Mixed	Mixed	Mixed
Provides-test-environment	[16, 23]	○	○	○	●	○	○	○
Sends device unavailable alert	[5]	○	○	○	○	○	○	○
Network resilience	[6]							
Local processing		●	●	●	●	●	○	○
Local control		○	●	●	●	●	○	○

Table 1: Smart home comparison; *Refs.* column lists example prior work we used to derive the corresponding property. ● indicates the smart home supports the property; ○ indicates it does not.

are home, but also when they are away (through the smartphone app on their mobile phones). Data captured by smart homes can reveal occupants' daily activities and potentially sensitive information about the occupants. We found significant differences in vendors' approaches in handling users' smart home data. As shown in Table 1, Apple Home and Google Home clearly state that data ownership is with users, and they offer users an option to delete their data, but with the other smart homes data ownership policies are unclear.

Data sharing between users. The smart homes we evaluated share three types of data between users: user's *location*, captured through the user's smartphone app (if enabled by the user); *automations* created by the user; and *device activity* log. For these data types, different smart homes offer sharing preferences. In Smart-Things everything (*location, automations, and device activity*) is shared with all users; in Vera *automation and device activity* are shared with all users; in Wink only *device activity* is shared; and in Apple Home only *automations* are shared between users (and users can edit each others automations). Furthermore, in Vera, users can see other users' *automation*, but the details vary depending on the user's access level.

Side-channel privacy leaks. Device activity log can reveal a user's habits and behavior that the other users in the home may

not otherwise notice. A smart home's decision on whether to share this information readily between users determines how easy (or difficult) it will be for a malicious user to track another user, and this, in turn, may influence how people use smart homes. Without easy access to this information through a smart home, spying on other users requires intent, skill, and effort; with smart home readily providing this information, spying on other users requires only intent. In addition to device activity logs, unintended private data sharing – privacy leaks – can happen in other ways. For example, in SmartThings, we found that a user can determine another user's presence at any arbitrary location by misusing the user-presence feature. SmartThings shows a user's presence (e.g., at home or away) based on the location of the user's phone and the hub's location. But any user in the home can change the hub's location to any location of interest to check whether other users are present at that location (e.g., is Bob really at work?).

3.3 Automation

For smart homes to reliably execute automations, they have to be aware of the state of the devices in the home and they have to be resilient to network failures [5].

Home state awareness. The communication model between the hub and the devices determine how quickly a hub would learn of any change in its devices. We considered three communication models: *pull* (hub periodically polls devices for their status), *push* (devices push their status when there is a change), and *mixed* (combination of push and pull). An aggressive polling approach can capture changes in device status quickly, but this approach is expensive in terms of energy, especially if we expect the battery operated smart devices to last for years. A push model is energy efficient but may lead to an inconsistent view of a home if there are network errors and the delivery of certain push messages fails. A mixed model can leverage the energy efficiency of the push model while using a relaxed pull strategy to maintain a consistent view of the home over time. We found that all smart homes have converged to the mixed communication model.

Network resilience. Much of a smart home's utility is due to it being connected to the internet, but network outages do occur, and therefore, a smart home should be resilient to network failures. We argue that in the event of a network outage smart homes should provide a minimum level of service, which includes supporting devices and services necessary to keep the home in a safe state. For instance, even in the event of a network outage, occupants should be able to turn on smart lights, a smart thermostat should operate normally and not accidentally leave the home in an undesired state – as it happened during the recent outage due to the widespread DDoS attack [20] – and smart door locks should still operate so people can enter or leave the home. We therefore tested smart homes for their support for *local processing*, i.e., whether the smart home can process automations and communicate with devices without internet access, and *local control*, i.e., whether a user can control the smart home without internet access. Overall, we found that smart homes are converging towards a local processing and local control design – a good design choice for a reliable smart home experience, even in the event of a network outage.

Broken automations. Automations can fail because of several reasons such as malfunction of the input (trigger) device, malfunction of the output (actuator) device, or a network failure. We tested how smart homes handle failures in automations due to the unavailability (malfunction) of the trigger device or the actuator device. Specifically, we investigated whether a smart home sends an alert to users when a device becomes unavailable, which is important because the failed device could be a trigger or an actuator for an important automation. In our experiments, none of the smart homes alerted their users if a device became unavailable (Table 1). When a device was unavailable, the device appeared as "unavailable" or "inactive" on the status dashboard of all the smart homes, but users were not notified of the device failure or the affected automation. We also tested how smart homes report execution of an automation when the automation is triggered but the actuator device is unavailable to complete the automation. In Vera, if the actuator was not responsive, the automation status was shown as failed, but in SmartThings and Philips Hue the automation was shown (incorrectly) as successful. Apple Home did not show status or log of previously run automation, so users would not be aware of the failed automation.

4 DISCUSSION

Informed by our understanding of current smart homes, we surface the social implications of current smart homes around access control and privacy in a home, the usability challenges of automation, and the tension between current approaches to address interoperability and reliability in smart homes.

4.1 Access Control

If access control in a smart home is not designed carefully, it could give one occupant more control and power over the devices in the home, compared to other occupants, which could affect interpersonal relationship in the home [24]. This raises an important design question: Should all occupants have equal access to the smart home? In non-smart homes, Johnson and Stajano argue that access policies for devices generally follow what they call the 'Big Stick' principle, which states whoever has physical access to a device is allowed to control that device [10]. Extending this principle to smart homes implies that an occupant should have at least the *operate* level of access for the devices in the same room. But this principle may not always apply, e.g., parents may not want their kids to access the smart TV during study time [18].

Tension: Current approaches to access control. The smart homes we tested used different access control models. SmartThings gave equal access privileges to all users, whereas Apple Home and Wink allowed for device-based access (i.e., primary user can grant other users access to certain devices). Vera provided more of a role-based access model, where the primary user defines roles for all other users, and access for each role is set by Vera. Between these two approaches (letting users decide for themselves vs. system enforcing equal access) it is not clear which one would be a better approach for a home setting. The equal-access-for-all approach (used by SmartThings) is simple and easy-to-understand for users, but does not support access control use cases like parental control or guest access, whereas the other approach (used by Apple Home, Vera, and Wink) supports some access control use cases but gives more power to the primary user.

Recommendation: Location-based access policy for guests. When a guest leaves, if their access is not revoked promptly, they can remotely access the devices in the home. The smart home owner may forget to promptly revoke a guest's access or may hesitate to do so, for fear that it might appear rude to remove access as soon as the guest leaves the home. If an owner does remember to revoke a guest's access, when the guest visits again, the guest would need to be granted access again. A location-based access policy, similar to what Apple Home provides, that leverages guests' mobile phone to determine their location could grant guests access to devices only when they are present in the home. Such context-based access control policy could simplify access control for guest users, by automatically limiting their access only when they are at home.

4.2 Privacy

The privacy implications of a smart home are not limited to the individuals who are registered users of the smart home but also extend to *all* the smart home occupants as well as *guests* that visit the home.

Recommendation: Reduce privacy leaks via side-channels. In a smart home, data is shared between users, and depending on how it is shared, privacy leaks may happen. For instance, consider device activity logs, which can help users understand their own behavioral patterns. If, however, the device activity log reveals device usage pattern of a particular user, that user could feel being watched. For example, in a shared smart home apartment, roommates may prefer if their trips to bathroom were not logged. Such privacy risks can be reduced by anonymizing device activity logs, storing activity logs only for a short period of time, or maybe for some devices the smart home could provide a "do not log" option.

Another example of privacy leak via side-channels is the misuse of the user-presence feature in SmarthThings. In our experiments, SmartThings shared users' presence status (determined by the location of the user's phone) in the home with other users. Some may find location sharing convenient to let their family know when they arrived home, or to create automations based on their location; others may see it as an invasion of privacy. There is a need to design a usable permission model for location sharing that gives users more control over who can access and use their location.

Tension: Guest privacy. We usually think about privacy of home occupants from visiting guests, but what about the privacy of guests from smart home occupants? Consider guests who are staying for a few days (or longer) while the smart home occupants are away on a vacation; or consider an Airbnb host who rents his/her smart home to visitors. In this case, should the smart home owner have remote access to the smart home while it is occupied by a guest? And, how should the smart home owner retain ownership privileges but without invading the guest's privacy? Disabling remote access to the smart home disables owner's remote access, but also disables the guest's remote access, which the guest may not want. So selectively disabling remote access for certain users may be desirable for such situations.

Tension: Utility vs. privacy with continuous sensing. Some smart devices, with their continuous sensing, can provide a lot of utility to users, but depending on where the data is stored, who has access to the data, and what that data is used for, there can be serious privacy implications for smart home occupants. For example, smart meters can provide users their detailed energy consumption and grid companies use this information to ultimately improve their service to the users, but this data can also be used to infer information about the appliances in the home and their use, and also users' activities in general. Smart assistants like the Amazon Echo or Google Home are always listening to readily respond to users' commands, and companies may store all the recorded audio to improve their service, but this data can also be used to infer information such as identifying the number of people in a room, guessing a user's mood (happy, stressed, depressed), or building a model of the user's speech; users of smart assistants may not be aware of these implications. And similarly, smart cameras (e.g., baby monitors, security cameras) record video and provide users with relevant notifications (e.g., baby woke up, a trespasser caught on camera), but companies may store the video, which can have serious privacy implications for the people captured in the videos. Some prior approaches to this problem span high-level privacy

guidelines for building ubiquitous systems [11], privacy-aware architectures for building smart home apps [8], and privacy-aware analysis algorithms [13], but there is need for effective solutions to reduce this tension and for mechanisms that enable users to make informed trade-offs.

4.3　Automations and Interoperability
When users create automations, they may not necessarily be aware of failure cases, particularly failure of the trigger device or the actuator device.

Recommendation: Ask for post-failure actions. When a user creates an automation, asking the user what the smart home should do when the automation fails may serve two goals: i) educating the user by informing that the automation could fail – something the user may not be aware of – and the system could offer some information on how that automation could fail; and ii) increasing user confidence in the smart home's reliability, by educating the user and giving her more control [23].

Recommendation: Detect possible failures. To detect failures in an automation, a smart home should know the status of the input trigger device and of the output actuator device. In our tests, all the smart homes were aware of the status of all their devices. So, current smart homes could easily detect a device that becomes unavailable and identify the affected automations. However, identifying all the affected automations may not be trivial if there are automations that dependent on other automations. For example, if an automation, say Q, is dependent on the successful execution of another automation P, but if P's trigger device becomes unavailable and P fails, should the smart home also mark Q as a failed automations and run Q's post-failure action? The correct choice is not obvious. Thus, implementing failure detection and notification would require careful design.

Tension: Interoperability at the expense of reliability. Interoperability between smart home devices and smart home hubs is one of the main challenge for smart homes [6]. To deal with this challenge, some device vendors are choosing the cloud approach, where a device and the hub communicate through the cloud even when the device and the hub are on the same local network and could communicate directly (locally). This cloud approach allows vendors to make their devices compatible with different smart home hubs, available now and in near future, but this same approach also increases network dependency and introduces additional privacy concerns, as the smart home data may reside in multiple servers. Thus, although interoperability can be addressed by integrating in the cloud, this approach introduces new privacy risks and makes smart homes less resilient to network failures.

5　RELATED WORK
Much of the prior work on modern smart home devices has been focused on individual IoT devices or individual smart homes. For example, Yang et al. conducted a user-experience study with people living with Nest smart thermostat, and found that participants had difficulty understanding how the system worked, which lead to reduced interaction with the thermostat [23]. In 2013, Ur et al. conducted access control cases studies of three smart home products [21], and one of their devices was Philips Hue, which we

also used in our evaluation and we found similar access control issues with Philips Hue. Woo and Lim conducted a 3-week study with participants using DIY smart homes and they identified six stages of DIY-usage [22]; their stages are similar to the phases we used in our evaluation. And more recently, Fernandes et al. analyzed security of SmartApps in emerging smart homes [7], and Alrawi et al. analyzed the security of various IoT devices [2].

In contrast with these previous works with particular smart home products, we take a broader approach and study seven different smart homes. Through such a collective analysis we can learn the similarities and differences in the design choices that smart home vendors make, we can identify past research recommendations that are being used (or not being used) in current smart home products, which can help guide future research.

6 CONCLUSION

In smart home computing, the mobility of the users, the changing context and needs, and the continuous sensing in the home, raise several design challenges. In this paper, we systematically studied seven popular, commercially available consumer smart homes, to compare their design choices around access control, privacy, and automation, and to understand how these smart homes handle certain edge cases (e.g., broken automations). We found, for example, that smart homes are converging on design choices related to smart home's reliability (e.g., local processing and local control), but that their approaches for access control and privacy are different; that access control and data sharing policies in some smart homes could enable occupants to spy on other occupants; and that alternate modes of interaction (e.g., voice-controlled devices) add convenience but could undermine access control policies in the smart home. From our evaluation of these design points and failure cases, we surface key issues around access control and privacy, the usability challenges of automation, and tensions between interoperability and reliability. These lessons and design alternatives can help inform future research and next-generation smart home technologies.

ACKNOWLEDGEMENTS

We thank our shepherd, Aakanksha Chowdhery, as well as our anonymous reviewers, for their valuable feedback. We also thank Anna Kornfeld Simpson for helpful feedback on earlier drafts. This work was supported in part by the National Science Foundation under Award CNS-1565252, the MacArthur Foundation, and the University of Washington Tech Policy Lab.

REFERENCES

[1] Gregory D Abowd and Elizabeth D Mynatt. 2000. Charting past, present, and future research in ubiquitous computing. *Proceedings of the ACM Transactions on Computer-Human Interaction (TOCHI)* 7, 1 (March 2000). https://doi.org/10.1145/344949.344988

[2] Omar Alrawi, Chaz Lever, Manos Antonakakis, and Fabian Monrose. 2019. SoK: Security Evaluation of Home-Based IoT Deployments. In *Proceedings of the IEEE Symposium on Security and Privacy (S&P)*. https://doi.org/10.1109/SP.2019.00013

[3] A J Brush, B Lee, R Mahajan, and S Agarwal. 2011. Home automation in the wild: Challenges and opportunities. In *Proceedings of the SIGCHI Conference on Human Factors in Computing Systems (CHI)*. https://doi.org/10.1145/1978942.1979249

[4] A. J. Bernheim Brush and Kori M. Inkpen. 2007. Yours, Mine and Ours? Sharing and Use of Technology in Domestic Environments. In *Proceedings of the International Conference on Ubiquitous Computing (UbiComp)*. Springer-Verlag, 18. http://dl.acm.org/citation.cfm?id=1771592.1771599

[5] Scott Davidoff, Min Kyung Lee, Charles Yiu, John Zimmerman, and Anind K. Dey. 2006. Principles of Smart Home Control. In *Proceedings of the International Conference on Ubiquitous Computing (UbiComp)*. Springer-Verlag, 16. https://doi.org/10.1007/11853565_2

[6] W. Keith Edwards and Rebecca E. Grinter. 2001. At Home with Ubiquitous Computing: Seven Challenges. In *Proceedings of the International Conference on Ubiquitous Computing (UbiComp)*. Springer-Verlag, 17. https://doi.org/10.1007/3-540-45427-6_2

[7] Earlence Fernandes, Jaeyeon Jung, and Atul Prakash. 2016. Security Analysis of Emerging Smart Home Applications. In *Proceedings of the IEEE Symposium on Security and Privacy (S&P)*. https://doi.org/10.1109/SP.2016.44

[8] Jason I Hong and James A. Landay. 2004. An Architecture for Privacy-sensitive Ubiquitous Computing. In *Proceedings of the International Conference on Mobile Systems, Applications, and Services (MobiSys)*. ACM, 13. https://doi.org/10.1145/990064.990087

[9] Iulia Ion, Niharika Sachdeva, Ponnurangam Kumaraguru, and Srdjan Čapkun. 2011. Home is Safer Than the Cloud!: Privacy Concerns for Consumer Cloud Storage. In *Proceedings of the Symposium on Usable Privacy and Security (SOUPS)*. ACM, Article 13, 20 pages. https://doi.org/10.1145/2078827.2078845

[10] Matthew Johnson and Frank Stajano. 2009. Usability of Security Management: Defining the Permissions of Guests. In *Trust, Privacy and Security in Digital Business*. Springer Berlin Heidelberg. https://doi.org/10.1007/978-3-642-04904-0_36

[11] Marc Langheinrich. 2001. Privacy by Design: Principles of Privacy-Aware Ubiquitous Systems. In *Proceedings of the International Conference on Ubiquitous Computing (UbiComp)*. https://doi.org/10.1007/3-540-45427-6_23

[12] Michelle L. Mazurek, J. P. Arsenault, Joanna Bresee, Nitin Gupta, Iulia Ion, Christina Johns, Daniel Lee, Yuan Liang, Jenny Olsen, Brandon Salmon, Richard Shay, Kami Vaniea, Lujo Bauer, Lorrie Faith Cranor, Gregory R. Ganger, and Michael K. Reiter. 2010. Access Control for Home Data Sharing: Attitudes, Needs and Practices. In *Proceedings of the SIGCHI Conference on Human Factors in Computing Systems (CHI)*. ACM, 10. https://doi.org/10.1145/1753326.1753421

[13] Stephen McLaughlin, Patrick McDaniel, and William Aiello. 2011. Protecting Consumer Privacy from Electric Load Monitoring. In *Proceedings of the ACM Conference on Computer and Communications Security (CCS)*. ACM. https://doi.org/10.1145/2046707.2046720

[14] Andrew R. McNeill, Lynne Coventry, Jake Pywell, and Pam Briggs. 2017. Privacy Considerations when Designing Social Network Systems to Support Successful Ageing. In *Proceedings of the SIGCHI Conference on Human Factors in Computing Systems (CHI)*. ACM, 13. https://doi.org/10.1145/3025453.3025861

[15] Sarah Mennicken and Elaine M Huang. 2012. Hacking the natural habitat: An in-the-wild study of smart homes, their development, and the people who live in them. In *Proceedings of the International Conference on Ubiquitous Computing (UbiComp)*. https://doi.org/10.1007/978-3-642-31205-2_10

[16] Sarah Mennicken, Jo Vermeulen, and Elaine M. Huang. 2014. From Today's Augmented Houses to Tomorrow's Smart Homes: New Directions for Home Automation Research. In *Proceedings of the ACM International Joint Conference on Pervasive and Ubiquitous Computing (UbiComp)*. ACM, 11. https://doi.org/10.1145/2632048.2636076

[17] Pardis Emami Naeini, Sruti Bhagavatula, Hana Habib, Martin Degeling, Lujo Bauer, Lorrie Faith Cranor, and Norman M. Sadeh. 2017. Privacy Expectations and Preferences in an IoT World. In *Proceedings of the Symposium on Usable Privacy and Security (SOUPS)*.

[18] Stuart Schechter. 2013. The User IS the Enemy, and (S)he Keeps Reaching for that Bright Shiny Power Button!. In *Proceedings of the Workshop on Home Usable Privacy and Security (HUPS)*.

[19] D. K. Smetters and Nathan Good. 2009. How Users Use Access Control. In *Proceedings of the Symposium on Usable Privacy and Security (SOUPS)*. ACM, Article 15, 12 pages. https://doi.org/10.1145/1572532.1572552

[20] Nick Statt. 2017. How an army of vulnerable gadgets took down the web today. Online at theverge.com. https://www.theverge.com/2016/10/21/13362354/dyn-dns-ddos-attack-cause-outage-status-explained

[21] Blase Ur, Jaeyeon Jung, and Stuart Schechter. 2013. The Current State of Access Control for Smart Devices in Homes. In *Proceedings of the Workshop on Home Usable Privacy and Security (HUPS)*. https://www.microsoft.com/en-us/research/publication/the-current-state-of-access-control-for-smart-devices-in-homes/

[22] Jong-bum Woo and Youn-kyung Lim. 2015. User experience in Do-It-Yourself-style smart homes. In *Proceedings of the ACM International Joint Conference on Pervasive and Ubiquitous Computing (UbiComp)*. https://doi.org/10.1145/2750858.2806063

[23] Rayoung Yang and Mark W. Newman. 2013. Learning from a Learning Thermostat: Lessons for Intelligent Systems for the Home. In *Proceedings of the ACM International Joint Conference on Pervasive and Ubiquitous Computing (UbiComp)*. ACM, 10. https://doi.org/10.1145/2493432.2493489

[24] Eric Zheng, Shrirang Mare, and Franziska Roesner. 2017. End User Security and Privacy Concerns with Smart Homes. In *Proceedings of the Symposium on Usable Privacy and Security (SOUPS)*. https://www.usenix.org/conference/soups2017/technical-sessions/presentation/zeng

AIDE: Augmented Onboarding of IoT Devices at Ease

Huanle Zhang[♮], Mostafa Uddin[§], Fang Hao[§], Sarit Mukherjee[§], Prasant Mohapatra[♮]

[♮]University of California, Davis   [§]Nokia Bell Labs

{dtczhang, pmohapatra}@ucdavis.edu   {mostafa.uddin, fang.hao, sarit.mukherjee}@nokia-bell-labs.com

ABSTRACT

In order to use and manage IoT devices, a prerequisite is to on-board them so that they can be initialized and connected to the infrastructure. This requires mapping each physical device with its digital identity. Doing so manually is tedious, error-prone and not scalable. In this paper, we propose AIDE, a mechanism that provides Augmented onboarding of IoT Devices at Ease. AIDE offers a streamlined on-boarding process by automatically associating devices at different locations with their corresponding Received Signal Strength (RSS) profiles, which can be applied to a wide range of wireless technologies such as WiFi, BLE and Zigbee. AIDE does not require additional infrastructure or hardware support, and can work by simply using a COTS smartphone as receiver. The mechanism employs a carefully designed measurement approach and a post-processing algorithm to mitigate multi-path effect and improve measurement accuracy. Preliminary experiments in different indoor environments show that AIDE achieves about 90% on-boarding accuracy when devices are 6 feet away from the measurement point, and 100% accuracy when devices are directly approachable.

ACM Reference Format:
Huanle Zhang, Mostafa Uddin, Fang Hao, Sarit Mukherjee, Prasant Mohapatra. 2019. AIDE: Augmented Onboarding of IoT Devices at Ease. In *The 20th International Workshop on Mobile Computing Systems and Applications (HotMobile '19), February 27–28, 2019, Santa Cruz, CA, USA*. ACM, New York, NY, USA, 6 pages. https://doi.org/10.1145/3301293.3302354

1 INTRODUCTION

The Internet of Things (IoT) continue to expand its reach into homes, industry, hospitals, and other environments, as more and more devices are connected with the purpose of gathering and sharing data. Apart from the convenience aspect, there are several potential benefits of IoT that can lead to increased energy efficiency, improved safety and security, and higher product quality. However, to achieve the benefits of IoT devices, it is critical to have an efficient *on-boarding* process that can initialize and provision the devices for accessing the network infrastructure. Unfortunately, often the process to on-board IoT devices is time consuming and labor intensive, which becomes the barrier to streamlined IoT adoption and deployment [1]. Furthermore, the complexity of deploying large

number of devices may also increase the vulnerability and security risk of the infrastructure.

To better understand the limitation of the current manual on-boarding process, consider a scenario where an enterprise has acquired many smart light bulbs and installed them on ceiling, wall or floor. These devices can be controlled through wireless communication such as BLE, WiFi and Zigbee. But before the system administrator or operator can operate these light bulbs, s(he) needs to know the device ID (MAC address or physical address) of each light bulb. Note that although the human-readable manufacturer names may be contained in the beacon packet, these names can only help to separate different types of devices (e.g. light bulbs vs. thermostats), or devices from different manufacturers. It is difficult to know (physically) which light bulb has which device ID just based on beacon packets in the case where all light bulbs are from the same manufacturer. To on-board these light bulbs manually, the operator may either try to find the MAC address on the original package of each device and enter them into the system one by one, or s(he) can try to onboard each light bulb one at a time, and turn it on/off and try to verify which device is under control. We can see that such manual on-boarding process is very tedious and error-prone, and can be very inefficient when the number of devices is large. In addition, for devices that do not give visual feedback about its operational status, e.g., sensors that do not show on/off status, it can be difficult to verify their device IDs without testing each of them in isolation.

In order to on-board IoT devices at large numbers, we need a streamlined mechanism to register each device to the infrastructure based on its unique digital identity (i.e., MAC or physical address). In addition to seamless registration, it is also essential to know, which digital identity corresponds to which physical device. Knowing this information enhances usability [2] and safety [1] in interacting with the surrounding IoT devices. In this paper, we refer to such methodology as *augmented on-boarding*.

Our basic idea is to differentiate the seemingly identical devices based on their Received Signal Strength (RSS) values. In a deployed environment, devices are typically separated from each other by a certain distance. For example, light bulbs may be installed on ceiling with several feet in between. Similarly, hand held devices can be separated from each other by moving them apart. Hence when we measure the RSS values of different devices, generally we should be able to find some difference in their signal strength due to their location differences. Note that RSS is available in almost all COTS receivers regardless of what wireless communication technology is used, e.g., WiFi, BLE and Zigbee, which makes RSS-based solution IoT-protocol independent.

One naive solution to identify a target device is to measure the RSS values by holding a smart phone closest to this device and then identify this device as the one with the highest RSS value. However, there are a number of challenges that make such naive solution not working well. First, RSS value drops exponentially with the increase in distance, which makes it difficult to reliably compare two signals beyond a certain distance range. Therefore, in order to create reliable RSS contrast, we need to conduct measurement at the close proximity of the target device. However, in many cases, due to physical constraint (e.g., devices on ceiling) or obstruction (e.g., furniture on the way), target devices may not be approachable. Furthermore, RSS measurements are affected significantly by the multi-path effect. A slight change in location or direction may cause significant changes in measurement results. To further complicate the matter, RSS values vary significantly across devices. Even for the same type of devices, their RSS values vary due to other factors such as battery levels or age.

Due to above signal and physical constraints, the naive approach of selecting maximum RSS measurement to identify devices shows only ~ 65% accuracy in our experiments. In this paper, we propose AIDE, a more carefully designed measurement approach that systematically samples across multiple locations, and then use a voting-based algorithm to process the RSS measurement results for different devices at different locations to infer the device identities. Through preliminary experiments in several different indoor environments, we find that our solution can significantly improve the measurement accuracy over the naive approach. In the case that the target device is directly reachable, we can achieve 100% accuracy. In the case, the target devices are installed on ceiling and not directly reachable, we can achieve about 90% accuracy. However, in order to make augmented on-boarding applicable in practical settings we need near perfect accuracy. As our first steps towards that goal, AIDE shows promising results in our evaluation.

2 USE-CASE SCENARIOS

Large-Scale Device Onboarding for Industry: IoT devices have been increasingly adopted by industries for many different applications. In the introduction we have shown one such example, where an enterprise that deploys smart light bulbs can use our solution to streamline on-boarding process. In addition, consider a retail store that uses IoT to improve the shopping experience, e.g., sending beacon alerts to customers or using smart shelves to show product information [4, 5]. This requires a large number of IoT devices deployed at various locations of the store. When such devices are initially deployed, they need to be registered in the system, so that correct device ID to location mapping can be established. In order to do so, the current de-facto process is to either enter each device ID into the system manually, if this can be found from device's original package; or through a trial-and-error process where the operator can try to connect to each device one-by-one, change its status (e.g. turn them off or change light color), and then observe which device is changed and hence make the association. However, such manual process may be error-prone and inefficient. Instead, if we use the proposed AIDE mechanism, the store operator can simply use a phone to do device's beacon measurement close to the shelf where each device is installed. Then after all the measurement is done, the AIDE app that runs on the smart phone will automatically associate all device IDs with their corresponding shelf locations.

Inventory Management in Hospitals: Our on-boarding solution can be used in managing day-to-day inventory in the medical sector. Consider a scenario, where a patient is admitted to an emergency care. In this environment, for efficient utilization of space and easy movement of the physicians, often patients are assigned to hospital beds that are close to each other, separated only by curtains (i.e., vertical treatment room [3]). Once a patient is admitted, (s)he wears a wrist band with bar-code that represents the identity of that patient. This identity is used by the hospital to maintain the record about the patient. Now assume that the hospital has an inventory of BLE heart-rate monitoring devices. Since these devices are typically acquired in batches, many of them are from the same manufacturing companies and have the same model numbers. One of the heart-rate monitors will be attached to the patient after (s)he is admitted. The de facto process requires to first register all devices in the inventory manually by entering their MAC addresses and serial numbers etc. into the database, and also attach a printed label with its unique ID to this device. Then when the device is assigned to the patient, again manually associate the device label with the patient's record. In this way, the hospital can monitor the patient status and at the same time keep record of their inventory. However, such manual process may be error-prone and inefficient. Instead, if we use the proposed AIDE mechanism,the physician or nurse can simply hold a smart phone close to the heart-rate monitor, and the AIDE app that runs on the smart phone will automatically identify the device based on its beacon signal, despite having other beacon signals from similar heart-rate monitoring devices of nearby patients. Later this device identity can be associated with the patent's record. Although the hospital environment requires stringent 100% accuracy, we have seen promising results from our experiments that this may be achievable when the devices are directly approachable.

Interactive Indoor Map: In an enterprise environment such as an office building, we may be surrounded by a large number of smart devices and appliances. As the usage of these devices grows, it becomes important for the employees to be able to interact with these devices seamlessly. One way to enable such interaction is to use a smart phone app with an interactive indoor map of the building [2], where the IoT devices are marked on the map. Users can then click on the devices on the map to control them. In this scenario, it is important to have a streamlined process to on-board all such devices whenever they are installed and replaced. If this is done manually, one would have to try to connect and control each device one by one and try to assign device IDs on the map. With AIDE, one can instead use a smart phone to collect measurement data at the proximity of each device for a few seconds, and then the algorithm will automatically assign all device IDs on the map in one shot. In this usage scenario, AIDE can help to associate the physical device to its beacon and MAC address.

3 CHALLENGES

In the proposed on-boarding solution, we passively measure RSS from the wireless communication of surrounding devices. Unlike many other metrics such as CSI and AoA, RSS is considered as the most generic and easily accessible measurement metric. In that regard, any COTS mobile device that is compatible with IoT wireless

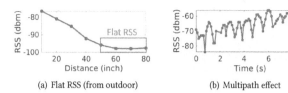

(a) Flat RSS (from outdoor) (b) Multipath effect

Figure 1: Signal constraint. (a) Flat RSS beyond some distance; (b) Noisy RSS due to multipath effect

communication protocol can be used as a receiver for our measurement. Thus, without any modification (software and hardware) in the already deployed IoT devices, and without any infrastructure support (e.g., access points), we can use any COTS smartphone for our on-boarding solution. Despite the practicality of RSS measurement, there are a number of challenges due to the characteristics of signals, and the physical settings at indoor environment.

RSS measurement can vary due to a number of reasons that include transmission power, distance, multi-path effect, etc. In the following list, we describe different challenges that we face for varying nature of RSS measurement and the complex layouts of indoor structure.

(1) Different devices have different transmission powers. Assume, we have two devices of same type (device 'A' and 'B') side-by-side, and their transmission powers differ because one has (device 'A') higher battery capacity than the other (device 'B'). Note that, increase of transmission power increases the RSS value of the received signal. Given the close proximity of device 'A' and 'B', even if we measure RSS of both devices at the position of device 'B', we may see higher absolute RSS value of device 'A' compared to device 'B'. Thus we cannot rely on absolute RSS value to infer the proximity of devices.

(2) Beyond certain distance, change in RSS is indistinguishable. Figure 1(a) shows a trace (collected outdoor at open-space on top of Crowford Hill, NJ) in which the RSS does not decrease much beyond ∼ 50 inches. Therefore, measuring RSS in close proximity helps in distinguishing target devices. However, it may not always be possible to get close to the target devices or devices may not be approachable. For example, if devices are deployed on ceiling, we cannot get very close to the target devices. In these circumstances, it is challenging to use RSS to distinguish target devices from distance, especially when the target devices are close to each other. In other words, it is more difficult to create sufficient contrast in RSS values of target devices to distinguish them when the measurements are conducted farther away from the devices.

(3) RSS data at indoor environment is noisy because of multi-path effect. Figure 1(b) shows a trace of RSS when we walk with a receiver directly toward a transmitter located at 80 inches away. Although the RSS increase is the general trend, the data fluctuates significantly. Due to the multi-path effect, measuring at larger distance may show higher RSS value compared to a shorter distance from the target device. Therefore, without proper techniques to combat multipath effect, the accuracy of onboarding based on RSS may degrade.

(a) Moving phones in a circular way when collecting data

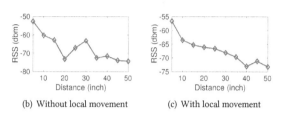

(b) Without local movement (c) With local movement

Figure 2: To mitigate multipath effect, we move our phone in a circle way as (a) shows. (b) and (c) plot one trace with and without local movement respectively

4 PROPOSED SOLUTION

Before describing the proposed solution, we first present the RSS measurement technique in mitigating multi-path effect. Second, we describe the RSS measuring procedure, and finally we describe the algorithm to identify devices. By putting them together, we propose an augmented on-boarding solution, AIDE.

4.1 Mitigating Multipath Effect

In Figure 1(b), we see how multi-path can have both constructive (multi-path components are in phase) and destructive (multi-path components are out of phase) interference effect on RSS measurement. In such phenomenon, for constructive case we see relatively higher RSS value, and relatively lower RSS value for destructive case. Therefore, instead of fixing the phone, we move our phone in a circular way (i.e., local movement) when we collect RSS data as Figure 2(a) shows. By doing this, we average RSS (spatially) within a small region, and thus we mitigate the multi-path effect in our measurement. Note that the radius of the circular movement has to be at least 2.5 inches, which is half of the wavelength (i.e., $\lambda = c/f = 3 \times 10^8 / 2.4 \times 10^9$ meters $\simeq$ 2.5 inch). Thus, we can have measuremnt across full wavelength. To show the effectiveness of our local movement method, we measure RSS at different distances from a transmitter, and average RSS data at each location. Figure 2(b) and Figure 2(c) plot the results with and without local movement, respectively. They clearly show that our local movement method results in a smoother and more consistent RSS curve over distance.

4.2 Measuring Procedure

Figure 3 depicts our measuring procedure. In this example, we want to on-board device IDs of three light bulbs on the ceiling. To on-board these devices, we collect RSS from all three light bulbs at fixed-locations, called *measurement locations*. There are three constraints in selecting a *measurement location*: First, each measurement location corresponds to a target device, whose device ID we are interested in finding. Therefore, in Figure 3, we have three measurement locations for three target devices. Second, a

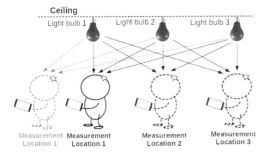

Figure 3: Measuring procedure in AIDE. We measure RSS at fixed positions closest to each target device. At each measurement location, we move our phone in a circular way when collecting RSS

measurement location of a target device is the position that is closest to that device compared to the other target devices. Third, a measurement location should be as close as possible to the target device. For example, in Figure 3, the measurement location 1 is the closest one (right below) to light bulb 1 compared to the left-most measurement location 1'. Hence location 1 should be used even though both locations satisfy the second constraint. This third constraint allows us to avoid the flat-like RSS region from Figure 1(a), and to have enough RSS contrast among multiple target devices.

For approachable case, a measurement location can be at the position of the target device, where as, for unapproachable case, a measurement location can be as close as possible to the target device. For example, as shown in Figure 3, the measurement location for light bulb 1 on ceiling (target device), which is unapproachable, is right below at *measurment location* 1. At each measurement location, we collect RSS of surrounding devices, both target and non-target, for a few seconds. Here non-target devices are the set of devices that the user is not interested in on-boarding or devices that may not be visually present (e.g., devices deployed in other rooms). Note that here we only focus on devices that are seemingly identical (e.g., same type and from same manufacturer). Devices of different types can be differentiated based on their device ID structure (i.e., MAC address) and device's name extracted from the beacon message. Furthermore, we also filtered out the already on-boarded devices from our measurement using their device IDs. After collecting the data, we derive statistical metric (i.e., mean, median, 95 percentile (close to maximum) and 5 percentile (close to minimum)) for each device or device ID to build RSS profile. Once we build the profiles for all device IDs, we apply our device identification algorithm to map the device ID to each measurement location, which physically represents a target device.

4.3 Identification Algorithms

Problem Formulation: For better understanding, let's first formulate the problem before describing the algorithms. Assume, we have N measurement locations for N target devices. For each measurement location, we have RSS profile for M number of device IDs that include both the target and the non-target devices ($M \geq N$). Correspondingly, we have an M-by-N matrix D, in which d_{ij} represents the RSS profile of ith ($i = 1, 2, ..., M$) device ID at j^{th} ($j = 1, 2, ..., N$) measurement location.

$$D = \begin{bmatrix} d_{11} & d_{12} & ... & d_{1N} \\ d_{21} & d_{22} & ... & d_{2N} \\ ... & ... & ... & ... \\ d_{M1} & d_{M2} & ... & d_{MN} \end{bmatrix} \quad (1)$$

Given the RSS profile matrix D, our objective is to associate the right device ID i for the measurement location j. Before describing the proposed algorithm, we describe two intuitive algorithms. Later, in evaluation, we compare these two algorithms with our propose algorithm.

Naive Algorithm. For each measurement location, this algorithm selects the device ID that has the strongest RSS. The outcome of this algorithm may vary due to the different transmission powers of different devices.

Greedy Algorithm. This algorithm improves on Naive Algorithm. It first finds the largest RSS in D, say RSS d_{ij}. Then it assigns measurement location j with device ID i. Afterwards, the row i and column j in D is set to $-\infty$. The procedure repeats N times until N devices at N measurement locations are identified. Compared to Naive Algorithm that considers a measurement location to be independent of other measurement locations, this algorithm starts with the largest RSS (normally higher confidence) and also avoids assigning same Device ID to multiple measurement locations.

Voting-based Algorithm: We propose a voting-based algorithm to consider the *likelihood* of each device ID at each measurement location. Each device i receives a vote for location j, reflecting its likelihood of being at location j. The vote is calculated as $\sum_{k=1}^{N}(d_{ij} - d_{ik})$. This is derived by comparing device i's RSS at location j with other locations. A higher vote for device i at location j means that device i has greater signal strength at location j compared to that at other locations. Since each device only compares its signal strength at different locations, the vote is not affected by the difference of transmission powers between devices. Also note that the vote is jointly determined by measurement result from all locations, which makes the result more robust than the result of the greedy algorithm where a single RSS value is used.

$$V = \begin{bmatrix} \sum_{j=1}^{N}(d_{11} - d_{1j}) & ... & \sum_{j=1}^{N}(d_{1N} - d_{1j}) \\ \sum_{j=1}^{N}(d_{21} - d_{2j}) & ... & \sum_{j=1}^{N}(d_{2N} - d_{2j}) \\ ... & ... & ... \\ \sum_{j=1}^{N}(d_{M1} - d_{Mj}) & ... & \sum_{j=1}^{N}(d_{MN} - d_{Mj}) \end{bmatrix} \quad (2)$$

Based on the vote matrix V, we search for the largest vote summation of N elements in V. These N elements are from unique devices (i.e., different rows) and unique measurement locations (i.e., different columns). Currently, we use a brute-force method, in which we traverse every combination of N devices out of M devices, and for those N devices we traverse every combination of N measurement locations. The result is given by the combination (device-wise and location-wise) that has the largest summation. The complexity of the brute-force algorithm is exponential. We plan to explore heuristic algorithms that have polynomial complexity.

4.4 Putting All Together: AIDE

Figure 4 shows a visual prototype of using AIDE in smartphone system that associates the visual objects (images or icons) with

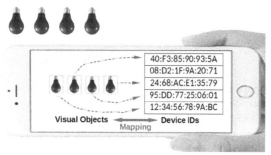

Figure 4: AIDE associates visual objects with device IDs using a smartphone

received device IDs. During the data collection phase, a user clicks a device object on screen and collects RSS at a position close to that device. The user repeats this procedure for all devices to on-board. Afterwards, AIDE automatically binds each visual object with its corresponding device ID. Then the user can control these devices, e.g., setting the brightness level of a light bulb. Note that in general, the system needs to (1) associate the physical device to its device ID, and (2) associate the physical device to its visual representation (e.g. image or icon) in the app. The mechanism we presented so far focuses on Step (1). In this simple prototype, Step (2) is done by requiring the user to click on the device image while measuring this device. This can also be done automatically by relying on the phone's camera to recognize and track the devices using machine learning [6], which we plan to investigate as part of our future work.

5 EVALUATION

For evaluation, we conduct preliminary experiments using BLE devices. However, AIDE supports other wireless communications such as WiFi and Zigbee because it only requires RSS information.

5.1 Experimental Setup

We deploy BLE devices at three sites: a small meeting room, a medium conference room and an office corridor. Devices are placed at various locations, some not directly approachable, e.g., on ceiling, some approachable, e.g., on table or floor. We create different topologies on the ceiling including line, grid and random, and also consider the scenario with mixed target and non-target devices. We implement the measurement app using a Google Pixel 2 smartphone. At each measurement location, we collect RSS data for 30 seconds, and use the mean, median, 95 percentile, or 5 percentile value. For better usability of AIDE, it is important to reduce the time of data collection. However, reducing the duration of collection time may affect the accuracy of measurement, especially when the distance between measurement locations and devices are large. As part of the future work, we are exploring this tradeoff.

5.2 Accuracy Versus Device Distance

In this evaluation, we investigate the impact of distance between devices on measurement accuracy when the devices are not approachable (i.e. on the ceiling). Here we use a pair of devices, with distance of either 2 feet or 4 feet in between. The phone is placed 6 feet below the measured device. Thus, the maximum difference of

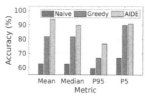 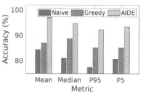

(a) Devices are 2 feet apart   (b) Devices are 4 feet apart

Figure 5: Accuracy of onbarding two devices on ceiling. AIDE achieves 93.4% and 97.1% in 2 feet case and 4 feet case respectively

distances between the pair of devices and the phone is only 0.3 feet (for 2 feet case) and 1.2 feet (for 4 feet case), respectively.

Figure 5 shows the overall accuracy comparison between naive, greedy and our voting-based algorithms. It clearly shows that voting-based algorithm outperforms the greedy algorithm which in turn outperforms the naive algorithm. The voting-based algorithm consistently achieves high accuracy using the Mean metric, with 93.4% and 97.1% accuracy in 2 feet and 4 feet device distance respectively. Given the fixed distance between the measurement location and the target device, we see the accuracy increases with the increase of distance between neighboring target devices. In the rest of evaluation, we use Mean in our algorithm, and compare to the other algorithms with whichever metric (e.g., 5 percentile) gives its highest accuracy.

5.3 Devices in Different Topology

We deploy multiple devices on ceiling to form two different topologies to study the accuracy. i) **Line Topology:** Where we deploy 4 devices in a line at different indoor environments. The distance between neighboring devices is 2 feet and thus the maximum difference of distance between neighboring devices to the phone is 0.3 feet. ii) **Grid Topology:** Where we deploy 6 devices into a 2-by-3 grid on ceiling in the medium conference room. The distance between neighboring devices is 4 feet and thus the maximum difference of distance between neighboring devices to the phone is 1.2 feet. Again the phone is placed 6 feet below the ceiling.

Table 1 tabulates the accuracy for both topologies. The accuracy of the voting-based algorithm is greater than the greedy algorithm, which in turn is better than the naive algorithm. More specifically, the voting-based algorithm achieves an average 86.2% accuracy for these two topology, with an average improvement of 15.7% and 28.2% compared to the greedy algorithm and the naive algorithm respectively. The accuracy in Table 1 differs from Figure 5 because here we need to separate out multiple devices instead of two. The accuracy of the grid topology is lower than the line topology because we need to onboard 6 devices in the grid topology whereas only 4 in the line topology.

5.4 Other Testing Scenarios

Target and Non-target Devices. We randomly deploy 5 target devices on ceiling at the conference room and 2 non-target devices on ceiling at corridor outside the room, imitating the case where some devices are not visually present. In this setting, the voting-based algorithm achieves 92.0% accuracy of identifying device IDs

Algorithm	Topology: Line 2 feet apart on ceiling	Topology: Grid 4 feet apart on ceiling
Naive	53.8% (median)	62.2% (mean)
Greedy	76.5% (mean)	64.4% (median)
AIDE	87.9%	84.4%

Table 1: Accuracy of onboarding multiple devices that are shaped into a line and a grid

for the target devices. We also calculate the percentage that target and non-target devices are falsely categorized as non-target (i.e., false negative) and target devices (i.e., false positive), which is 6.0% and 15.0% respectively. In general, the false ratio does not depend on the number of target and non-target devices, but rather depends on the relative signal strength of these devices. False ratio is lower when target devices have larger difference of signal strength at the measurement locations compared to non-target devices.

Approachable Scenario. In approachable setting, where we deploy 5 devices at various positions such as on table, floor and TV top in the medium conference room. In this case the voting-based algorithm achieves 100% accuracy. Here the result is as expected, as we have measured RSS very close to the target device, and thus the likelihood of that device at its measurement location is significantly higher than at other measurement locations.

6 RELATED WORK

Previously researchers have addressed the challenges of associating the physical device and the device identity under different circumstances. For instance, recently [7], researchers have used on-board inertial-sensors to correlate between motion information sensed by the sensors and the physical object detected by the camera [8]. This solution assumes target devices to be in motion, and to have on-board motion sensors. In other circumstances [9, 10], RF-aided localization techniques have been used, which require additional infrastructure support (i.e., anchor points, directional antennas [10], etc.). Furthermore, using only RSS for localization has an average estimation error of 2 meters for BLE [11], which makes it challenging to distinguish devices that are less than 1 meter apart. Unlike previous works, our proposed solution does not require infrastructure support or special hardware requirements for IoT devices.

7 DISCUSSION AND FUTURE WORK

In this paper, we have proposed AIDE that targets at an emerging necessity to on-board IoT devices in more intuitive and easy way. At the center of this solution is the voting-based algorithm that process RSS measurement to associate device identification at different physical locations. Through evaluation, we have shown that the proposed algorithm can achieve over 90% accuracy in different physical settings.

Although RSS profiles are subject to environmental changes, our data measurement procedure mitigates the effect because we collect data with the phone making circular movement for a period of time. During our data collection in the building, people occasionally walked nearby, but our system still shows promising performance. In fact, as long as there is a direct line-of-sight path between the target device and its corresponding measurement location, any blockage between this measurement location and other devices

actually improves the accuracy because the signal strength of other devices at this measurement location is reduced, which makes vote value higher for the target device for this location compared to other locations. As a result, voting based algorithm is more likely to produce the correct device mapping. Currently, we allocate 30 seconds at each measurement location. We plan to reduce the measurement time length by designing an indicator that automatically prompts to the user when to stop measuring at each location, and thus mitigate user's burden of data collecting.

In general, our algorithm is not affected by the transmission power because it does not directly use absolute RSS values. Instead it is based on the difference of RSS at different measurement locations. Presence of WiFi devices may potentially affect the measurement for BLE devices due to channel overlap. However, during our experiment the inference of WiFi signal does not seem to have much impact. Nevertheless, we plan to explore the environment with mixture of WiFi and BLE more carefully in our future work.

Considering that BLE signals transmit at different channels (i.e., hopping) and each channel has its own characteristics, we want to explore techniques such as channel separation [12] and leverage different channels separately to improve the accuracy. In addition, we want to explore whether machine learning can result in a better RSS profile representation than the metric mean which is used in our current implementation. We also plan to study the system performance with other wireless standards such as Wi-Fi, Zigbee, etc. Finally, as part of our future work, we plan to implement and integrate the visual part of AIDE to build a user-friendly augmented on-boarding solution.

REFERENCES

[1] Jennifer Gilburg. Zero Touch Device Onboarding for IoT Control Platforms. RSA Conference, 2017.
[2] CUBICASA. Integrate Floor Plans into Your Smart Home and Home Automation Applications. https://www.cubi.casa/floor-plans-smart-homes-iot/. Accessed on Jan. 9, 2019.
[3] Hamedani AG, Liu SW, Brown DF, Asplin BR, and Camargo Jr. Vertical Patient Flow, an Innovative Approach to Crowding In US Academic Emergency Departments. *Annals of Emergency Medicine*, 2010.
[4] Cameron Klotz. IoT Applied in Retail 5 Real Examples. https://hardwaremassive.com/resources/guest-articles/iot-applied-in-retail-5-real-examples. Accessed on Jan. 9, 2019.
[5] Alexander Coolidge. Kroger Tests "Smart Shelf" Technology. https://www.cincinnati.com/story/money/2015/10/02/next-shelves-giving-cues-kroger/73612252/. Accessed on Jan. 9, 2019.
[6] Jongwon Choi, Hyung Jin Chang, Tobias Fischer, Sangdoo Yun, Kyuewang Lee, Jiyeoup Jeong, Yiannis Demiris, and Jin Young Choi. Context-aware Deep Feature Compression for High-speed Visual Tracking. In *CVPR*, 2018.
[7] Carlos Ruiz, Shijia Pan, Adeola Bannis, Xinlei Chen, Carlee Joe-Wong, Hae Young Noh, and Pei Zhang. IDrone: Robust Identification through Motion Actuation Feedback. *Proceedings of the ACM on Interactive, Mobile, Wearable and Ubiquitous Technologies*, 2018.
[8] Shijia Pan, Carlos Ruiz, Jun Han, Adeola Bannis, Patrick Tague, Hae Young Noh, and Pei Zhang. UniverSense: IoT Device Pairing through Heterogeneous Sensing Signals. In *ACM HotMobile*, 2018.
[9] Swarun Kumar, Stephanie Gil, Dina Katabi, and Daniela Rus. Accurate Indoor Localization with Zero Start-up Cost. In *ACM MobiCom*, 2014.
[10] Souvik Sen, Jeongkeun Lee, Kyu-Han Kim, and Paul Congdon. Avoiding Multipath to Revive Inbuilding WiFi Localization. In *ACM MobiSys*, 2013.
[11] Dongyao Chen, Kang G. Shin, Yurong Jiang, and Kyu-Han Kim. Locating and Tracking BLE Beacons with Smartphones. In *ACM CoNEXT*, 2017.
[12] Rahul Majethia and Krishnan Rajkumar. Mining Channel State Information from Bluetooth Low Energy RSSI for Robust Object-to-Object Ranging. In *ACM IOT*, 2018.

Browsing the Web of Things in Mobile Augmented Reality

Thomas Zachariah
University of California, Berkeley
Berkeley, California
tzachari@berkeley.edu

Prabal Dutta
University of California, Berkeley
Berkeley, California
prabal@berkeley.edu

ABSTRACT

With the current augmented reality and low-power radio technology present on mobile platforms, we can imagine a standard and physically tangible browsing mechanism for objects in the Web of Things. We explore a model for user interaction with IoT devices that makes use of mobile augmented reality to allow users to identify new devices or easily access regularly-used devices in their environment, enables immediate interaction with quickly-obtainable user interfaces from the web, and provides developers a convenient platform to display custom interfaces for their devices. This model represents a step towards software-based interaction that might, one day, feel as intuitive, accessible, and familiar as the physical interfaces we commonly encounter in our daily lives.

CCS CONCEPTS

• **Human-centered computing** → **Web-based interaction**; **User interface design**; **Mixed / augmented reality**; *Ubiquitous and mobile computing systems and tools*;
• **Information systems** → **Service discovery and interfaces**; *Web interfaces*; Users and interactive retrieval;
• **Networks** → Mobile ad hoc networks.

KEYWORDS

Internet of Things, Mobile, Augmented Reality, Device Discovery, Web Browsing, User Interfaces

ACM Reference Format:
Thomas Zachariah and Prabal Dutta. 2019. Browsing the Web of Things in Mobile Augmented Reality. In *The 20th International Workshop on Mobile Computing Systems and Applications (HotMobile '19), February 27–28, 2019, Santa Cruz, CA, USA*. ACM, New York, NY, USA, 6 pages. https://doi.org/10.1145/3301293.3302359

1 INTRODUCTION

As the Internet of Things (IoT) grows, the issue of accessibility becomes more apparent. The benefits of connecting everyday things to the Internet are limited by a prevailing walled-garden approach to accessing the services provided by each device. Currently, most consumer IoT devices require installation of a separate app on a mobile phone or tablet to enable any form of user interaction. This is reminiscent of the heyday of America Online, whose business model of providing separately-packaged, single-purpose online services thrived for a brief period, but ultimately limited the potential content and resources that a browser with open access to the World Wide Web would later provide. This approach has been moderately successful in piquing initial interest and enabling an entry-point for societal acceptance of the new technology, but it limits the ability for discovery, prevents regular engagement from users, and discourages developers from creating useful services and products.

This issue, of course, has not gone entirely unnoticed. Major players have come together to create a variety of standards, most of which struggle to become widely adopted by developers. Apple and Google have introduced standards in which devices are organized into a "home" and can be managed with a unified controller on a mobile phone, tablet, or smart speaker. This single scoping limits which devices are accessible, what controls are provided, and how data is displayed in the user interface. Additionally, it requires users to make their own associations with devices and utilize recall more often than recognition when trying to interact with a specific device. It also limits the discovery of new "things" in their environment.

With the rising prevalence of reliable and capable mobile augmented reality (MAR) on personal phones and tablets, we may already have the tools necessary to develop a solution that provides a more intuitive approach to discovery, a more tangible approach to interaction, and a more creative approach to presentation. This may also lay the groundwork for a compelling, practical, and useful application for MAR.

In this paper, we examine a potential model for user interaction with IoT devices that makes use of MAR to allow users to identify new devices and easily access regularly-used devices in the physical space of their environment. It could enable immediate interaction with quickly-obtainable user interfaces (UIs) from the web, and provide developers with a convenient platform to display, within perceived physical space, custom interfaces for their devices that can be created using standard web tools. This mobile augmented reality browsing concept is depicted in Figure 1. In our study, we consider a few of the driving applications that could be supported and we explore some of the opportunities and challenges that arise in the development of such a system.

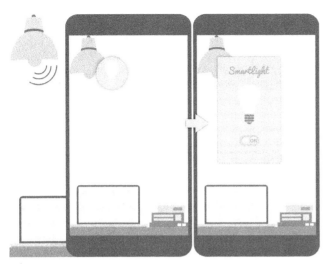

Figure 1: Concept overview. In this model, users can open a "browser" on their smartphone or tablet, which uses the camera to identify devices and discover their associated web interfaces in physical space. When an interface is opened, it can use a JavaScript Bluetooth API or network protocol to interact with the device.

2 RELATED WORK

Interaction Standards for IoT Devices. Device-specific apps are the current standard for interaction in the Internet of Things. They allow fine-grain setup and control of specific devices in an interface aesthetic of the developer's choosing. But this requires knowledge of the device and download of its app. It is also typically only accessible by the owners of the device, which discourages opportunities for ephemeral discovery and interaction.

Unified Control on Mobile Platforms. Unified control systems like Apple Home and Google Home begin to alleviate the problem by providing a single interface to control multiple devices in a house [1, 7]. As their names indicate, they are primarily intended for use in the home and limit scope to devices that implement specific proprietary protocols and are owned by the user. This still often requires download of the devices' apps for setup. It also imposes a standard aesthetic and provides a limited offering of control interfaces (e.g switches and sliders).

Device Discovery. Google's Physical Web allows discovery of nearby devices via Bluetooth Low Energy [6]. The device broadcasts a URL which a phone can detect and open in a browser. The URL can point to a web page that acts as an interface for the device. If the device is connected to the Internet or the page uses a JavaScript Bluetooth API, users can interact with the device in real time. This enables immediate interaction in an interface of the developer's choosing. Unfortunately as the number of devices scales up, the listing model becomes overwhelming and it is often difficult for users to map the appropriate interface to device. This may be, in part, why Google has removed Physical Web support on Android and iOS. However, the concept of associating nearby physical devices with web content via a broadcast service may be useful in the context of an MAR browser that more tangibly connects interfaces to devices.

Early Inspirations for AR-Like Modalities. In 1987, a Bell Labs study on human-system communication discovered that users struggle to identify canonical names and keyword commands for systems using voice or type interfaces [5], indicating that visual articulation might be more effective. This problem continues today in IoT, where users must identify available devices, brands, and associated apps prior to any form of interaction, even with voice-control agents. A 2000 Microsoft study on emerging interfaces for smart devices examined user experiences of touch and speech interfaces [3]. While the study did not discuss AR as a modality, it suggested that the functionality of systems could improve when interfaces are reinforced with an input that provides location-awareness (e.g. gaze or gesture) to help disambiguate a target device.

AR and MAR in Consumer Space. Recently, Apple and Google released AR software development kits for mobile platforms, ARKit and ARCore [1, 7]. With native support for AR and more capable hardware on smartphones and tablets, mobile augmented reality has become a practical reality and exposes the technology to a large user-base. Prior to this, third-party MAR frameworks existed, but much work in AR tended to focus on head-worn display devices rather than mobile. Still, surveys of existing consumer AR technologies from the last decade indicate that while industry interest in AR is high, it lacks compelling practical applications [15, 22].

MAR Systems in Practice. MAR systems designed to enable interaction with objects in an environment usually only work with a specific set of devices, and limit the type of controls devices can have and how they are presented to the user. Some of the most popular MAR applications work only in highly specific environments like an outfitted office, classroom, or exhibit [2, 9, 17]. Many of these employ computer vision with limited training sets, which is made easier with built-in machine learning frameworks on mobile platforms, like Google's ML Kit and Apple's Core ML [1, 7]. HP Reveal is an example that uses image recognition to identify objects "anywhere", but requires the user to manually narrow the search-space by subscribing to a "channel" of objects [18]. It is primarily used to demonstrate object identification, rather than interaction.

Target Identifiers Standard visual identifiers like QR codes or AprilTags are often used for general use cases. The MAR browser could potentially make use of such identifiers, but they may be obtrusive or distracting in the long run. They still generally require users to be somewhat informed about the environment around them and limit discovery when markers are not visible on screen. Early tablet-based AR control systems for appliances in homes with preset interfaces and tags have been studied, but not widely adopted [14]. Some work has been done to create AR systems with more subtle or visually appealing markers [8, 19]. Recent work in visible light communication (VLC) enable data dissemination through modulation of LEDs, which can be captured on a smartphone camera, while remaining mostly imperceptible to the human eye [10, 20]. This can potentially act as a visual "landmark" for devices in MAR.

Localization. Recent work has demonstrated integration of novel indoor localization techniques in AR. ALPS makes use of ultrasound beacons that broadcast audio that can be picked up on smartphone microphones and used to accurately determine location and orientation of the user [11]. Similarly, use of ultra-wideband (UWB) can accurately locate tags that can be attached to phones or other objects [21]. The location information obtained from these techniques can be used to help render an accurate and persistent AR environment for all users and between multiple uses [12, 13].

3 APPLICATIONS

In the MAR browsing model, a user would be able to point their phone at the device of interest, and immediately discover the interface for it. The interface would link to a web page which can make use of a cloud service, a local network protocol, or a browser-provided JavaScript Bluetooth API to interact with the device. We explore a few applications for which an MAR-based browsing model might be useful.

3.1 Smart Home Devices

The smart home has been the primary focus for the consumer IoT market. Home apps, like Apple Home and Google Home, provide a single console interface for all the smart devices in a house. When a moderate number of compatible devices are present, it is often difficult to remember which interface corresponds with which device, even when each one is appropriately labeled on the console, and used regularly. Additionally, to be compatible with such consoles, devices must utilize specific proprietary protocols, and are limited in the type of interface they can display on the console. For this reason, many IoT manufacturers struggle to or opt not to integrate with these consoles. Regardless of compatibility, each device still typically requires installation of its own mobile app to function.

With the MAR browser, finding the interface for a device would be similar to finding one in the physical world. Instead of the Home apps' strategy of relying on the user's recall of a particular device, the MAR browser would utilize the user's recognition by allowing the user to find the appropriate interface by pointing to the device of interest, much like inspecting a lamp to find a switch.

3.2 Device Setup

To ease the process of connecting devices to the Internet in a home, the MAR browser could potentially enable a quicker and more convenient method for device setup and configuration. Instead of requiring the user to download an app and to go through a setup process of entering ID numbers or accessing settings to initiate a connection, the device's interface can be opened in the browser and it can use visual verification methods and a direct connection via Bluetooth to sync with a particular device. Additionally, users can place target locations for device interfaces in the augmented reality space during this process.

3.3 Ephemeral Devices

Breaking out of the confined scope of the smart home, an MAR browser could potentially be utilized to enable new opportunities for quick, ephemeral interaction with new and easily-discoverable interfaces in the global Internet of Things. Interactive devices and interfaces could be deployed in public (e.g. stores, sidewalks, conference rooms, exhibits). Users would explore these spaces by effectively using the browser as an MAR "window" into the public web. Support for device discovery and ephemeral interaction of this kind would be a major departure from the app-per-device and single-scoping models that are prevalent in IoT. Enabling this, however, will require important consideration of the methods for retrieval of data about devices in public and both the virtual and physical association of the appropriate interfaces to those systems.

4 OVERVIEW

To begin developing an AR-based browsing architecture, we consider design decisions about platform, target identification, user interfaces, and scope. To help aid the understanding of requirements and limitations, a prototype implementation, shown in Figure 2, has been created. This demonstrates one mechanism for AR-based discovery and interaction in a known environment, and helps inform some of the design decisions that would need to be considered.

4.1 Platform

The most straightforward implementation of the MAR browser requires an Internet-connected mobile phone or tablet that has sufficient hardware and processing support for augmented reality. Most flagship smartphones released in the last 4 years are capable of this at least with third-party software. More recent iOS (iPhone 6s, 7, 8, X, XS, XR, SE; iPad 5th Gen, Pro) and Android (Google Pixel 1, 2, 3; Samsung Galaxy S7, S8, S9, Note8, Note9) platforms have official support for MAR with dedicated software development kits from Apple and Google. Making this a mobile-based system, rather than one based on a head-worn device or a webcam, makes it more accessible to a larger population of current users and the touch interface can make it intuitive to use. Our implementation is built on iOS using ARKit.

4.2 Targets

One of the more challenging parts of this system is defining how smart devices are identified as "targets"—locations which, when viewed on the phone's camera, prompt the phone to overlay associated content (e.g. images, videos, or, in our case, a linked fully-functioning user interface for the device).

One of the common ways to do this is with image recognition. If the phone's AR browser is trained to recognize the image of the device, it can overlay the interface relatively easily. The prototype is an implementation of such a system, as depicted in Figure 2. In this example, the target is identified visually using a trained image of the lamp. The challenge with this is one of scalability. It is unlikely that the browser can be trained to recognize every device in every angle and lighting scenario.

Alternatively, the geolocation (GPS coordinates) of devices can be obtained during the setup of the device. This, however, would likely only apply to stationary devices and would not account for mobile or wearable devices. Additionally, geolocation on phones is still quite coarse-grained (m-level accuracy) and development of a global map of devices may prove to be an intractable problem.

More recent phones are capable of creating their own local mapping of targets in their environment. It is possible for local mappings to be shared from phone to phone, but the variance in data and lack of a common origin point of reference may render the data useless when trying to load it on a different phone or even reload it on the same phone at a different time. A possible method to improve accuracy with local mappings might be to have users initially place their devices on a designated origin when they enter an IoT-outfitted space. This could re-calibrate the device's orientation to allow the phone to more accurately place known targets in a space, and to enable persistence of location between uses. One could also envision using a mount outfitted with NFC (near-field communication) or

Figure 2: Screenshots of a demo implementation of a mobile augmented reality browser. In this proof-of-concept implementation, the smartphone camera identifies the target and displays an indicator (the favicon for the target's URL) which the user may touch to open the device's linked web interface. Once opened, the interface, an HTML web page, uses JavaScript and a local network protocol to allow the user to interact with the Wi-Fi-connected device, and toggle the light on or off.

Bluetooth as the designated origin, which could provide a URL to load a space's map on to the phone. This way, any smartphone or tablet entering the space can retrieve the appropriate local mapping instead of needing to rely on global geolocation.

The devices themselves can broadcast their presence to the phone over the local Wi-Fi network or Bluetooth Low Energy. Like with Google's Physical Web, the devices can provide a URL in their broadcast advertisements that would both help to identify the device and point to an address where the device's user interface is served. This can also help to simplify how devices are found. While fine-grained location (cm-level accuracy) cannot be obtained from the detection of Wi-Fi or Bluetooth, it indicates the relative proximity of the device, which can 1) inform the user of its presence and 2) provide a more simplified, scoped search-space for the phone to identify targets.

For example, a light bulb can advertise `https://lightswit.ch/control`, the address of its user interface, over Bluetooth Low Energy. Once detected on a user's phone, the device can be listed on-screen as a nearby "thing". At the same time, the phone can also refine its search-space of targets to objects that look like light bulbs associated with the `lightswit.ch` URL or, perhaps, known geolocations of such devices. If the phone is unable to identify the device, but the user has knowledge of its location, he or she can potentially contribute a picture or an updated coordinate to help identify the device in the future.

4.3 Target Proxies

The reality in many environments is that the device itself may not be a desirable target. For instance, a smart power meter outlet may not be visible when in use since the plug for the appliance it is metering may obscure it. Additionally, the data is directly related to

the metered appliance, and the user may more naturally associate the interface for the meter with the appliance rather than the meter itself. The user may prefer that the interface for the meter be placed closer to the actual appliance. Figure 2 is also an example of this. The lamp was a chosen as the target location for the interface rather than the smart switch device at the outlet, as it more closely relates to the object of the intended activity of interaction. Consideration for these situations provide greater reasoning for allowing users to define/modify the placement of interfaces for the devices they own, or utilizing standard visual identifiers like QR codes that can be placed at the desired location.

4.4 Interfaces

Once a target has been identified, the browser should be able navigate to and display a linked user interface for the device that can display data from and interact with the device. To facilitate this in a general and scalable manner, standard web tools can be used to create the interface content. This means that the UIs are, in effect, web pages created with HTML, JavaScript, and CSS. This would allow developers to maintain their own creative liberties with the interaction model and interface aesthetic. The interface can make use of a browser-provided JavaScript Bluetooth API or a local networking protocol to enable local communication between the browser and the device. Alternatively the interface can continue the trend used by mobile apps of proxying commands through a cloud service.

In the case of the example shown in Figure 2, the interface is a web page that is served on the local Wi-Fi network. Whenever the user presses the switch displayed on the interface, it issues a server-side command to the network-connected smart switch device through a UPnP protocol.

4.5 Scope

Though it potentially limits a range of possibilities with public and ephemeral discovery, the browsing model can work as a local system that is focused on operating with devices in a user's home or work environment. Users can easily feed the system images of the devices in the actual environment they reside, providing targets that can be recognized more reliably. Alternatively, the user can define or correct an object's location using a drag and drop interface which will then be stored as coordinates in the phone's local mapping of the environment.

However, a system that is capable of working at a larger scale is more desirable. Identifying things as targets by image recognition is made more feasible when using the devices' Bluetooth or Wi-Fi broadcasts to refine the search-space. Use of standardized visual identifiers such as QR codes or AprilTags may improve performance, especially when devices are not stationary. Locations can be defined/corrected by the crowd using a drag-and-drop style interface to obtain new images of the target or modified geolocation.

Overall, defining and determining how the physical scope for interaction is interpreted will be important. Depending on the technologies used, a "nearby" device could be considered one within the device's Bluetooth range, on the device's Wi-Fi network, in identifiable visual range of the phone's camera, or within an arbitrary distance of the phone's geolocation.

5 RESEARCH QUESTIONS

In this section, we discuss some research challenges and questions that should be considered when designing and implementing the MAR browsing architecture.

5.1 Location Determination & Accuracy

A key consideration for the MAR browser is determining where interfaces are placed in augmented reality and ensuring that the placement corresponds with a user's intuitive understanding of how that interface relates to the physical environment. What are the methods to accomplish this? Can we do this without — or at least with minimal — user setup? Can we support both stationary and mobile objects of interest? How do we properly identify and distinguish interfaces for multiple targets in close proximity? How will different types and levels of lighting affect the accuracy of target identification and interface placement? We discussed some of these considerations in Sections 4.2 and 4.3. Some solutions for improvement might include updating location by crowd-sourcing user location (verification by proximity), storing device location meta-data in the cloud which can be downloaded based on user location, or "annotating" locations and devices of interest with QR codes that link to well-defined schema.

5.2 Communication Topology

Once a web-based user interface is opened, how do we enable direct interaction with the device? We suggest enabling support for local interaction using a JavaScript Bluetooth API for Bluetooth devices. Interfaces for Wi-Fi devices can implement local network protocols if the web content is served on the local network. Alternatively, as many mobile apps currently do, the interface can issue commands through a dedicated cloud service for devices with continuous Internet connectivity. This would effectively allow developers to create and deploy app-like UIs for their own devices.

5.3 Usability & User Experience

The intention of this browsing model is to begin taking steps to make software-based interaction with IoT devices feel as intuitive as physical interaction with our surrounding environment. Besides physical placement of interfaces, what are the design decisions that help interface feel more tangibly and physically tied to the devices they control? Can we make interaction via mobile as convenient as on-device interfaces? Can we give creators the power to create interfaces suitable for their product rather than constrain the types of services that are available? How do we design the browser to better promote ephemeral discovery and interaction in public?

Augmented reality, while intuitive in many ways, can still generally feel awkward to users. Will users adjust to the paradigm of placing a phone between them and the world around them? Interesting approaches have been taken in the past to help reduce awkwardness in MAR, like using camera attachments to facilitate a more comfortable screen angle [4] or incorporating novel methods of feedback [16].

While not entirely important at least with initial prototypes, consideration of occlusion and other visual features that help provide a sense of realism to the virtual objects in physical space will eventually be useful for improving the user experience.

5.4 Developer Experience

Ideally, the process of creating devices that are compatible with the browser and developing interfaces that are discoverable, operable, and associated on the browser should be a relatively convenient process compared to the current siloed mobile app approach. What should the programming environment look like and what tools should be made available to developers?

Because the browser would essentially run on an extension of web standards, developers could still make use of a typical web programming environment to create the interfaces. Some browser-specific APIs will likely need to be defined to help facilitate functions like Bluetooth communication and establish some camera and visual verification protocols. Determining the exact set of functions that is required will be important. For device development, standard advertisement services over Bluetooth or Wi-Fi (e.g. mDNS) can be used to broadcast URL and other metadata to the phone. The developer can also set up a server to host a UI on the device itself.

5.5 Browsing Model

The UIs displayed on a user's smartphone can be physically tied to the devices they control or to a relevant point in physical space. But does this present a larger benefit than previous paradigms, like simple linking through Physical Web or QR codes alone? While Physical Web provides a convenient means for content discovery, it can either overwhelm the user with notifications for a long list of web pages or prevent relevant results from being presented in an attempt to filter that list. Additionally, it could be difficult for the user to determine which interface is associated with which device.

QR-linking does enable more physically-tied associations of content to target objects. However, at present, the common uses for QR seem to be very deliberate, single-time actions like linking to a download for an app or to a configuration web page within a browser. It also requires switching back and forth between camera and browser to open multiple interfaces. The MAR browser would effectively be combining camera, browser, and local network protocols to allow for a more seamless experience when inspecting and interacting with a space.

Once a model for linking interactive web interfaces to target devices is established, are there more interesting and novel features that could be supported through the MAR browser? Perhaps, for instance, a method could be established to allow users to easily perform trigger-action programming connecting multiple devices in their environment.

5.6 Data & Privacy

Because the system uses camera, location, and data about devices in local and private environments, there are risks associated with the size and sensitivity of the data. It is important to determine exactly what data is necessary to save locally or send online, and develop measures to ensure that no more than the necessary amount is retained, transmitted, or shared. Additionally, the browser model will likely require some defined notions of ownership and permission, and rules to enforce them. Safeguards will also need to be put in place to detect and prevent links to malicious web interfaces. It is essential that, at least, the standard practices of web security are preserved and supported through the browser.

5.7 Power Usage

Currently, use of augmented reality is a notable drain on phone batteries, which may discourage people from using the browser, especially in public, where phone charging is often limited. Phone companies seem to be allocating a considerable amount of effort into making it more efficient. Considering what practices make more efficient use of energy will be useful when implementing the design. For example, using flat imagery like favicons and rectangular web page interfaces in MAR will generally require less energy than rendering 3D objects and controls.

6 CONCLUSIONS

The technology to support mobile augmented reality exists, and there is high interest and effort put into continuing to improve it. Creation of an MAR-based browsing architecture would primarily consist of putting the right pieces together and making concrete decisions on standards, particularly for target recognition and device discovery. Further studies will be required to better assess and improve the usability of a such a system, but utilization of this architecture may enable us to begin taking steps to break free of the walled-garden infrastructure that is stifling the Internet of Things, while also providing compelling use cases for the augmented reality technology that is becoming more prevalent on our mobile devices.

7 ACKNOWLEDGMENTS

We wish to thank our shepherd, Xia Zhou, and the anonymous reviewers for their detailed comments and feedback. This work was supported in part by the CONIX Research Center, one of six centers in JUMP, a Semiconductor Research Corporation (SRC) program sponsored by DARPA. This material is also based upon work partially supported by the National Science Foundation under grant CNS-1824277, as well as by the NSF/Intel Partnership on CPS Security and Privacy under grant CNS-1822332.

REFERENCES

[1] Apple. 2018. Apple Developer Documentation. (Oct 2018). https://developer.apple.com/documentation/

[2] P. Belhumeur, D. Chen, S. Feiner, D. Jacobs, W. Kress, H. Ling, I. Lopez, R. Ramamoorthi, S. Sheorey, S. White, and L. Zhang. 2008. Searching the World's Herbaria: A System for Visual Identification of Plant Species. 116–129. DOI: https://doi.org/10.1007/978-3-540-88693-8_9

[3] B. Brumitt and J. Cadiz. 2001. "Let There Be Light": Examining Interfaces for Homes of the Future.. In INTERACT, Vol. 1. 375–382.

[4] A. Colley, W. Van Vlaenderen, J. Schöning, and J. Häkkilä. 2016. Changing the Camera-to-screen Angle to Improve AR Browser Usage. In Proceedings of the 18th International Conference on Human-Computer Interaction with Mobile Devices and Services (MobileHCI '16). ACM, New York, NY, USA, 442–452. DOI: https://doi.org/10.1145/2935334.2935384

[5] G. Furnas, T. Landauer, L. Gomez, and S. Dumais. 1987. The Vocabulary Problem in Human-system Communication. Commun. ACM 30, 11 (Nov. 1987), 964–971. DOI: https://doi.org/10.1145/32206.32212

[6] Google. 2017. The Physical Web. (Jun 2017). https://google.github.io/physical-web/

[7] Google. 2018. Google Developers. (Jul 2018). https://developers.google.com/products/

[8] V. Heun, S. Kasahara, and P. Maes. 2013. Smarter Objects: Using AR Technology to Program Physical Objects and Their Interactions. In CHI '13 Extended Abstracts on Human Factors in Computing Systems (CHI EA '13). ACM, New York, NY, USA, 961–966. DOI: https://doi.org/10.1145/2468356.2468528

[9] N. Kumar, P. Belhumeur, A. Biswas, D. Jacobs, W. Kress, I. Lopez, and J. Soares. 2012. Leafsnap: A Computer Vision System for Automatic Plant Species Identification. In Computer Vision – ECCV 2012. Springer Berlin Heidelberg, Berlin, Heidelberg, 502–516.

[10] Y. Kuo, P. Pannuto, K. Hsiao, and P. Dutta. 2014. Luxapose: Indoor Positioning with Mobile Phones and Visible Light. In Proceedings of the 20th Annual International Conference on Mobile Computing and Networking (MobiCom '14). ACM, New York, NY, USA, 447–458. DOI: https://doi.org/10.1145/2639108.2639109

[11] P. Lazik, N. Rajagopal, O. Shih, B. Sinopoli, and A. Rowe. 2015. ALPS: A Bluetooth and Ultrasound Platform for Mapping and Localization. In Proceedings of the 13th ACM Conference on Embedded Networked Sensor Systems (SenSys '15). ACM, New York, NY, USA, 73–84. DOI: https://doi.org/10.1145/2809695.2809727

[12] P. Lazik, A. Rowe, and N. Wilkerson. 2018. ALPS: The Acoustic Location Processing System. https://www.microsoft.com/en-us/research/uploads/prod/2017/12/Patrick_Lazik_2018.pdf. (2018).

[13] P. Lazik, A. Rowe, and N. Wilkerson. 2018. Realty and Reality: Where Location Matters. https://www.microsoft.com/en-us/research/uploads/prod/2017/12/John_Miller_2018.pdf. (2018).

[14] J. Lee, J. Kim, J. Kim, and J. Kwak. 2007. A Unified Remote Console Based on Augmented Reality in a Home Network Environment. In 2007 Digest of Technical Papers International Conference on Consumer Electronics. 1–2. DOI: https://doi.org/10.1109/ICCE.2007.341516

[15] H. Ling. 2017. Augmented Reality in Reality. IEEE MultiMedia 24, 3 (2017), 10–15. DOI: https://doi.org/10.1109/MMUL.2017.3051517

[16] C. Liu, S. Huot, J. Diehl, W. Mackay, and M. Beaudouin-Lafon. 2012. Evaluating the Benefits of Real-time Feedback in Mobile Augmented Reality with Hand-held Devices. In Proceedings of the SIGCHI Conference on Human Factors in Computing Systems (CHI '12). ACM, New York, NY, USA, 2973–2976. DOI: https://doi.org/10.1145/2207676.2208706

[17] D. Marques and R. Costello. 2015. Skin & bones: an artistic repair of a science exhibition by a mobile app. MIDAS. Museus e estudos interdisciplinares 5 (2015).

[18] Hewlett Packard. 2018. HP Reveal. (Mar 2018). https://www.hpreveal.com/

[19] J. Platonov, H. Heibel, P. Meier, and B. Grollmann. 2006. A mobile markerless AR system for maintenance and repair. In 2006 IEEE/ACM International Symposium on Mixed and Augmented Reality. 105–108. DOI: https://doi.org/10.1109/ISMAR.2006.297800

[20] N. Rajagopal, P. Lazik, and A. Rowe. 2014. Visual light landmarks for mobile devices. In IPSN-14 Proceedings of the 13th International Symposium on Information Processing in Sensor Networks. 249–260. DOI: https://doi.org/10.1109/IPSN.2014.6846757

[21] N. Rajagopal, J. Miller, K. Kumar, A. Luong, and A. Rowe. 2018. Welcome to My World: Demystifying Multi-user AR with the Cloud: Demo Abstract. In Proceedings of the 17th ACM/IEEE International Conference on Information Processing in Sensor Networks (IPSN '18). IEEE Press, Piscataway, NJ, USA, 146–147. DOI: https://doi.org/10.1109/IPSN.2018.00036

[22] D. Van Krevelen and R. Poelman. 2010. A Survey of Augmented Reality Technologies, Applications and Limitations. International Journal of Virtual Reality 9, 2 (June 2010), 1–20. http://www.ijvr.org/issues/issue2-2010/paper1%20.pdf

Toward Practical Volumetric Video Streaming On Commodity Smartphones

Feng Qian[1]   Bo Han[2]   Jarrell Pair[3]   Vijay Gopalakrishnan[2]

[1]University of Minnesota – Twin Cities   [2]AT&T Labs – Research   [3]AT&T

ABSTRACT

Volumetric videos offer six degree-of-freedom (DoF) as well as 3D rendering, making them highly immersive, interactive, and expressive. In this paper, we design Nebula, a practical and resource-efficient volumetric video streaming system for commodity mobile devices. Our design leverages edge computing to reduce the computation burden on mobile clients. We also introduce various optimizations to lower the perceived "motion-to-photon" delay, to dynamically adapt to the fluctuating network bandwidth, and to reduce the system's resource consumption while maintaining a high QoE.

ACM Reference Format:
Feng Qian, Bo Han, Jarrell Pair, and Vijay Gopalakrishnan. 2019. Toward Practical Volumetric Video Streaming On Commodity Smartphones. In *The 20th International Workshop on Mobile Computing Systems and Applications (HotMobile '19), February 27–28, 2019, Santa Cruz, CA, USA.* ACM, New York, NY, USA, 6 pages. https://doi.org/10.1145/3301293.3302358

1 INTRODUCTION

This paper examines *volumetric videos*[1], an emerging immersive media, and explores how to efficiently stream them to mobile devices. Compared to regular videos and 360° panoramic videos that recently became popular, volumetric videos are unique in two key aspects. First, regular and 360° video content is on either a plane or a sphere. Volumetric videos are instead truly *three-dimensional*: they consist of not 2D pixels, but elements such as voxels (volume pixels) or 3D meshes (polygons). Second, volumetric videos provide six degrees of freedom (6DoF), allowing a viewer to freely change both the position (X, Y, Z) and the orientation (yaw, pitch, roll) of her viewport. By contrast, regular videos provide no viewport freedom, and 360° videos allow only 3DoF as the viewer's translational position is always fixed.

Both features above make volumetric videos highly immersive, interactive, and expressive. They can support numerous innovative applications from entertainment to medical and education. Volumetric videos can be represented in different ways. In this paper, we exemplify our approaches using the *Point Cloud* (PtCl) representation where each video frame consists of multiple voxels or

---

[1]A demonstration of high-quality volumetric video streaming can be found at https://www.youtube.com/watch?v=feGGKasvamg.

points [13]. Nevertheless our high-level approaches are applicable to other sophisticated representations such as 3D meshes [17]. PtCl is a popular way to represent 3D objects due to its simplistic data structure and good rendering performance. Static PtCls have been well studied in the computer graphics and multimedia communities (§5). However, existing work has not studied the delivery of volumetric videos that consist of a *stream* of PtCls to resource-constrained mobile devices and over bandwidth-limited wireless links, which is the focus of this paper.

Streaming volumetric videos is challenging due to several reasons. First, they are extremely bandwidth-consuming (§3), and thus their wireless delivery may require the support from future 5G networks [1]. Second, unlike regular pixel videos that can be decoded using dedicated hardware, decoding volumetric videos can only be done by software today. This results in high computational overhead. Third, adaptive-bitrate (ABR) video streaming systems typically have several key components such as rate adaptation, QoE inference, and buffer control. Little research has been done on any of these aspects for volumetric video streaming on mobile devices.

In this paper, we begin with developing a proof-of-concept PtCl player on Android platform (§3), and use it to conduct measurements to demonstrate several key challenges described above. Based on our observations, we present a holistic design of a practical PtCl video streaming system for commodity smartphones. We call our system Nebula, whose key design aspects consist of the following.

- **Layered Content Organization** (§4.1). We devise a DASH-style scheme to organize the content on the server side. By leveraging the unique characteristics of PtCl data, we delta-encode each video chunk into *layers* to allow its quality to be incrementally upgraded.

- **Edge Assistance** (§4.2). Since directly decoding a compressed PtCl video on a phone is expensive, we introduce an edge (proxy) server in Nebula. The proxy *transcodes* the PtCl stream into a regular pixel-based video stream, which captures the viewer's viewport and can be efficiently decoded on smartphones. We propose various optimizations to reduce the motion-to-photon delay [2] between the client and the proxy.

- **Rate Adaptation** (§4.3). Nebula integrates two separate rate adaptation mechanisms, with one running between the phone and proxy, and the other between the proxy and the server, to adapt the video quality to the varying network condition. In particular, we propose directions toward developing a robust rate adaptation algorithm for volumetric videos.

- **Viewport Adaptation** (§4.4). For a spatially large PtCl or a scene with multiple scattered PtCls, fetching or decoding the entire PtCl may be infeasible. In this case, Nebula applies *viewport adaptation* that allows the proxy to fetch only the portions that the viewer is seeing or about to see, based on predicting the 6DoF movement of the viewport. We further propose optimizations that reduce the resource utilization while maintaining a high QoE for viewport adaptation.

2 VOLUMETRIC VIDEOS: A PRIMER

Capturing. Volumetric videos are captured using multiple RGB-D cameras with *depth* sensors, *e.g.*, offered by Microsoft Kinect, Intel RealSense, and various LIDAR scanners [23], which acquire 3D data from different viewpoints. The acquired data is then merged to obtain the entire scene. During the merging process, frames captured by different cameras should be properly synchronized, their coordinates be unified, and noises be removed. The whole processing pipeline can be realized by open-source software such as LiveScan3D [14], a 3D data acquisition system supporting multiple Kinect devices.

Representation. Point cloud (PtCl) and 3D mesh are two popular ways to represent volumetric videos. 3D mesh has been extensively investigated by the computer graphics community for a long time [17]. It employs a collection of meshes, which can be triangles, quadrangles, or general polygons, to represent the geometry of 3D models. Although 3D mesh can accurately model objects, its algorithms are complex as they need to maintain the topological consistency in the processing pipeline [13]. In contrast, PtCl is a much more flexible and simpler representation as introduced in §1.

Compression (*i.e.*, encoding) of 3D objects has been well studied in the literature, with the state-of-the-art compression scheme being *octree*-based approaches [7, 11, 18]. An octree is a tree data structure that partitions a 3D region by recursively dividing it into eight subregions [24], with the levels of detail being controlled by the height of the tree. When applied to a PtCl, an octree efficiently stores the points in such a way that its nodes correspond to regions that contain at least one point, and the best estimation of the points' locations is given by the leaf nodes. In addition to compressing a single PtCl (or a single PtCl video frame), the octree can be extended to perform delta encoding between two PtCls (or inter-frame compression for a PtCl video) [12]. Note that as of today, decoding volumetric videos is typically performed by software. But as volumetric video becomes more popular, dedicated hardware support for volumetric video decoding may appear in the future.

3 PTCL STREAMING ON SMARTPHONES

We examine the performance of volumetric video streaming on mobile devices, to motivate the design of Nebula.

PtCl Video Player. Despite existing efforts on volumetric video streaming [10, 21], fewer studies, if any, have been conducted on understanding its performance on commodity smartphones. We thus first develop a PtCl video player for Android. Our player was written in Java and C++ in 2,800 LoC. It is capable of playing PtCl videos hosted locally or remotely (fetched over TCP). The videos can be in either raw or compressed format. A raw video contains a series of *frames* to be played at a fixed rate (*e.g.*, 24 or 30 FPS). Each frame consists of a PtCl *i.e.*, a list of 3D points. Each point occupies 9 bytes: its position (X, Y, Z, 2 bytes each) and its color (R, G, B, 1 byte each). A compressed video has a similar format except that each frame (PtCl) is encoded using an octree (we have not yet implemented inter-frame compression). The player maintains

a playback buffer of up to 50 frames, and plays each frame by rendering its PtCl using OpenGL/GPU.

During a playback, the viewer can freely change the viewport's position (X, Y, Z) and orientation (yaw, pitch, roll). For intuitive interactions, the viewer can select one of three modes and swipe the screen to change the viewport: *Orbit* (rotating the viewport around the Y axis), *Zoom* (moving the viewport along the Z axis, closer or further to the origin), and *Pan* (moving the viewport along the X or Y axis).

Dataset. We use a volumetric video captured at AT&T Shape [1]. Depicting a female singer, it allows viewers to immersively watch her performance. The video consists of 3,188 frames, and each frame contains on average 50,360 points. Using this video, we further construct four other videos with sparser or denser points: 12.6K, 25.2K, 75.5K, and 100.7K on average in a frame. We make the points sparser by performing random sampling, and make them denser by adding noises (randomly generated points) to each frame.

Measurements. We next use our player to measure the streaming performance. All experiments were conducted on Samsung Galaxy S8, a state-of-the-art smartphone as in 2018. Unless otherwise stated, all reported measurement results are averaged over 5 playbacks of our test video described above.

Observation 1. Rendering an uncompressed (decoded) PtCl video is fast. We begin with playing uncompressed PtCl videos locally. As shown in the "Avg Render FPS" column in Table 1, depending on the frame density, the average FPS ranges from 173 to 1110, considerably higher than the required frame rate of 24 FPS. This is attributed to the simplicity of the PtCl structure that allows fast rendering, compared to other complex representations such as 3D mesh [11, 13].

Observation 2. Transferring uncompressed PtCl video is challenging over today's wireless networks. We next stream the uncompressed videos from a server to a client over commercial LTE networks. Despite the high bandwidth (up to 40Mbps) offered by LTE, the playback experienced unacceptably long stalls for almost all videos. The reason is simply the large frame size as shown in Table 1. For a PtCl video with 50K points per frame, the required bandwidth for streaming uncompressed frames at 24 FPS is $9 \times 50\text{K} \times 24 \times 8 = 86.4$Mbps.

Observation 3. Decoding performance on today's mobile devices is poor. Given the above observation, a natural idea is to encode (compress) a PtCl video before its transmission. We thus cross-compile the Point Cloud Library (PCL [3]), a production-quality library for PtCl processing, on Android. We integrate PCL into our player by using PCL's built-in functions for efficient octree-based PtCl encoding and decoding. Surprisingly, as shown in Table 1, the decoding performance on SGS8 is very poor, with the FPS ranging from 1.5 to 13.9, due to the costly operations of walking through the octree, inspecting each node, and reconstructing the decoded data to be consumed by the OpenGL shader.

Octree-based encoding is typically lossy. Therefore PCL supports different resolution profiles that control the video quality by adjusting the height of the octree. The results in Table 1 are for the low-resolution profile (favoring faster decoding, higher compression ratio). Table 2 shows the phone-side decoding performance for medium- and high-resolution profiles, whose FPS and compression ratio further degrade.

Avg # Points	Frame Size	Avg Render FPS (Phone)	Dec. FPS (Phone)	Dec. FPS (Server)
12.6K	0.11MB	1110.8	13.9	41.7
25.2K	0.23MB	776.0	7.2	20.2
50.4K	0.45MB	351.6	3.5	10.1
75.5K	0.68MB	233.3	2.1	6.1
100.7K	0.91MB	173.3	1.5	4.4

Table 1: PtCl stream rendering performance on SGS8 and decoding performance on SGS8 and an edge server (1 thread, low-resolution profile).

Res. Profile	Dec. FPS (Phone)	Comp. Ratio
Low	3.5	36.3%
Med	3.2	25.4%
High	3.0	15.7%

Table 2: Decoding performance on SGS8 for different resolution profiles (1 thread, 50K points per frame).

# Threads	Dec. FPS (Phone)	Dec. FPS (Server)
1	3.5	10.1
2	7.0	19.0
4	8.6	34.3
6	8.2	41.3
8	6.7	47.0

Table 3: Multi-core decoding performance on SGS8 and an edge server (low-res profile, 50K points per frame).

Similar to regular videos, there are two opportunities one can leverage: *intra-frame* compression, which compresses a single PtCl, and *inter-frame* compression, which delta-encodes a PtCl based on another PtCl (*e.g.*, of a previous frame). The above results as well as most existing studies only concern with intra-frame compression (as a result the compression ratios in Table 2 are low). Applying inter-frame compression can further reduce the video size, but at the cost of even slower decoding speed on smartphones.

Observation 4. Multi-core decoding provides limited performance improvement on smartphones. A straightforward idea to boost the decoding performance is to leverage the multiple CPU cores to concurrently decode multiple frames. We implement multi-threaded decoding in our player. Our SGS8 phone is equipped with an octa-core CPU. However, as shown in Table 3, when using 4 threads, the decoding FPS only increases by 1.5× compared to single-threaded decoding. Also, launching more than 4 threads causes the performance to degrade. This may be possibly attributed to multiple factors such as shared I/O and limited CPU cache. Note that PtCl decoding may also be accelerated by GPU. Nevertheless, GPUs on mobile devices are significantly weaker than those on PCs/servers due to the fundamental constraints of energy consumption and heat dissipation.

4 THE DESIGN OF THE NEBULA SYSTEM

We now detail the design of the Nebula system whose architecture is shown in Figure 1.

4.1 Video Content Organization

To store the PtCl content, Nebula employs a scheme that is compliant with DASH (Dynamic Adaptive Streaming over HTTP). Video frames are properly compressed using both intra-frame and inter-frame encoding. The PtCl stream is then segmented into *chunks* each having a fixed duration. A manifest file will be provided to the client to inform the URL of each chunk.

Layered Representation. In traditional DASH schemes, a chunk has multiple *independently* encoded versions corresponding to different quality levels. Nebula instead leverages the unique characteristics of PtCl chunks by organizing the chunk data (the points) into *layers*. Assume a PtCl chunk has n versions/layers. Among all versions, only the lowest version (layer L_0), which contains the smallest number of points, is self-contained; the next lowest layer L_1 only contains the *delta* from L_0. In general, the client needs to fetch all layers from L_0 to L_i, and to combine their points to form the actual chunk data belonging to the version of the i-th quality level. Such a layered representation greatly improves the flexibility

of the rate adaptation algorithm by allowing *incrementally* upgrading a chunk's quality (§4.3). For intra-frame encoding using an octree, different layers' encoded data can be generated by vertically partitioning the tree. The partition method for inter-frame encoding can also be developed, with the constraint that encoded data of a given layer should only depend on the same or lower layers of other frames within the same chunk.

We note that the underlying concept of layered encoding is not new. It has been proposed in the context of regular pixel-based videos, known as Scalable Video Coding (SVC). However, SVC has never registered commercial deployment due to its high complexity and high encoding overhead [15]. In contrast, our layered encoding scheme for PtCl is simple due to the very nature of PtCl, whose points belonging to different layers can easily be merged.

4.2 Edge Offloading

Our findings in §3 suggest that directly decoding a PtCl video stream on today's COTS smartphones might be challenging. Nebula therefore offloads the PtCl decoding to an edge server (proxy). Specifically, the client keeps reporting its viewport's position and orientation to the edge proxy. Meanwhile, the proxy fetches the PtCl stream from the remote server, decodes it, and transcodes it (based on the viewport's position and orientation) into a regular pixel-based video stream. The transcoded video is then sent to the client, which can efficiently decode the video through, for example, its hardware H.264/H.265 decoders.

We demonstrate that a commodity edge server is capable of decoding PtCl streams at the line rate. We repeat the decoding experiments in §3 on a commodity server with Intel Xeon E3-1240 processor at 3.5GHz (launched in 2015), 16GB memory, and 1TB SATA HDD. As shown in Table 1, for single-core decoding, the server outperforms our SGS8 smartphone by about 200% in terms of FPS. Table 3 compares the multi-core decoding performance between the phone and server. The server's performance scales well with the number of threads, and outperforms the phone by up to 450% under multi-core. For 12.6K, 25.2K, 50.4K, 75.5K, and 100.7K points per frame, our server achieves decoding FPS of up to 190, 95, 47.0, 29.2, and 21.4, respectively.

The Overall Processing Pipeline on the proxy side consists of the following five tasks: (1) fetching the PtCl data from the server (I/O bound), (2) decoding the PtCl stream (CPU bound), (3) rendering the PtCl stream based on the client's viewport position and orientation (GPU bound), (4) encoding the rendering result into a pixel video stream (DSP), and (5) sending the pixel video to the client (I/O). Note that the above tasks consume different types of system resources and thus can be executed in a pipelined manner.

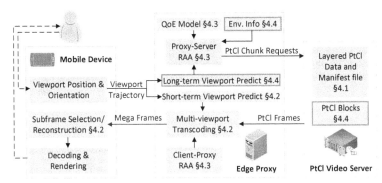

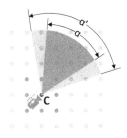

Figure 1: The Nebula **architecture. Components in red boxes relate to viewport adaptation (§4.4) that may be optionally enabled.**

Figure 2: Transcoding a PtCl frame to multiple subframes, each with a different viewport, to reduce the motion-to-photon latency.

Now let us consider the actual transcoding process. A simple approach is to take a single "snapshot" for the current viewport position and orientation reported by the client. Let t_1 be the time when the client reports its viewport v, and t_2 be the time when the frame transcoded for v is displayed. Under the above transcoding approach, the delay $t_2 - t_1$ is the so-called "motion-to-photon" latency [2] (*i.e.*, the time taken for a viewport movement to be reflected on the screen).

We next examine this critical QoE metric. In the five tasks described above, Tasks (1) and (2) do not depend on the client's real-time viewport information so the decoded PtCl data can be buffered beforehand. Only (3), (4), and (5) contribute to the motion-to-photon latency. To quantify it, we conduct experiments on a DELL laptop (as an edge server) with an NVIDIA GTX 1080 GPU. On this laptop, rendering a PtCl frame with 50K points takes less than 1ms, and the per-frame encoding time for 4K, 2K, and 1080p H.264 videos is 10ms, 5ms, and 3ms, respectively. We then measure the per-frame decoding time on SGS8, which is 11ms, 5ms, and 3ms for 4K, 2K, and 1080p frames, respectively. Thus, the motion-to-photon delay for 4K, 2K, and 1080p resolutions are 21ms, 10ms, and 6ms, respectively, plus their corresponding network transmission time (including the uplink latency for reporting the viewport).

Multi-viewport Transcoding. We consider further reducing the motion-to-photon delay. Recall that when a motion occurs, the user's intended viewport at t_2 may be different from the displayed viewport *i.e.*, the one at t_1 (t_1 and t_2 defined previously). Such a discrepancy degrades the QoE. Our basic idea is thus to let the proxy transcode one PtCl frame into multiple pixel-based frames (called *subframes*), which include not only the reported viewport (at t_1), but also its nearby viewports for t_2 based on predicting the (short-term) viewport movement. Ideally, if the prediction is accurate, then at t_2, one of these subframes' viewports will match the user's intended viewport. Displaying it effectively eliminates the motion-to-photon delay. In reality, we anticipate that some of these viewports will be at least close to the user's intended viewport, thus reducing the impact on QoE.

Consider the two-dimensional example shown in Figure 2. The current viewport position is C and covers the dark blue area with a FoV (field-of-view) of α. When actually generating the subframes, the proxy will take two approaches. First, it generates subframes at nearby locations (in red dots) to accommodate the potential translational movement of the viewport. Second, the proxy may enlarge

some subframes' viewports (*e.g.*, to $\alpha' > \alpha$) to tolerate the possible rotational movement. A larger-than-FoV subframe will be generated using a panoramic representation such as Equirectangular or CubeMap so any FoV covered by it can be restored.

To facilitate deciding which viewports to transcode, Nebula employs effective algorithms to predict the 6DoF viewport movement. This is inspired by the fact that in 3DoF panoramic video streaming, there were studies showing that the yaw, pitch, and roll can be accurately predicted in the near future (less than 0.5 seconds or so) [22]. Then, leveraging the *short-term* prediction algorithms, Nebula can dynamically decide how many and which viewports (subframes) to include, as well as each viewport's position and size (α'). Several factors affect the decision: the speed, direction, and mode (orbit, zoom, pan) of the viewer's viewport movement as well as its prediction accuracy.

Client-side Subframe Decoding, Selection and Reconstruction. The proxy then encodes the multiple subframes (transcoded from a PtCl frame) into a "mega frame" and sends it to the client. Due to their proximity, typically the subframes are visually similar, allowing efficient cross-subframe compression. During a playback, the client picks one subframe from each mega frame, decodes it, and displays it. To reduce the decoding overhead, Nebula can leverage new codec features such as the Tiling Mode [19] in H.265 to let the client decode only its selected subframe in a mega frame. Regarding the actual selection policy, the selected subframe's viewport should be the closest to the user's intended viewport. We will also investigate the feasibility of using fast 2D scene reconstruction [8] to achieve better viewport approximation by "interpolating" the received subframes when user's viewport C is not aligned exactly with the red dots in Figure 2.

4.3 Rate Adaptation

A rate adaptation algorithm (RAA) dynamically adjusts the video quality based on the available network bandwidth. In Nebula, due to the transcoding proxy, we need to consider two types of RAAs: one runs between the client and the proxy for the pixel video stream, and the other operates between the proxy and the server for the PtCl stream.

The Client-proxy RAA is overall similar to a traditional RAA. However, one key difference is the multi-viewport (subframe) nature in Nebula. Therefore a challenge here is how to assign quality levels to different subframes. A simple approach would be to treat a mega frame as a single unit by assigning the same quality level to all its subframes. An advanced solution would be to assign different quality levels to them based on their probabilities of being selected.

The Proxy-server RAA differs vastly from existing RAA due to two reasons. First, it operates on PtCl streams whose many characteristics such as bitrate dynamics and QoE metrics are very different from those of traditional pixel-based videos. Second, recall from §4.1 that PtCl chunks are progressively encoded into layers; therefore, to be more bandwidth-adaptive, the RAA should have the capability of incrementally upgrading an existing chunk by fetching additional layer(s). We next describe two essential steps toward developing a robust RAA for PtCl videos: deriving QoE metrics and designing the actual RAA.

Deriving QoE Metrics. For traditional videos, a commonly agreed QoE metric is a weighted sum of several components: bitrate, stall duration, video quality switch, *etc.* [25]. QoE metrics for volumetric videos, however, still remain an open problem (see §5).

We exemplify several interesting research questions we would like to answer. (1) Compared to users watching regular videos (0DoF) and 360° videos (3DoF), are PtCl video viewers more sensitive to stalls as they exercise their 6DoF when navigating in the 3D space? (2) How do quality changes in a PtCl stream impact the viewer's QoE? (3) A new dimension in 6DoF videos is the distance from the viewer to the PtCl. As the viewing distance becomes larger, how should we reduce the PtCl quality while still maintaining a good QoE?

To get the QoE ground truth, we plan to conduct IRB-approved user studies. We will play strategically crafted PtCl videos to the subjects and ask them to give subjective scores. The ground truth will be leveraged to build a comprehensive QoE model of PtCl video streaming on mobile devices.

Designing RAA for Layered PtCl Stream. Among many candidate solutions, Nebula employs an RAA under a discrete optimization framework [25], which provides a principled way for rate adaptation. Specifically, it periodically examines a finite window of the next N chunks, and searches for a quality assignment that maximizes a utility function derived from the QoE model (the above task). Incremental chunk upgrade can be easily integrated into the optimization framework: even if a chunk has already been downloaded, it will still be considered by our RAA as follows. Assume a fetched chunk has a current quality level of l. The RAA will set a search space from l to the highest quality level. Then if the RAA computes a level higher than l, the additional layer(s) will be fetched to upgrade the chunk.

A challenge we need to overcome is the potentially high runtime overhead of our RAA, whose single invocation incurs an overhead of $O(Q^N)$ if an exhaustive search is performed (N is the search window size and Q is the total number of quality levels). Such an overhead may be effectively reduced by, for example, reusing previous computation results and applying various heuristics.

4.4 Viewport Adaptation

Use Case: a PtCl Zoo. So far we assume a PtCl video contains only one point cloud, whose entire stream is fetched by the proxy. We now consider a more general scenario where the entire scene, oftentimes consisting of multiple PtCls, is too large to be fetched

as a whole. Consider a virtual zoo application. It is comprised of a static 3D background and many animals each being rendered as a PtCl video. At a given time, a user "walking" in the zoo can see only a small subset of all animals. For large animals such as a dinosaur, the user may see only part of it when standing close to it.

Streaming this virtual zoo is very different from and consumes much higher bandwidth than today's VR apps, whose dynamic objects typically consist of very short animation sequences [5]. To efficiently stream the PtCl zoo to a mobile device, our previous building blocks such as edge transcoding, rate adaptation, and layered representation remain useful. In addition, we need the mechanism of *viewport-adaptation* where the proxy prefetches only the content that the viewer is about to see. This is the key mechanism for reducing the server-to-proxy traffic and the proxy-side workload.

3D Point Cloud Blocks. A prerequisite of viewport-adaptive streaming is to segment (when necessary) a PtCl chunk into *blocks* [20]. A block has the same duration as a chunk but only occupies a smaller, bounded 3D region. With their URLs listed in the manifest file, blocks can be independently fetched and decoded, thus providing a mechanism of partially fetching a PtCl. In addition, as a block may move, the client needs to be aware of the block's position during its playback (we will shortly see why). To realize this, for each block, we include the moving trajectories of the eight corners of its *bounding box* in the manifest file.

Viewport Adaptation. Let us first assume an ideal scenario where the viewer's 6DoF movement trajectory is perfectly known. Then at any given time, by knowing the position and orientation of the viewport, as well as the positions of the eight corners of each block's bounding box, the proxy can quickly compute the set of blocks (more accurately, their bounding boxes) that the viewer sees and therefore should be fetched.

In reality, however, due to the viewer's movement randomness, we need to *predict* her 6DoF viewport movement. This prediction differs from the short-term prediction described in §4.2 (for multi-viewport transcoding) in the time scale: here the prediction needs to be more ahead of time (*e.g.*, 1 to 2 seconds) due to the extra delay the proxy takes to fetch, decode, and render the PtCl blocks. Unfortunately, even for 3DoF viewport movement, its predictability decreases considerably as the prediction window becomes longer [22]. We expect that *long-term* 6DoF prediction may also be challenging. We plan to conduct a user study that collects real users' 6DoF movement traces, and study their predictability.

Despite the potential challenges described above, we do believe it is feasible to design a practical viewport-adaptive streaming scheme by leveraging an edge proxy. We highlight several high-level design principles below.

• The proxy should account for both the bandwidth and its decoding capability when deciding which blocks to fetch.

• The proxy can use the environment (walls, obstacles, *etc.*) to quickly filter out blocks that the viewer cannot see.

• To minimize the risk of stalls, even if a block has a low probability of being perceived, the proxy may still need to conservatively fetch it at a low quality, and incrementally upgrade it later when necessary (§4.3).

• Distant blocks are shown in small sizes to the viewer, so they can also be fetched at a low quality per the QoE model. For such distant blocks, when the resource is limited, the proxy may even just fetch a single frame that is statically displayed to satisfy a minimum user experience requirement.

5 RELATED WORK

Compression of PtCl and 3D mesh has been well investigated in the literature. In particular, several variations of octree-based (§2) compression have been proposed (*e.g.*, [7, 11, 24]). Kammerl *et al.* extended the octree to perform inter-frame compression for real-time 3D data acquisition [12]. Another inter-frame compression scheme based on iterative closest points (ICP) algorithm was proposed by Mekuria *et al.* [18]. We refer readers to [17] for 3D mesh compression.

Streaming volumetric videos is a new topic. Very recently (2018), Park *et al.* [21] sketched a greedy volumetric video streaming algorithm that considers video bitrate, visibility, and the distance from the viewer. DASH-PC [10] extends DASH to PtCl streaming. It proposes sub-sampling dense PtCls to create different quality representations, as well as designs a DASH-style manifest file format. Compared to both proposals, Nebula is a holistic PtCl video streaming system designed specifically for mobile devices, with unique features such as edge assistance, perceived delay reduction, principled rate adaptation, and incremental quality upgrade.

QoE Metrics have been well studied for regular videos, but remain an open problem for volumetric video streaming. Most of the existing work focuses on assessing the quality of a static 3D model, with the reference model known, using simple metrics such as point-to-point distance or angular similarity [4]. For volumetric videos, researchers have done limited subjective tests or simply used the above per-frame distortion metrics [6]. However, it is well known that (for regular videos) traditional image quality metrics such as PSNR and SSIM do not correlate well with subjective measures (QoE). The same likely holds for volumetric videos. We thus plan to thoroughly investigate their QoE metrics by considering the impact of, for example, stalls, quality changes, viewing distance, and the motion-to-photon delay.

VR and 360° Video Streaming Systems. Finally, there exist a plethora of systems on mobile VR and 360° video streaming. Representative research prototypes include FlashBack [5] (boosting mobile VR quality through caching rendered scenes), Furion [16] (cloud-assisted VR through separating foreground and background content), Rubiks [9] (tile-based 360° video streaming), and Flare [22] (another viewport-adaptive 360° video streaming system for smartphones with further optimizations). Compared to VR and 360° video streaming, PtCl streaming faces numerous challenges such as poor decoding performance on smartphones, a lack of rate adaptation algorithms, and the difficulty for predicting the 6DoF viewport movement, as well as unique opportunities such as the specific data structure of PtCl data. All these challenges and opportunities are considered in Nebula's design.

6 ON-GOING WORK AND CONCLUSION

Motivated by the poor PtCl streaming performance on smartphones, we present Nebula, a holistic system for high-quality mobile volumetric video streaming. Our central idea is to use an edge server to judiciously transcode a PtCl stream into a regular pixel-based

video that can be efficiently transmitted to and decoded by mobile devices. We further describe various optimizations such as incremental quality upgrade, motion-to-photon delay reduction, principled QoE-aware rate adaptation, and viewport adaptation.

We are now prototyping Nebula according to our design detailed in §4, as well as conducting the IRB-approved user studies as described earlier. We will thoroughly evaluate Nebula using PtCl video content on real mobile devices and under diverse network conditions. We also plan to extend Nebula to support 3D mesh based volumetric videos.

ACKNOWLEDGEMENTS

We thank the anonymous reviewers for their comments. We also thank Dr. Aakanksha Chowdhery for shepherding our paper.

REFERENCES

[1] AT&T Future of 5G Technology. http://bit.ly/2NRvNQF.
[2] Google VR – Fundamental Concepts. https://developers.google.com/vr/discover/fundamentals.
[3] Point Cloud Library (PCL). http://pointclouds.org/.
[4] E. Alexiou and T. Ebrahimi. Point Cloud Quality Assessment Metric Based on Angular Similarity. In *IEEE ICME*, 2018.
[5] K. Boos, D. Chu, and E. Cuervo. FlashBack: Immersive Virtual Reality on Mobile Devices via Rendering Memoization. In *MobiSys*, 2016.
[6] E. Dumic, C. R. Duarte, and L. A. da Silva Cruz. Subjective Evaluation and Objective Measures for Point Clouds – State of the Art. In *Intl. Colloquium on Smart Grid Metrology*, 2018.
[7] T. Golla and R. Klein. Real-time Point Cloud Compression. In *Intl. Conference on Intelligent Robots and Systems*, 2015.
[8] A. Hamza and M. Hefeeda. Adaptive Streaming of Interactive Free Viewpoint Videos to Heterogeneous Clients. In *MMSys*, 2016.
[9] J. He, M. A. Qureshi, L. Qiu, J. Li, F. Li, and L. Han. Rubiks: Practical 360-Degree Streaming for Smartphones. In *ACM MobiSys*, 2018.
[10] M. Hosseini and C. Timmerer. Dynamic Adaptive Point Cloud Streaming. In *ACM Packet Video*, 2018.
[11] Y. Huang, J. Peng, C.-C. J. Kuo, and M. Gopi. A Generic Scheme for Progressive Point Cloud Coding. *IEEE Trans. on Vis. and Computer Graphics*, 14(2):440–453, 2008.
[12] J. Kammerl, N. Blodow, R. B. Rusu, S. Gedikli, M. Beetz, and E. Steinbach. Real-time Compression of Point Cloud Streams. In *Intl. Conference on Robotics and Automation*, 2012.
[13] L. Kobbelt and M. Botsch. A Survey of Point-Based Techniques in Computer Graphics. *Computers & Graphics*, 28(6):801–814, 2004.
[14] M. Kowalski, J. Naruniec, and M. Daniluk. LiveScan3D: A Fast and Inexpensive 3D Data Acquisition System for Multiple Kinect v2 Sensors. In *Intl. Conf. on 3D Vision*, 2015.
[15] C. Kreuzberger, D. Posch, and H. Hellwagner. A Scalable Video Coding Dataset and Toolchain for Dynamic Adaptive Streaming over HTTP. In *MMSys*, 2015.
[16] Z. Lai, Y. C. Hu, Y. Cui, L. Sun, and N. Dai. Furion: Engineering high-quality immersive virtual reality on today's mobile devices. In *Proceedings of MobiCom 2017*, pages 409–421. ACM, 2017.
[17] A. Maglo, G. Lavoué, F. Dupont, and C. Hudelot. 3D Mesh Compression: Survey, Comparisons, and Emerging Trends. *ACM Computing Surveys*, 47(3), 2015.
[18] R. Mekuria, K. Blom, and P. Cesar. Design, Implementation and Evaluation of a Point Cloud Codec for Tele-Immersive Video. *IEEE Trans. on Circuits and Systems for Video Technology*, 27(4):828–842, 2017.
[19] K. Misra, A. Segall, M. Horowitz, S. Xu, A. Fuldseth, and M. Zhou. An overview of tiles in HEVC. *IEEE Journal of Selected Topics in Signal Processing*, 7(6):969–977, 2013.
[20] A. Nguyen and B. Le. 3D Point Cloud Segmentation: A Survey. In *International Conference on Robotics, Automation and Mechatronics*, 2013.
[21] J. Park, P. A. Chou, and J.-N. Hwang. Volumetric Media Streaming for Augmented Reality. In *GLOBECOM*, 2018.
[22] F. Qian, B. Han, Q. Xiao, and V. Gopalakrishnan. Flare: Practical Viewport-Adaptive 360-Degree Video Streaming for Mobile Devices. In *ACM MobiCom*, 2018.
[23] H. Qiu, F. Ahmad, F. Bai, M. Gruteser, and R. Govindan. Augmented Vehicular Reality. In *Proceedings of MobiSys*, 2018.
[24] R. Schnabel and R. Klein. Octree-based Point-Cloud Compression. In *Euro. Symp. on Point-Based Graphics*, 2006.
[25] X. Yin, A. Jindal, V. Sekar, and B. Sinopoli. A Control-Theoretic Approach for Dynamic Adaptive Video Streaming over HTTP. In *SIGCOMM*, 2015.

Multi-Year GPS Tracking Using a Coin Cell*

Manuel Eichelberger
ETH Zurich
manuelei@ethz.ch

Ferdinand von Hagen
ETH Zurich
vhagenf@ethz.ch

Roger Wattenhofer
ETH Zurich
wattenhofer@ethz.ch

ABSTRACT

We present a small, light and low-power GPS tracking device. Powered by a coin cell, the novel receiver design enables a tracking lifetime of two years with quarter-hourly position recordings. A snapshot receiver design is employed which allows for arbitrarily adjustable duty cycles. Offloading data processing into the cloud reduces the hardware complexity and the energy consumption of the receiver. Compared to conventional GPS trackers, our design minimizes the tracker's cost, size and weight, which enables new applications. Our prototype implementation weighs 1.3 grams, has a size of 23mm × 14mm and highlights an operating time of 683 days with quarter-hourly positioning when powered by a coin cell.

CCS CONCEPTS

• **Information systems** → **Global positioning systems**; • **Hardware** → **Sensor devices and platforms**;

KEYWORDS

coin cell, Coarse-Time Navigation, Collective Detection, computation offloading, GNSS, hardware, implementation, low power, millisecond, snapshot

ACM Reference Format:
Manuel Eichelberger, Ferdinand von Hagen, and Roger Wattenhofer. 2019. Multi-Year GPS Tracking Using a Coin Cell. In *The 20th International Workshop on Mobile Computing Systems and Applications (HotMobile '19), February 27–28, 2019, Santa Cruz, CA, USA*. ACM, New York, NY, USA, 6 pages. https://doi.org/10.1145/3301293.3302367

---

*The authors of this paper are alphabetically ordered.

---

1 INTRODUCTION

Global localization is a driver for so many applications that it is often considered to be a key technology of our time. However, all GPS receivers today have a high energy consumption. Mobile phones and smart watches can run days or even weeks on a single battery charge, but with GPS enabled, they barely make it through a single day. While personal devices such as smartphones can be recharged regularly, GPS trackers cannot.

Applications for GPS tracking include animal tracking, both wildlife and domestic animals. In addition, one may like to track personal items such as wallets or keys. More generally, we believe that the availability of a low energy GPS receiver will open up a unforeseen number of surprising applications, in tracking and beyond. Many of these applications also need a small footprint in terms of size and weight.

Current commercial GPS receivers include a lot of signal processing hardware, mostly so-called correlators, which are used to find and track satellite signals. These correlators collectively consume much power and the hardware is active continuously, because receivers constantly decode timing and satellite orbit information from the satellite signals.

In this paper, we present a novel GPS tracker hardware design. Our design is a snapshot GPS receiver which captures only a few milliseconds of satellite signals for each position computation. The active time of snapshot receivers for a single position request is three orders of magnitude lower than that of conventional receivers. The latter require about six or even 30 seconds of data at startup, depending on available prior satellite orbit information. Snapshot receivers can be designed either with a storage or a wireless communication component. We choose the first option, as it consumes less power and space. Loggers such as our device can be used for applications which do not need real-time positioning, like wildlife tracking, collecting workout statistics or geotagging photographs.

Besides the hardware design, we present a corresponding prototype implementation using a suitable selection of components. An evaluation of the actual energy consumption shows that such a tracker, powered from a single coin cell, is not limited by the energy consumption, but rather by the size of the storage for the recorded signals. The used 2 Gb flash storage can hold 65600 signal snapshots of one millisecond length. This corresponds to a lifetime of 683 days with quarter-hourly positioning. Our prototype GPS tracker weighs a mere 1.3 grams and its dimensions are 23 x 14 mm. This makes it suitable for weight-constrained applications like bird tracking and enables it to be concealed for instance in valuable belongings like wallets, handbags or bicycles.

With our hardware receiver design and the insights we gained when designing and testing our receiver, we want to provide the GPS research community with a platform to test and build snapshot receiver algorithms. Furthermore, our receiver design is a step towards a practically usable hardware building block, which can be integrated into a real product, like for instance a low-power, long-term animal tracking device.

1.1 Related Work

Commercially, no GPS hardware is available to implement snapshot receivers. One way to test snapshot GPS is to use a *software defined radio (SDR)*. SDRs are relatively large, heavy and consume orders of magnitude more power than a dedicated GPS receiver. Therefore, SDRs are most useful for static testing, but not for mobile scenarios. The same holds for the only alternative, which is using a *SiGe GN3S*[1] USB GPS sampling dongle together with a laptop. This is a problem for the GPS tracking research community, because snapshot receiver algorithms cannot be tested in their intended application environment. So far, mostly simulations or data cut out from longer recorded signal sequences have been used to show the performance of these methods [1, 2, 6].

In research, snapshot GPS receivers are known for several years [1, 2, 6]. They drastically reduce the power consumption of a GPS receiver, because signal processing can be offloaded to a web service [6]. This simplifies the hardware design and moves the most energy consuming part of the receiver into the cloud. However, most proposals focus on the software of such a receiver. While Liu et al. [6] propose a snapshot receiver hardware design, their first version used additional, large hardware for time synchronization. We use the same MAX2769 GPS front-end chip. However, our prototype implementation is almost 12 times smaller than Liu et al.'s second version, *CLEON*, that drops the time synchronization hardware. Also, our hardware draws a standby power of 4.5 µA instead of 2.5 mA [6], effectively increasing its lifetime for long duty cycles by a factor of 500. And our receiver's active power during a signal capture is reduced by a factor of 100, from 62 mJ [6] to 0.74 mJ, while capturing only 10 times less data, namely one millisecond instead of 10, and while improving the localization accuracy.

1.2 Applications

We give two example applications which can directly benefit from the availability of snapshot GPS receivers and do not require real-time positioning. One has to keep in mind that due to the drastic improvements in size, weight and power consumption, snapshot receivers may spark a variety of unexpected applications.

Bird Tracking. Ornithologists use tracking devices to study bird behavior. Large birds like geese or birds of prey can be equipped with traditional GPS tracking devices. Due to weight constraints, batteries can only be small and will thus last for a short time only, limiting the usefulness of such trackers. Small songbirds can only carry additional weights of less than two grams [3], which is not enough for a conventional GPS receiver and a battery. A current technique is to equip such small birds with small and low-power light-level sensors and a real-time clock. Reading the light levels and matching them with timestamps from the clock allows determining the length of the day at a bird's location and thus determining its latitude approximately. Errors are on the order of 200 km or more [3]. This allows for a limited set of studies like observing approximate migratory bird movements and their timing. Our receiver, which

weighs 1.3 grams only, fits into the weight budget for equipping such small birds with GPS, while providing several months long observation times. Due to our receiver's accuracy in the range of tens of meters (see Section 4.3), our hardware enables more detailed studies on bird behavior.

Holiday Logging. Many travelers like to tag their holiday photographs with the location where those were taken. Due to the high energy consumption and the multi-second latency from activating a receiver to getting the first position estimate, many cameras do not include a GPS receiver. Therefore, some people buy stand-alone GPS trackers which run a day or two on a single charge and whose computed positions can be combined with the holiday pictures afterwards on a computer. Our receiver eliminates recharging. After initial setup, our tracker can be forgotten about, even for a world tour! In the end, one can extract all positions with 15 minute resolution and has a log of the complete holiday journey.

Summarizing, our work lays the foundation for inexpensive, accurate and low-power GPS localization. It enables a new range of objects and animals to be equipped with global localization.

2 HARDWARE DESIGN

A snapshot GPS receiver samples a few milliseconds of GPS signal and stores or transmits this data for computing the receiver position from it. *Raw* data is needed, meaning I/Q or real samples of the signal and not processed data that commercial GPS chips provide.

The goals of our snapshot receiver design are:

- Capture raw GPS signal samples
- Store them on the device
- Keep track of the current time
- Allow simple configuration and data transfer
- While consuming minimum power

Our design addresses all of these goals and allows for large duty cycles with minimum sleep power.

2.1 Sampling

The frequency of the L1 GPS data modulation is 1.023 MHz. Therefore, by the Nyquist-Shannon sampling theorem, a sufficient minimum sampling rate with a single channel (*real*) receiver is 2.046 MHz and half of that for a dual channel (*I/Q*) receiver. Using a higher sampling frequency will usually yield a better quality of the received signal. But more importantly, the Galileo GNSS is also transmitting ranging signals at the L1 frequency, but with a sub-carrier rate of 6.138 MHz. Therefore, it is beneficial if a sampling rate of at least 6.138 MHz (I/Q) or 12.276 (real) is used. In our design, we settle for a real receiver and a sampling frequency of 16.368 MHz, which allows for the simultaneous reception of GPS and Galileo signals, increasing accuracy and robustness.

As seen in Table 1, most GPS front ends use 2-bit quantization levels. Using such low sampling precision degrades the signal-to-noise ratio by only 0.55 to 0.72 dB [7, Section 6.12], while the reduced data size allows capturing more snapshots with the same energy and storage space.

---

[1]The product is not available any more: https://www.sparkfun.com/products/retired/10981

Table 1: List of all commercial GPS front-end chips that we found through an extensive search (web, books, emails, phone calls). The following abbreviations are used to denote the different GNSS systems. US: GPS, R: GLONASS, E: Galileo, C: BeiDou.

Manufacturer	Model	GNSS	Sampling rate	Sample format	Max. power	Min. quantity	Price
Analog Devices	ADSST-GPSRF01	US	max. 32 MHz	2 bit real	195 mW	unavailable?	on request
IMST	[unnamed]	US/E	*unknown*	2 bit real	*unknown*	unavailable	*unknown*
Maxim	MAX2769	US/R/E	max. 50 MHz	2 bit I/Q or 3 bit real	62.7 mW	2500?	on request
Maxim	MAX2769B	US/R/E/C	max. 50 MHz	2 bit I/Q or 3 bit real	88.4 mW	2500?	on request
Navika	AST-GPSRF	US/E	16.368 MHz	2 bit real	> 48.9 mW	discontinued	*unknown*
NTLab	NT1065	US,R,E,C	≥ 99.231 MHz	4 x 2 bit real	> 306 mW	*unknown*	*unknown*
SAPHYRION	SM1027U	US/R/E/C	50 MHz	3 bit I/Q	≥ 76.9 mW	*unknown*	*unknown*
SiGe	SE4110L	US	max. 19.5 MHz	2 bit real	> 28.4 mW	1	$ 3.59
Skyworks	SE4150L	US	16.368 MHz	2 bit real	59.4 mW	1	$ 3.20
STA	STA5620	US	16.368 MHz	2 bit real	51.3 mW	221 (obsolete)	$ 4.78
STA	STA5630	US/E	16.368 MHz	3 bit real	25 mW	3000	$ 1.05
Zarlink	GP2015	US	5.71 MHz?	2 bit real	254.1 mW	discontinued	*unknown*

2.2 Component Selection

The main parts required for our hardware design are:

- GPS Front End
- Microcontroller
- Flash Storage
- Battery
- Power Converters

GPS Front End. The front end is the circuit converting the received RF signals into digital samples. Although we spent quite some time searching GPS front-end chips, there seem to be only a dozen manufacturers producing standalone chips. All the models we could find are listed in Table 1. Note that the reason for this short list is probably due to the fact that most GPS receivers in commercial products integrate the position computation and are not designed to output the raw signal samples. Even though some commercial receiver seem to offer "raw" data output, mostly only computed values like pseudoranges to all satellites or navigation data is provided, which is insufficient for our application, which requires raw GPS signal samples. For the front end we selected the Maxim MAX2769 GPS front end as it allows testing a wide range of RF, data format and filter settings. The raw GPS signals are output at 16.368 MHz with two bit precision. Both active and passive antennas can be connected. It uses less than 22 mA at 2.7 V. Unfortunately shutdown current is about 20 µA which requires the use of an external switch to not exhaust the power budget. An alternative would be the SE4150L GPS front end, which requires less external components and therefore is easier to integrate. It also has fewer necessary settings and slightly lower power consumption.

Microcontroller. The microcontroller needs to fulfill two important constraints: 1) It must read incoming samples, two bits at a time, at the designed rate of 16 MHz and 2) it should have a low standby power consumption to allow for long tracking periods with large duty cycles. During inactive times of the receiver without signal sampling, the microcontroller needs to keep track of the current time and all other receiver components can be cut off from the power source to save energy. Thus, the microcontroller's standby power consumption is one of the factors limiting the battery longevity. For our design, we select the Atmel SAM4L, as it offers a *parallel input capture interface (PARC)*, which reads up to 8 bits concurrently at a maximum rate of 24 MHz. The PARC is a perfect interface for reading the data of the GPS front end. At less than 3.1 µA, the SAM4L offers low standby power consumption with activated *real-time clock (RTC)*.

Flash Storage. The flash storage must offer big storage size while consuming little power during write operations. The NAND flash memory MT29F2G01 offers 2 Gb storage and a maximum current during data write operations of 25 mA. At our sampling rate of 16.368 MHz, the flash memory size allows collecting one GPS signal snapshot every fifteen minutes during 683 days. Combined GPS and Galileo snapshots could be captured hourly during the same time period.

Battery. Many conventional batteries are heavy (cylindrical batteries) or have significant self discharge (LiPo cells, supercapacitors), making them unsuitable for our purpose. Coin cells offer high power density, low weight and are cheap, which makes them ideal for our requirements. We use the CR2032 [4] which has a maximum usable capacity of 235 mA h. With a target runtime of 2 years, an average power consumption of 26 µA cannot be exceeded. Accounting for battery degradation, the power consumption has to be restricted to significantly lower values. Real-world evaluations of coin cells [5] show that high peak currents or qualitatively low coin cells often only offer half their rated capacity. To ensure stable operation and account for temperature, coin cell quality and high peak currents, the average power consumption should remain around 10 µA. Our average power consumption of 6 µA (cf. Section 4) is a factor 4 below the maximum of 26 µA and therefore our tracker requires only a quarter of the coin cell's capacity for a two year runtime.

Power Converter. The coin cell offers an initial voltage of 3 V which will drop to 2 V during high load or towards the end of the cell's lifetime. We use two controlled power domains. One domain with 1.8 V for the microcontroller and one domain for the GPS

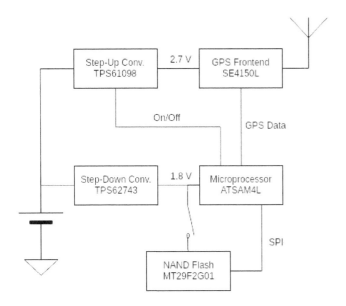

Figure 1: Overview of the components in the system.

Figure 2: Size comparison of our GPS tracking hardware with a wristwatch.

front end with at least 2.7 V. While it would be possible to design the entire system for 2.7 V, 1.8 V reduces the external components required for the processor and minimizes standby power consumption because an efficient step-down converter can be used. The TPS63743 step-down converter powers the 1.8 V domain and its quiescent current is only 360 nA, which allows it to be active continuously. The TPS61098 provides 2.7 V to the GPS front end even when the coin cell voltage drops.

Standby Power Consumption. Both the flash and GPS front end consume a couple of μA during shutdown. While this might be negligible in most applications, the shutdown power consumption of these chips combined will empty the coin cell in less our targeted two years lifetime. Using a controlled high-side load switch like the ADP199, the power consumption during shutdown can be reduced to below 100 nA.

As even ceramic capacitors can have leakage currents in the range of nanoamperes to hundreds of microamperes which will exceed the power budget, it is crucial to remove and minimize all capacitors wherever possible. Resistors have to be planned carefully to not waste any energy too. An alternative is to use different switched power domains, decoupled for example by the aforementioned load switch.

3 IMPLEMENTATION

An overview of the final architecture can be seen in Figure 1. The microcontroller is powered continuously by the step-down converter. To save energy, the NAND flash is connected through a load switch to the power domain of the microcontroller. The switch is controlled by the microcontroller and only enabled when the flash is necessary. Communication with the flash is performed via the *Serial Peripheral Interface (SPI)* at data rates of up to 24 Mbps. The GPS data is transferred in parallel with 16.368 MHz to the capture

interface of the microcontroller, where it is first cached in RAM and then written to memory.

3.1 PCB Design

To minimize PCB size and allow using small parts, the board is designed with four layers and a minimum design width of 100 μm. To reduce PCB cost, only vias through the whole stack are used, but no blind or buried vias. Passive components are reduced to the smallest size available, often 01005 (0.4mm × 0.2mm). The resulting board is only 23mm × 14mm big and weighs 1.3g. A size comparison with a wristwatch is shown in Figure 2. GPS front end, power management and microcontroller are mounted on the (visible) top side of the board while the flash chip and USB connector are mounted on the bottom side.

Two challenges are matching the impedance of the antenna connection and reducing the electromagnetic interference of digital signals with the RF signals. The antenna RF connector is mounted on the bottom through an impedance-controlled via buildup. The GPS front end is prepared for a shielding enclosure and RF traces are shielded by surrounding grounded vias and ground layers.

4 EVALUATION

This section gives an evaluation of the power consumption and signal reception. Power measurements are difficult to obtain due to the high dynamic range between the active and standby currents. Even attached debugging circuits can have much higher leakage currents than our device's standby power consumption. Special care was taken during the hardware development to make all debugging circuits detachable for measuring the power consumption. Furthermore, the GPS data is analyzed to verify proper operation of the receiver.

4.1 Standby Power Consumption

During standby only the microcontroller is powered. The boost converter is in low-power mode and the flash memory switched

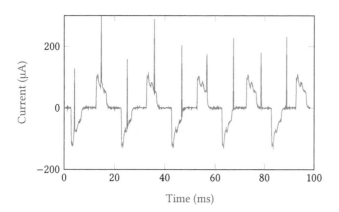

Figure 3: Total standby power consumption of the GPS tracking device. The processor is in deep-sleep mode with only the *real-time clock (RTC)* running, the step-up converter for the GPS front end disabled and the flash disconnected by the load switch. The operation of the step-down converter powering the microcontroller is visible. The average current is 3.2 μA.

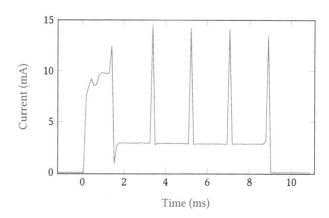

Figure 4: Current consumption of the flash device. After initialization for the first 1.7 ms, four blocks of data are transferred and written. Data writing is clearly visible as peaks in the power consumption.

off, which should consume less than 1 μA combined. The microcontroller is powered by the TPS62743 and should consume less than 3.5 μA combined. Therefore, a total standby power consumption of under 4.5 μA can be expected which is well below our maximum power budget.

Our measurements (Figure 3) show that the current during standby varies between -125 and 300 μA over time due to the switching voltage converter powering the processor. The average power consumption measured with different devices showed values ranging from 2.9 up to 5.1 μA and is within the expected range.

4.2 Active Power Consumption

The active time can be split into multiple parts. After wakeup, the processor initializes the GPS front end and starts sampling the received data through the parallel interface. Then, the GPS front end is disabled and the processor formats the data for storing it. The final step is to power up the flash memory, transfer and write the data to the flash memory. The power profile of the flash chip during this procedure is shown in Figure 4. The full process takes around 13.5 milliseconds to complete. To estimate the power consumption, the maximum values from the data sheets are used. At full speed and with the required peripherals activated, the microcontroller consumes approximately 20 mA. This does not account for low-power modes or lower clock rates that could be used to reduce power consumption. The GPS front end and crystal oscillator consume at most 25 mA. During write, the flash memory will consume at most 25 mA. Depending on the efficiency of the power converters and other peripherals, these values can vary.

Our measurements (Figure 5) reveal that the power consumption of the flash and microcontroller are in the expected range, while the power consumption of the GPS front end is higher than expected, leading to an initial peak power of 60 mA. This probably originates

from the initial charging of the stabilizing capacitors and setup of the GPS front end.

The average power consumption for the 13.5 ms active time is 18.3 mA. Our initial example of storing one GPS signal snapshot per hour corresponds to a duty cycle of 13.5 ms/3600 s = 3.75e−6. The contribution of the power during the active time to the average power consumption is 18.3∗3.75e−6 = 68.6 nA. In case of snapshots every 15 minutes, the contribution increases to 274.4 nA. Both values are negligible compared to the standby current.

4.3 GPS Data Analysis

In a field test, our receiver is positioned on top of a university building. The recorded snapshots with one millisecond of data are evaluated with a branch-and-bound Collective Detection implementation [2]. *All* calculated positions are within 25 meters to the true receiver position. Although we did not do an extensive evaluation of the positioning accuracy, this is an encouraging preliminary finding. In comparison, Liu et al. evaluated the snapshot positioning accuracy with a GPS sampling dongle instead of their presented snapshot receiver and used 10 milliseconds of data instead of one. Still, they achieved less than 25 m error only in about 80 % of all cases and observed a maximum positioning error of 725 m [6]. Our result therefore seems to confirm that Collective Detection improves positioning robustness [2].

5 CONCLUSION

Our hardware design, implementation and evaluation show that low-power GPS receivers which offload the position computation to the cloud are a viable concept. Our receiver periodically takes snapshots of GPS signals and stores them locally. The mean power consumption of the device is under 18 μW, allowing our receiver to run for two years on a single coin cell. This enables new applications that were impossible to date. Our design exhibits a thousandfold improvement in standby power consumption and a hundredfold improvement in active power consumption over previous work.

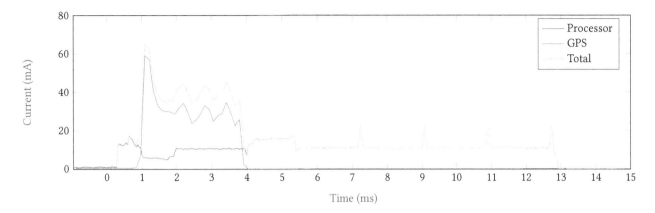

Figure 5: Active power consumption measured before the power converters by a power analyzer. The processing phases are visible. After the processor has run initial setup, the step-up converter is enabled and powers the GPS front end. After a short settling time the processor reads raw GPS data for one millisecond. Starting at 4 ms the processor prepares the data for transfer to the flash. At 5.5 ms to 13 ms the data is transferred in 4 blocks to the flash memory. The peaks in power consumption indicate when the data is written. After the last write has finished, the processor disables all peripherals and returns to sleep mode.

REFERENCES

[1] Penina Axelrad, Ben K Bradley, James Donna, Megan Mitchell, and Shan Mohi-uddin. 2011. Collective Detection and Direct Positioning Using Multiple GNSS Satellites. *Navigation* 58, 4 (2011), 305–321.

[2] Pascal Bissig, Manuel Eichelberger, and Roger Wattenhofer. 2017. Fast and Robust GPS Fix Using One Millisecond of Data. In *Information Processing in Sensor Networks (IPSN), 2017 16th ACM/IEEE International Conference on*. IEEE, 223–234.

[3] Eli S Bridge, Jeffrey F Kelly, Andrea Contina, Richard M Gabrielson, Robert B MacCurdy, and David W Winkler. 2013. Advances in tracking small migratory birds: a technical review of light-level geolocation. *Journal of Field Ornithology* 84, 2 (2013), 121–137.

[4] Energizer. 2018. Product Datasheet: Energizer CR2032. http://data.energizer.com/pdfs/cr2032.pdf

[5] Texas Instruments. 2010. White Paper SWRA349. https://e2echina.ti.com/cfs-file/__key/communityserver-discussions-components-files/104/7510.swra349-Coin-cells-and-peak-current-draw.pdf

[6] Jie Liu, Bodhi Priyantha, Ted Hart, Yuzhe Jin, Woosuk Lee, Vijay Raghunathan, Heitor S Ramos, and Qiang Wang. 2016. CO-GPS: Energy Efficient GPS Sensing with Cloud Offloading. *IEEE Transactions on Mobile Computing* 15, 6 (2016), 1348–1361.

[7] James Bao-Yen Tsui. 2000. *Fundamentals of Global Positioning System Receivers - A Software Approach*. John Wiley and Sons, Inc., New York.

Evaluating Energy-Efficiency using Thermal Imaging

Huber Flores
Jonatan Hamberg
Xin Li
Department of Computer Science
University of Helsinki
Helsinki, Finland
first.last@cs.helsinki.fi

Titti Malmivirta
Agustin Zuniga
Eemil Lagerspetz
Department of Computer Science
University of Helsinki
Helsinki, Finland
first.last@cs.helsinki.fi

Petteri Nurmi
Lancaster University
Lancaster, United Kingdom
Department of Computer Science
University of Helsinki
Helsinki, Finland
first.last@cs.helsinki.fi

ABSTRACT

Energy-efficiency remains a critical design consideration for mobile and wearable systems, particularly those operating continuous sensing. Energy footprint of these systems has traditionally been measured using hardware power monitors (such as Monsoon power meter) which tend to provide the most accurate and holistic view of instantaneous power use. Unfortunately applicability of this approach is diminishing due to lack of detachable batteries in modern devices. In this paper, we propose an innovative and novel approach for assessing energy footprint of mobile and wearable systems using *thermal imaging*. In our approach, an off-the-shelf thermal camera is used to monitor thermal radiation of a device while it is operating an application. We develop the general theory of thermal energy-efficiency, and demonstrate its feasibility through experimental benchmarks where we compare energy estimates obtained through thermal imaging against a hardware power monitor.

CCS CONCEPTS

• **Computer systems organization** → **Embedded systems**; • **Hardware** → *Power and energy*; *Power estimation and optimization*; *Temperature monitoring*.

KEYWORDS

energy measurement, IoT, smart devices, wearable, drones, thermal imaging, thermal sensing

ACM Reference Format:
Huber Flores, Jonatan Hamberg, Xin Li, Titti Malmivirta, Agustin Zuniga, Eemil Lagerspetz, and Petteri Nurmi. 2019. Evaluating Energy-Efficiency using Thermal Imaging. In *The 20th International Workshop on Mobile Computing Systems and Applications (HotMobile '19), February 27–28, 2019, Santa Cruz, CA, USA.* ACM, New York, NY, USA, 6 pages. https://doi.org/10.1145/3301293.3302364

1 INTRODUCTION

Computing and sensing capabilities of smartphones, wearables and other Internet of Things (IoT) devices are continually increasing.

Indeed, most contemporary smartphones are equipped with powerful CPUs and wide range of sensors such as GPS or heart rate sensors – with new sensing modalities regularly emerging. As an example, the Caterpillar CAT S61 smartphone[1] integrates built-in thermal imaging and air quality sensors. These advances in sensing, however, have only been followed by moderate improvements in battery technology, making it difficult to fully take advantage of the available sensing capabilities. Indeed, *energy-efficiency* remains a critical design goal.

Despite the importance of energy, assessing the energy footprint of mobile and wearable solutions has become increasingly difficult in recent years. The most widely accepted solution has been to use a hardware power monitor (such as Monsoon power meter) to measure energy footprint while the device is being operated. This method generally provides the most accurate and holistic view of instantaneous power usage. Unfortunately, power meters need to be connected between the device being measured and its battery (or other power source). Hence, this approach only works on devices that have a detachable battery. While common in the past, detachable batteries are becoming infrequent on latest generations of smartphones and wearables. Furthermore, as computing and sensing capabilities are integrated into small-scale affordable IoT devices, a method for measuring power without access to the device battery is needed. Indeed, rather than consuming power, devices may even generate it, e.g., energy harvesting [10] or fuel cells [4]. While some alternatives to hardware monitors have been developed, such as energy profiles or software based measurements (see section 2), these solutions also are insufficient as they are sensitive to platform and test-bed configuration. Moreover, in the case of software measurements, the energy measurements are affected by the software mechanism gathering them. Novel solutions that are capable of overcoming these limitations of current techniques are thus needed for assessing energy footprint of emerging mobile, wearable, and IoT solutions.

In this paper, we contribute by proposing *thermal imaging* as an innovative and novel way to estimate power drain of emerging mobile, wearable and IoT devices. In our approach, an off-the-shelf thermal camera is used to monitor thermal radiation emitted by a device while it is operating an application whose energy footprint is being measured. By capturing changes in thermal footprint of the device, differences in energy consumption can be identified. We contribute by developing the general theory behind thermal energy-efficiency, and demonstrating its feasibility through benchmark experiments conducted on two different devices and using three

---

[1] https://www.catphones.com/

different applications. We demonstrate that, while not sufficient for deriving absolute estimates of energy consumption, our approach is capable of capturing relative differences in energy footprints of different applications.

2 RELATED RESEARCH

Energy Measurement: For devices with detachable batteries, it is possible to measure the energy drained by the device, by replacing the battery with a laboratory power source. In this case voltage and current can be captured by typical multimeters. For smart TVs and smart refrigerators, we can connect multimeters directly between the wall socket and the appliance. A more advanced alternative for multimeters is a combined power source and measurement device, such as the Monsoon Power Monitor[2]. However, for newer smartphones and IoT devices, batteries are not detachable, making measurement difficult. For some devices, with partial disassembly we can gain access to the battery and measure energy consumption. For others, the battery may be soldered to other components, making measurement impossible.

Power Profiling: Measurements collected with the above methods can be either used directly or they can be used to create a *power profile* that gives approximate estimates during runtime use [11]. While this approach can be highly accurate, particularly when estimating instantaneous power drain, it is only applicable to devices with detachable batteries as capturing measurements requires using a controlled power source instead of the battery.

Energy modelling: Energy modeling attempts to construct mathematical models that help to explain energy consumption from computational operations of devices. While models can be used, e.g., to understand long-term effects of sensors on battery life [8] and to develop new mechanisms to mitigate energy consumption issues [13], they are usually limited by factors such as the method used to sample energy use [15], characteristics of the devices or contexts of usage [14]. Embedded software sampling [2] overcomes some of these issues, but the sampling of energy on the device increases power consumption of the device. On the other hand, models that profile energy through hardware measurements by dedicated instruments [1, 9, 12] are not intrusive, but they offer poor generality as the measurements are sensitive to platforms and test-beds used for measurements. Another possibility is to use collaborative large-scale data collection [6, 16] to characterize energy consumption. While these crowd-based approaches can characterize energy usage across a wide range of contexts, they tend to have coarse granularity and only be suitable for aggregate level information.

Mobile thermal sensing: The energy that is periodically radiated by mobile devices makes them heat sources. Several studies have used thermal readings to illustrate the heating behaviour of components in smartphones. Xie et al. [18] recognize the CPU, GPU and battery as the principal heat generators. Therminator [17] simulates how the temperature of parts of the device is linked with its layers. Paterna et al. [7] models the thermal patterns at circuit board-level considering the variations in ambient condition. While several work offers insights about hot-energy metrics in mobile

devices, most of it requires intrusive methods of instrumentation. In this work, we mitigate this issue by modelling the energy profile of devices using thermal images. Unlike existing work, our approach does not require devices to be instrumented with mechanisms to measure energy consumption.

3 THERMAL ENERGY-EFFICIENCY

Our proposed method for energy footprint estimation relies on common off-the-shelf thermal camera that is used to monitor how the thermal radiation of a device changes as it is being used. In this section we detail the general theory of thermal estimation, and give details of a prototype system that we have developed as a proof-of-concept.

Theoretical Background: In practice, a sensing device always absorbs some of the thermal energy conducted by its heat generating components such as the CPU and battery. Assuming the device is in thermal equilibrium with its environment before any thermal energy is generated, any operations of the device cause heat conduction to the outermost parts of the device, eventually warming up its casing. The casing then radiates thermal power proportional to the fourth power of its temperature, as described by the Stefan-Boltzmann law: $P = A\epsilon\sigma T^4$, where A is the surface area, ϵ is the *emissivity* of the casing material, σ is the constant of proportionality[3], and T is the observed surface temperature in degrees Kelvin.

Surface Area Estimation: To estimate size of the surface area A, we can either conduct a manual measurement to get the dimensions or estimate them programmatically from a cropped thermal image of the surface if distance between camera and target device is known. There are standard approaches for detecting and cropping to a Region Of Interest (ROI) in thermal images, such as the segmentation algorithms presented by Duarte et al. [3]. For calculating the distance, we can either use an inbuilt depth sensor (CAT S61) or exploit the availability of separate RGB and thermal cameras to perform stereo imaging. Another option would be to use a multi-device setup where 2-4 thermal cameras monitor the device being evaluated from different vantage points. By establishing visual correspondence between multiple ROI, the surface area of the object can be estimate when the size of the imaging sensor is known.

Emissivity: Another challenge for thermal imaging is related to emissivity of objects. Emissivity ϵ is the ratio in which the target emits its energy as radiation compared to an ideal black surface, or blackbody (which has $\epsilon = 1.0$). Different materials have different emissivity values, e.g., black plastic has $\epsilon \approx 0.95$ while emissivity of glass ranges from $\epsilon \approx 0.70$ to 0.97 depending on production process[4]. On contemporary smartphones, the cover is typically designed from polycarbonate, which is capable of absorbing a significant portion of the thermal radiation emitted by the device. However, even with these devices, it is possible to capture thermal radiation through the camera aperture which has better thermal reflectivity. Emissivity of the target surface can also be estimated by comparing it against an object with well-known emissivity value,

---

[2]https://www.msoon.com/online-store

[3]Also known as the Stefan-Boltzmann constant, $\sigma = 5.670367 \cdot 10^{-8}$
[4]https://www.thermoworks.com/emissivity_table

such as a glass of water. For this, both objects need to have a uniform temperature (e.g. room temperature) after which we can set $P_1 = P_2$ and solve for $\epsilon_1 = \frac{\epsilon_1 A_1}{A_2}$ since we know both temperatures. This procedure takes some time, but only needs to be performed once for each measured device and its surface materials.

Mobile Thermal Imaging: To estimate the power drain of a device, we measure its thermal radiation using a forward looking infrared (FLIR) camera. In our feasibility evaluation, described in the section 4, we build a prototype based on an integrated FLIR camera of a Caterpillar S61 device as the sensor. Besides thermal cameras becoming highly available and integrated into smartphones, affordable USB connected cameras (such as FLIR One) are also increasingly available. The alternative to a smart phone sensor would be using a standalone thermal camera (e.g. FLIR TG167). These, however, usually lack the capabilities for automatic capturing – convenient for measuring continuous changes in thermal radiation over time.

4 FEASIBILITY EVALUATION

We next demonstrate feasibility of thermal energy-efficiency assessment through proof-of-concept benchmarks conducted using three computationally intensive applications and smartphone models. As reference we consider energy measurements obtained on a Monsoon power monitor.

4.1 Experimental Setup

Devices: We consider S5 (i9505) and Nexus (i9250) smartphones as we need models that can be instrumented with the power meter to obtain ground truth energy measurements. We used a thermal camera of the smartphone CAT S60 for capturing the thermal footprint of these devices while running the applications. We used the pre-installed software of S60 to take thermal images.

Applications: We consider three apps downloaded from Google Play store and chosen as representative examples of apps with high resource consumption. To generalize our results, the apps were chosen from different categories. Only apps compatible with both devices were chosen.

Augment:[5] is an augmented reality application where one can manipulate and view virtual objects in the physical environment. We used the app to display a virtual chair for 5 minutes, and repeated the experiment 5 times. The average time and power were stable, $t = 303.24\ s$ and $p = 3138.92\ mW$, respectively.

Chess:[6] is a puzzle game that implements a minimax algorithm to challenge users. We ran the application with a new game of Chess each time, keeping the game running for 5 minutes at a time. The average time and power were stable, $t = 304.11\ s$ and $p = 2067.49\ mW$, respectively.

Face recognition:[7] is an application that allows the device to identify a registered person based on their facial features. We ran the face detection feature of the application for roughly 5 minutes and

---

[5]https://play.google.com/store/apps/details?id=com.ar.augment
[6]https://github.com/huberflores/CodeOffloadingChess
[7]https://play.google.com/store/apps/details?id=ch.zhaw.facerecognition

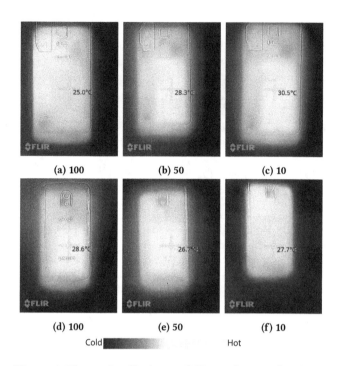

(a) 100   (b) 50   (c) 10

(d) 100   (e) 50   (f) 10

Cold ▬▬▬ Hot

Figure 1: Thermal radiation at different battery levels, S5 (a,b,c) and Nexus (d,e,f)

repeated the experiment 5 times. The average time and power were stable, $t = 297.55\ s$ and $p = 2509.736\ mW$, respectively.

4.2 Battery thermal footprint

As battery life is critical to primary operations of most mobile, wearable and IoT devices, the devices typically employ power saving techniques that can influence the energy usage. These can potentially influence energy estimates even if the device load remains approximately constant over time. Before using thermal images for evaluating energy of apps, we first analyze the differences in thermal footprint when the battery is charged at different levels. To achieve this, we analyze the overall discharging of a battery from 100% to 0%. We took thermal images from the backside of both smartphones. Images are captured each time in intervals of 10, e.g., when battery level is 100%, 90% until 10%. In the last interval, the battery of both devices is drained until reaching 2%. Lastly, a thermal image is taken when the device was completely depleted (off). The draining of the battery between intervals is induced by running a separate resource intensive application (Youtube) on the phone. Right before approaching an interval, each phone is left to cool down for 10 minutes before taking the thermal image for the interval.

Results: We find that thermal radiation captured by the images is similar at different battery levels with an average error in temperature (Celsius) of ±0.77 (Figure 1), i.e., the thermal images correctly suggest that device load remains stable over time. However, this is more difficult to observe in power meter measurements since notifications, background services, and other operations of the device cause spikes in instantaneous energy footprint. To highlight

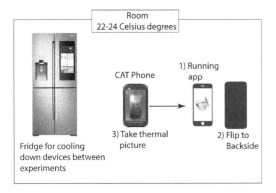

Figure 2: Experimental setup. The FLIR camera of a CAT S60 smartphone is used for taking thermal images of devices running different applications.

this, we measure the average time and power when the device does not have any application in the foreground and just the screen is on, we perform each experiment 5 times, for S5; $t = 301.60\ s$ and $p = 1167.30\ mW$; and Nexus; $t = 310.28\ s$ and $p = 2038.21\ mW$, respectively. When the device is completely idle and screen is off, we have, for S5; $t = 306.78\ s$ and $p = 27.98\ mW$; and Nexus; $t = 308.09\ s$ and $p = 87.938\ mW$, respectively. Despite devices activating internal operations in the background, or even going to idle mode, thermal imaging can identify resource usage footprints that depict the normal operations of the device.

4.3 App usage thermal footprint

We then proceed to capture the thermal footprint during application usage. Our experimental setup is illustrated in Figure 2. The goal of this experiment is to identify how a thermal image translates into energy footprint for a particular application. In this experiment, we execute three test applications for 5 minutes each, and took thermal images at minute 1, minute 3 and minute 5. We then place the phone into a refrigerator for 5 minutes to cool down the thermal camera before carrying out the next set of measurements. This ensures that the thermal image is representative of the load experienced by the CPU of devices. Cooling down the thermal camera is essential to correctly identify the unique thermal footprint of each application. Five thermal images are taken each time, we use the difference of the temperature between the five consecutive thermal images and take the mean value of them at each time slot as the delta to indicate the energy footprint. In addition, the cooling down period helps to preserve the accuracy of thermal imaging, which otherwise requires continuous re-calibration of the camera [5].

Results: The thermal footprint of applications used in the study is shown in Figure 3 for one minute of execution. We can observe that the thermal radiation emitted by the device intensifies based on the resource intensiveness of the app. For instance, for S5 (top row), we can observe the thermal footprint to be larger for the Augmented app and smaller for the Chess app. Moreover, we can observe a similar pattern for the Nexus device (bottom row). This matches the *relative ordering* of energy footprint given by our baseline measurements obtained with the Monsoon power meter appliance (see Figure 4 and 5), which suggests that it is possible to estimate - at

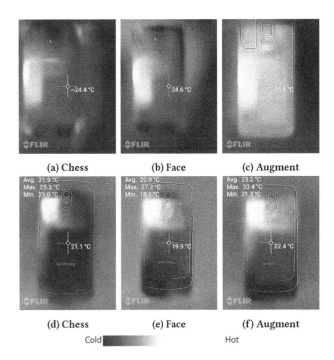

Figure 3: Thermal footprint of different applications running in devices, S5 (a,b,c) and Nexus (d,e,f). We can observe that each application has its own thermal footprint during runtime.

least on a relative level - variations in the expected energy consumption of an app from its thermal footprint. In addition, when we proceed to estimate energy consumption from thermal imaging (Table 1), we can still observe that same relative estimations between both remain.

4.4 Limitations

While visual inspection of thermal regions indeed correlates well with energy estimates obtained using the power monitor, several considerations need to be taken into account before *automatic estimates* of energy can be obtained. First, the thermal radiation area needs to be accurately pointed by the camera, otherwise estimates are misleading as radiation is not uniform due to it being absorbed by the device material. As a result, the leaking of radiation is slow and difficult to spot. For instance, Figure 3 shows for Nexus (d,e,f) that the relative temperature measurements do not match the size of the thermal area that is estimated by the camera. Since we used a single value in our experiments to take thermal measurements, the energy estimates drawn from temperature values are not as accurate as what we can observe visually. For instance, Figure 6 shows differences in temperature as given by our estimates. From the figure we can observe that the results are sensitive to how well we are able to associate the thermal values with the appropriate regions where thermal radiation occurs. The best result is obtained for the augment application, in which case the thermal radiation is reflected throughout the backside of the device. This issue can be mitigated through careful segmentation of the thermal image.

	Augment	**Face**	**Chess**
Monsoon S5	3138.93	2509.74	2067.50
Thermal S5	15544.51	14654.03	14917.53

Table 1: Temperature to energy estimation using thermal sensing: Conversion from Celsius degrees to micro watts using a standard coefficient of 1.8991. **Total energy consumption is estimated in the interval of** $1-5$ *min* **using an integral of** 30 *s* **periods.**

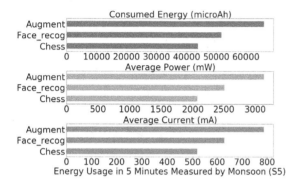

Figure 4: Energy profile of different applications running in S5 device. Energy estimation is obtained by using Monsoon measurements (baseline).

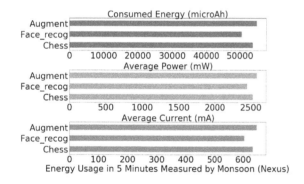

Figure 5: Energy profile of different applications running in Nexus device. Energy estimation is obtained by using Monsoon measurements (baseline).

5 DISCUSSION

Naturally, there is room for further research and improvements. We discuss the most relevant points here.

Accuracy: While we show that it is possible to relate thermal radiation to application usage, many further details need to be addressed to reach a higher level of accuracy. In our experiments, we took thermal images from the back cover of a device. However, different application heat up different components of the device which cannot be solely captured by a backside picture, e.g., the front screen when using a camera app such as augment. One way in which this can be overcome is by taking multiple pictures from different angles of the device, such that the overall estimation of energy is

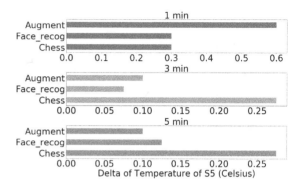

Figure 6: Difference in estimated temperatures for different applications running on S5 device. Energy profile obtained from thermal imaging.

aggregated from several images. Other anomalies such as hardware failures, sub-optimal settings of devices, and environmental factors can cause overheating that can influence the accuracy of the thermal imaging estimations.

Sealed devices: Increasingly many devices do not have a detachable battery and cannot be disassembled to gain access to the internal battery. Indeed, devices with sealed batteries are more convenient for device manufactures to provide better designs, e.g., thinner and smaller devices; and enhanced features, e.g., water resistance. As a result, accessing the battery of devices will require a higher cost of instrumentation. Our method works with all devices, without the need to access the battery. Moreover, it also reduces significantly the cost of examining energy of devices. This is very relevant for large-scale deployments of devices in the wild[8].

Older vs newer devices: Since the computational capabilities of devices are increasing constantly, the cost of executing an app differs between older and newer devices. This suggest that thermal footprint of applications varies between devices. Thus, before estimating energy consumption via thermal imaging, the characteristics of devices need to considered for tailoring thermal imaging for a particular device. We rely on older devices as they provide better visualization of thermal footprint to distinguish easily different applications.

Multiple contexts: With a charging measurement device such as the Charger Doctor[9], we can measure the charging voltage and current when a battery-powered device is being charged via a USB cable. Other traditional measurement tools also work in this type of scenario. However, when we take the device off the charger, we can no longer use such a device. The method presented in this paper is independent of the power source and charging/discharging state of the device. Activity that results in high energy drain on the device will generate heat, and the resulting thermal radiation can be captured with our method, and energy drain estimated.

Heat conduction: In our method, we need to consider other effects, such as external and internal heat conduction. *External heat*

---

[8]http://mitsloan.mit.edu/ideas-made-to-matter/energy-efficiency-new-mit-company-tests-thermal-imaging-and-analytics-drone
[9]https://www.adafruit.com/product/1852

conduction only becomes evident when both the measured device casing and the testbed are coated with highly conductive materials, e.g., aluminum, and they share the surface area. Fortunately, this type of interference is easily corrected by securing the device on a tripod or any weakly conductive platform. *Internal heat conduction* is observed as thermal energy being transferred through the wires, components, and soldering of the device — especially its copper elements. Non-conducting components shield heat from the thermal camera, slowing its progress to the case. The thermal energy originating from a CPU or the battery also spread over a wide area or conduct to a whole different part of the casing, making component-wise measurement difficult. Another source of heat that can be transferred to devices, it is the one produce when the device enters in contact with the user, e.g., hand holding the device.

Surface emissivity: The emissivity of the casing affects how much of the thermal output can be measured. Measuring the thermal radiation of surface materials with a very low emissivity value (e.g. polished aluminium, $\epsilon \approx 0.05$) may not be possible because of software and hardware limitations. However, this is limitation can be overcome by attaching any highly conductive material with a known emissivity value to the surface, e.g., adhesive copper tape. It should be noted that when attempting to measuring specific components or other areas, only those should be covered with the emissive material to prevent heat distribution. In practice, most devices are made of materials suitable for using our approach.

Additional considerations: While our preliminary results demonstrate relative matching between estimated energy appliance and thermal imaging, additional considerations such as ambient temperature, thermal estimation duration period, proximity to target (device) estimation, and thermal imaging quality/resolution, among others; are factors to be taken into consideration to further tune our approach. For instance, thermal imaging may need calibration to work in a cold outdoor environment to provide accurate energy estimations. Another example, a drone flying over an IoT deployment needs to get close enough to devices to correctly monitor their energy consumption.

Other applications: While our study focuses on estimating energy consumption of devices, the thermal footprint can be used also to identify heating patterns of individual components and get insights about the relationship between their location and energy efficiency within the structure of devices. In addition, our approach can be utilized to identify anomalies in components, e.g., battery, by distinguishing abnormal behaviors; and to detect energy bugs and computationally heavy applications.

6 SUMMARY AND CONCLUSION

We contributed by developing a novel approach for measuring energy footprint of mobile and wearable systems through thermal sensing, and demonstrated the feasibility of our idea through controlled benchmarks. Our initial results suggest that thermal imaging can indeed be used to assess *relative* differences in energy across applications run on the same device, even if their *absolute* energy footprint cannot be estimated. Our approach is useful for emerging sensing solutions running on devices lacking detachable batteries,

such as recent smartphones (latest Apple or Samsung phones have non detachable batteries), smartwatches and fitness trackers.

7 ACKNOWLEDGMENTS

This research has been financially supported by Academy of Finland grants 296139, 297741, 303825 and 317875, and by the Jorma Ollila Grant from the Nokia Foundation.

REFERENCES

[1] Niranjan Balasubramanian, Aruna Balasubramanian, and Arun Venkataramani. 2009. Energy consumption in mobile phones: a measurement study and implications for network applications. In *Proceedings of the 9th ACM SIGCOMM Conference on Internet Measurement (IMC 2009)*. ACM, Chicago, Illinois, 280–293.

[2] Mian Dong and Lin Zhong. 2011. Self-constructive high-rate system energy modeling for battery-powered mobile systems. In *Proceedings of the 9th international conference on Mobile systems, applications, and services (MobiSys 2011)*. ACM, Washington, DC, USA, 335–348.

[3] A Duarte, L Carrão, M Espanha, T Viana, D Freitas, P Bártolo, P Faria, and HA Almeida. 2014. Segmentation algorithms for thermal images. *Procedia Technology* 16 (2014), 1560–1569.

[4] Rutvik Vasudev Lathia, Kevin S. Dobariya, and Ankit Patel. 2017. Hydrogen Fuel Cells for Road Vehicles. *Journal of Cleaner Production* 141 (2017), 462.

[5] Titti Malmivirta, Jonatan Hamberg, Eemil Lagerspetz, Xin Lin, Ella Peltonen, Huber Flores, and Petteri Nurmi. 2019. Hot or Not? Robust and Accurate Continuous Thermal Imaging on FLIR cameras. In *In Proceedings of the IEEE International Conference on Pervasive Computing and Communications (PerCom 2019)*. IEEE, Kyoto, Japan.

[6] Adam J Oliner, Anand P Iyer, Ion Stoica, Eemil Lagerspetz, and Sasu Tarkoma. 2013. Carat: Collaborative energy diagnosis for mobile devices. In *Proceedings of the ACM Conference on Embedded Networked Sensor Systems (SenSys 2013)*. ACM, Rome, Italy, 1–14.

[7] Francesco Paterna, Joe Zanotelli, and Tajana Simunic Rosing. 2014. Ambient variation-tolerant and inter components aware thermal management for mobile system on chips. In *Proceedings of IEEE Design, Automation and Test in Europe Conference and Exhibition (DATE 2014)*. IEEE, Dresden, Germany, 1–6.

[8] Ella Peltonen, Eemil Lagerspetz, Petteri Nurmi, and Sasu Tarkoma. 2015. Energy modeling of system settings: A crowdsourced approach. In *Proceedings of International Conference on Pervasive Computing and Communications (PerCom 2015)*. IEEE, St. Louis, MO, USA, 37–45.

[9] Andrew Rice and Simon Hay. 2010. Decomposing power measurements for mobile devices. In *Proceedings of IEEE International Conference on Pervasive Computing and Communications (PerCom 2010)*. IEEE, Mannheim, Germany, 70–78.

[10] Sujesha Sudevalayam and Purushottam Kulkarni. 2011. Energy harvesting sensor nodes: Survey and implications. *IEEE Communications Surveys & Tutorials* 13, 3 (2011), 443–461.

[11] Sasu Tarkoma, Matti Siekkinen, Eemil Lagerspetz, and Yu Xiao. 2014. *Smartphone energy consumption: modeling and optimization*. Cambridge University Press.

[12] Narendran Thiagarajan, Gaurav Aggarwal, Angela Nicoara, Dan Boneh, and Jatinder Pal Singh. 2012. Who killed my battery?: analyzing mobile browser energy consumption. In *Proceedings of the 21st ACM International Conference on World Wide Web (WWW 2012)*. ACM, Lyon, France, 41–50.

[13] Narseo Vallina-Rodriguez and Jon Crowcroft. 2013. Energy management techniques in modern mobile handsets. *IEEE Communications Surveys & Tutorials* 15, 1 (2013), 179–198.

[14] Narseo Vallina-Rodriguez, Pan Hui, Jon Crowcroft, and Andrew Rice. 2010. Exhausting battery statistics: understanding the energy demands on mobile handsets. In *Proceedings of the second ACM SIGCOMM workshop on Networking, systems, and applications on mobile handhelds*. ACM, New Delhi, India, 9–14.

[15] Thomas Vincent and Olivier Philippot. 2018. Software Measurement of Energy Consumption on Smartphones. In *Greening Video Distribution Networks*. Springer, 127–132.

[16] Jiangtao Wang, Yasha Wang, Daqing Zhang, and Sumi Helal. 2018. Energy Saving Techniques in Mobile Crowd Sensing: Current State and Future Opportunities. *IEEE Communications Magazine* 56, 5 (2018), 164–169.

[17] Qing Xie, Mohammad Javad Dousti, and Massoud Pedram. 2014. Therminator: a thermal simulator for smartphones producing accurate chip and skin temperature maps. In *Proceedings of the ACM International symposium on Low power electronics and design (ISLPED 2014)*. ACM, La Jolla, CA USA, 117–122.

[18] Qing Xie, Jaemin Kim, Yanzhi Wang, Donghwa Shin, Naehyuck Chang, and Massoud Pedram. 2013. Dynamic thermal management in mobile devices considering the thermal coupling between battery and application processor. In *Proceedings of IEEE/ACM International Conference on Computer-Aided Design (ICCAD 2013)*. IEEE, San Jose, CA, USA, 242–247.

Reconfigurable Streaming for the Mobile Edge

Abhishek Tiwari
Department of Computer Science
University of Toronto
atiwari@cs.toronto.edu

Brian Ramprasad
Department of Computer Science
University of Toronto
brianr@cs.utoronto.ca

Seyed Hossein Mortazavi
Department of Computer Science
University of Toronto
mortazavi@cs.toronto.edu

Moshe Gabel
Department of Computer Science
University of Toronto
mgabel@cs.toronto.edu

Eyal de Lara
Department of Computer Science
University of Toronto
delara@cs.toronto.edu

ABSTRACT

Deploying stream computing applications on edge networks brings a new set of challenges including frequent reconfigurations due to client mobility and topology changes, geographical constraints from application semantics, state management over wide-area networks, and more. Current stream processing frameworks do not adequately address these challenges since they are designed for use inside data centers and rely on global coordination between participating nodes. Merlin is a new stream processing framework designed from the ground up for stream processing on the edge. Merlin supports fast reconfiguration without disrupting applications by decoupling data delivery from data processing and removing the need for global coordination.

CCS CONCEPTS

• **Information systems** → **Stream management**.

KEYWORDS

Edge Computing; Streaming; Dynamic Reconfiguration

ACM Reference Format:
Abhishek Tiwari, Brian Ramprasad, Seyed Hossein Mortazavi, Moshe Gabel, and Eyal de Lara. 2019. Reconfigurable Streaming for the Mobile Edge. In *The 20th International Workshop on Mobile Computing Systems and Applications (HotMobile '19), February 27–28, 2019, Santa Cruz, CA, USA.* ACM, New York, NY, USA, 6 pages. https://doi.org/10.1145/3301293.3302355

1 INTRODUCTION

Our ability to support the acquisition, processing, and storage of huge volumes of data has transformed business and culture, technology and science [7]. Yet, if the technical challenge of last decade was the exponential increase in the volume of data, then the challenge of the next decade is the proliferation of geographically distributed data. The advent of the Internet-of-Things (IoT), mobile devices, and sensor networks is expected to lead to an exponential increase in the number of distributed data sources, with a predicted 27 billion connected devices by 2021 [4]. The prevailing cloud computing paradigm is not a good match for this flood, and scaling computational resources in the cloud will not help if we cannot get the data into the data center in the first place, due to bandwidth and latency constraints.

Edge or fog computing is an emerging alternative [13, 14] that uses nearby resources, as well as nodes on the path to the cloud, to provide computation and storage over very large number of geographically distributed sites. Such multi-tier hierarchies are beneficial when latency requirements are stringent enough to render cloud processing unviable, where client devices are too weak, and when the computation requires both locally and globally relevant information. Processing data near to the point of creation has several benefits: it reduces wide-area network bandwidth demands by aggregating data locally, it lowers the latency to compute results that depend on local data, and it helps limit the geographic area where sensitive data propagates.

Unfortunately, existing distributed stream processing frameworks [1, 3, 6, 8, 17] are a poor match for edge computing. They were designed to work inside data centers on nodes that connect over high capacity, low-latency links. Moreover, these designs assume a mostly static environment where data is produced by a comparatively small and stable set of data sources, and a network topology that changes infrequently. In contrast, edge deployments are characterized by geographically distributed nodes connected over links that (relative to the data center) have low bandwidth and high latency. Moreover, in edge deployments, data is produced at a large number of geographically distributed sources (e.g., smart phones, intelligent transportation), and client mobility results in frequent changes in network topology as clients move between edge nodes.

We propose a new stream processing framework for running applications on edge data centers. We assume a hierarchy of edge data centers that has a traditional wide-area cloud data center at its root, and additional layers of data centers that become progressively smaller as we approach the edge of the network. We assume that the data center hierarchy is shared infrastructure that will run a large number of data streaming applications. Moreover, since most data centers in the hierarchy have limited capacity, application components have to be dynamically removed or deployed in response to changes in usage patterns.

Consider for example a smart city traffic monitoring system deployed over a wide area. The system collects streams of data from

HotMobile '19, February 27–28, 2019, Santa Cruz, CA, USA
© 2019 Association for Computing Machinery.
ACM ISBN 978-1-4503-6273-3/19/02...$15.00
https://doi.org/10.1145/3301293.3302355

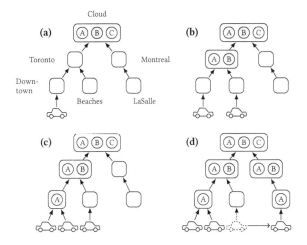

Figure 1: Reconfiguration in a traffic monitoring application: (a) initially all components run in the cloud; (b) additional instances of A and B started in Toronto to handle increase in load; (c) extra instance of A added to Downtown data center to handle load spike; (d) reconfigure deployment as traffic shifts to a new city.

road sensors, GPS-equipped vehicles, environmental monitors, and other sources and aggregates them at multiple levels to manage traffic. This huge volume of data could overwhelm network capacity at the cloud data center, yet correct operation requires aggregating data from multiple streets, neighborhoods, and cities. An edge architecture provides an elegant solution, as data can be aggregated locally and put to use exactly where it is needed, without flooding network links at the upper layers.

Figure 1 illustrates how the deployment of the monitoring system's components evolves over time on a hierarchical data center network with three layers. Initially, all the application's components (A, B, C) are only running at the cloud data center. At this stage there is only a modest load and it is most convenient to send all data for processing to the cloud. In the second stage, additional instances of A and B are started on the Toronto data center to handle an increase in data originating from this city. In stage three, an instance of A is started on the Downtown data center to address a sudden increase in traffic concentration. Finally, as traffic shifts from Toronto to Montreal, new bolts are instantiated along this route.

Dynamic deployment of streaming applications on a hierarchical data center network, however, presents several important challenges: the framework needs to be able to support the addition and removal of computational elements with minimal disruption; the state of the application needs to be rebalanced; developers must be able to specify geographical constraints on placement; and the system needs to be able to handle failure and intermittent connectivity.

In this paper we take an initial step toward addressing the challenge of reconfiguration. We first introduce our vision for stream processing on a hierarchical network of data centers, and discuss key challenges.We then discuss the limitations of existing stream

processing architectures and illustrate the detrimental effects of reconfiguration with experiments using the popular Apache Storm [6] framework. We then introduce Merlin, our dynamic hierarchical streaming prototype and show that it enables frequent dynamic application reconfiguration without any stoppage time. Merlin achieves this by decoupling data delivery from data processing and by removing the need for global coordination.

2 VISION AND CHALLENGES

We next describe our vision for enabling dynamic stream processing on a hierarchical network of edge data centers.

We assume the common operator graph model: stream processing applications are represented as directed acyclic graphs (DAG) consisting of *nodes* that originate or process streams of data. A stream is made of individual data units called *tuples*, and nodes in the graph are either *spouts* that emit tuples, or *bolts* that consume and process tuples, and (optionally) emit new tuples[1].

A developer parallelizes their application by decomposing their algorithm into a collection of connected bolts and spouts, called a *logical plan*, which can process tuples concurrently. The framework then compiles a *physical plan* that determines the number of instances of each bolt and spout to create and their placement on the cluster. The logical plan for the sample traffic monitoring application consists of: a spout that generates tuples with traffic, GPS, and environmental data; bolt-A, which aggregates traffic by neighborhood and emits new tuples with traffic predictions and per-neighborhood summaries; bolt-B, which aggregates data by city, provides traffic management, and emits a new tuple every few seconds with the per-city summaries; and finally, bolt-C, which aggregates the data for the entire country. When deployed on a cloud data center, road sensors and vehicles upload information to a central database on the cloud, from which they can be retrieved by the spout.

Our goal is to enable the deployment of stream processing applications on a hierarchical network of data centers. We assume that the data center hierarchy is organized as a tree that has a traditional wide-area cloud data center at its root, and an arbitrary number of additional layers of data centers that get progressively smaller as we approach the edge of the network. We also assume that the data center hierarchy is shared infrastructure that will run a large number of data streaming applications, and that data centers that are closer to the edge have limited capacity. For example, Figure 1(a) illustrates a hierarchical network consisting of three levels: a traditional wide-area cloud data center, two city-scale data centers, and several neighborhood-scale data centers.

We further assume that an application's logical plan consists of nodes that can all run at the cloud data center at the root of the hierarchy. In addition, we assume that some (and potentially all) of the nodes can also be instantiated on data centers closer to the edge of the network, subject to developer-provided constraints that indicate how close to the edge it is safe to place a node without altering application semantics. In our traffic monitoring example, bolt-A (neighborhood aggregation) can run correctly at any level of the data center hierarchy. In contrast, bolt-B (city aggregation and management) can only run at the root on a city-level data

---

[1]For simplicity, we adopt the nomenclature of Apache Storm [6].

center. Running this bolt at a neighborhood-level data center will result in an inaccurate statistics for the city as traffic reports from other neighborhoods will be missed. In this scenario, sensors and cars operate as spouts emitting reports (i.e., tuples) to the closest neighborhood-level data center. Tuples are then either processed by a locally-installed bolt, or get propagated up towards the root of the hierarchy.

By default, an application is initially deployed on the cloud data center. As the data stream starts to flow through the data center hierarchy, additional instances of nodes can be dynamically added progressively closer to the edge of the network, subject to developer constraints and the load on the shared network. Figure 1 shows how the deployment of our sample application evolves over time. Initially, all three application bolts are only installed at the cloud data center. At this stage the application is only experiencing modest load and it is most convenient to send all reports to the cloud. In the second stage, additional instances of bolt-A and bolt-B are started on the Toronto data center to handle an increase in reports emanating from this city. In stage three, an instance of bolt-A is started on the Downtown data center to address a sudden increase in traffic concentration in this neighborhood. In our traffic monitoring application, placing bolts close to the edge of the network dramatically reduces the number of tuples that must be sent to the the wide-area cloud data center, as the majority of the tuples get processed locally, and only a much smaller number of updates will propagate to the city-wide and wide-area cloud data centers. This approach also reduces the latency for calculating neighborhood and city-level statistics, as there is no need to wait for the data to propagate all the way to the cloud and back. Finally, the approach is better for privacy as individual reports are no longer available on the cloud.

Stream processing on a multi-tier hierarchy of edge data centers, however, introduces a new set of unique challenges:

- Frequent reconfiguration. Since data centers (particularly those close to edge of the network) have limited resources, it is unreasonable to assume that all applications will be pre-installed and run all the time at all locations. Instead, the physical map of an application will have to change dynamically as users move between edges, or as the need to run different applications on a given edge arises. This requires mechanisms for reconfiguration without disruption as well as policies that optimize system performance.
- Programming interface. The developer needs to have a way to instruct the streaming framework where to place elements. Specifying the parallelism factor for a bolt is not sufficient as the number and location of data sources (e.g., road sensors and vehicles) changes over time. In addition, the structure of the data centre hierarchy may not be known to the developer, and the hierarchy may not be uniform. (i.e., different parts of the hierarchy may consist of different number of levels or may vary in their geographic coverage).
- Support for failures and disconnection. Edge deployments may involve large networks with a large number of links that may experience intermittent failures. In addition, some scenarios may require support for disconnected operation.

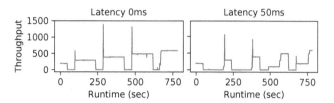

Figure 2: Storm's throughput drops to zero at the start of the reconfiguration operation, and can take many seconds to recover. Latency exacerbates this affect.

- Optimal resource allocation on a hierarchical data centre network is challenging as there is a need to balance the multiple application requirements in the face of heterogeneity in data center resource and application demands. For example, the decision to deploy a new instance of bolts A and B in the neighborhood data center must be taken in the face of performance, load management, and geographical constraints.

In the rest of this paper, we take an initial step to address the first of these challenges – the need for frequent reconfiguration. Addressing the other challenges is left for future work. Before we introduce our new approach, however, we present results from a simple experiment with Apache Storm that shows that existing cloud-based streaming systems are poorly suited to the task of handling frequent reconfiguration requests. While Apache Storm is just one of many existing cloud-based streaming systems, we argue that it is representative of a broad class cloud-based streaming frameworks that would be expected to perform in a similar way.

3 APACHE STORM

We next explore the suitability of using an existing cloud stream processing system on a hierarchical edge network. We focus our evaluation on Apache Storm [6] because it is a widely-used framework; however, we argue that our evaluation is representative of a wide class of cloud-based stream processing systems, such as Twitter Heron [8], Apache Flink [3], Spark [17], and Drizzle [15]. In all these systems application components are tightly coupled: the element that emits a tuple also directly delivers it to the element that is meant to consume it. All these frameworks also rely on global coordination, and require the topology to stop and restart in order to add or remove nodes.

In our experiment, we deploy the spout and first two bolts of an example aggregation application on an emulated two-tier hierarchical edge network composed of one wide-area cloud data center and nine edge data centers connected over network links with 50 msec of latency.

We configured the cloud data center to run the Storm Master (i.e., Nimbus), Zookeeper, and a single Storm worker, which ran bolt-B for the duration of the experiment. We configure each of the edge data centers to run two Storm workers: a spout and a bolt. At the start of the experiment, we run a single instance of bolt-A and a single spout on one of the edge data centers. After three minutes, we use the Storm *rebalance* command to start an extra instance of bolt-A and a new spout on one of the idle edge data centers. We repeated this process every 3 minutes until we ran out of idle edge data centers.

Figure 2 depicts the throughput measured at the cloud data center for the first 10 minutes of the experiment. The figure shows that the throughput drops to zero at the start of every reconfiguration operation, and can take many seconds to recover. To be fair, reconfiguration is very rare in the cloud environments for which Storm was designed. It is therefore not surprising that Storm experiences multi-second disruption times when adding new components to the topology. While this may not be a significant issue for traditional cloud deployment where reconfiguration is indeed rare, it will significantly disrupt the operation of an edge network where reconfiguration is expected to occur frequently.

Reconfiguration in Storm is a high latency operation that requires the complete network topology to synchronize before making any changes. Upon receiving the rebalance command, Storm halts all spouts and bolts and allows them to flush their data. Storm coordinates the entire process by communicating via Zookeeper and this communication is based on a polling mechanism where the Storm slave workers poll the Zookeeper server. Essentially the 'stop the world event' causes the topology to be down for a significant amount of time, making dynamic topology changes an extremely expensive operation. The early-binding or tightly coupled design of the framework where the component emitting data is directly connected with the component processing the data is good for performance; however, it makes reconfiguration hard. We conclude that current stream processing engines are a poor match for the edge computing setting due to their reliance on global coordination between participating nodes.

4 MERLIN

Merlin is a new framework for stream processing on a hierarchical network of data centers. Merlin supports dynamic application deployment and enables the frequent reconfiguration of an application's physical plan without requiring global coordination. Merlin's design in based on two key principles: decoupling tuple delivery from processing, and the use of only local knowledge for routing tuples. Merlin assumes that each data center in the hierarchy runs four components: a local data store, one or more executors, a pusher, and a router module. The data store provides reliable persistent storage for tuples and can be locally replicated for performance and durability. The executors run instances of locally installed application bolts. In Merlin, bolts do not communicate directly with each other. Instead, the Merlin *router* reads tuples from the data store, and decides for each tuple whether to pass it to one of the *executors* for processing by a local bolt, or leave it for the *pusher*, which will propagate it to the next level of the hierarchy by inserting the tuple into the data store of its parent. New tuples emitted by a local bolt are written to the local data store and are subsequently handled by the router.

For example, in the scenario shown in Figure 1 (c), tuples created by road sensors in the Beaches neighborhood are initially stored in the local store of the Beaches data center. The router running on this data center reads the tuples and copies them to the Toronto data center as there are no locally installed bolts that could process them. In turn, the router running on the Toronto data center reads

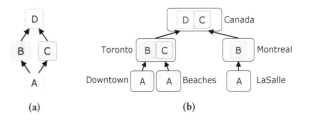

Figure 3: Application logical plan (a) and different mappings on to the edge network (b).

tuples from its local data store and forwards them to the locally installed instance of bolt-A. Tuples emitted by bolt-A are initially stored on the local data store of the Toronto data center where the router will forward them to the locally installed instance of bolt-B. Finally, tuples emitted by bolt-B are copied to the cloud data center where they will be eventually passed to bolt-C.

The above design makes it possible for Merlin to handle the addition and removal of bolts from a data center as a local operation. Adding or removing a bolt only requires updating information on the local router, which can then start forwarding compatible tuples for local processing. Similarly, changes made to a data center do not affect the routing decisions made by the rest of the data centers in the network. Individual data centers do not know the global placement of bolts, and their local router module only needs to make a simple decision: consume the tuple locally or push it to the parent. To ensure that it is always safe for the Merlin router to propagate tuples towards the root of the data center hierarchy, Merlin assumes that all application bolts are installed by default on the root data center (Section 2). Merlin's store-and-forward approach is also a good match for applications that experience intermittent connectivity, as tuples meant to be propagated up the hierarchy can be kept in local storage until the connection to the parent is re-established.

While Merlin assumes a simple hierarchy in the shape of a tree to forward tuples, the framework supports more complex streaming application topologies and allows bolts to emit tuples for multiple destinations. For example, Figure 3(a) shows a logical plan consisting of 4 bolts. Bolt A emits two types of tuples, which get consumed by either bolt B or bolt C. Figure 3(b) shows a possible deployment of this application on Merlin. The example assumes that the application developer has indicated that application correctness would not be impacted by running bolt A and bolt B, on neighborhood and city-level data centres, respectively.

4.1 Prototype

We implemented a prototype of Merlin that provides *at-least once* and *out-of-order* processing of data streams on a hierarchy of data centers. Figure 4 illustrates the various components that Merlin deploys on each data center. The prototype uses Cassandra DB [9] as its local data store. As the figure shows, each data center deploys an independent Cassandra ring. Every Merlin data center also runs a *router* that reads tuples from its local Cassandra ring and either delivers them to an *executor* for consumption by an application bolt or to the *pusher*, which will transfer the tuple to the Cassandra ring of the parent data center. The design provides at-least once

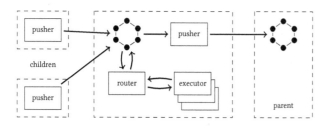

Figure 4: Merlin architecture.

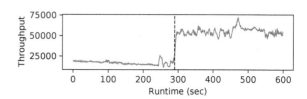

Figure 5: Merlin throughput over 10 minutes. A new edge data center was added after 5 minutes.

processing guarantee: in event of a failure, the data is available in the Merlin node's local data store; on recovery, the router will pick up undelivered tuples and route them again. Merlin implements a simple flow control algorithm that throttles pushers when available free space on the parent drops below a configurable threshold. Bolts in Merlin are Java objects that adhere to an API for consuming and emitting tuples.

The prototype does not support the replication or migration of application-specific bolt state, which is required to handle the addition or removal of bolts that depend on application state to operate. For example, adding an instance of bolt-A (neighborhood-aggregation) to the Downtown data center (see Figure 1(c)) requires replicating information about all Downtown streets that was up to this point kept by the instance of bolt-A running on the Toronto data center. We plan to explore the use of CloudPath [11] to run bolts as *stateless* functions that rely on a hierarchical distributed database (such as PathStore [10]) for application state management.

4.2 Preliminary Evaluation

Figure 5 presents experimental results for a topology that starts with one Merlin edge data center and one Merlin data center. At the 300 second mark, we add another Merlin edge data center to the topology. As the figure depicts, the new Merlin data center assimilates into the topology and starts functioning with no disruption or delay. The reconfiguration would be similarly immediate if an edge data center were to leave the topology. By design, Merlin is a loosely coupled system; Merlin nodes maintain no knowledge of the global topology and only know their parent node. The tuples are not emitted directly to the destination bolt for consumption but are rather inserted into the local store of the parent node, which routes them upstream. All a node has to do to join the topology is to get the parent node information and start writing to it via a Cassandra session. This loosely coupled design is well suited for a dynamic edge architecture and IoT streaming applications as it does not require stopping and synchronizing the entire topology in order to reconfigure it.

5 RELATED WORK

Existing work on edge stream processing focuses on resource allocation, task placement, and effective parallelization. For example, work on video streaming applications deals with optimizing for lag-sensitive applications or pushing computation towards the edge [16, 18, 19]. These works assume a static network topology, and also use global optimization.

Most existing stream processing engines require *global coordination*. They are designed for large cloud data centers [1–3, 6, 8, 17], and assume that data is first propagated to the cloud and that all nodes in the cluster communicate over low latency and high bandwidth links. For example, adding new workers to a running Apache Storm [6] topology requires checkpointing and stopping the entire topology, reconfiguring it, and starting it again. Similarly, Apache Flink [3] requires global coordination of the dataflow [5] for failure recovery and for reconfiguration.

Kafka Streams similarly relies on global coordination (for example to provide end-to-end message processing guarantees) and low-latency communication between all nodes and the Kafka brokers. Drizzle [15] introduces group scheduling which reduces reconfiguration to within several seconds for small groups, but still requires 10 to 100 seconds when adding new nodes, and requires centralized scheduling which is infeasible across data centers. SpanEdge [12] allows placing of processing tasks at the edge for applications that require low latency and to reduce bandwidth usage on the WAN. It is built on top of Storm which suffers from the same restart delay when reconfiguration of the topology is required. To maintain their low latency goals, only a static topology can be used. In contrast, Merlin is designed from the ground up to enable fast and frequent reconfiguration by avoiding global coordination and by decoupling tuple delivery from processing.

6 CONCLUSION AND FUTURE WORK

This paper lays the groundwork for a new kind of streaming platform designed for edge computing and mobile settings. Unlike existing stream computing engines such as Storm and Flink, Merlin's loosely-coupled design allows quick and non-disruptive reconfiguration – regardless of network size. There are many research and engineering challenges that we plan to tackle including state management for stateful operators, exactly-once processing semantics, in order execution semantics, an Application Programming Interface (API) for user code, a higher level query processing engine, a mechanism to specify geographic constraints for deployment, load balancing and more sophisticated flow control, dynamic scaling of routers on the nodes, and generation of a physical plan from the logical plan.

REFERENCES

[1] Tyler Akidau, Alex Balikov, Kaya Bekiroğlu, Slava Chernyak, Josh Haberman, Reuven Lax, Sam McVeety, Daniel Mills, Paul Nordstrom, and Sam Whittle. 2013. MillWheel: Fault-tolerant Stream Processing at Internet Scale. *Proc. VLDB Endow.* 6, 11 (2013), 1033–1044.

[2] Tyler Akidau, Robert Bradshaw, Craig Chambers, Slava Chernyak, Rafael J. Fernández-Moctezuma, Reuven Lax, Sam McVeety, Daniel Mills, Frances Perry, Eric Schmidt, and Sam Whittle. 2015. The Dataflow Model: A Practical Approach to Balancing Correctness, Latency, and Cost in Massive-scale, Unbounded, Out-of-order Data Processing. *Proc. VLDB Endow.* 8, 12 (2015), 1792–1803.

[3] Paris Carbone, Asterios Katsifodimos, Stephan Ewen, Volker Markl, Seif Haridi, and Kostas Tzoumas. 2015. Apache Flink: Stream and Batch Processing in a Single Engine. *IEEE Data Eng. Bull.* 38 (2015), 28–38.

[4] Cisco VNI. 2017. Cisco Visual Networking Index: Forecast and Methodology, 2016-2021. (2017).

[5] Apache Software Foundation. [n. d.]. Apache Flink: Data Streaming Fault Tolerance. https://ci.apache.org/projects/flink/flink-docs-master/internals/stream_checkpointing.html. ([n. d.]).

[6] Apache Software Foundation. 2015. Apache Storm. http://storm.apache.org/index.html. (2015).

[7] Rob Kitchin. 2014. *The Data Revolution: Big Data, Open Data, Data Infrastructures and Their Consequences.* SAGE Publications Ltd.

[8] Sanjeev Kulkarni, Nikunj Bhagat, Maosong Fu, Vikas Kedigehalli, Christopher Kellogg, Sailesh Mittal, Jignesh M. Patel, Karthik Ramasamy, and Siddarth Taneja. 2015. Twitter Heron: Stream Processing at Scale. In *Proceedings of the 2015 ACM SIGMOD International Conference on Management of Data (SIGMOD '15)*. 239–250.

[9] Avinash Lakshman and Prashant Malik. 2010. Cassandra: A Decentralized Structured Storage System. *SIGOPS Oper. Syst. Rev.* 44, 2 (2010), 35–40.

[10] Seyed Hossein Mortazavi, Bharath Balasubramanian, Eyal de Lara, and Shankaranarayanan Puzhavakath Narayanan. 2018. Toward Session Consistency for the Edge. In *USENIX Workshop on Hot Topics in Edge Computing (HotEdge 18)*.

[11] Seyed Hossein Mortazavi, Mohammad Salehe, Carolina Simoes Gomes, Caleb Phillips, and Eyal de Lara. 2017. CloudPath: A Multi-Tier Cloud Computing Framework. In *2nd ACM/IEEE Symposium on Edge Computing (SEC)*.

[12] H. P. Sajjad, K. Danniswara, A. Al-Shishtawy, and V. Vlassov. 2016. SpanEdge: Towards Unifying Stream Processing over Central and Near-the-Edge Data Centers. In *2016 IEEE/ACM Symposium on Edge Computing (SEC)*. 168–178.

[13] M. Satyanarayanan. 2017. The Emergence of Edge Computing. *Computer* 50, 1 (2017), 30–39. https://doi.org/10.1109/MC.2017.9

[14] W. Shi, J. Cao, Q. Zhang, Y. Li, and L. Xu. 2016. Edge Computing: Vision and Challenges. *IEEE Internet of Things Journal* 3, 5 (2016), 637–646.

[15] Shivaram Venkataraman, Aurojit Panda, Kay Ousterhout, Michael Armbrust, Ali Ghodsi, Michael J. Franklin, Benjamin Recht, and Ion Stoica. 2017. Drizzle: Fast and Adaptable Stream Processing at Scale. In *Proceedings of the 26th Symposium on Operating Systems Principles (SOSP '17)*. 374–389.

[16] Shanhe Yi, Zijiang Hao, Qingyang Zhang, Quan Zhang, Weisong Shi, and Qun Li. 2017. LAVEA: Latency-aware Video Analytics on Edge Computing Platform. In *Proceedings of the Second ACM/IEEE Symposium on Edge Computing (SEC '17)*. Article 15, 13 pages.

[17] Matei Zaharia, Reynold S. Xin, Patrick Wendell, Tathagata Das, Michael Armbrust, Ankur Dave, Xiangrui Meng, Josh Rosen, Shivaram Venkataraman, Michael J. Franklin, Ali Ghodsi, Joseph Gonzalez, Scott Shenker, and Ion Stoica. 2016. Apache Spark: A Unified Engine for Big Data Processing. *Commun. ACM* 59, 11 (2016), 56–65.

[18] Haoyu Zhang, Ganesh Ananthanarayanan, Peter Bodik, Matthai Philipose, Paramvir Bahl, and Michael J. Freedman. 2017. Live Video Analytics at Scale with Approximation and Delay-Tolerance. In *14th USENIX Symposium on Networked Systems Design and Implementation (NSDI 17)*. 377–392.

[19] Tan Zhang, Aakanksha Chowdhery, Paramvir (Victor) Bahl, Kyle Jamieson, and Suman Banerjee. 2015. The Design and Implementation of a Wireless Video Surveillance System. In *Proceedings of the 21st Annual International Conference on Mobile Computing and Networking (MobiCom '15)*. 426–438.

Mobility Control of Mobile Sensing for Time-Varying Parameter

Yuichi Nakamura
Institute of Industrial Science,
The University of Tokyo
y-nakamura@mcl.iis.u-tokyo.ac.jp

Masaki Ito
Institute of Industrial Science,
The University of Tokyo
m-ito@iis.u-tokyo.ac.jp

Kaoru Sezaki
Center for Spatial Information
Science, The University of Tokyo
sezaki@iis.u-tokyo.ac.jp

ACM Reference Format:
Yuichi Nakamura, Masaki Ito, and Kaoru Sezaki. 2019. Mobility Control of Mobile Sensing for Time-Varying Parameter. In *The 20th International Workshop on Mobile Computing Systems and Applications (HotMobile '19), February 27–28, 2019, Santa Cruz, CA, USA.* ACM, New York, NY, USA, 1 page. https://doi.org/10.1145/3301293.3309553

1 INTRODUCTION

The rapid spread of mobile devices such as smartphones, the paradigm of mobile sensing has attracted much attention from many different areas including disaster mitigation, public health, urban planning and so on [1]. As for estimating the scalar or vector field mobile sensing is relatively lower-costed and offers better spatial resolution of result compared to conventional stationary sensor.

There is, however, still no practical methods for determining the placement of sensors in such a system for dynamic environment. For example, [2, 3] suggests the method of node movement but it regards the parameter being measured is time-invariant.

2 MOBILITY CONTROL OF SENSOR NODES IN MOBILE SENSING

This paper aims to develop a method to determine how to move sensor nodes in a sensing system to collect data that provides the quality of resulting field estimation. Here we assume a system as follows: 1) The system consists of multiple sensor nodes with certain mobility that conduct homogeneous measurements. 2) Each node conducts measurement for multiple times and moves to a new location between them. 3) By integrating sensing data, the scaler/vector field will be estimated for the entire area.

The proposal includes the way of mobility control of sensor nodes to enhance the estimation from the measured data with regard to spatio-temporal resolution.

3 METHOD

In our method, the gradient of confidence of interpolation is used to determine the movement of sensor.

Kriging was used to interpolate the measured value with regard to three axes: two spatial axes x, y and time axis t. The variance of the estimation is called kriging variance and that is defined for $\forall x, y, t$ as $V(x, y, t)$. At each time step, sensor nodes will be moved

towards the direction that has the steepest descent. In other words, at time $t = t_1$, the sensor node at (x_1, y_1) will be moved to the direction $\vec{e}$, given by

$$\vec{e} = \arg\max_{|\vec{e}|=1} \left\{ \left[\nabla_{x,y} V(x, y, t) \big|_{t=t_1} \right] \cdot \vec{e} \right\}. \tag{1}$$

This way, in the next time step, measurements will be conducted at points where the estimation is less confident.

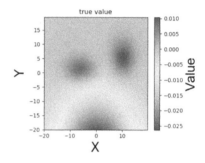

Figure 1: The ground truth.

4 EVALUATION

To test the proposed method, we conducted a simulation with time-varying 2-d scalar field (**Figure 1**). We compared the proposed method with random movement. Among numerous trials, the proposed method showed statistically significant advantages over the baseline with regard to the MSE between the estimation and the ground truth.

5 CONCLUSION

In this paper we proposed a method of mobility control of sensor nodes in sensor nodes to estimate the entire vector / scalar field which is time-variant. In this paper we merely conducted simulation for the evaluation, evaluation using the real sensing data is also expected, which would reveal further challenges for real applications. For example, the kriging along space / time axis might not work for parameter without spatial / temporal continuity.

REFERENCES
[1] C. Zhang, and Y. Zhao, "High Precision Deep Sea Geomagnetic Data Sampling and Recovery with Three-Dimensional Compressive Sensing," IEICE TRANSACTIONS on Fundamentals of Electronics, Communications and Computer Sciences, vol.E100-A, no.9, pp.1760–1762, 2017.
[2] C.J. Sullivan, "Radioactive source localization in urban environments with sensor networks and the Internet of Things," 2016 IEEE International Conference on Multisensor Fusion and Integration for Intelligent Systems (MFI), pp.384–388, IEEE, sep 2016.
[3] A. Krause, A. Singh, and C. Guestrin, "Near-Optimal Sensor Placements in Gaussian Processes: Theory, Efficient Algorithms and Empirical Studies," Journal of Machine Learning Research, vol.9, pp.235–284, 2008.

Poster: Retroreflective MIMO Communication

Yue Wu, Kenuo Xu, Hao He, Zihang Wu, Chenren Xu

Peking University, China

MOTIVATION

Retroreflective communication has the intrinsic advantage of ultra low power and flexible pointing requirement, and thus is suitable for IoT [1] and V2X [2] applications. While LCD is commonly used as optical modulator due to the low cost, its slow response time becomes the performance bottleneck, when it is used in the SISO setting. Therefore, it is desirable to develop MIMO techniques.

DESIGN

We propose to design retroreflective MIMO channel based on polarization division multiplexing (PDM), with multiple LCD modulators and photodiode (PD) receivers. LCD shutter works as a bi-state modulator which rotates the polarized light by $0°$ or $90°$. With polarizer on each side of LCD, it could retroreflect incoming light or absorb it. The retroreflected light is polarized to the angle of front polarizer, which is imperceptible by human eyes but could be separated using polarizer on PD receivers.

Given M individual LCDs and N PD receivers (Fig. 1a), the received signal R_n could be expressed using channel matrix H_{nm}, retroreflected signal strength T_m and their angles θ_{t_i}, also background noise signal R_{0n}.

$$R_n = R_{0n} + H_{nm}T_m, \quad H_{nm} = \cos^2(\theta_{r_n} - \theta_{t_m})$$

Note that the maximum rank of H_{nm} is 3 when $M \geq 3$ and $N \geq 3$, which means even if we have arbitrary amount of transmitters and receivers, there are only 3 independent communication channels in this system [3], which means the PDM is limited in up to 3 times throughput gain.

Our key insight is that LCD as a bi-state modulator cannot always utilize bandwidth efficiently since it cannot generate arbitrary level of signal strength. This leads to our idea of generating more channels even if they are not independent.

The receiving signal constructs a M-dimensional space, while N LCDs have only 2^N symbols. If all the 2^N symbols could be recognized, we could say that we get N binary code channels, which improves the throughput by N times. Note

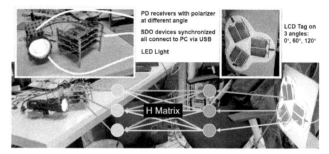

(a) Experimental Setup

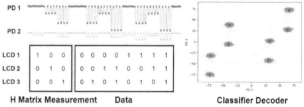

H Matrix Measurement　　　Data　　　Classifier Decoder

Three binary code channels with 2 receivers and 3 transmitters

(b) Raw Waveform
Figure 1: Preliminary Results

that this scheme works even if M is less than N, which could be seen in the example Fig. 1b.

Exceeding the limit of independent channel requires elaborate design of polarization angles, thus it is limited to single user MIMO. With an extra LCD in front of the tag, it can perform channel selection when two angles are too close to decode signals, by rotating the polarized light by $0°$ or $90°$.

PRELIMINARY RESULTS

We built a prototype system to evaluate our design. Reader send carrier signal on LED light and receive retroflected signal. The optical part includes an array of PDs and amplifiers, while multiple output is connected to readers.

Our preliminary results show that we could successfully decode three channels using only 2 receivers, with a classifier decoder.

REFERENCES

[1] Xieyang Xu, Yang Shen, Junrui Yang, Chenren Xu, Guobin Shen, Guojun Chen, and Yunzhe Ni. Passivevlc: Enabling practical visible light backscatter communication for battery-free iot applications. In *ACM MobiCom*, 2017.

[2] Guojun Chen, Purui Wang, Lilei Feng, Yue Wu, Xieyang Xu, Yang Shen, and Chenren Xu. Long range retroreflective v2x communication with polarization-based differential reception. In *ACM SenSys*, 2018.

[3] Darko Ivanovich, Samuel B Powell, Viktor Gruev, and Roger D Chamberlain. Polarization division multiplexing for optical data communications. In *SPIE Optical Interconnects XVIII*, 2018.

Platform Variability in Edge-Cloud Vision Systems

Ali J. Ben Ali
University at Buffalo
alijmabe@buffalo.edu

Sofiya Semenova
University at Buffalo
sofiyase@buffalo.edu

Karthik Dantu
University at Buffalo
kdantu@buffalo.edu

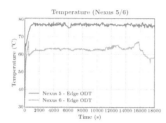 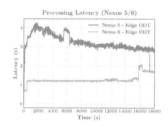 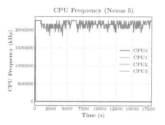 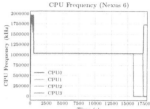

Figure 1: (1) CPU temperature, (2) per-frame processing latency, and (3-4) CPU core frequency for Nexus 5/6

ABSTRACT

Modern edge devices such as smartphones, tablets, smart glasses, VR and AR headsets have gotten more capable with high-resolution displays, powerful CPU/GPUs, multiple sensing modalities and multiple connectivity options. These platform capabilities are enabling complex sensing applications that integrate visual, inertial, and other sensing modalities in real-time to enable applications such as indoor navigation, object recognition, face recognition, activity recognition, and others. Typically, such applications are computationally-intensive and require execution of complex computer vision pipelines for effective execution.

While edge devices are getting more powerful, it is still challenging to run such computationally intense applications exclusively on the edge. To address this challenge, several solutions propose splitting the computing between the cloud and the edge. However, these solutions are typically tested for a few seconds/minutes. Our observation is that this ignores platform constraints when multiple apps are running on the same edge device and/or long-term operation, resulting in platform variability such as voltage/frequency scaling, shutting down of CPU cores, etc. all of which affect the application performance.

To demonstrate this concern, we perform the following experiment. We build an example edge-cloud vision system - performing Object Detection and Tracking (ODT) using

TensorFlow using the SSD-MobileNet-v2 model. We run the application on two devices - Google Nexus 5 (Qualcomm Snapdragon 800 2.26 GHz quad-core processor with 2 GB memory) and Google Nexus 6 (Qualcomm Snapdragon 805 2.7 GHz quad-core processor with 3 GB memory). Figure 1 shows the CPU temperature, processing latency per image frame, and CPU frequency over five hours run. Due to the processing load, the CPU temperature goes above an acceptable threshold at time=30s (Nexus 5) and time=250s (Nexus 6). These temperature variations cause the OS to reduce the CPU frequency in both cases, increasing the processing latency per frame. Further, on the Nexus 6, we observe that the OS turns off some cores to reduce platform temperature after running for more than four hours, while Nexus 5 only runs on one core for most of the time.

These observations have been made while running one application only. As is typical, if multiple applications were running on these edge devices, their performance would be affected further due to the platform load. We also have results from running multiple applications, as well as running the ODT application in a split manner between the edge and fog/cloud for improved performance. In each of these cases, we observe a similar behavior. Our proposal is that future edge-cloud systems need to explicitly test for platform variation due to long-term operation in order to demonstrate feasibility.

ACM Reference Format:
Ali J. Ben Ali, Sofiya Semenova, and Karthik Dantu. 2019. Platform Variability in Edge-Cloud Vision Systems. In *The 20th International Workshop on Mobile Computing Systems and Applications (HotMobile '19), February 27–28, 2019, Santa Cruz, CA, USA*. ACM, New York, NY, USA, 1 page. https://doi.org/10.1145/3301293.3309555

Heimdall: A Case for Encrypted Displays

Extended Abstract

Animesh Srivastava[*]
sranimesh@gmail.com

ABSTRACT

It can be argued that among all the personal devices, a smartphone carries the most private information of one's life. The improved hardware, computing resource, ever-increasing storage, ubiquitous connectivity, and innovative ways of accessing useful information has slowly and steadily integrated smartphones in our lives. Whether it is interacting on social media, planning for the day using productivity apps or getting things done at work, the smartphone screen is the primary gateway between a user and the world of information accessible through the smartphones. There is always a risk of leaking sensitive information while accessing such information on one's smart-device in a public setting.

Visual information can be easily taken advantage of by a malicious bystander. Even if the screen is not comprehensible to the human eye, an off-the-shelf recording device can capture the finer details displayed on the victim's smartphone. A popular way of protecting visual information displayed on smartphones is to use privacy screens [1]. However, privacy screens fail to protect visual privacy when the bystander or the recording device is pointed at it directly. To address this issue, in the poster, we propose, *Heimdall*, an augmented reality (AR) based system.

The primary reason for the failure of privacy screens is that the medium used to broadcast the visual information is shared by the intended user and the bystanders. An AR based solution isolates the medium used to receive the visual information by the intended user from any other receiver. The primary guiding force behind the design of *Heimdall* are as follows:

- **On-demand Privacy Mode**: The user should be able to interact with her smartphone without the need of the AR equipment. The user can enable privacy mode when sensitive information needs to be accessed and disable otherwise.
- **Minimal computation on AR device**: We do not assume that the AR device will be capable of performing an intensive computation. AR glasses under *Heimdall* should be able to stream the user's view and replace it with an augmented view.

Heimdall consists of the following three components: (1) **Heimdall Client**: an application installed on user's smartphone that encrypts or decrypts the screen on user's request, (2) **Heimdall AR**: an application running on user's AR device that overlays the decrypted visual information on the smartphone, and (3) **Heimdall**

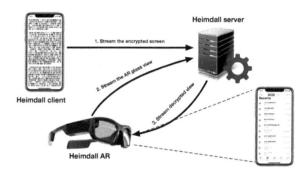

Figure 1: The figure presents a high level overview of the interaction between the three components of *Heimdall*.

Server: a server software to continuously decrypt an encrypted stream of visual information, stream it back to the AR glass, and relay every interaction made by the user with the AR view to the smartphone device. Figure 1 shows a high level interaction of all the three components under *Heimdall*.

A typical *Heimdall* usage scenario is as follows: Alice is at the airport about to board her flight. She receives an important email from work and she decides to respond to the email sooner than later. Alice triggers the privacy mode by invoking *Heimdall* client on her phone. The screen immediately gets encrypted (garbled for any onlookers.) Alice puts on her AR glass and looks at the phone. She could interact with the email app, read and compose a reply, and send it. After she closes the email app, she taps the AR glass on the side to stop the privacy mode.

With the growing number of AR glass products [2], we find that *Heimdall* addresses a real-world problem and provides huge value to the users.

CCS CONCEPTS

• **Security and privacy** → **Usability in security and privacy**.

KEYWORDS

Visual privacy leaks

ACM Reference Format:
Animesh Srivastava[*]. 2019. Heimdall: A Case for Encrypted Displays: Extended Abstract. In *The 20th International Workshop on Mobile Computing Systems and Applications (HotMobile '19), February 27–28, 2019, Santa Cruz, CA, USA.* ACM, New York, NY, USA, 1 page. https://doi.org/10.1145/3301293.3309556

REFERENCES

[1] 3M. 2019 (accessed Jan 3, 2019). *Privacy and Screen Protectors.* https://www.3m.com/3M/en_US/privacy-screen-protectors-us/
[2] wearable.com. Nov 9, 2018 (accessed Jan 6, 2019). *The best augmented reality glasses 2019: Snap, Vuzix, ODG, Sony & more.* https://www.wareable.com/ar/the-best-smartglasses-google-glass-and-the-rest

---

[*]Now at Google.

HotMobile '19, February 27–28, 2019, Santa Cruz, CA, USA
© 2019 Copyright held by the owner/author(s).
ACM ISBN 978-1-4503-6273-3/19/02.
https://doi.org/10.1145/3301293.3309556

EmerGence: A Delay Tolerant Web Application for Disaster Relief

Udita Paul
Department of Computer Science
UC Santa Barbara
u_paul@ucsb.edu

Michael Nekrasov
Department of Computer Science
UC Santa Barbara
mnekrasov@cs.ucsb.edu

Elizabeth Belding
Department of Computer Science
UC Santa Barbara
ebelding@cs.ucsb.edu

ABSTRACT

The number and intensity of natural disasters have drastically increased in recent years and are anticipated to continue doing so. In addition to directly threatening human lives, disasters cripple communication and electric infrastructure, compounding the negative impact on humans, as observed for instance during Hurricane Maria in Puerto Rico [1]. This inevitably puts more strain on the remaining infrastructure resulting in failure of many people to effectively communicate. In this work, we have developed a progressive web application, EmerGence, designed to leverage opportunistic internet connectivity to relay messages from individuals trapped in disaster-hit areas. EmerGence works by bypassing the crippled/downed communication infrastructure to connect disaster victims with needed resources (both human and material) through a combination of a new web development concept called the Progressive Web App (PWA) and served by an Unmanned Aircraft System (UAS).

EMERGENCE OVERVIEW

Unlike a traditional web page, PWAs look and feel like native applications using Javascript ServiceWorker that allows background processing and pre-caching of pages and data. Furthermore, unlike native applications, PWAs do not need prior installation, and work across devices and operating systems. We use the UAS as a delay tolerant edge server. This allows EmerGence to work on opportunistic connectivity setting it apart from other disaster relief applications [2-4]. EmerGence allows users to see posts made by other users as well as post their own content with or without network connectivity. In absence of network connection, the app renders locally stored contents to the users. Similarly, when users post during break in internet connection, the app buffers the posts locally and once connection is established, it pushes the contents without requiring further user action. Users are also notified in the event a new post is made. Each post is geo-tagged to locate people in need of help.

EmerGence looks at how to provide delay tolerant edge connectivity to existing devices in a disaster-struck area. To this end, it makes several novel contributions: (1) implements PWA for delay tolerant communication with a mobile edge server and (2) evaluates optimal transmission strategies for a PWA under poor network conditions.

We conducted preliminary tests to analyse performance of EmerGence. We introduced various level of delay in the network (to better emulate a congested network environment) to assess the time taken for the app to load and post a varying number of messages. In the absence of network connectivity, when loading up to 20 posts, results show that the app responds within 100ms as the contents are served from the local browser cache. However, with 1000ms delay in the network; it takes up to 800ms to load the same number of posts using the network. With the same amount of delay in the network, it is seen that the app takes about 25 seconds to post all 20 locally buffered messages.

In future work, we are evaluating novel transmission strategies, such as pre-generating static pages on drone to minimize connection time. We are also looking at expanding data delivery to include real time analysis performed on drone such as a natural language processing model to parse through the various user messages to categorize users into those who possess certain resources and those in need of such resources. We are also looking at tools for first responders such as automatic network coverage mapping.

REFERENCES

[1] FCC. Communications Status Report for Areas Impacted by Hurricane Maria – September 21, 2017, https://transition.fcc.gov/DailyReleases/Daily Business/2017/db0921/DOC-34680A 1:pdf, September 2017. (Accessed on 01/07/2019).

[2] A. J. M. Schwab, J. E. C. Omaña, K. V. Roazol, T. A. Y. Abe and B. S. Fabito, "iSagip: A Crowdsource Disaster Relief and Monitoring Application framework," 2017 *International Conference on Soft Computing, Intelligent System and Information Technology (ICSIIT)*, Denpasar, 2017, pp. 327-330.XXXXXXXXXXXXXXXXXXXX https://www.acm.org/publications/proceedings-template.

[3] F. Shih, O. Seneviratne, I. Liccardi, E. Patton, P. Meier, and C. Castillo, "Democratizing mobile app development for disaster management," In *Joint Proceedings of the Workshop on AI Problems and Approaches for Intelligent Environments and Workshop on Semantic Cities*, pages 39–42. ACM, 2013.

[4] M. B. Greer Jr. and J. W. Ngo, "Personal Emergency Preparedness Plan (PEPP) Facebook App: Using Cloud Computing, Mobile Technology, and Social Networking Services to Decompress Traditional Channels of Communication during Emergencies and Disasters," *2012 IEEE Ninth International Conference on Services Computing*, Honolulu, HI, 2012, pp. 494-498.

An Opportunistic mHealth Architecture for Remote Patient Monitoring

Esther Max-Onakpoya, Aggrey Jacobs, Corey E. Baker

ema273,awja223,baker@cs.uky.edu

Department of Computer Science, University of Kentucky

The widespread use and recent advancements in mobile technology have spurred improvements in access to healthcare through remote patient monitoring. As a result, chronically-ill patients can be remotely monitored using noninvasive or invasive body sensors connected to mobile phones. This has led to a decrease in mortality rates and improved quality of life for patients who are able to utilize such technology [5]. Ideally, remote patient monitoring (RPM) should benefit patients regardless of geographical and financial barriers. However, limited or nonexistent access to broadband connectivity has restricted the benefits of connected health services for many people in rural areas [4].

Additionally, the cost of deploying broadband or updating traditional technology has proved to be a large financial burden. Furthermore, the prevalence of chronic disease is approximately 20% higher in rural areas than other areas [3]. Consequently, the need for cost-effective patient monitoring technologies that can operate in the midst of intermittent connectivity is essential in rural and developing areas. A promising solution to this lies in the use of delay tolerant networks (DTN) [2]. Hence, this abstract discusses the design and viability of an architecture that leverages the ubiquity of mobile devices, DTNs and intermittent broadband connectivity to facilitate the transmission of medical information through a remote patient monitoring iOS application.

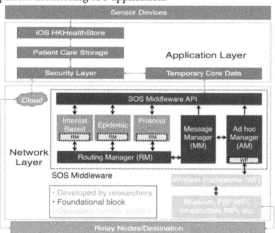

Figure 1: A system architecture for communication of health data from an iOS device to other devices and the cloud.

The proposed architecture in figure 1 maximizes the potential of DTN and intermittent Internet connectivity, similar to a regular DTN-mesh network, where source nodes can harness the current or future connectivity of relay nodes in other to transmit information to destination. It is designed to be deployable in the real-world by using the inner workings of iOS and current standards of RPM as a template to build a mobile application.

The state-of-the-art methods of RPM utilize a combination of objective and subjective patient health information to draw conclusions on patient health and disease progression. Objective patient data is obtained from sensor devices and transmitted asynchronously to an aggregator such as Apple's iOS HealthKit. Similarly, subjective data is collected from the patient's interaction or with the mobile application. Consequently, the data can be collected through a secure access point such as iOS HealthKit's healthstore. Following this, the data can be transferred to a central secure database that persists on the user's phone (the application's Patient Care Storage). While an iOS device is locked, data neither be read from the Health Kit health store nor care plan store by an application. Hence, data can be transmitted to a temporary database from which, pertinent routing data can be read from and medical information can be securely routed through the Secure Opportunistic Schemes (SOS) middleware system stack [1].

While there has been a lot of literature addressing general DTN problems like RF communications and routing, problems relating to the practical deployment and evaluation of DTN applications for RPM have not been thoroughly researched. These problems include security and privacy requirements (e.g. encryption methods, maintaining patient privacy through source or destination integrity, etc), methods of incentivising relay nodes, routing protocols that evolve with/adapt to culture of various rural settings, technology adoption in rural areas, and the like. The architecture described above allows researchers to harness the inner working of iOS to create delay tolerant health applications than can be easily deployed in the real world.

REFERENCES

[1] Corey E Baker, Allen Starke, Tanisha G Hill-Jarrett, and Janise McNair. 2017. In Vivo Evaluation of the Secure Opportunistic Schemes Middleware using a Delay Tolerant Social Network. In *Distributed Computing Systems (ICDCS), 2017 IEEE 37th International Conference on*. IEEE, 2537–2542.

[2] Mrinmoy Barua, Rongxing Lu, and Xuemin Shen. 2011. Health-Post: A delay-tolerant secure long-term health care scheme in rural area. In *Global Telecommunications Conference (GLOBECOM 2011), 2011 IEEE*. IEEE, 1–5.

[3] CDC. 2018. National Center for Health Statistics. https://www.cdc.gov/nchs/hus/contents2017.htm#Table_039

[4] S Jane Henley, Robert N Anderson, Cheryll C Thomas, Greta M Massetti, Brandy Peaker, and Lisa C Richardson. 2017. Invasive cancer incidence, 2004–2013, and deaths, 2006–2015, in nonmetropolitan and metropolitan counties—United States. *MMWR Surveillance Summaries* 66, 14 (2017), 1.

[5] Ernest Moy. 2017. Leading causes of death in nonmetropolitan and metropolitan areas – United States, 1999–2014. *MMWR. Surveillance Summaries* 66 (2017).

Poster: Towards Self-Managing and Self-Adaptive Framework for Automating MAC Protocol Design in Wireless Networks

Hannaneh Barahouei Pasandi, Tamer Nadeem
{barahoueipash,tnadeem}@vcu.edu
Virginia Commonwealth University
Richmond, Virginia, USA

CCS CONCEPTS

• **Networks** → *Network protocol design*;

KEYWORDS

Communication Protocols, Machine Learning, MAC protocol

ACM Reference format:
Hannaneh Barahouei Pasandi, Tamer Nadeem. 2019. Poster: Towards Self-Managing and Self-Adaptive Framework for Automating MAC Protocol Design in Wireless Networks. In *Proceedings of The 20th International Workshop on Mobile Computing Systems and Applications, Santa Cruz, CA, USA, February 27–28, 2019 (HotMobile '19)*, 1 pages.
https://doi.org/10.1145/3301293.3309559

1 MOTIVATION

Wireless protocols are continuously evolving to meet new and more complex service requirements. The current methods for protocol design are mainly human-based and thus are burdened with various limitations. Design of new protocols is time-consuming and requires a specialized knowledge that is not trivial to acquire. This is especially limiting in the context of modern networking domain, i.e., IEEE 802.11 protocol that is continuously evolving nowadays to meet new requirements and conditions through the addition of new amendments. In this poster, we explain the design steps of an intelligent framework that designs MAC protocols by interacting with environment. In this framework IEEE 802.11 MAC protocols are decomposed into core functionalities in which the intelligent Deep Q-Learning (DQL) agent designs an efficient protocol by selecting the optimum set of building blocks in response to network dynamics.A preliminary version of this system has been implemented in [1, 2]. In the following, we explain briefly the main design parts of the proposed system.

2 SYSTEM DESIGN

Developing the basic modules and components of IEEE 802.11 standards for automatic network protocol design. In our framework, we consider the modular design principle that decouples a MAC protocol into independent blocks. This principle allows fast reconfiguration and adaptation of the MAC design. We decompose MAC protocols into their main functionalities (timer, carrier

sensing, backoff, etc.,) using data flow model. We also develop an extended state machine that keeps the logical and temporal relations, as well as the dependencies between blocks. The quality of learning is tightly depend of the quality of the provided input for the Deep Q-learning agent. In order to provide more insight into the quality of obtained building blocks and to design more efficient automatic block selection mechanism, we propose to evaluate the richness of information space given by them. We propose a three-way approach for computing information richness measures of examined sets of protocol building blocks. Firstly, we will count how many different values can be obtained to estimate the size of information space given by each set of blocks. Secondly, we will measure Shannon and Renyi's quadratic entropies of these values to further measure richness of the space. Finally, we will compute Renyi's quadratic cross entropy and Cauchy-Schwarz Divergences between projection distributions of each of building block sets to measure the diversity among them.

Designing and developing a DQL approach for centralized and distributed agents. After finalizing the building block set, DQL agent uses these blocks as well as a batch of previous experiences as input. The output is a vector of corresponding Q-values for all the possible actions from the current state. We expand this architecture for centralized and distributed approach. In centralized agent scenario, a single DQL agent is responsible for managing the protocol design task. One of the vital challenges in DL is in the possible strong temporal correlations embedded in the agent learning procedure. In our framework, we faced long-range time dependencies that materialize only after many transitions of the environment. Therefore, we alleviated this by embedding LSTM networks within our deep architecture. In Multi-agent scenario, we model the actual protocol design task where multiple protocols are created at the same time. We assume a cooperative scenario in which all agents work together towards a common goal. We finally evaluate our framework in terms of DQL agent convergence and adaptation to network conditions as well as comparing the designed protocol by our agent against series of the state-of-the-art MAC protocols.

REFERENCES

[1] Hannaneh barahouei Pasandi and Tamer Nadeem. 2019. Challenges and Limitations in Automating the Design of MAC Protocols Using Machine-Learning. In *International Conference on Artificial Intelligence in Information and Communications (ICAIIC)*. IEEE.
[2] Hannaneh Barahouei Pasandi and Tamer Nadeem. 2019. Towards A Machine Learning-Based Framework For Automated Design of MAC Protocols. In *IEEE International Conference on Pervasive Computing and Communications Workshops (PerCom Workshops)*. IEEE.

CARE: Campus-wide Accessible Route Estimation through Surface Analysis

John Hata
Department of Computer Science and
Software Engineering
Miami University
Oxford OH USA
hatajm@miamioh.edu

Md Osman Gani
Department of Computer Science and
Software Engineering
Miami University
Oxford OH USA
ganim@miamioh.edu

Vaskar Raychoudhury
Department of Computer Science and
Software Engineering
Miami University
Oxford OH USA
raychov@miamioh.edu

ABSTRACT

Travelling is not always fun for wheelchair users in the built environment (both indoor and outdoor) in presence of various unknown barriers, such as, uneven sidewalks, curb heights, stairs, ramps, cobbled streets, etc. [1] [2]. Also, elderly individuals are more likely to require assistance while using self-propelled and non-motorized wheelchairs. However, along with barriers there are also various wheelchair-friendly facilities, such as, supervised crosswalks and elevators, which improve accessibility of environments and facilities.

Various indoor environments, including buildings, might have infrastructure in place for wheelchair accessibility, but it is not always easy to find a path to the nearest accessible entrance and exit, especially in the face of an emergency, such as a fire, tornado, or the worst, campus violence. The challenges are manifold.

- *Firstly*, the user may not know exactly where s/he is located and how far it is from the emergency event's location. This is even more difficult for indoor locations void of GPS coverage or missing information about the area. Moreover, the user should be able to share their location to external emergency personnel in case of requiring assistance or extraction.

- *Secondly*, an emergency event, such as a fire, can spread rapidly, requiring real-time alternative path finding. In addition, some surfaces are inaccessible for wheelchair users, such as, stairs, gravels, grass, mud, etc.

- *Finally*, the suggested path must exclude hindrances to wheelchair users customized to their needs depending on the wheelchair type and the capability of the user.

In this project, we plan to develop a Campus-wide Accessible Route Estimation (CARE) System which works through a large-scale vibration data analysis (created by wheelchair movement) from different built or natural surfaces and aims to classify the surfaces into accessible and inaccessible. The goal is to find accessible routes for wheelchair users. We have the following three concrete objectives to achieve through the project.

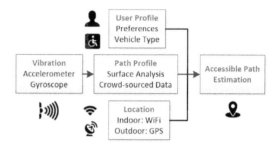

Figure 1: Accessible Route Estimation System

(1) We develop a Wi-Fi based indoor localization scheme for wheelchair users using their smartphones. The system will capture wireless probes and received signal strength values in a secured and non-intrusive manner (protecting user privacy) and it will determine the relative location of a wheelchair user with respect to the nearest wireless access points. User locations in the outdoor environment are estimated through their GPS coordinates.

(2) An Android app has been developed to collect vibration (accelerometer and gyroscope sensors) data during wheelchair movement through various indoor and outdoor surfaces in the Miami University campus. We have used a manual wheelchair and two different Android smartphones for data collection. Based on that, we label the data and train the machine learning system using several features in order to classify the surfaces into accessible and inaccessible categories. At a later stage, multiple crowd-sourced wheelchair vibration data streams are forwarded to the system to successfully classify the surfaces.

(3) Based on the user location and desired destination, we can then generate accessible routes adaptively and in real time customized to the user and wheelchair requirement.

ACKNOWLEDGMENTS

This work is partially supported by the UG Summer Scholarship and the Faculty Research Grant from Miami University, OH, USA.

REFERENCES

[1] D. Ding, et al., 2007. Design considerations for a personalized wheelchair navigation system. IEEE EMBS 2007, Lyon, France, 4790–4793.
[2] Thorsten Völkel, et al., Mobility Impaired Pedestrians Are Not Cars: Requirements for the Annotation of Geographical Data, ICCHP 2008. Lecture Notes in Computer Science, vol 5105. Springer, Berlin, Heidelberg.

Forecasting Mood Using Smartphone and SNS Data

Chaima Dhahri
KDDI Research, Inc., Japan
ch-dhahri@kddi-research.jp

Kazushi Ikeda
KDDI Research, Inc., Japan
kz-ikeda@kddi-research.jp

Keiichiro Hoashi
KDDI Research, Inc., Japan
hoashi@kddi-research.jp

1 INTRODUCTION

This poster demonstrates a mood forecasting system that forecasts tomorrow's mood based on today's data collected from SNS and smartphone sensors. Forecasting user's mood plays an important role in diverse topics such as recommendation systems. We define the mood as the variation in the feeling of a person. It can be either positive, negative or neutral.

Previous works can be divided into two groups: SNS-based and sensor-based methods. For the former group, the prediction coverage depends on user's activeness on SNS. Besides, they focused on text-only posts and ignore other types of posts such us link-only, image-out posts which may contain important insights [2], [3]. For the latter group, conventional methods have been focused on collecting data using extra devices to measure body physiological signal [4] and/or on smartphone sensors [1] along with user inputs. These methods suffer from the noise introduced by the user.

The research question for this study was whether it is possible to built an autonomous mood prediction system by sensing the user's smartphone sensors and SNS activities over cyber, social and physical spaces.

2 MOOD FORECAST MODEL

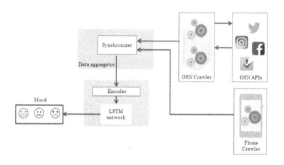

Figure 1: Mood Forecast Framework

We propose the system framework as shown in Fig. 1 for automatic mood forecasting using SNS and smartphone sensor data. To build our model, we crawl user's SNS accounts (Twitter, Instagram and Foursquare) and collect smartphone sensor data. We summarize the extracted features in Table 1. These features form the input vector to our neural network (LSTM). The output is the mood; positive, neutral and negative.

HotMobile '19, February 27–28, 2019, Santa Cruz, CA, USA
© 2019 Copyright held by the owner/author(s).
ACM ISBN 978-1-4503-6273-3/19/02.
https://doi.org/10.1145/3301293.3309561

Table 1: SNS and Smartphone Features

Feature Source	Feature Name
SNS(cyber)	negative/positive text count, hashtag/media/retweet count, source, day vs. night, active vs. passive, hue, sturation, brightness
SNS(social)	mention/favourites/like/comment count
SNS(physical)	geo-tag shared, location category
Smartphone	accelerometer, gyroscope, total/incoming/outgoing/missed call count, call duration, call/SMS unique number count, location, total/inbox/sent SMS count, WiFi

Table 2: Accuracy for Predicting Tomorrow Mood

	Active Users	Non-active Users
RF (SNS-only)	66	54
LSTM (SNS-only)	74	71
RF (SNS+smartphone)	73	69
LSTM (SNS+smartphone)	81	78

3 EXPERIMENT AND RESULTS

We run an experiment for 100 users over one month to test the performance of our proposal. The goal is to predict tomorrow's mood of each user individually using their own data (today's data). We compare the performance of our proposal with vector-based method using random forest (RF) algorithm. We use 4-fold cross validation method. We evaluate the performance of the prediction on a subset of features (SNS-only and SNS+smartphone) and a subset of users(active users and non-active).

Table 2 summarizes the result in terms of accuracy averaged over the number of users. The results show that LSTM method outperforms vector-based method (RF) in all conditions. It suggests ,also, that using features from both SNS and smartphone enhances the performance by 7 percentage points compared to the condition when using features from SNS only, regardless the learning algorithm. We can conclude that by combining SNS and smartphone data, we could achieve a maximum accuracy of 81% using LSTM as predictive algorithm.

REFERENCES

[1] Mahnaz Roshanaei et al. 2017. EmotionSensing: Predicting Mobile User Emotion. In *ASONAM*.
[2] Zunaira et al. Jamil. 2017. Monitoring Tweets for Depression to Detect At-risk Users. In *Proceedings of the Fourth Workshop on Computational Linguistics and Clinical Psychology — From Linguistic Signal to Clinical Reality*. Association for Computational Linguistics, 32–40.
[3] Mahnaz Roshanaei et al. 2017. *Having Fun?: Personalized Activity-Based Mood Prediction in Social Media*. Springer International Publishing.
[4] Sachin Shah et al. 2015. Towards affective touch interaction: predicting mobile user emotion from finger strokes. *Journal of Interaction Science* (2015).

Reliable Collaborative Vehicle-to-Vehicle Communication for Local Video Streaming

Mohamed Azab
City of Scientific Research &
Technological Application, Egypt.
mazab@vt.edu

Effat Samir
Alexandria University, Egypt
effat_samir@mena.vt.edu

Rawan Reda
Alexandria University, Egypt
rawan1reda@gmail.com

ABSTRACT

Vehicular Cloud Communication (VCC) gained huge momentum enabling local efficient data exchange. In this paper, we propose Network as a service (NaaS) architecture enabling internet-independent video-sharing in VCC.

INTRODUCTION

Video streaming services and selective TV in modern cities became the main source of entertainment. Unfortunately, the high bandwidth usage involved is a major challenge to Internet Service Providers. The situation is even worse when we consider mobility. The cellular networks based Internet traffic is very costly due to the limited network ability to cover the user requests compared to landlines. In this paper, we present a novel ad-hoc P2P Network as a Service (NaaS) architecture enabling internet-independent local video-streaming among moving vehicles. The presented approach manages to provide efficient service to sustain streaming traffic for the vehicles on highway with limited access to the cellular network like (4G) [1].

V2V framework for local video-streaming

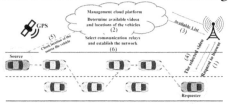

Figure 1: Network Architecture for Reliable V2V Communication

The goal of this system is offload communication intensive data transfer from the cellular network to local P2P connections. This in turn reduces the cost of bandwidth usage. As shown in figure 1, we used customized mobile application to communicate with a remote management service running on the cloud and to report the subscribers' location on the road. The application broadcasts a list of sharable content on the subscribers' phones and on the RSUs. Further, it also sends download/stream requests to the cloud for connection establishment. The request triggers the NaaS to calculate the optimal number of hops "communication relays" between the requester and the source, considering the

current vehicles locations, and the capabilities of the wireless communication device onboard. Once the route is determined, the vehicles involved are notified "communication relays" and a multi-hop P2P network is constructed. This is the only Internet dependent traffic that the application uses. The heavy file transfer process is done offline using the onboard Dedicated Short Range Communication (DSRC) device. The management service also monitors the connection and handles interruptions by real-time network reconstruction. The appropriate selection of these relays reduces the number of hops, which minimizes the chance of networking failure [2].

1.Evaluation

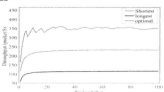

Figure 2: throughput Vs payload

Table 1: Selected relays between S and R.

	Relays number	Delay/link (ms)
Minimizing path link	22	8.4
Maximizing path link	7	44
Averaging path link	11	14.4

We simulated a hypothetical model assuming generic data representing video packets among a group of simulated moving vehicles on a road. The best selection of relaying vehicles influences the performance of the system. Figure 2 and Table 1 show the transmission throughput versus the number of selected relays. Minimizing the distance between the selected relays, resulted in higher packets losses and retransmissions was reported. On the other hand, maximizing the distance between the relays lead to a huge throughput reduction with an increased signal to noise ratio indicating potential data corruption. Optimally selecting such relays based on average distance provided efficient transmission and limited number of relays

Ongoing work & research challenges

Currently, we are exploiting machine learning techniques to optimize bracket loss and to ensure long-term stable Connections.

REFERENCES

[1] Baiocchi, A., & Cuomo, F. (2013). Infotainment services based on push-mode dissemination in an integrated VANET and 3G architecture. Journal of Communications and Networks, 15(2), 179-190.

[2] Boban, M., Barros, J., Tonguz, O. K., (2014). Geometry-based vehicle-to-vehicle channel modeling for large-scale simulation. IEEE Transactions on Vehicular Technology 63 (9), 4146–4164.

Fine Grained Group Gesture Detection Using Wearable Devices

Yongjian Zhao
Colorado School of Mines
Golden, CO, USA
yzhao2@mines.edu

Stephen New
Colorado School of Mines
Golden, CO, USA
snew@mines.edu

Kanchana Thilakarathna
The University of Sydney
Sydney, Australia
kanchana.thilakarathna@sydney.edu.au

Xiaodong Zhang
University of New South Wales
Sydney, Australia
ken.zhang@unsw.edu.au

Qi Han
Colorado School of Mines
Golden, CO, USA
qhan@mines.edu

ACM Reference Format:
Yongjian Zhao, Stephen New, Kanchana Thilakarathna, Xiaodong Zhang, and Qi Han. 2019. Fine Grained Group Gesture Detection Using Wearable Devices. In *The 20th International Workshop on Mobile Computing Systems and Applications (HotMobile '19), February 27–28, 2019, Santa Cruz, CA, USA.* ACM, New York, NY, USA, 1 page. https://doi.org/10.1145/3301293.3309564

1 MOTIVATION

People tend to form groups in real world activities. One way to detect groups is to first recognize each user's activity and then analyze their cooperative or collaborative relationship [1]. However, in some cases we may just want to find out whether people belong to the same group rather than identifying the specific activity they are performing, so groups may be detected based on either proximity[2] or gesture similarities[3].

Nowadays wearable devices are extremely popular as personal health and fitness tracking devices. These wearables can be effectively used for the identification of user status in groups that perform the same activity at the same location, which can be helpful in many applications such as emergency response, disaster recovery, and sport activities. For instance, we can help guide people towards emergency exits during a fire evacuation or identifying the group of supporters of a particular team in a sports game.

In this work, we utilize the sensor data collected from smartwatches and apply signal processing algorithms to accurately identify the group synchronization status.

2 GROUP GESTURE DETECTION

In this work, we mainly use accelerometer data collected from each user's smartwatch. In order to identify different status of users, the server first selects a user as reference, each user is then compared with the reference and the status is identified. We first determine whether the user is performing different gesture by extracting the amplitude of the signals at each axis and calculate the average amplitude of peak values from each axis for each user. If the difference between the values of the two users exceeds the predefined

threshold θ, the two users are performing different gestures. If two users are performing the same gesture, we then determine whether the user is synchronized with the reference. We apply two approaches to identify each user's status: time domain analysis where and extrema is detected and frequency domain analysis where Fast Fourier Transformation (FFT) is performed to determine the difference between two series of data.

3 SYSTEM IMPLEMENTATION

A Nexus 5 with Android 6.0.1, API 23 and a LG Watch Urbane with Android 7.1.1, API 25 were used in the implementation. The PC server was hosted on a 2017 Macbook Pro. Two types of periodic motions were examined: an upwards-facing stationary watch and a waving motion restricted to the $y-z$ plane with a period of 5 seconds. All of the processing is handled by the PC server. After collecting 10 seconds of sensor data from the watch, the SensorManager preforms the FFT on all the collected accelerometer data. If the most occurring frequency for a particular watch was not within a range (± 0.005Hz) of the designated leader, then the PC server would send back either Fast or Slow. Otherwise the server would send back Sync. Once the phone receives the message, it notifies the current wearer. The latency for the round trip time between the watch and the server is about 0.1 second on average. Table 1 shows the experimental results when applying our algorithm on the dataset we collected where the user waved his hand from left to right.

Status	Sync	Lag	Fast	Slow	Precision	Recall
Sync	360	0	0	0	0.986	1
Lag	0	120	0	0	0.857	1
Fast	0	0	60	0	1	1
Slow	5	20	0	35	1	0.583

Table 1: Experimental results on left dataset

REFERENCES

[1] D. Gordon, J. Hanne, M. Berchtold, A. A. N. Shirehjini, and M. Beigl. 2013. Towards Collaborative Group Activity Recognition Using Mobile Devices. *Mobile Networks and Applications* (2013), 326–340.
[2] R. Sen, Y. Lee, K. Jayarajah, A. Misra, and R. K. Balan. 2014. GruMon: Fast and Accurate Group Monitoring for Heterogeneous Urban Spaces. In *SenSys*.
[3] N. Yu, Y. Zhao, Q. Han, W. Zhu, and H. Wu. 2016. Identification of Partitions in a Homogeneous Activity Group Using Mobile Devices. *Mobile Information Systems* 2016 (2016), 3545327:1–3545327:14.

Poster: A Testbed Implementation of NDN-based Edge Computing For Mobile Augmented Reality

Rehmat Ullah
Hongik University
Sejong, Republic of Korea
rehmat_ciit@hotmail.com

Muhammad Atif Ur Rehman
Hongik University
Sejong, Republic of Korea
atif_r@outlook.com

Byung-Seo Kim
Hongik University
Sejong, Republic of Korea
jsnbs@hongik.ac.kr

ABSTRACT

Future Augmented Reality (AR) applications require fast information response time and significant computational power and memory for many of its tasks. To enable future AR applications, in this poster, we combine Named Data Networking (NDN) and Edge Computing (EC) in order to achieve fast information response time. The outcomes are implemented and evaluated through testbed and simulations.

KEYWORDS

Edge Computing; Augmented Reality; Future Internet; Named Data Networking; Fast Response Time

ACM Reference Format:
Rehmat Ullah, Muhammad Atif Ur Rehman, and Byung-Seo Kim. 2019. Poster: A Testbed Implementation of NDN-based Edge Computing For Mobile Augmented Reality. In *The 20th International Workshop on Mobile Computing Systems and Applications (HotMobile '19), February 27–28, 2019, Santa Cruz, CA, USA*. ACM, New York, NY, USA, 1 page. https://doi.org/10.1145/3301293.3309565

1 PROPOSED FRAMEWORK

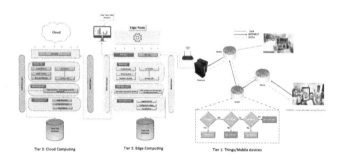

Figure 1: An architectural diagram of the proposed framework

Fig. 1 illustrates our proposed framework. At the things Tier, all the mobile devices/IoT devices communicate locally via NDN network. If there are some tasks that cannot be handled by NDN, then it is forwarded to the edge device. In addition, if edge device

is not able to perform computation on these requests then the edge device will forward the requests to the Cloud data center, where further processing will take place [1].

Figure 2: NDN based edge cloud computing testbed

2 PROTOTYPE AND EVALUATION

In our prototype implementation [1] as depicted in Fig. 2, the Edge application is hosted at one hop distance from ndnSIM and has 16 GB RAM, core-i7, 4710HQ-CPU and @2.40 Ghz core. For Cloud application we have used Microsoft Azure Window Server 2016 Data Center located in Virginia, Washington, USA, and has 8 GB RAM and Intel(R) Xeon(R) CPU E5-2673 v4 @2.30Ghz, 2.29Ghz.

ACKNOWLEDGMENT

This research was supported by the International Research & Development Program of the National Research Foundation of Korea (NRF) funded by the Ministry of Science and ICT. (No. NRF-2018K1A3A1A39086819)

REFERENCES

[1] Lemuel Soh, Jeff Burke, and Lixia Zhang. "Supporting Augmented Reality: Looking Beyond Performance". In *Proceedings of the 2018 Morning Workshop on Virtual Reality and Augmented Reality Network (VR/AR Network '18)*, ACM, New York, NY, USA, 7-12.

[1] https://github.com/atifrehman/NEC or https://github.com/rehmatkhan/NEC

Demo: A Spatial Audio System for the Internet-of-Things

Frank Liu, Robert LiKamWa
Arizona State University
Tempe, Arizona
fwliu1@asu.edu, likamwa@asu.edu

ABSTRACT

Current speakers on IoT hubs are limited, as they do not provide spatial audio experiences. Current spatial audio techniques do not scale to IoT needs, due to high cost, maintenance, and latency. To provide spatial audio for existing IoT environments, we propose and demonstrate a distributed spatial audio system that uses time-domain crosstalk cancellation among a multi-speaker IoT system to position virtual audio throughout a room.

1 The need for spatial audio in IoT

Spatial audio – the ability to discern directionality of sound – would add significant richness to the Internet of Things (IoT) application space. Virtual multidirectional sounds could bring to life an audio-based home guidance system or search engine. Smart speakers on IoT hubs, e.g. Amazon Echo or Google Home, do not currently provide spatial audio to the users; audio sounds like it emanates directly from the device. We propose to develop a system that leverages existing IoT infrastructure to create sounds that seem to emanate from arbitrary physical locations.

1.1 The state-of-the-art of spatial audio

Binaural synthesis processing frameworks, e.g., Resonance Audio, translate spatial virtual sound environments into two-channel audio signals delivered through headphones. However, delivering spatial audio through loudspeakers creates *crosstalk*, where unwanted sound from each speaker reaches the opposite ear. *Wave field synthesis* creates the effect by carefully synchronizing speaker arrays, which is both expensive and non-scalable. *Ambisonic* [3] and *amplitude panning* [2] systems create the effect by controlling the amplitude of surrounding loudspeakers, limiting the virtual sounds to a line segment between

loudspeakers. *Dynamic crosstalk cancellers* use pairs of loudspeakers to create spatial audio for a tracked user through frequency-domain audio processing but have issues with high latency and inaccuracy [4] or require significant calibration to model a room and user's transfer function [1].

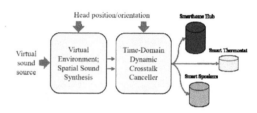

Figure 1: Diagram of the dynamic spatial audio system

2 Our demo: a proposed spatial audio system

We need spatial audio systems built from *existing* IoT infrastructure, and that adapt to the user and environment. We propose a distributed spatial audio system (Fig. 1), revolving around a time-domain dynamic crosstalk cancellation technique which uses amplitude gain and time delay modifications for real-time low-latency spatial audio.

In this demonstration we integrate: (i) The Unity Game Engine to place virtual sounds, (ii) Google Resonance Audio to generate spatial audio, (iii) HTC Vive tracking to provide user head location, (iv) our time-domain crosstalk cancellation algorithm, (v) multiple speakers, representing IoT devices. We compare our system against a headphones-based system to assess efficacy against the state-of-the-art.

REFERENCES

[1] M. Song, C. Zhang, D. Florencio, H. Kang. 2011. An Interactive 3-D Audio System with Loudspeakers. In IEEE Transactions on Multimedia (Volume: 13, Issue: 5, Oct. 2011)
[2] V. Pullki. 1997. Virtual sound source positioning using vector base amplitude panning. J. Audio Eng. Soc., vol. 45, pp. 456–466.
[3] D. Artega. 2018. Introduction to Ambisonics.
[4] H. Kurabayashi, M. Otani, K. Itoh, M. Hashimoto, M. Kayama. 2013. Development of dynamic transaural reproduction system using non-contact head tracking. In Proc. of IEEE Global Conference on Consumer Electronics (GCCE), (Tokyo, Japan).

Demo: Helping to Tackle Social Isolation and Loneliness of Older Adults Using Mobile Applications

Peter Shaw
Lancaster University, UK
p.shaw@lancaster.ac.uk

Mateusz Mikusz
Lancaster University, UK
m.mikusz@lancaster.ac.uk

Nigel Davies
Lancaster University, UK
n.a.davies@lancaster.ac.uk

Christopher N. Bull
Lancaster University, UK
c.bull@lancaster.ac.uk

Mike Harding
Lancaster University, UK
m.harding@lancaster.ac.uk

Niall Hayes
Lancaster University, UK
n.hayes@lancaster.ac.uk

1 INTRODUCTION

We live in a society with an ageing population in which the number of 65+ will significantly increase within the next 50 years. In parallel, we observe an increasing amount of technology deployed to people – both in the form of more sophisticated mobile phones as well as in the amount of technology ubiquitously integrated into the environment. With the ageing population, it will become increasingly important to accommodate the needs and requirements of older adults when designing systems and applications. We believe that mobile devices offer a unique opportunity to support older adults by, for example, providing access to citizen services to address the risks of social isolation and loneliness of older adults. Related work has been focussed on designing systems (fixed and mobile) that address the physical, cognitive and sensory needs of older adults [2, 3, 5] and on exploring HCI-related issues when designing applications for older adults (e.g. [4, 5]). We have previously conducted a series of co-creation workshops with older adults in which we determined a set of broader design considerations and requirements for developing mobile applications and systems for this demographic [1].

In the context of this demo, we draw on the co-creation workshops in which we have designed and developed a citizen services platform specifically for older adults. The platform consists of a dedicated mobile application (fig. 1) and a series of backend system components. The mobile application was designed for smartphones and tablets and provides a gateway for older adults to major services such as nearby social events and personalised transport information. Through a set of backend components, we analyse interactions with users and provide opportunities to automatically determine opportunities to provide recommendations to older adults, e.g. for relevant social activities nearby.

2 DEMO OVERVIEW

We plan to demonstrate our mobile application on a collection of mobile phones and tablets and allow attendees to interact with the application freely. We will provide insights into the underlaying

Figure 1: Mobile Age application.

architecture and its specific characteristics to accommodate the needs of older adults. Using a dedicated analytics dashboard deployed on our backend system, we will further visualise the types of interaction data collected from the mobile application and how the captured insights can be used to improve the quality of the mobile application and specific citizen services in the context of supporting older adults.

ACKNOWLEDGMENTS

We thank AgeUK, SLDC and our user group participants. Mobile Age has received funding from the European Union's Horizon 2020 research and innovation programme under Grant No.: 693319.

REFERENCES

[1] C. Bull, M. Harding, M. Mikusz, B. Knowles, N. Davies, and N. Hayes. 2018. Designing Mobile Applications for Older Adults. HotMobile'18.
[2] Miranda A. Farage, Kenneth W. Miller, Funmi Ajayi, and Deborah Hutchins. 2012. Design Principles to Accommodate Older Adults. *Global Journal of Health Science* 4, 2 (2012). https://doi.org/10.5539/gjhs.v4n2p2
[3] Peter Gregor, Alan F. Newell, and Mary Zajicek. 2002. Designing for Dynamic Diversity: Interfaces for Older People. In *Proceedings of the Fifth International ACM Conference on Assistive Technologies (Assets '02)*. ACM, New York, NY, USA, 151–156. https://doi.org/10.1145/638249.638277
[4] B. Knowles and V. L. Hanson. 2018. The Wisdom of Older Technology (Non-)Users. Commun. ACM. (2018). (in press).
[5] A. Petrovčič, S. Taipale, A.Rogelj, and V. Dolničar. 2017. Design of Mobile Phones for Older Adults: An Empirical Analysis of Design Guidelines and Checklists for Feature Phones and Smartphones. *International Journal of Human-Computer Interaction* (2017). https://doi.org/10.1080/10447318.2017.1345142 (in press).

Demo: *XREmul* - An Emulation Environment *for* XR Application Development

Jaewon Choi, Seungchan Jeong, and JeongGil Ko
Ajou University

CCS CONCEPTS

• **Human-centered computing** → **Mixed / augmented reality**;

1 INTRODUCTION

EXtended Reality(XR), which includes the concepts of virtual reality, augmented reality and mixed reality, is a promising technology for the research community and also the commercial domain in the sense that it can open a variety of new applications in a novel computing environment.

Most XR applications are "interactive" and this interactivity is realized using immersive equipments such as XR headsets and controllers. Compared to applications in traditional computing environments, an XR application requires more sophisticated and careful design given that diverse dimensions of interaction is allowed and also because users can be more sensitive to the application/functional quality due to the higher levels of immersion.

To achieve a high quality XR interaction experience, large amounts of repetitive testing is required. However long playtimes using immersive XR headsets, even for the purpose of testing, can cause discomfortness (e.g., VR sickness). Therefore, the testing process itself becomes a heavy burden for XR application developers.

To address such issues, we propose *XREmul* , a framework for emulating the XR experience for the interaction design and development process. *XREmul* provides a framework for recurrent testing with application-level transparency and extensible input abstractions for XR-related equipments. In this demo, users will experience the *XREmul* framework with a VR headset and experience how its features can help ease the application testing process.

HotMobile '19, February 27–28, 2019, Santa Cruz, CA, USA
© 2019 Copyright held by the owner/author(s).
ACM ISBN 978-1-4503-6273-3/19/02.
https://doi.org/10.1145/3301293.3309569

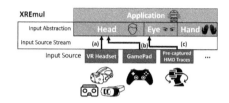

Figure 1: *XREmul* system architecture.

2 SYSTEM ARCHITECTURE

A major problem in developing and testing an XR application is that the input dimensions for their target devices are large and complex compared to traditional computing environments. Input device that interact with the XR platforms are diverse and the types/dimensions of input that they provide cannot be easily reproduced for testing purposes. Naturally, the testing of XR applications becomes complex and cost-ineffective. Continuous testing in XR environments can also lead to VR sickness [1], leading to additional testing burden.

To solve such issues, *XREmul* provides an *input emulation interface* and a *record-and-replay* feature for simplifying the repetitive testing process. *XREmul* is implemented on Unity3D to support cross-platform interface.

As Figure 1 shows, *XREmul* is composed of the following two core components.

Input Abstraction, an abstracted interface for application developers to use the *XREmul* features.

Source Stream, is a mapping function between the input abstraction and input source(s).

3 DEMO APPLICATIONS

In our demo, we present the development process of a simple sphere observing application.In this application, there is a white sphere in the user's view and if the user's head direction points to the sphere, the sphere's color is set to red. This is used to represent a simple interactive task in XR.

ACKNOWLEDGEMENTS

This work was supported by the the Basic Science Research Program through the National Research Foundation of Korea funded by the Ministry of Science and ICT (2018R1C1B6003869).

REFERENCES

[1] Wikipedia. Virtual reality sickness. Available at https://en.wikipedia.org/wiki/Virtual_reality_sickness.

Demo: A Low-power Graphics Library for Mobile AR Headset Application Development

Jaewon Choi, Hyeonjung Park, Jeongyeup Paek*, Rajesh K. Balan[†], JeongGil Ko

Ajou University, *Chung-Ang University, [†]Singapore Management University

CCS CONCEPTS

• **Human-centered computing → Mixed / augmented reality**;

1 INTRODUCTION

We present *LpGL*, a *Low-power Graphics Library* designed to extend the usage time of mobile AR headsets. *LpGL* offers a transpatent layer to the application to intercept graphics-related calls to reduce unneeded graphics processing overhead without any quality loss for saving mobile device power. Our system reduces power consumption up to ~22%, with only 46μsec of latency induced per visible object.

2 LOW-POWER GRAPHICS LIBRARY

The lifetime of state-of-the-art AR headsets, such as the Magic Leap One, is only 2-3 hours; however, longer active hours are needed to realize future mobile AR applications. A major factor affecting the battery efficiency are the computation units (e.g., CPU, GPU) for graphics rendering. Therefore, we propose Low-power Graphics Library (*LpGL*), which is a layer between the application and the GPU designed to extend the lifetime of mobile AR headsets by harmonizing the computation-quality trade-off based on the following goals.

- The AR developer should not have to modify the source code to apply our system to their application.
- Our system should be lightweight enough to not increase the power consumption due to the added computation cost.
- Despite reducing power consumption, the system should not adversely affect the user experience.

Specifically, *LpGL* offers a transparent interface to access the platform's native graphics APIs and optimizes the system's power usage using the following sub-components.

○ **Scene Dynamics Scoring-based Frame Rate Control**: Scenes with less dynamics do not show differences in user-perceived quality even when rendered at low frame rates [1].

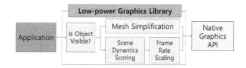

Figure 1: *LpGL* **System Architecture**

Scene dynamics scoring quantifies the current scene dynamics, and determines a suitable frame rate on a per-scene basis.

○ **Mesh Simplification**: Increasing object complexity results in higher power usage for graphics rendering. *LpGL* identifies objects away from the user's core view-point and tries to reduce the number of triangles for such objects. The simplified versions of all objects used in an application are created in compile time to minimize operation-time latency.

○ **Culling**: To draw a 3D object, an app issues "draw calls". However in the traditional graphics pipeline, rendering is performed even for objects that can not be seen in the user's field of view. *LpGL* suppresses draw calls for such un-seen objects to minimize power usage at the graphics pipeline.

3 DEMO APPLICATIONS

We present three applications to show the benefits of *LpGL*.

○ **Floating Sphere Observation**: This application contains a static scene (no object motion), in which the spheres float around the user and are simply observed.

○ **Sphere Shooting**: In this application, the user is asked to shoot floating spheres using a controller. This application represents a case with high level of object motion dynamics.

○ **Abnormal Bunny Search**: This sample application asks the user to identify abnormal bunnies under three conditions: with *LpGL*, without *LpGL* and using a naïve energy saving technique, where the bunny qualities are uniformly sacrificed to meet the energy savings level of *LpGL*. This application shows how using *LpGL* can minimize energy cost without sacrificing user perceived object fidelity.

ACKNOWLEDGEMENTS

This work was supported by the the Basic Science Research Program through the National Research Foundation of Korea funded by the Ministry of Science and ICT (2018R1C1B6003869).

REFERENCES

[1] C. Hwang, S. Pushp, C. Koh, J. Yoon, Y. Liu, S. Choi, and J. Song. RAVEN: Perception-aware Optimization of Power Consumption for Mobile Games. In *Proceedings of the International Conference on Mobile Computing and Networking (MobiCom'17)*, pages 422–434, 2017.

Author Index